Spirits of Our Whaling Ancestors

SPIRITS
OF OUR
WHALING ANCESTORS

Revitalizing Makah and Nuu-chah-nulth Traditions

CHARLOTTE COTÉ

Foreword by MICAH McCARTY

A Capell Family Book

UNIVERSITY OF WASHINGTON PRESS   Seattle & London
UBC PRESS   Vancouver & Toronto

THE CAPELL FAMILY ENDOWED BOOK FUND supports the publication of books that deepen the understanding of social justice through historical, cultural, and environmental studies. Preference is given to books about the American West and to outstanding first books in order to foster scholarly careers.

Published in the United States of America by
UNIVERSITY OF WASHINGTON PRESS
www.washington.edu/uwpress

Library of Congress Cataloging-in-Publication Data and Library and Archives Canada Cataloging in Publication can be found at the end of the book.

The paper used in this publication is acid-free and 90 percent recycled from at least 50 percent post-consumer waste. It meets the minimum requirements of American National Standard for Information Sciences—Permanence of Paper for Printed Library Materials, ANSI Z39.48–1984.∞

FRONTISPIECE: Whaler photograph by Edward S. Curtis; Courtesy Royal British Columbia Museum, Victoria.

Published in Canada by
UBC PRESS
University of British Columbia
2029 West Mall, Vancouver, B.C. V6T 1Z2
www.ubcpress.ca

This book is dedicated to my mother, the late Evelyn Georg,

whose love nurtured me, whose wisdom guided me,

whose knowledge of our language and culture educated

and enlightened me, and whose spirit continues to support

and nourish me through life's journey.

Contents

Foreword

IN THIS VERY RELEVANT STUDY OF MAKAH AND NUU-CHAH-NULTH whaling traditions and practices, the reader is afforded an inside perspective on modern aboriginal self-determination from the point of view of a Native scholar.

The Native drive to sustain the ancient traditions of whaling is forced to adapt to the pressures of Western civilization, an experience that can make for a "two-world" sense of identity. The realities of the Native homeland and those of the outside world are often an ocean apart; most people are far from their ancestral homes and disconnected from a natural experience of an organic environment. On the other hand, there is a place we Natives call home, where we understand one another better then most mainstreamers will ever know and where we return throughout our lives. We are taught from a place-based perspective, with a multi-generational, long-term observation of the world that provides the means by which we define ourselves. Charlotte Coté will introduce you to a "West Coaster's" place in the world heritage.

As a Makah who steadfastly values what it means to know who you are and where you come from, I find this book to be a proud affirmation of family history and a sense of belonging, demonstrating a thread that connects and a chord that resonates with Makah and Nuu-chah-nulth, regardless of the legal divisions of colonial borders. Dr. Coté makes an important contribution to indigenous scholarly resources, a contribution from the heart of the West Coast. Because she herself was active in the movement to revitalize Makah whaling, she sees the need for a two-pronged campaign: one that is a culturally grounded education of our people, by our people, for our people, and one that is steeped in the diplomacy of educating peoples of the outside world. She takes the reader along on a "canoe journey" to explore both approaches, so that the Native and the non-Native worlds can better understand each other. This canoe journey is a fitting metaphor for cultural sensitivity in light of the recent United Nations Declaration of Indigenous Rights. Only four member nations voted against the Declaration—New Zealand, Australia, Canada, and the United States of America—which is an interesting fact about English-speaking colonialism.

Dr. Coté introduces the reader to our people and provides identifying elements of our history, and then her canoe takes us to the heart of an emotionally charged debate on the philosophical differences between Native beliefs and those founded in the animal rights movement. She assertively confronts the school of thought that animals, and especially whales, are not for human consumption. She exposes a New Age dogma that is both pious and inflexible, a dogma that may well be a product of the corporate "Save the Whales" culture, in which the financial sustainability of a nongovernmental organization (NGO) can compromise its ethics and may have spawned another brand of supremacist with another style of ethnic cleansing.

This book is profoundly important to the advancement of a better understanding of cultural diversity. It is also a must-read for Native students and scholars. Dr. Coté takes a proud stand on a controversial issue; she sheds light on our sacred traditions and helps safeguard their endurance.

MICAH McCARTY
Vice-Chair, Makah Tribal Council
April 2010

Kleko Kleko / Thank You

THIS BOOK WOULD NOT HAVE BEEN POSSIBLE WITHOUT THE LOVE, support, and encouragement of my beautiful family, my Tseshaht community, my *haw'iih*, and my entire Nuu-chah-nulth Nation. It was their words, stories, and teachings, their strength and honesty, that guided my hands as I wrote the book. They encouraged me to pursue my scholastic dreams, but at the same time to stay always rooted in my culture and community. They have all given me so much in my life and made me the proud Tseshaht woman I am today. My deep appreciation also goes to the many Makah people whose wisdom threads throughout these pages. To all, kleko kleko! I hope with this book to humbly give something back.

To my parents, Jack and the late Evelyn Georg, kleko kleko for their unconditional love and support and for encouraging me to *thlulh silh a*, to do something good with my life. My mother's spirit is always with me, and knowing this keeps me going. I will hold her in my heart forever. Kleko kleko to my late grandparents, Hughie and Grace Watts, for their wonderful teachings and beautiful stories. Kleko kleko to my late brother-in-law, Art Thompson, and my sister, Charlene Thompson-Reid, for opening their home and their hearts to me. I will forever carry with me the utmost respect for and gratitude to Art, who was always available to share his knowledge and his amazing and insightful whaling stories, which were filled with passion and sincerity.

A special kleko kleko to my friend Makah Tribal Council vice-chair Micah McCarty. In the many conversations we had over the years, Micah demonstrated to me how important the whaling tradition was and still is to the Makah people. His passion for his culture, his whaling identity, and his devotion to community continue to empower me. I am grateful to him for graciously sharing family whaling stories and his knowledge of Makah history. Throughout this process, Micah has become a dear friend.

My sincere gratitude goes to my cousin Lena Ross and my late aunty Linda Watts, who work/ed extensively with the Nuu-chah-nulth language and helped me understand and write our words. Kleko kleko to *Haw'ilth* Tom Mexsis Happynook for sharing his knowledge and being available at any time to answer my questions; to Makah linguist and cultural expert Maria Pascua for cordially providing me with the Makah words I use in this book; to Makah whaler/harpooner Theron Parker for sharing with me thoughts and reflections on his own whaling history and identity and for providing me with rich details of the 1999 hunt; and to Makah whaler Wayne Johnson for our conversations, which, although brief, displayed his great passion for his whaling identity.

I would respectfully like to thank my elders Nelson Keitlah and Stanley Sam for taking the time to sit with me and share their personal stories about our whaling tradition. I still smile when I think of some of the candid stories Stanley told me. Kleko kleko to anthropologist/historian/archaeologist Denis St. Claire for helping me write my history and gather information about my great-great-grandfather Sayach'apis, and for showing such a deep love and respect for my elders and culture. Kleko kleko to my aunty Misbun (Eileen) Haggard and cousin Anne Hunter for sharing their cultural knowledge with me throughout many years. Thank you to my uncle Bob Soderlund, my sister Gail Peterson Gus, and my nieces Evelyn and Carmen Thompson for providing me with photographs, many of which I have used in this book. Thank you to Robin Wright and the Burke Museum and to Debbie Preston and the Northwest Indian Fisheries Commission for additional photographs.

My deep thanks go to my friends Susan McCallum and Marty Sands not only for proofreading my manuscript but, more importantly, for providing me with love, support, and encouragement during those times when I felt that I could not write another word. Thank you to my colleague Sasha Harmon for reading, critiquing, and editing my chapters. Thank you to University of Washington Press managing editor Marilyn Trueblood for guiding me through the manuscript revisions, to Tom Eykemans for his wonderful design, and special thanks to acquiring editor Jacqueline Ettinger for being so supportive and most of all patient as we worked through the process of turning my manuscript into this book. I am also extremely grateful to the Capell Family, who have shown keen interest in the book and given generous support to it.

A special kleko kleko to all the Makah people who showed me great hospitality when I was in Neah Bay in 2000 conducting interviews and who have continued to help me throughout the years. To all my friends, colleagues, siblings, aunts, uncles, cousins, nieces, nephews, elders, and community members, kleko kleko for providing me with guidance, support, love, patience, and knowledge, for never doubting me as I struggled to complete this book, and for always encouraging me. And finally, to the spirit of my great-great-grandfather Sayach'apis and to all the spirits of my whaling ancestors whose presence warmed and comforted my heart and soul as I wrote this book, kleko kleko!

Orthography

T**HE LANGUAGE OF MY PEOPLE IS THE SOUTHERN WAKASHAN, A LAN-**
guage group that consists of Nuu-chah-nulth (Nootka), which itself has
several dialects; Ditidaht (Nitinat, Nitinaht); and Makah. The Wakashan
language family is made up of seven related languages, spoken along the coast of
British Columbia, on Vancouver Island, and on the Olympic Peninsula of Washington State.[1]

There have been various phonetic systems developed throughout the years
to write the Nuu-chah-nulth, Ditidaht, and Makah languages. In the early
1900s, anthropologist/linguist Edward Sapir conducted fieldwork in Tseshaht
territory, where he analyzed and recorded our language. He worked with Tseshaht member Alex (Alec) Thomas to develop a notation system based on Franz
Boas's system that could be used to write Nuu-chah-nulth words.[2] Even after
Sapir's death in 1939, Alex continued to work on a writing system for our language and sent thousands of pages of language and cultural material to the
National Museum of Canada. Alex died in 1969, and in 1974 a practical orthography based on his work was published to help Nuu-chah-nulth people learn
their language.[3] Other writing systems were also developed by linguist Morris Swadesh, ethnographer/linguist Randy Bouchard, anthropologist Philip
Drucker, and anthropologist Eugene Arima. In 2005 linguist John Stonham
published *A Concise Dictionary of the Nuu-chah-nulth Language*, much of it
based on Sapir's fieldwork materials.

In the last thirty years, the Makah and Nuu-chah-nulth peoples have made
great efforts to revitalize and preserve their languages. The Nuu-chah-nulth
Tribal Council initiated a language program in the 1970s and began collect-

ing language resource materials. Nuu-chah-nulth elders and linguists worked together to develop a system of writing the Nuu-chah-nulth language by modifying the International Phonetic Alphabet (IPA). In 1989 the NTC produced the first Nuu-chah-nulth dictionaries based on this new language system: *Our World: T'aat'aaqsapa Cultural Dictionary* and *Our World–Our Ways: T'aat'aaqsapa Cultural Dictionary*. Each includes a brief introduction of the writing system used, a guide to the reading and pronunciation of words, and the writing of words in the various Nuu-chah-nulth dialects.[4] The Makah also undertook to preserve their language and established the Makah Language Program through the Makah Cultural and Research Center. In 1978 the tribe created a dictionary using a modified form of the IPA and developed curriculum materials for their school.[5]

Although there is a system for writing our language, I have chosen instead to write the Nuu-chah-nulth and Makah words phonetically. I did this because the two languages have some sounds and symbols that are not used in English, and that notation can be difficult to understand, to read, and to say. Spelling the words as closely as possible to how they are pronounced makes them easier to read by those unaccustomed to reading symbols. My goal is to allow all readers to focus more on the meaning of the words. As I have not followed an established writing system, readers should use my spelling of Native words for pronunciation only and not for study of the Nuu-chah-nulth or Makah languages.[6] Readers who would like to know more about systems to transcribe Wakashan languages are encouraged to consult the works described in the notes to this section.

◆　◆　◆

I have provided a sample of the Nuu-chah-nulth words I include in my book to demonstrate the differences in how I write the words and how the words are written today in the Nuu-chah-nulth writing system. The sample shows the words written in English; written with a phonetic spelling, which I use; and written in the Tseshaht/Nuu-chah-nulth style, which is used by linguists in my community. For clarification, I use an apostrophe (') to denote a glottal stop, a hyphen to denote a break in the word, and a line under a letter to denote a breath sound (see also the Nuu-chah-nulth Pronunciation Guide, below).

English	Phonetic Spelling	Nuu-chah-nulth Language System
chief	*haw'ilth*	*hawʔił*
chiefs (plural)	*haw'iih*	*hawʔiih*
lineage group	*ushtak̲imilh*	*ushtak̲imilh*
Native name	*qu'atsiic imtii*	*quʔaćiic ʔimtii*
Nuu-chah-nulth	Nuu-chah-nulth	Nuučaanʔuł
one	*tsawalk*	*ćawaak*
ritual bathing	*oo-simch*	*uu-simč*
thank you	*kleko kleko*	*łʔekoo łʔekoo*
Tseshaht	*Tseshaht*	*ćišaaʔath*

NOTE: The words written in our Nuu-chah-nulth language were provided to me by Tseshaht First Nation Education Services Manager Lena Ross, who is one of the Tseshaht language specialists.

NUU-CHAH-NULTH PRONUNCIATION GUIDE

Vowels

a   has the sound in English *what*, or the "u" in *cup*

aa   has the sound in the British pronunciation of *father*, the first part of a sneeze, *ah-choo*

e   has the sound in *pet*

ee   sounds like the e in *eggs*

i   has the sound in English *it*

ii   has the sound in *greed* or *see*

oo   has the sound in *only*

u   has the sound in *took* or *note*

uu   has the sound in *boot* or *road*

Consonants

c   pronounced like "ts" in *nuts* or *bats*

ć   glottal sound, sounds like "ts" in *hats* pronounced explosively

č   sounds like "ch" in *chop*

c   sounds like *watch it* with the "ch" pronounced forcefully

h   has the sound in *home*

ḥ   sounds like an "h" made deep in the throat

k	has the sound in English *kite*
k̓	pronounced like a hard "k" with a popping sound
kʷ	sounds like "qu" in *queen*
k̓ʷ	sounds like "qu" in *quack* followed by a popping sound
ł	barred "l" sounds like "l" and blowing
ƛ	barred landis, sounds like "tla" and placing your tongue behind your teeth
ƛ̓	sounds like "tla" with an "a"
m	has the sound in *morning*
m̓	sounds like an "m" with an "a," "ma," pronounced forcefully
n	has the sound in *nose*
n̓	has an "n" sound but pronounced forcefully
p	has the sound in *pig*
p̓	pronounced as an explosive or forceful "p"
q	sounds like a "k" made deep in the throat
qʷ	sounds like a "q" with a "w"
s	has the sound in *six*
š	sounds like the "sh" in *shoe*
t	has the sound in *toast*
t̓	sounds like a "t" with an "a," pronounced as an explosive "t"
w	has the sound in *wish*
w̓	sounds like an explosive "wa"
x	sounds like a cat's hiss
x̱	sounds like clearing the throat with an "x"
xʷ	sounds like a hiss plus a "w"
x̱ʷ	sounds like clearing your throat with your lips rounded
y	has the sound in *yes*
y̓	sounds like a "y" with an "a" with an explosive sound
ʕ	pharyngeal, sounds like an "i" made deep in the throat
ʔ	glottal stop, denotes a pause between vowels

Notes

1   For more information on languages in the Pacific Northwest, see Lawrence C. Thompson and M. Dale Kinkade, "Languages," 30–50, and M. Dale Kinkade, "History of Research in Linguistics," 98–106, both in *Handbook of the North American Indians*, vol. 7: *Northwest Coast*, ed. Wayne Suttles (Washington, D.C.: Smithsonian Institution, 1990). For more information on Southern Wakashan languages, specifically the Nuu-chah-nulth and Makah languages, see Toshihide Nakayama, *Nuu-chah-nulth (Nootka) Morphosyntax* (Berkeley: University of California Press, 2001); Eun-Sook Kim, "Theoretical Issues in Nuu-chah-nulth Phonology and Morphology," Ph.D. diss., University of British Columbia, 2003; Matthew Davidson, "Studies in Southern Wakashan (Nootkan) Grammar," Ph.D. diss., SUNY Buffalo, 2002; Suzanne Marie Rose, "The Kuquot Grammar," Ph.D. diss., University of Victoria, 1981; and *Our World: T'aat'aaqsapa Cultural Dictionary* and *Our World—Our Ways: T'aat'aaqsapa Cultural Dictionary* (Nuu-chah-nulth Tribal Council, 1989

and 1991). The Southern Wakashan languages are closely related, with the main differences being phonological and lexical; see Davidson, "Studies in Southern Wakashan," 17–18. Also see the University of Washington Web site http://www.depts.washington.edu/wll2/languages.html.

2   See Edward Sapir and Morris Swadesh, *Nootka Texts: Tales and Ethnological Narratives with Grammatical Notes and Lexical Materials* (Philadelphia: University of Pennsylvania Press, 1939), 8–13. Edward Sapir et al., *Whaling Indians: Tales of Extraordinary Experience*, Part 1, Sapir-Thomas Texts (Ottawa: Canadian Museum of Civilization, 2000), x–xii.

3   *Nuu-chah-nulth Phrase Book and Dictionary. Barkley Sound Dialect* (Banfield, B.C.: Barkley Sound Dialect Working Group, 2004).

4   Four Nuu-chah-nulth Groups—Huu-ay-aht, Ucluelet, Uchucklesaht, and Toquaht—also created a dictionary and phrase book, *Nuu-chah-nulth Phrase Book and Dictionary. Barkley Sound Dialect* (see note 3).

5   From the Makah Nation Web site: http://www.makah.com/language.htm.

6   I use a style of writing similar to the one that Chief Umeek (Richard Atleo) utilized in his book *Tsawalk: A Nuu-chah-nulth Worldview* (Vancouver: UBC Press, 2004). In *Tsawalk* (p. xx), Umeek says that he spelled the Nuu-chah-nulth words roughly according to the Ahousaht accent rather than following any phonetic system.

Abbreviations

EA	environmental assessment
EIS	environmental impact statement
FONSI	finding of no significant impact
ICRW	International Convention for the Regulation of Whaling
IFA	Indian Fisheries Association
IHS	Indian Health Service
IWC	International Whaling Commission
MCRC	Makah Cultural and Research Center
MMPA	Marine Mammal Protection Act
MTC	Makah Tribal Council
NEPA	National Environmental Policy Act
NMFS	National Marine Fisheries Service
NMML	National Marine Mammal Laboratory
NTC	Nuu-chah-nulth Tribal Council
NOAA	National Oceanic and Atmospheric Administration
PAWS	Progressive Animal Welfare Society
PBR	potential biological removal
PCFA	Pacific Coast Feeding Aggregation
PETA	People for the Ethical Treatment of Animals
PSA	Public Service Announcement
S/SPAWN	Steelhead-Salmon Protection Action for Washington Now
UPOW	United Property Owners of Washington
WCW	World Council of Whalers

Spirits of Our Whaling Ancestors

INTRODUCTION

Honoring Our Whaling Ancestors

I̲T WAS MAY 17, 1999, THE DAY MY SISTER CHARLENE CALLED FROM VIC-
toria, B.C., to share the news that members of the Makah Nation had been suc
cessful in their whale hunt in the ocean waters near Neah Bay, Washington. A
thirty-foot *maa'ak*¹ (gray whale) gave its life to feed the Makah people, an act that
elicited in me a sense of excited disbelief. "What! No way!" I shouted. I was sitting
at my computer immersed in writing my dissertation, nearly 1,000 miles away at
the University of California, Berkeley. I was overwhelmed and ecstatic at what
the Makah tribe had just achieved. For the previous couple of weeks, my niece
Katherine Thompson, who lives in Neah Bay, had been calling me with updates
on the hunt that was about to take place. "Keep me posted," I told her. "And, if
you come across any newspaper articles on the hunt, please keep them for me."
Then, the call came from Charlene . . .

"Sis, the hunt has been on every TV station," she said. "There are hundreds of
people over there right now." She told me that she and her husband, Art Thompson, were going to Neah Bay that weekend to attend the potlatch the Makah
tribe was holding to commemorate their first whale hunt in more than seventy
years. "It's so exciting," Charlene exclaimed, "we're going to get to eat whale!" My
brother-in-law came on the line. "Lottie, they did it!" he yelled excitedly into the
phone, "You need to get your butt over to Neah Bay immediately!"

At the time I was teaching and working on my dissertation that analyzed the
cultural significance of the revival of whaling for the Makah tribe and my people,
the Nuu-chah-nulth, two groups that are related to each other culturally, linguistically, and geographically. I had planned to go to Neah Bay after I completed
teaching in a couple of weeks, with the hope that I would be there when a whale

was caught. I hung up the phone, sad and disappointed that I could not be there to share in the celebration with my Makah and Nuu-chah-nulth relatives. And I was also upset that I was not going to get the opportunity to taste whale meat.

A week later I received a large package in the mail. I opened it and, to my delight, found numerous newspaper articles about the Makah whale hunt. My niece had not forgotten my request. Every article on the hunt that she had come across she clipped and sent to me. Immediately I phoned to thank her for such a wonderful gift, and then I spread out all the articles on my living room floor and slowly and meticulously read through them. The newspaper captions read: "Makah Hunt Brings Back Memories of Whaling on B.C.'s Coast," "Makah Relish Link to Their Past," "Hunting for Pride," "Such a Sensation: Joyous Makah Kill Whale." I read each article intently. When the Makah announced that they were going to begin their hunt that May, newspaper and television reporters immediately went to Neah Bay, many of them camping near the community. As they waited for the "big event" to happen, they reported on the day-to-day activities leading up to the morning the whale was caught. In their daily reports, they commented that the whaling crew had already gone out and had come upon a whale but had been unable to harpoon it; they reported on how the anti-whaling protesters were attempting to thwart the hunt by steering their boats between the whaling crew and the whale and by playing killer whale sounds from a boat close by; they mentioned how calm the sea was on the morning of the day the whaling crew caught the whale; they reported on how the harpooner stood up in the boat and heaved his harpoon, how it successfully struck the whale, and how the whale reacted when it realized it had been struck.

Each story was accompanied by one or more pictures, each capturing in vivid detail a moment in time that will never be forgotten by the Makah people. The pictures showed the Neah Bay shoreline teeming with hundreds of people, many of them proud Makah tribal members who were holding drums and singing songs as the esteemed whale was being towed to shore. The photos captured one of the most powerful images of the hunt: the harpooner, Theron Parker, standing on top of his beached prize and ceremonially sprinkling it with eagle feathers.

The newspaper articles also covered the activities that took place once the whale was on land. They described how the Makah people prayed and sang songs to the whale, to show it respect and to thank it for giving itself to their community. They discussed how, after all the proper rituals were performed, the whale was cut up and readied for distribution in the Makah community, with some meat and blubber saved for the potlatch that was to follow. A couple of days later the Makah held their potlatch, and the newspaper reporters and camera crews were there once again to report on the ceremonies. The reporters noted that people from all over the world attended—people from as far north as Alaska and from as far south as Fiji; people of all ages and racial backgrounds; and people from the neighboring Native communities and from my own Nuu-chah-nulth Nation.

Newspaper photos showed images of proud Makah men, women, children, elders, and tribal leaders, smiling and shaking hands with all the guests who came to Neah Bay to share this very special day with them. There were pictures of the Makah dressed in their finest ceremonial regalia, holding their most powerful drums, singing and dancing their traditional songs, many of which were directly linked to their whaling heritage. There were pictures of the guests eating a traditional Makah meal of salmon, halibut, and shellfish. And, finally, there were images never before captured: pictures of the curious faces of the guests and of the proud faces of the Makah members as they sampled, chewed, and ate a food that a majority of them had never tasted before, the prized cuisine of the evening, the meat and blubber of the whale.

I put down the newspaper articles and thought about everything I had just read. I thought about the Makah and how proud they must be feeling to have accomplished something so culturally significant. I thought about my Nuu-chah-nulth people and how important the capture of this whale by our Makah relatives was to us, since we, too, were planning to revive our whale hunts.

Five years earlier, following the removal of the gray whale from the Endangered Species list, the Makah tribe had made the announcement that they were going to revive their whale hunts, an integral right of their culture that they had not exercised since the early 1900s, when the gray whale was hunted by commercial whalers to near extinction. Following their announcement, the Nuu-chah-nulth declared that we were also going to revive our hunts. The Makah and Nuu-chah-nulth peoples' decision to revive their whaling practices was met both with support and with vehement opposition. Many people, Native and non-Native, supported what we planned to do and understood its cultural relevance. But there were also people who opposed the revival of the whale hunts because they did not understand how important this practice was to us. They claimed that since whaling was no longer part of our material culture it was obsolete. Then there were the anti-whaling and animal rights activists, who seemed to make no effort to understand why we wanted and needed to hunt whales—they did not want whales killed for any reason, cultural or not. And that brings me to why I wrote this book.

I explain in this book how reviving our whaling tradition has cultural, social, and spiritual significance and will reaffirm our identities as whaling people, enriching and strengthening our communities by reinforcing a sense of cultural pride. Historically, whaling served important social, subsistence, and ritual functions that were at the core of our societies. Whaling held economic importance as well as spiritual significance and prestige for the Makah and Nuu-chah-nulth peoples. Stories contained within our oral traditions that have been passed down through generations tell of the great Thunderbird, T'iick'in, and how he brought the whale, *iiḥtuup*, to our people to feast upon. We have stories about great Makah and Nuu-chah-nulth whaling *haw'iih* (chiefs) who spent years physically, mentally, and spiritually preparing for a whale hunt. Some of them were such great whalers that they could bring home up to five whales in one season. After a whale was caught, it was brought back to the community to be ceremoniously divided up among the village members, providing an enormous amount of food for the community. Killing a whale was considered the highest glory, and the more whales a chief caught, the more prestige, respect, and physical wealth he received.

Until the late 1920s, whaling was still a very important component of both groups' cultures and was intertwined in the intricate web of social interactions that constructed our identities. By the early 1920s, however, over-harvesting of whales by commercial whalers had severely depleted the whale populations. As the Makah and Nuu-chah-nulth whale hunts declined, the ritual and spiritual elements that were central to our tradition also began to diminish. The loss of whaling also meant a weakening of the social connections that were integral to this tradition. Simultaneously, the U.S. and Canadian governments were initiating policies that effectively undermined our social system. The introduction of new subsistence pursuits, such as sealing and fishing, provided the Makah and Nuu-chah-nulth with the ability to acquire food, prestige, and wealth from new sources. And, finally, the introduction of a European cash economy into both communities created a shift in emphasis away from whaling, as our people were pulled into the global market. From the mid-1800s to the early 1900s, the Makah and Nuu-chah-nulth societies underwent major economic, political, social, and spiritual transformations that weakened our traditions and destabilized our cultures. As a result, our entire social fabric began to unravel.

When investigating indigenous cultures and the impact that non-Indian contact had on our societies, many scholars focus on cultural disruption and the breaking down of social networks and traditions. In this book I focus on cultural *resience* continuity. I demonstrate how, even though our societies faced disease epidemics and federal policies that harmed our cultures, we have remained connected to our traditions. This connection can be viewed as a line that threads from our precontact cultures to the present day. That line has been stretched, it has been tattered, and it has been weakened—but it has not been destroyed.

◆ ◆ ◆

Beginning in the 1850s, our societies began to face rapid economic, political, social, and cultural changes that ultimately led to the end of whale hunts in the 1920s. My ancestors faced diseases that severed many of the hereditary lineages that had helped structure and maintain our social systems. We faced government policies that took our children away, banned our ceremonies, and taught us that our way of life was savage. We were introduced to new technologies and new economies, which we successfully adapted into our societies. Although whaling was no longer part of Makah and Nuu-chah-nulth material cultures, our whaling tradition continued to inform our lives and remained firmly connected to our cultures and our identities.

Throughout the years, the commercial whaling industry continued to threaten the whale population, and international rules and regulations were enacted in the 1960s that prohibited whaling on the Northwest Coast. Even though the Makah have the right to whale secured in their 1855 treaty with the United States, they, along with the Nuu-chah-nulth, supported the international bans and stopped whaling. As prohibitions took effect and whaling became more regulated, most of the whale populations began to recover from the devastation caused earlier by commercial whaling. The California gray whale population was so decimated, however, that it did not rebound the way other whale stocks did, and as a safeguard it was placed on the Endangered Species list in 1970. Because of this extra protection, by the 1990s the gray whale population had successfully recovered, and in 1994 it was removed from the list. When the Makah tribal leaders heard that the gray whale was no longer endangered, they announced that they were going to revive their whale hunts. The Nuu-chah-nulth made their announcement shortly after.

The revitalization of the whaling tradition is part of a larger cultural revitalization and self-determination movement that Native peoples throughout the world began experiencing in the 1960s. Our leaders saw that many of the social problems that plagued our communities could be overcome by strengthening our cultures. They recognized that traditions, customs, and languages were important elements of our cultures that needed to be rejuvenated and reinforced for community growth and development.

Taiaiake Alfred, a leading Kanien'kehaka (Mohawk) scholar, has dedicated his life to indigenous struggles and to articulating ways for Native people to make self-determination a reality. In his book *Peace, Power, Righteousness*, Alfred urges Native people to ground their communities in traditional values and principles that will provide them with the strength to move beyond the five hundred years of pain, loss, and suffering inflicted on them following colonization. In order to decolonize, Alfred says, Native communities must "commit themselves to self-conscious traditionalism," whereby community members and leaders work together to selectively re-adopt core values and traditions and make these the center of their social and political lives.[2] In his book *Wasáse*, Alfred maintains that by revitalizing our core philosophies and traditions, we will effectively control our own destinies.

> Survival is bending and swaying but not breaking, adapting and accommodating without compromising what is core to one's being. Those who are emboldened by challenges and who sacrifice for the truth achieve freedom. Those who fail to find balance, who reject change, or who abandon their heritage altogether abandon themselves. They perish. The people who live on are those who have learned the lesson of survival: cherish your unique identity, protect your freedom, and defend your homeland.[3]

The Makah and Nuu-chah-nulth no longer need to hunt whales for subsistence. However, the whale's nutritional value could help alleviate some of the health problems that plague our communities. Clinical health studies have found that sea mammal oil can be used to ameliorate diseases that afflict our people, such as high blood pressure and diabetes. Putting whale oil and meat back on our dinner tables means a return to a healthier lifestyle at the same time that the harvesting, use, and sharing of these foods unites our communities. The umbilical cord that connects us to our whaling tradition has remained unbroken and continues to nourish and strengthen our communities. The tradition is in our family names, in the names of the land we live on, and in the names of waterways we subsist on. It has continued to live on through the stories contained within our oral traditions, through our ceremonies, songs, and dances, and through our artistic expression. We have always been known as a whaling people; as former Makah Whaling Commission Chairman Keith Johnson maintains, "It's who we are."[4]

I am a member of the Tseshaht First Nation, one of the fifteen culturally and linguistically related groups coming under the name Nuu-chah-nulth, which means
"all along the mountains and sea." Our traditional territories are on the west
coast of Vancouver Island. I was born and raised in my community and grew
up understanding that our whaling tradition informs every aspect of our lives.
Tseshaht names refer to sacred places in our territory. The name Tseshaht itself
directly links my people to our whaling tradition. We received the name from
our former principal village, Ts'ishaa, meaning "people from an island that reeks
of whale remains," which referred to the rancid smell left from whales brought up
onto the beach following a hunt.[5] Traditional names, and their continued usage,
serve as constant reminders of how important whales and whaling were to our
past and still are to our present-day community. Place-names can be utilized to
encode, enrich, and structure accounts of the past. Place-names act as a memory
aid to glue history together. These names are key to understanding our history
because important historical events can often be recalled by a term for a feature
of a particular place or landscape.[6]

Whales and Nuu-chah-nulth whalers are central characters in our stories and
legends, which are passed down orally from one generation to the next. When I
was a young girl, my grandfather, Hughie (Watts), would gather his grandchildren together and tell us stories that he had heard as a child. I still have vivid
memories of all of us gathered at his feet in the middle of my grandparents' living room, staring up at my grandfather, captivated by and hanging onto every
word that flowed from his lips. He told us stories about Pitch Woman stealing
the little children, stories about the marriage of Mink. And then there were those
wonderful stories about Thunderbird and Whale, and the grand stories about our
powerful Tseshaht whalers. Native scholar Angela Cavender Wilson (Tawapaha
Tank Win) says that stories in the oral tradition "provide a sense of identity and
belonging, situating community members within their lineage and establishing
their relationship to the rest of the world."[7]

Our whaling ancestors continue to breathe life into our rich whaling narratives, preserved and reinforced through oral traditions. They give power to our
drums as we dance and support our voices as we sing. They continue to guide the
hands of our artists as they create powerful images of the great Thunderbird and
majestic Whale. We perform the ceremonies that keep us connected to and reaffirm our identities as whaling people.

My goal in writing this book is to provide an understanding of our whaling tradition. I achieve this through the utilization of written and archival material and archaeological data, balancing these with Native oral stories and narratives, as well as my own personal reflections, so that a multitude of voices emerges from the text. The writing process was challenging and deeply personal. I also found the experience to be rewarding because in many ways it felt liberating to tell "our" story, to be able to offer my own Nuu-chah-nulth perspective on a tradition that means so much to me and my people. For Native scholars, as First Nations writer Janice Acoose asserts, "the act of writing thus becomes an act of resistance, an act of re-empowerment."[8]

All but one of the newspaper articles, journal articles, and book chapters, and the sole book that was published on the topic of Makah and Nuu-chah-nulth whaling were written by *mamalhn'i* (non-Native) scholars. In fact, in examining the larger picture of Native studies, I found that over 90 percent of the literature on Native peoples and their histories is written by non-Indians.[9] Native scholar Donald Fixico (Shawnee, Sac & Fox, Seminole, and Muscogee Creek) notes that Native American Studies has been dominated by non-Native scholars who have defined its parameters. Non-Native scholars, Fixico argues, "attempted to determine its forms of evidence only as written accounts, professed limited theories, and devised methodologies from a non-Indian tradition."[10] Thus, there is a need for Native histories to be written by Native people.

On the other hand, as Choctaw/French scholar Devon Mihesuah points out, "using the Native voice exclusively may not yield a precise picture of past events, but neither will the sole use of skeletal remains, midden heaps, or non-Indians' diaries, government records, and letters."[11] We cannot ignore the material that has been written by non-Indians. In fact, much of the material that has been written about my people was invaluable to my research. Linguists and anthropologists who worked with my people in the early and mid-1900s have left rich and detailed ethnographic accounts that came from the words of our ancestors. For example, I use linguist/anthropologist Edward Sapir's and linguist Morris Swadesh's ethnographic data throughout this book. Between 1910 and 1923, Sapir conducted fieldwork in Tseshaht, and while there he interviewed many Nuu-chah-nulth elders and worked extensively with one of them, Sayach'apis, my great-great-grandfather. Sapir made every attempt to write the stories and present the ethnographic material he gathered in a manner that was true to the way they were told to him. He worked closely with Sayach'apis's grandson Alex

Thomas, who recorded and translated the data for Sapir. The Tseshaht and English versions are included in his published texts. The writing of the original texts in our language allowed the cultural nuances to remain and people within my community have utilized these as educational and language tools. The English-version stories were also published as close as possible to the way they were originally collected by Sapir and by Thomas, so that even these stories can still be read through a Tseshaht and Nuu-chah-nulth lens. When I was in Neah Bay interviewing the Makah whaling crew involved in the 1999 hunt, one of the crew members, Theron Parker, told me that he had read some of Sapir's material on whaling, and it provided him with valuable information that he never knew about whaling, information that had never been passed down to him by his elders. So this is why these types of texts can work alongside our own Native-based narratives and the stories that have been passed down to us. The challenge, then, is finding a way to successfully merge vastly different methodological approaches, supporting this written data with our oral traditions, so that the Native voice is evident and directs the narrative.

This is what I have set out to accomplish in this book. I have combined these methodologies, writing from both an academic space and a Native-centered space. Native scholar Duane Champagne (Chippewa) says that Native scholars who have grown up in their communities, immersed in their cultures, can provide considerable insight into their societies, insight that could take non-Native scholars conducting fieldwork years to achieve. And, he adds, this cultural and historical knowledge that the Native scholar has will often lead to critical investigations of issues that non-Native scholars might not recognize. This does not mean that a Native scholar will, by virtue of being Native, be better at writing Native history than non-Native scholars. Champagne writes: "The mere presence of Indian blood within a scholar, however, does not ensure better or more sensitive historical or cultural understandings of Indian peoples. This can come only with training, motivation, sensitivity, knowledge, and study."[12] As a scholar, I have endeavored to present a study that is comprehensive and critically and academically rigorous but, at the same time, keep my writing sensitive to my community and respectful of my people.

In her book *Decolonizing Methodologies,* Maori scholar Linda Tuhiwai Smith discusses some of the critical issues that indigenous scholars face in conducting "insider" research. At a general level, Native scholars need to establish ways of thinking critically about their disciplinary processes and relationships, and about the richness of their data and analysis. But, she argues, "[that person] also needs to be humble because the researcher belongs to [an indigenous] community as a member with a different set of roles and relationships, status and position."[13] My research and analysis are grounded in my experiences growing up in a Native community, and I utilize the knowledge I have gained from elders and family members. My knowledge comes from the family I was born into and the community in which I was raised. My education comes from my relatives and my elders. The words I write come from the spirit of my ancestors who have guided my hands and my heart throughout this process. As a Native person, you never write for yourself or by yourself. Cree scholar Winona Wheeler says that the knowledge Native people acquire comes through listening, because we are an oral culture. And, she further explains, our knowledge also comes from the relationships we form "with the Creator, the past, the present, the future, life around us, each other, and within ourselves. And, like my ancestors, I am here on this earth to learn."[14]

As I began the research for this book, I began to "really" listen to what was being told to me by family members and elders. Our discussions would bring me back to when I was a child and how I was raised to understand and respect where I came from and to be proud of who I was. I would think about things that I never had thought about before, how, even though the main language in our community is English, we still use certain words and phrases in our own language to explain where someone comes from and to make references to certain geographical locations. I remember my grandparents, who lived next door to me, saying in Tseshaht the names of the things around us, attempting to keep our language alive.

Memories are powerful. As Wheeler exclaims, "Memory is a beautiful gift." She says that there are very few historians, or few scholars for that matter, who realize the "deep effect that the oral transmission of knowledge has on the individual."

Memories are also experienced at the somatic level and in the soul. To remember those times spent listening to old people tell histories at the kitchen table, on a road trip, or in the warm glow of a campfire, is to relive them. Memory, in the context of Indigenous oral traditions, is a resonance of senses—it evokes the relationship the listener had with the storyteller, and it evokes the emotional responses and the feeling of total absorption experienced at the time. The smells, nuances, facial expressions, body language, and range of audience response are as much a part of the memory of the story as the story itself.[15]

I had one of the best childhoods anyone could ever have experienced. Too many times, when scholars write Native American histories or about our contemporary communities, they focus on negative aspects: the cultural and social breakdown, the pain and violence stemming from the boarding-school system, family dysfunction, social problems of alcoholism and drug addiction, and the health issues that plague our communities today. I was raised in a world that included each of the things I just mentioned, but the family that I was raised in gave me the strength and the wisdom to see beyond these social problems in our communities and to write about what makes us strong, not what has caused us pain and sorrow.

Each day that I walk on this earth I come to appreciate more and more the teachings I was raised with. Each time I sit down with my relatives, with my aunts, uncles, siblings, cousins, and elders, the learning process continues. Each time I communicate with them by phone or through an e-mail, I gain more knowledge and strengthen the ties I have to them and to my community. I am always thankful that I have a family who has stayed close, united in our cultural and familial ties and in our love for one another. Even though my career as a professor has physically removed me from my community, my heart has never left it. And at every opportunity, I take that five-hour trek to be physically home with my family and immerse myself in my community to reinvigorate my mind, heart, and spirit with more cultural teachings.

I am the second person in the Nuu-chah-nulth Nation to pursue doctoral studies and receive a Ph.D. The first person to attain a doctoral degree is one of our respected hereditary chiefs, Umeek (Richard Atleo), who taught First Nations studies at Malaspina University-College and is currently the research liaison at the University of Manitoba and associate adjunct professor at the University of Victoria in British Columbia. Chief Umeek wrote an excellent book, *Tsawalk: A Nuu-chah-nulth Worldview*, that combines Nuu-chah-nulth and Western views of the nature of existence to advance our understanding of the universe. In *Tsawalk*, he discusses our law of generosity and the ways in which Nuu-chah-nulth-aht are raised to be generous. He connects giving and generosity to our overall well-being. "The collective Nuu-chah-nulth experience teaches not only that a generous person is never without the necessities in life, but also that the art of giving generates a sense of personal well being, a sense of balance and harmony."[16] This is my way of giving back to my Tseshaht community, to my family, and to the Nuu-chah-nulth and Makah peoples.

◆　◆　◆

In chapter 1, I examine the Makah and Nuu-chah-nulth whaling tradition before the arrival of *mamalhn'i*, illustrating how whaling was connected to our economic, political, and religious systems, entwined in a complex system of social interactions that served important social, subsistence, and ritual functions. Chapter 2 details the history following contact with *mamalhn'i* to show how Makah and Nuu-chah-nulth interactions with non-Indians and colonial policies produced increased political, economic, spiritual, and societal changes that challenged my ancestors' ability to maintain their cultural traditions, which led to the end of our whaling practices.

While Makah and Nuu-chah-nulth societies underwent dramatic transformations leading to the demise of our whale hunts, I demonstrate in chapter 3 how our whaling tradition has been maintained through place- and personal names, songs, ceremonies, and artistic expression, and, thus, how it continued to be significant to Makah and Nuu-chah-nulth cultures and identities. The decision to revive our whaling practices was sparked by events in the 1960s and 1970s, and in chapter 4, I explore how the movement toward self-determination influenced Makah and Nuu-chah-nulth cultural revitalization. Makah and Nuu-chah-nulth leaders saw the revival of whaling as a way to reinvigorate cultural traditions and reaffirm our identities as whaling people, but the revitalization was contested by some environmental and animal rights groups. Chapter 5 looks at the rise of the anti-whaling movement. Through the utilization of the "Indian as savage" image, the whaling opponents undermined the Makah efforts to initiate a whale hunt in the late 1990s and challenged their cultural and treaty right to whale. The anti-whaling coalition grew, drawing in politicians known for their anti-Indian and anti-treaty positions. In chapter 6, I focus on how this anti-whaling/anti-Indian coalition developed a successful legal campaign, utilizing federal environmental laws, to stop the Makah from whaling.

In the final chapter, I examine the cultural, social, and dietary reasons why the Makah and Nuu-chah-nulth want to bring whale meat, oil, and blubber back into our diets. I discuss the diseases plaguing Native communities today and the renewed focus on traditional foods as a way to overcome health problems. And, finally, I examine Native whaling communities in Alaska and northern Canada to illustrate how, through their annual whale hunts, these people have maintained strong community ties by communal hunting, processing, distributing, sharing, and consuming whale products.

1 / *Tsawalk*

THE CENTRALITY OF WHALING TO MAKAH AND NUU-CHAH-NULTH LIFE

STORIES CONTAINED WITHIN INDIGENOUS ORAL TRADITIONS PRO-
vide a window into Native societies and cultures, helping to define and
explain their way of life. In Nuu-chah-nulth and Makah oral tradition, a
story has been passed down from one generation to the next, one that is central
to our identity as whalers. T'iick'in, the great mythical Thunderbird, was the first
great whale hunter. The flapping of his wings caused thunder and his flicking
tongue brought lightning. There were once four Thunderbirds that lived in our
area, but three of them were killed by Kwatyat, the creator of all things. T'iick'in
was known to feed on whales (*iiḥtuup*). He utilized Itl'ik, Lightning (Sea) Serpent, as a kind of harpoon or spear to throw at a whale to stun it. Once he had
dazed the whale, T'iick'in swooped down and picked it up in his mighty claws
and took it back to the mountains, where he enjoyed a feast of succulent whale
meat and blubber. T'iick'in demonstrated that the *iiḥtuup* could be caught and
utilized for food and tools.[1]

In another version of this story, Thunderbird and whale saved the Nuu-chah-
nulth people from starvation. It was a very bad season for fishing and people
were having a difficult time finding food to eat. Thunderbird saw how hungry we
were and went out in search of a whale. He took Lightning Serpent and wound it
around his waist as he flew along the coast hunting for a whale. Finally, he spot-
ted one, and he took the serpent and threw it down at the whale, hitting and stun-
ning it. While the whale was stunned, it remained floating on the surface of the
water, making it easy for Thunderbird to grab. Thunderbird dived down, picked
up the whale in his powerful talons, and brought it to the village for all the people
to eat, so that they would no longer be hungry.[2]

I heard Thunderbird, Whale, and Lightning Serpent stories when I was a young girl. The legends have been passed down the generations and throughout the years have been recorded by ethnologists, anthropologists, and historians. There are many different versions, but they all contain the same message: the whale was, and still is, central to our culture and identity. In this chapter, I discuss how, before the arrival of the *mamalhn'i*, whaling traditions were central to our very existence as a people and were intricately connected to Makah and Nuu-chah-nulth economic, political, religious, and social systems.

MAKAH AND NUU-CHAH-NULTH CULTURAL SYSTEMS

The Makah and Nuu-chah-nulth peoples' traditional territory is on the central Northwest coast, the Makah in the Cape Flattery area at the northwestern tip of the Olympic Peninsula in Washington State and the Nuu-chah-nulth on the west coast of Vancouver Island in British Columbia. Topographically, the Makah's and Nuu-chah-nulth's traditional territory consists of steep and rocky terrain, with the Coast mountain range in British Columbia and the Cascades mountains in Washington and Oregon acting as natural dividers, cutting off these seafaring, maritime peoples from the inland hunting-and-gathering societies. These natural boundaries surrounding the various indigenous groups resulted in a large number of small, autonomous societies along the coast.[3]

The Makah and Nuu-chah-nulth are among the Wakashan-speaking peoples, sharing linguistic ties, cultural patterns, and a tradition of hunting whales. Early explorers' accounts noted the similarities in Makah and Nuu-chah-nulth social organization, language, subsistence patterns, and ceremonialism.[4] Since the Makah are the only tribe in the United States who speak the Wakashan language, this led some scholars to suggest that they moved to the Cape Flattery area from Vancouver Island. This conjecture is supported by both Makah and Nuu-chah-nulth oral histories, which not only link the two groups but also provide a clue as to how the tribes became territorially disconnected. This is a story passed down through the Makah oral tradition and recorded by James Swan, the first non-Indian to live among the Makah in the mid-1800s.

> A long time ago . . . the water of the Pacific flowed through what is now swamp and prairie between Waatch village and Neah Bay, making an island of Cape Flattery. The water suddenly receded, leaving Neah Bay perfectly dry. It was four days reaching its lowest ebb, and then rose again without any waves or breakers till it had submerged the Cape, and in fact the whole country except

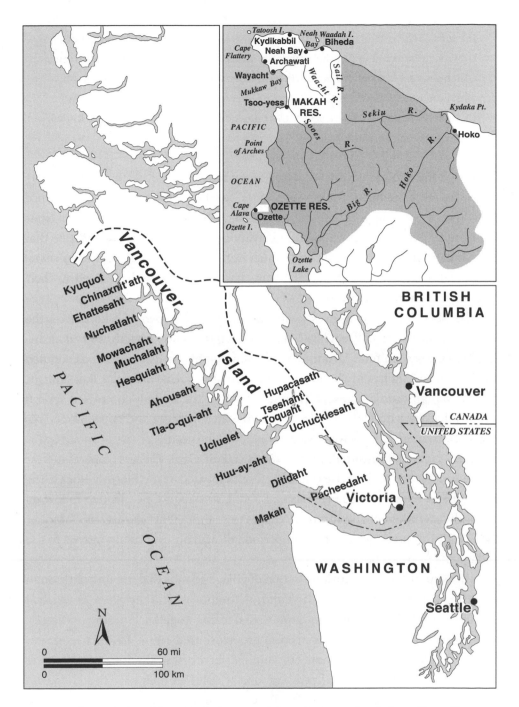

Territory of Nuu-chah-nulth and Makah groups. Adapted by Barry Levely from *HuupuKw anuum Tupaat: Nuu-chah-nulth Voices*, ed. Alan Hoover (Victoria: Royal British Columbia Museum, 2000). Inset: Mid-nineteenth-century Makah settlements. From Renker and Gunther, "Makah," in *Handbook of North American Indians*, vol. 7.

the tops of the mountains at Clyoquot. The water . . . as it came up to the houses, those who had canoes put their effects in them, and floated off with the current, which set very strongly to the north. Some drifted one way, some another; and when the waters assumed their accustomed level, a portion of the tribe found themselves beyond Nootka, where their descendents now reside, and are known by the same name as the Makahs.[5]

Although the two groups are separated by land, they are connected by the water-ways that were the major travel routes of the coastal peoples. Historical evidence and oral history support the cultural linkages between the Makah and Nuu-chah-nulth peoples. Archaeological excavations and carbon dating indicate that the Makah villages of Ozette and Wa'atch were occupied for at least 1,500 years. Radiocarbon dating shows that the Nuu-chah-nulth people have lived in their territory for more than 4,000 years.[6]

The Makah call themselves kwih-dich-chuh-ahtX, "people who live on the cape near the rocks and seagulls." They received the name Makah, a word meaning "generous with food," from their Clallam neighbors. The name was adopted by American officials in the 1850s. Before the 1855 Treaty of Neah Bay brought all the Makah onto one reservation in Neah Bay, the Makah comprised several groups that were divided into five principal winter villages and two summer villages. The winter villages were Neah (Diah), which was on the site of an old Spanish fort; Wa'atch (Wayatch), on the south side of Cape Flattery; and Tsoo-yess (Tsu-yess, T'sues) and Ozette (Hosette, Osett), located at the Flattery Rocks. The fifth village, named Biheda (Bahaada, Ba'ada), was abandoned in 1852 following a smallpox epidemic. The summer villages were located at Klasset and Tatooche Island. In the post-1855 reservation period, all Makah eventually moved to the village site in Neah Bay.[7]

The Nuu-chah-nulth are a collection of village groups that are linked through a common language and similar cultural components. They were established as small, socially independent groups that came together in single villages. The members of these villages or local groups shared rights to the use of specific resources within geographically limited territories. The local groups were composed of *ushtakimilh*, or lineage groups, which had their own head, *haw'ilth* (chief), who represented the line of descent from an original ancestor. The village also had a *taayii haw'ilth* (head chief), who was from the highest-ranking *ushtakimilh*. Archaeological and historical evidence shows that the structure of the Nuu-chah-nulth villages continually changed during both the pre- and the post-contact periods. This was a result of tribal warfare over territory, resources, and after-contact disease epidemics, which ultimately led to amalgamations that transformed the villages into the fifteen distinct groups that exist today.[8]

My people were mistakenly called Nootka or Nootkans (also spelled Nutka), a name given to one of the Nuu-chah-nulth groups (Mowachaht) by Captain Cook when he visited the territory in 1778. The name was later extended to include all of the groups, including the Makah. At this time, we did not have one specific overarching name to define ourselves as a larger tribal group, but we had names for local groups that were linked to places of origin. Gilbert M. Sproat, a Scottish businessman who came to our territory—to what became known as the Alberni Valley—in 1860, referred to us as the "aht" people, which is the general ending of our ancestral names (Ahousaht, Tseshaht, Toquaht, etc.). "Aht" translates literally as "people of."[9] However, Cook's name, Nootka or Nootkan, was the name that was eventually adopted by Canadian Indian agents, anthropologists, and others, and was used externally and internally to refer to these coastal groups.

[handwritten margin note: these names are a product of colonialism]

My great-aunt Winnie (Winifred David) heard a story when she was a young girl about how we became known as the Nootkan people. She carried many of the stories she heard as a child into adulthood, thus continuing our oral tradition. As an elder, she was interviewed by numerous anthropologists and historians, and her remembrances were important in creating comprehensive written accounts of Nuu-chah-nulth culture and history. The story of how the Nuu-chah-nulth people got their erroneous name begins with Captain Cook and his initial visit to the region in 1778. Cook's ship sailed into an area of Nuu-chah-nulth territory that he later named Nootka Sound. His ship came upon the Mowachaht village of Yuquot, which was renamed Friendly Cove by Cook. He was met by the local village members, who paddled out to the ship in their canoes in an attempt to help Cook's crew navigate the rocks. The people yelled to the crew a word that sounds like Nootka, a word in our language that in English means "to circle about or around." Aunty Winnie discussed this in an interview in 1977:

> They started making signs and they were talking Indian and they were saying: *nu-tka-icim nu-tka-icim*, they were saying. That means, you go around the harbour. . . . So Captain Cook said, "Oh, they're telling us the name of this place is Nootka." That's how Nootka got its name. . . . But the Indian name is altogether different. Yeah. It's Yuquot, that Indian village. So it's called Nootka now and the whole of the West Coast (Vancouver Island), we're all Nootka Indians now.[10] *[handwritten: rip]*

Throughout the years, the Nuu-chah-nulth groups on Vancouver Island worked at establishing a unified political voice for all the groups. In 1958, we formed a collective body and renamed ourselves the West Coast Allied Tribes (later changed to the West Coast District Council). A year after Aunty Winnie told her story to W. L. Langlois, the so-called Nootkan people officially adopted the more appropriate name of Nuu-chah-nulth, which means "all along the mountains and sea."

WHALING AND NUU-CHAH-NULTH AND MAKAH ECONOMIES

Whalebones found in archaeological sites in Makah and Nuu-chah-nulth territories show that whales were significant to Native cultures as far back as 4,000 years.[11] Before Native economies shifted following contact with *mamałn̓i*, Makah and Nuu-chah-nulth were marine people who derived most of their subsistence from the ocean, inlets, and nearby rivers. The people fished primarily for halibut and salmon, harvested the local shellfish, and hunted sea mammals. While they did not focus on developing land resources for subsistence, they did hunt deer, bear, and elk and gathered roots and berries, which contributed to their diet. The majority of the food gathering took place during the summer months, and the two groups traveled to areas along the waterways where they could extract the resources; while there, they erected dwellings. As a result, these coastal peoples had both summer and winter residences: semi-permanent summer residences along the ocean and river shores, and more permanent winter houses also close to the waterways but in more sheltered areas to protect them from the harsh winter climate.

The Makah and Nuu-chah-nulth relied on the sea for most of their subsistence and placed much emphasis on hunting sea mammals, such as seals, sea lions, and whales. Archaeological data provide evidence that their greatest economic resource was whaling.[12] Early historical documentation gives varying non-Native viewpoints on the economic significance of whaling. Some early writers suggested that the prestige value of whaling was more significant to the Makah and Nuu-chah-nulth than the economic value, whereas others saw whaling as an important subsistence resource. However, nineteenth- and twentieth-century literature reassessed the economic significance of whaling, with studies based on new archaeological data and oral histories. This new ethnographic research shows the importance of whaling to a subsistence life, with whales providing an enormous amount of food, particularly in the springtime when winter provisions were exhausted and food was more difficult to obtain. The faunal remains uncovered during excavations at the Makah village of Ozette established that whales accounted for 75 percent of all meat and oil consumed; 846.6 metric tons of blubber and meat were recovered from whales, which is a substantial amount

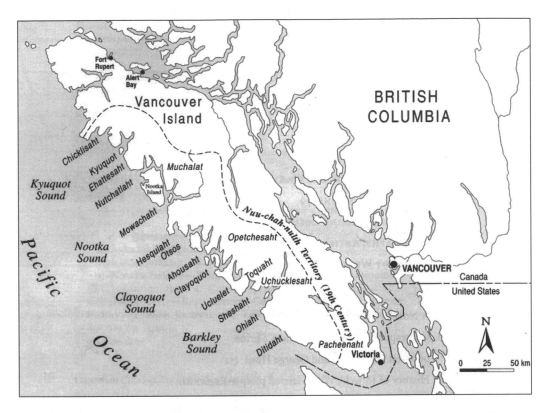

Nuu-chah-nulth groups, nineteenth century. From Aldona Jonaitis, *The Yuquot Whaler's Shrine* (Seattle: University of Washington Press, 1999).

of edible food. Whale meat, blubber, and oil were considered tasty and appetizing. The people used the oil as a dipping sauce to complement other foods, and, because of its high nutritional value, whale meat was also one of their most wholesome foods.[13]

Archaeological excavations in traditional territories in the 1960s and 1970s uncovered thousands of artifacts, many of which were connected to whaling. These discoveries showed the variety of uses for the whale bones. They were carved into rattles for use in rituals and ceremonies and reconstructed into tools and implements, such as bark shredders, clubs, and spindle whorls. They were utilized in the construction of water diversion systems that ran alongside the houses and channeled rainwater away from the villages. The bones were also used to stabilize small mudslide areas around the village centers. Whale sinew was used to make rope and cord, and the stomach and intestines were inflated and dried to make containers to hold the oil.[14]

An important component of Makah and Nuu-chah-nulth pre- and early-contact cultures, whaling was entwined in a complex web of social interactions and served important social, subsistence, and ritual functions. It was the unifying interactions of these various activities that formed an elaborate and interconnected network of economic, ceremonial, and redistribution rights and privileges.[15] The Makah and Nuu-chah-nulth lived in small kin-related village groups that centered on their *haw'iih* and their *ushtakimilh* (lineage group). Social organization was based on a stratified rank-and-prestige system. Societal distinctions between individuals and between groups permeated every aspect of social life. Social organization was based on the hereditary transmission of status and privilege, which was affirmed and enhanced through the accumulation and giving away of material wealth.[16]

The villages consisted of people from all ranks; those in the higher echelons were *haw'iih*, the chiefs or titleholders who were the heads of their family units based on their hereditary birthright. The *haw'iih* were also the wealthiest members of the local group, acquiring and sustaining wealth and status by holding great potlatches, where food, goods, and ceremonial items were distributed. The head chief held the largest and most lavish potlatches, which provided him with great esteem and further elevated his status.

The next in this ranked social order were the *maschimes*, or the commoners, who were related to respected *haw'iih* of some standing in their community but who did not generally accumulate wealth or potlatch. *Maschimes* could raise their status by mastering skills, such as by becoming great canoe makers, respected warriors, or esteemed healers.[17]

The lowest members of this social organization were the *kohl*, or slaves. *Kohl* were considered a group unto themselves and did not really fit into the graduated system of ranking. Slaves were captives, mostly women and children, who were taken during warfare. Although they were considered part of the tribal unit, because they were not free, they could not achieve higher status. They were considered possessions of the chiefs, and only their owner had authority over them. The more slaves a *haw'ilth* had, the more prestige he acquired, since ownership implied success at war or great wealth.[18]

All people from all social categories lived under the same roof. Housing structures consisted of permanent posts with detachable walls and roofs made out of cedar, which could be carried from the larger winter villages to the smaller summer villages. The winter houses were from 30 to 40 feet wide and could reach a length of 100 feet. Each house was overseen by a *haw'ilth*, who had ultimate authority over his *ushtakimilh*. The people living in the big houses in this large extended family social structure worked together for their *haw'ilth* and for the common good of the *ushtakimilh*.[19]

The chief's position was tied to many social obligations and it was up to each *haw'ilth* to make sure that his lineage group was looked after. His connection to powerful ancestral spirits provided him with an extraordinary ability to manage the resources that were tied to his position and to make sure that these resources were distributed to all members of his local group. The *maschimes* received housing, protection, and access to resources through their association with a chief; in return, they exploited the resources of the chief's land and marine space, creating a social system that was both stable and mutually supportive. The members of an *ushtakimilh* always had the ability to leave and join another village group, which could lessen the power of one chief and heighten the power and status of another.[20]

Birth into the differing social categories determined not only one's status and position within the society but also how an individual would be raised, the labor he or she would perform, the food eaten, the clothing worn, choice of marriage partners, and burial rites. Rank and status distinctions were most marked in Makah and Nuu-chah-nulth ceremonial life but also extended to subsistence activities and productive labor. Fishing for ordinary subsistence was carried out by the *maschimes* and the *kohl*, but activities that required great skill, such as killing a whale, were inherited privileges reserved for chiefs.

The whaling tradition reflected aspects of the stratified social system. Killing a whale was considered the highest glory: the more whales a chief caught, the more prestige, respect, and physical wealth he received, thus serving to elevate his status and position inside and outside his village or social group.[21]

OO-SIMCH: WHALING AND SPIRITUAL PREPARATION

Our whaling tradition was immersed in spiritual, ritual, and religious practices. The whaling *haw'iih* underwent months of complex rituals and ceremonial preparation to assure their success in whaling. It was believed that a chief's ability to catch a whale was derived from the spiritual world that provided him with power or medicine that other members of the tribe did not possess.[22] In the Pacific Northwest, there was a common belief among all the indigenous peoples that human beings could obtain extraordinary power from spiritual entities in the nonhuman world. This tradition is known as the Guardian Spirit complex, and it was a fundamental aspect of the coastal peoples' cultures and traditions.[23]

In this tradition, individuals would go on a spiritual quest to seek out a spirit known as *tumanos,* or *tamanawas* in Chinook Jargon. Once acquired, this spirit would assist them in being successful in fishing, hunting, or other pursuits. Many individuals would also seek out spirit power to live long and healthy lives. These spirits would make themselves known during an individual's vision quest or journey, which was held at a young age. Once the spirit was obtained, the individual would be responsible for maintaining this relationship through respectful rituals and ceremonies so that the guardian spirit would continue to provide him or her with certain abilities and protections.[24]

An individual could obtain a powerful spirit through rigorous ritual cleansing, observances of taboos, fasting, and prayer. This ritual cleansing is known in Nuu-chah-nulth as *oo-simch.*[25] The first syllable, "oo," means "be careful." When used in a spiritual context, "it invokes supernatural fear," or as Chief Umeek, Richard Atleo, explains, it is "human fear in the presence of spiritual mystery."[26] Therefore, *oo-simch* could be interpreted as "careful seeking" within a "fearsome" surrounding or environment.[27]

Oo-simch continues to be an important ritual that Nuu-chah-nulth-aht perform before fishing, hunting, or preparing for a potlatch and for overall spiritual well-being. Born in 1908, the late Ahousaht elder Peter Webster was taught the *oo-simch* ritual by his father and grandfather. Peter said that each family had its own rituals that consisted of bathing in the sea, scrubbing the body with twigs and branches, and singing prayer songs. These rituals cleansed the body, mind, and soul and would be carried out each day in a secret and secluded place. *Oo-simch,* he said, was to make the body "clean inside and outside" out of respect for the guardian spirit.[28]

When my cousin Linsey turned sixteen in 2003, her mother, Eileen Haggard, held a *iiclhuutla,* or "coming of age" potlatch, to acknowledge her daughter's passage into adulthood.[29] My aunt asked me to be one of her daughter's chaperones, to sit with Linsey and watch over her during the potlatch. In our culture, during the time leading up to a coming-of-age ceremony, the young girl is secluded and cannot come in contact with anyone other than older female relatives who *haahuupa,* educate her about life.[30] During Linsey's potlatch, female relatives were designated to watch over her and take care of her needs. Because of the importance of keeping the young girl clean and pure, her attendants also need to be ritually purified. Leading up to the potlatch, each morning before dawn, I went with my aunts, Eileen and Pauline, and my cousin, Gail, up a mountain to a secluded stream, where we would *oo-simch,* cleansing and purifying our bodies with cedar boughs.

My great-great-grandfather, Sayach'apis, born in 1843, was known to be a great hunter of sea mammals. He was brought up understanding the importance of *oo-simch* and received constant instruction from his father and uncle on ritual cleansing. He knew that if he wanted to be a successful hunter he needed to observe the proper protocol and spiritual preparation. At certain times of the year, Sayach'apis would go to his secret sites in the mountains, where he would stay for many days. While in the forest he would ritually bathe, rubbing himself with hemlock branches until his body ached from the pain. Nuu-chah-nulth have a belief in four *haw'iih*: Above (or Sky) Chief, Horizon Chief, Land Chief, and Undersea Chief. These chiefs were called upon during all ritual bathing and preparation. As Sayach'apis conducted his rituals, he would pray to the chiefs, asking Sky Chief for a long life and success. Sayach'apis caught many sea mammals in his lifetime, and he credited this to his careful and diligent adherence to *oo-simch*.[31]

This same kind of ritual behavior and ceremonial preparation was essential for all subsistence activities and many social practices, but, because of the social, economic, and spiritual significance of whaling, the *oo-simch* connected to that activity was even more rigid, strenuous, and complex.[32] Peter Webster's great-uncle was one of the last Nuu-chah-nulth whalers of the early 1900s. He told Peter that the ritual preparation he went through was lengthy and strenuous and involved abstaining from certain foods and from sexual activity in order to preserve all of his strength for whaling.[33]

Haw'ilth Umeek comes from a long line of whalers from the village of Ahousaht,[34] one of the northern Nuu-chah-nulth groups. He says that before a whale hunt, his great-grandfather, Keesta, born around 1866, would go up into the mountains to his special cleansing site, where he would spend eight months conducting spiritual and physical preparations, believing that "the great personage of the whale demanded the *honor* of extended ceremony."[35]

> In his preparations of a whaling expedition Keesta fasted, abstained from conjugal sex, performed ritual cleansing, and sang prayer songs over a period of eight months. He took with him the curled tail feather of a mallard duck. Since a curly tail feather does not uncurl under natural conditions, Keesta said that he would know whether his prayers were strong medicine when the curly tail feather straightened out of its own accord. Eventually the curly tail feather did just that, and only then did Keesta come down from the mountain. . . . Keesta "captured" three whales in the traditional Nuu-chah-nulth way.[36]

Umeek says that Keesta attributed the capture of those whales to the effectiveness of his prayers and that "the straightened tail feather was a supernatural sign indicating the tangible relationship between spiritual powers and physical powers."[37]

THE CENTRALITY OF THE *HAQUUM* TO THE WHALE HUNT

The whaling chief and his *haquum* (queen) underwent the same rigid and complex rituals and spiritual preparation and obeyed similar taboos to demonstrate their connected spirituality and power.[38] Husband and wife abstained from sex during their ritual preparation. Sometimes the husband even moved into another house during the whaling season. Within these complex and elaborate ritual ceremonies was the underlying concept of imitative power, meaning that the whaling chief's and his wife's actions during their preparation affected how the whale would act during the hunt as well as after it was caught.[39]

An aspect of the rituals that the whaler conducted before the hunt involved performing certain movements while bathing that imitated a whale's movements or actions. The whaler would begin his ritual bathing early in the morning in a freshwater lake or pond. He submerged himself four times and after each time rubbed himself with hemlock branches. As the whaler emerged from the water, he would blow mouthfuls of water toward the center of the lake or pond, emulating the way a whale moved in the ocean. He performed these movements very slowly and quietly in the belief that his actions would induce the whale to act in the same way.[40] While the whaler conducted the rituals, his wife held a rope tied to her husband's waist, which represented the harpoon line. As the chief sang his whaling songs, he walked calmly around his wife, making slow movements that mimicked the movements of the whale. In turn, the wife sang her songs, repeating over and over, "This is the way the whale will act."[41]

Once the whale hunt commenced, the wife also had to take great care in her actions, because even after her husband left for the hunt, her movements affected how the whale acted while being pursued. After the whaler and his crew left the shore, the wife returned to her home and did not go out for the duration of the hunt. She lay very still in a dark room. Any movements she made had to be calm and slow. It was believed that her power was so strong at this point that she could actually become the whale. If she made any quick or shaky movements, she would cause the whale to become unruly, making it difficult to catch. The wife was not allowed to comb her hair because it was thought that if the comb broke it would cause her husband's whaling harpoon line to snap. It was believed that the wife exerted such a "special influence over the whale" that she could actually "call it" to the shore.[42]

Although all crew members were expected to observe intense rituals, training, and taboos, it was only the whaler and his wife who went through the most elaborate rituals and ceremonial bathing that influenced the whale's spirit and induced the whales to allow themselves to be captured.[43]

WHALING SHRINES AND THE DRIFT WHALE RITUAL

The chiefs utilized shrines in their ritual preparation for all subsistence activities. Rituals conducted in these shrines served to bring strong runs of salmon, herring, or other resources.[44] However, the more elaborate shrines were used by whaling chiefs to prepare spiritually and ritually for their whale hunts. These whaling shrines, also called whalers' washing houses, held great spiritual significance in both Nuu-chah-nulth and Makah societies. They were utilized exclusively by the whaling chiefs for their purification rituals.

Whaling *haw'iih* inherited secret sites where these shrines were erected. They would go there to perform their sacred rituals and prayers to the spirits, asking them for what Mowachaht *haw'ilth* Jerry Jack called *cheesum*, or "whaling magic," which was needed to capture a whale. Even the techniques utilized by the whalers were connected to the spirit world. It was understood that whalers' ancestors were instructed by spirits on the proper rituals to be performed in these secret locations. This sacred knowledge and the methods used in preparation were then passed down and closely followed by the next generation of whalers.[45]

The shrines were also used by whaling chiefs to conduct rituals to entice dead whales onto their beaches. A drift whale was considered a chief's property, and once it was brought to shore, it would become the possession of the *haw'ilth* on whose beach it had landed. In the Makah and Nuu-chah-nulth belief system there was an understanding that the power an individual received from the spirit world could be transferred to another person after that individual died. The drift whale ritual incorporated this philosophy and involved the use of human corpses. The dead, especially the cadavers of successful whaling chiefs, were believed to have "mysterious power over whales."[46] *Haw'ilth* Jerry Jack said that the whaling *haw'iih* would tell other whaling chiefs, "When I die, I want you to use me, to cut my head off and use me for *cheesum*. I'll help you reach the creator to give you that strength that you need to get that whale."[47]

The great Mowachaht chief Maquinna had an elaborate whaling shrine hidden on an island close to the village of Yuquot.[48] The shrine contained over eighty anthropomorphic carvings and numerous human skulls. There is a story that says that one of Maquinna's ancestors was taught by Thunderbird how to use this shrine. Thunderbird told the chief to ritually bathe and to make implements to harpoon whales. Once the chief received his training from Thunderbird, he swam out to the island, where he prayed to the "Great Chiefs" and to the carvings and skulls, asking them to give him the strength to whale.[49] In his prayers the chief addressed the spirits of his ancestors who had allowed their corpses to be used for these sacred ceremonies.

> Now, my father, I have come to you, although you are dead; but your spirit is alive and is standing alongside of me now, in this house that your great-great-grandfathers built for you to come and pray to the four chiefs of this world; to whom you used to pray for help, in this house of the great spirits. You used to bring me with you here to hear you saying your prayers to our four great protectors and helpers; and I used to see you take your father's dead body on your back and carry him into the lake and dive with him into the water, to find the spirit of the whale that you were going to harpoon and to kill; and whenever you said that you had found the spirit of the whale you would take it into the house of the spirits and would give it to the wooden images in the house of prayer; and they would hold it for you until your time was ended for washing. And now I ask you to come, my father, on my back and help me in trying to find the spirit of the whale: and I will leave it in your charge now; for you used to do everything to help me while I was a little boy, the son—your son; and even now your spirit is taking care of me; so come with me now, and I will carry you on my back.[50]

THE QUEST FOR GOOD LUCK

During their ritual and spiritual preparation, whalers would continue their quest for help from the spirit world and also seek out material objects that would provide them with additional power or "luck" needed to hunt and kill a whale. These tangible objects could be used like a charm or amulet and would be sought for all hunting and fishing activities, but the most powerful ones would be sought for whaling. Once a charm was acquired it was kept secret, because secrecy was supposed to help in maintaining its power and effectiveness.[51] In Makah oral tradition there is a legend, "The Whale and the Little Bird," which tells the story of a whaler who noticed a connection between a whale and a little black bird called a *gakatas*. The whale and the *gakatas* lived together, and the little bird provided protection for the whale. It was considered very lucky to find one of these little birds, and if a whaler obtained one for his whaling power it would bring him many whales.[52]

Charms were sought for more than just subsistence activities. They were also sought after for wealth, love, and healing. They provided an individual with a material connection to the spirit world, and amulets were often obtained when individuals were conducting their rituals to seek a spirit helper. These charms could be blind snakes, crabs, and spiders or fragments of supernatural animals.[53] In Huu-a-uyaht oral tradition, there is a story about a young boy who got his strength to hunt whales by coming in contact with a supernatural power called a *michtach*. The young boy told his father that he wanted to become a great whaler. The father responded that in order to become a great whaler the boy must prepare himself by cleansing his mind and his body through physical preparation and spiritual cleansing. He told his son to find a secluded area to *oo-simch*, which the son did for an entire year. While he was in his sacred place conducting his prayers and rituals, the boy saw a strange creature. He tried to catch the creature but it was too quick and got away. He followed the creature up a mountain, where he came upon another strange creature. The son told his father about the unusual creatures, and his father explained that these were spirits and that he needed to seek out the one that was for whaling.[54]

Months went by and the young boy persisted with his ritual bathing and prayers in his attempts to seek out this strange creature that would provide him with the powers to whale. He ate very little during his *oo-simch*, only small strips of whale blubber that provided him with the strength to continue his purification. He was determined to get his whaling spirit, his *michtach*. Finally, he came in contact with the supernatural creature again. The creature was creeping along the side of the mountain bluff and did not notice the young boy. The boy slowly and quietly sneaked up behind the creature and grabbed the tip of its arm. The creature wiggled out of the young boy's grip, but as it fled, it left behind a piece of its tentacle. The young boy was very happy and wrapped his new "power" in a soft skin and returned home. On the fourth day after acquiring his spirit power, the young boy went out into the ocean and caught four humpback whales. His determination and perseverance in his ritual cleansing and bathing, and his respectful prayers asking the spirit world for supernatural power, paid off. He was now a "proven whaler" and his village would never go hungry now that he had the power to bring home whales to feed them.[55]

In Makah oral tradition there is a story about Thlu-kluts, Thunderbird, a giant who lives in the highest mountains and who feeds on *ch'ih-t'uh-pook* (whales).

When Thlu-kluts is hungry, he puts on his Thunderbird clothing and soars over the ocean in search of the whale. When he spots a *ch'ih-t'uh-pook*, he takes the Ha-he-to-ak, the Lightning Serpent, which he has tied around his waist, and throws it at the whale, first dazing and then killing it. He seizes the whale and brings it up the mountain to eat. The Makah whaling chiefs believed that the Ha-he-to-ak possessed great power, and when lightning struck a tree or land, they would go to that area in search of a piece of the Lightning Serpent. If they were fortunate enough to find even a small piece of its bone, this would provide the chief with supernatural strength, helping him to excel as a whaler.[56]

PREPARING FOR A WHALE HUNT

The Makah and Nuu-chah-nulth pursued various species of whales, but the *maa'ak* (*sih-xwah·wiX* in Makah), or gray whales, and the *iiḥtuup* (*ch'ih-ch'ih-wad* in Makah), or humpback whales, were the most sought after and most commonly caught. The *iiḥtuup* and *maa'ak* are relatively slow swimmers and travel close to the shores, making them easy to hunt. The gray whales have one of the longest migration routes of any cetacean, traveling 5,000 miles in each direction, beginning in Mexico and ending in Alaska. They pass Washington State and Vancouver Island in April and May and reach the Bering Sea in late June. Their southward migration begins in the fall, reaching Vancouver Island and Washington in late October to mid-December. The humpback has a similar migratory pattern, passing along the coast of Washington State and Vancouver Island in May and June and then returning on its southward migration in October and November. Some gray and humpback whales stay in the Makah and Nuu-chah-nulth marine space throughout the summer months as well.[57]

Archaeological excavations at the Makah village of Ozette, occupied for at least 1,500 years, indicate that the Makah whaling activities focused more on the gray than the humpback whale. Of all the whalebones excavated, more than 95 percent of the bones identified were from gray and humpback whales. Slightly over 50 percent were from the gray whale and 46 percent were from the humpback whale.[58] Archaeological excavations in Nuu-chah-nulth territory in Barkley Sound found that approximately 80 percent of the whalebones collected were from the humpback whale, while only 13 percent came from the gray whale. These figures demonstrate that many of the Nuu-chah-nulth groups pursued the humpback whale over the gray whale. The reasons for this could be that the humpback whales were larger and more plentiful than the gray whales; they contained a lot more oil than other whales; and they stayed in the Nuu-chah-nulth marine space for longer periods of time.[59] Our language could also provide a clue to the preference of whale species. In the Nuu-chah-nulth language, the generic name for whale is *iihtuup*, which is the same word for humpback whale. In the Makah language, the generic name for whale is *ch'ih-t'uh-pook*, which is not connected to any of the whale species; all the whales have their own distinct names.[60]

In 1792, Spanish explorer Juan Francisco de la Bodega y Quadra sailed into Nootka Sound on an expedition to investigate Spanish claims to the area and to negotiate with British captain George Vancouver the terms of the 1790 Nootka Convention. Quadra brought with him a young botanist, José Moziño, whose duty it was to compile a written ethnographic study of the indigenous cultures in the area. While there, Moziño took exhaustive notes concerning the Mowachaht people's traditions, lifestyle, and language. During his five-month residence in Nuu-chah-nulth territory, he was able to gather valuable and detailed information on indigenous lifestyles before contact with non-Indians began to change the Native cultures. In his personal journal, Moziño produced the first known written account of a Nuu-chah-nulth whale hunt. He notes:

> They thrust into the whale, with great force, a sharp harpoon attached to a long and heavy shaft so that it will pierce more deeply. This shaft is then recovered by means of a rope, and at the same time they slacken another [rope], tied at one end to the harpoon and at the other to an inflated bladder, which floats over the water like a buoy, marking the place to which the wounded animal has fled during the short time in which it stays alive.[61]

Moziño could sense by the way the whale hunt was conducted that it was a very important Mowachaht tradition. He noted: "Among all the types of fishing, none is more admired that that for the whale."[62]

James Swan was employed as the first schoolteacher in Neah Bay and resided among the Makah in the mid-1800s. During that time he collected data on their customs and lifestyles and was greatly intrigued by the seagoing capabilities of the Makah. Swan wrote extensively on Makah whaling: the types of harpoons used, the rituals surrounding the hunt, the distribution of the meat, and the feast that followed the cutting up of the whale. He noted the Makahs' marine skill and how they excelled in maneuvering their canoes, especially when pursuing whales.[63]

Canoes were central to marine-based cultures. They were the main mode of travel, transporting coastal peoples up and down the coast to exploit the sea resources, conduct trade, and attend potlatches and for warfare with other indigenous groups along the coast. Since most of their subsistence came from the oceans and rivers, the canoe played a central role in sea resource extraction, the fishing and hunting of sea mammals. The canoe was constructed out of the western red cedar tree. The canoe maker would take great care in choosing a tree for his canoe. Once a tree was chosen, proper rituals and prayers would be conducted, asking its spirit for success in the pursuits the canoe was to be used for. It was then felled and split in two, with one side being used to make the canoe. Because of the great importance placed on whaling, even greater care was taken in the selection of a tree that was to be made into a whaling canoe. The whaling canoe was large, between 28 and 38 feet in length and sturdy enough to carry eight men. Other canoes would accompany the whaling canoe and would assist the whaling crew when a whale was captured.[64]

A harpoon was used to kill the whale. The harpoon head was a sharp blade made of a large mussel shell. This shell was situated between a pair of antler or bone barbs and held together with spruce gum. A thin cord of sinew was wrapped tightly around the head and another coat of gum was added. Attached to this were a harpoon staff and a long line. Buoys made out of inflated sealskins were attached to the line and were used to help keep the whale afloat.[65]

PHYSICAL AND SPIRITUAL PREPARATION:
PAYING RESPECT TO THE WHALE

> Every protocol had been observed between the whaling chief and the spirit of the whale. Keesta [Chief Umeek's great-grandfather] had thrown the harpoon, and the whale had accepted it, had grabbed and held onto the harpoon according to the agreement they had made through prayers and petitions. Harmony prevailed, whale and whaler were one.—Umeek, Richard Atleo (*Tsawalk,* x)

Proper religious observances were also conducted during the hunt. The whaling crew continued their prayers throughout the hunt, maintaining their connection to the spirit world and to their spirit helpers who provided them with "more than human strength" to capture the whale.[66] My ancestors believed that a whale was not caught, but, with the proper rituals and utmost respect shown to the whale, it would give itself up to the whaler and to the people who had shown it the most esteem. This is why the rituals had to be conducted with great care and commitment before, during, and after the hunt. Songs and prayers were sung by the whaling crew during the hunt to demonstrate to the whale their appreciation for its gift of itself.

Makah whaler, ca. 1915. Photograph by Edward S. Curtis;
courtesy of the Royal British Columbia Museum, Victoria.

Whale, I have given you what you wish to get—my good harpoon. And now you have it. Please hold it with your strong hands. Do not let go. Whale, turn towards the fine beach . . . and you will be proud to see the young men come down . . . to see you; and the young men will say to one another: What a great whale he is! What a fat whale he is! What a strong whale he is! And you, whale, will be proud of all that you hear them say of your greatness.[67]

Once harpooned, a whale usually responded by heading toward the open sea, and it could drag the whaling crew for days. However, if a whaler had obtained strong whaling power, had correctly prepared for the hunt, and properly honored the whale's spirit, the whale would head toward the shore. If the whale thrashed about and the canoe capsized or was damaged by the whale, this was evidence that the whaler had not adequately prepared for the hunt and was careless in his ritual observances.[68]

The Nuu-chah-nulth name for whale, *iiḥtuup*, means "big mystery." Huu-ay-aht elder Willie Sport said that the chief's ability to establish such an intimate connection to a whale was seen as being both spiritual and mysterious.

A whaler believed that a specific whale gave itself to him, through a mysterious power. Prayer and cleansing the mind and body made the whaler worthy of the great whale's gift of life. When the whaler went out to sea and reached the place where thousands of whales were migrating up the coast, when he got there he didn't harpoon the first whale he saw, he identified the one that he was intended to kill. That one was looking for him, too. They recognized each other. The whale gives himself to the hunter who has been praying and who is clean.[69]

A whaler's success was regarded as proof that he had not only acquired a powerful whaling spirit but had also shown proper respect to the whale's spirit. The more success in whaling a *haw'ilth* had throughout his lifetime, the more powerful a spirit he was believed to have obtained.

When the whale tired, the crew in the other canoes would throw their lances into the whale until it finally died. A crew member then dived into the water and cut a hole through the whale's upper lip and lower jaw and sewed its mouth shut, to hold in the buoyant gases that would keep the carcass afloat.[70] Floats were hooked to this and other lines attached to the rest of the whale's body. The whale could then be towed to shore, to the accompaniment of songs and prayers to make the task less difficult. When the crew finally reached the village shores, they were greeted by community members with shouts of praise for the whaling crew and with songs to welcome the whale, an honored guest, to the village. The Nuu-chah-nulth community of Ahousaht had a tradition of having all the young children grab hold of one of the lines attached to the whale, to help pull it the last few yards up onto the beach.[71]

When the whale was brought to shore, the whaler's wife was usually the first person to greet it and would sprinkle it with eagle down. A song called *chuchaa* was sung to the whale and then the *chakwa'si*,[72] or dorsal fin, was removed. The chief kept the saddle of skin and blubber from the *chakwa'si*, which was considered the prize part of the whale. It was believed that the whale's anthropomorphic spirit resided in the dorsal fin. The body of the whale was its canoe, which carried the human spirit. After the *chakwa'si* was cut from the whale, the saddle was put on display and treated to four days of ritual prayers to pay respect to the whale and "to make [its] spirit feel at home."[73] Songs called *ts'its'ihiimik'yak* were sung to the *chakwa'si* to induce the human spirit to leave it and enter another "canoe," or whale.[74] In my family, we have a song passed down by my great-great-grandfather that was sung to the *chakwa'si* after it was brought into our whaling ancestor's house to be honored. The song was sung after the four days of rituals and prayers. The main chorus of Sayach'apis's song is "I finish coming to the land";[75] it was a way to complete the ceremony and confirm that the whale spirit had finished its journey as well.

After these prayers and rituals were performed, the whale was divided among the community members. Strict and careful protocol would oversee the allocation of the whale parts. First the crew and the other village members who helped capture the whale were given choice pieces of blubber. Then the rest of the whale pieces were given out according to inherited privilege.[76] Whale bones that were not utilized for specific purposes were stacked up on the beach in front of the chief's house as a testament to his whaling prowess.[77] The distribution of the whale helped fulfill a chief's responsibilities to his community while also serving to reinforce his social position.

PA-CHITLE: REINFORCING COMMUNITY THROUGH THE WHALING CHIEF'S POTLATCH

The West Coast peoples had, and still have in the twenty-first century, a ceremony or social gathering known as the potlatch.[78] The word comes from the Chinook trade language and was derived from the Nuu-chah-nulth word *pa-chitle*, which means "to give."[79] The potlatch reflected and perpetuated the Makah and Nuu-chah-nulth social organization and was utilized to validate status and hereditary privileges acquired at birth. The *haw'iih* and the *maschimes* had certain privileges, but the titleholders and their families were the ones who hosted the potlatches to announce and make a claim to these rights or to acknowledge the rights and status of those below them. In the precontact and early-contact period, only the higher ranking *haw'iih* potlatched and only those people who were free could attend the potlatch; thus, slaves were excluded.[80] Although high rank was a birthright,[81] *haw'iih* had to hold potlatches throughout their lives to "keep up" their names through the ceremonial gifting of foods and goods.

These public events were held by high-ranking families to bestow names and rights, to validate marriages, to recognize a youth's coming of age, and to mourn the death of a tribal member. All Northwest Coast peoples had a variety of highly ritualized ceremonies, each having its own specific name and objectives. For example, the Nuu-chah-nulth have a sacred ceremony called a *tloo-qua-nah* (Makah, *klukwalle*),[82] which is an initiation ceremony dramatizing the capture by wolves of human initiates, who are then recovered by former initiates after they have received special powers and privileges from the wolves.[83] At the end of the performance, a potlatch takes place, where the initiates dance and display the ceremonial privileges bestowed on them by the wolves.[84] *Mamalhn'i* settlers who witnessed our ceremonies mistook the verb *pa-chitle* for the name of the ceremonies because it was used repeatedly throughout. Eventually the word was transformed into "potlatch" and came to be used to refer to all the coastal peoples' ceremonies.[85]

As anthropologist Franz Boas asserted, the potlatch was a system of public record-keeping that served as a substitute for writing.[86] It also served an economic function through the ceremonial distribution of food and material goods. While the purpose of potlatches was to pass on titles of rank and their associated privileges to designated heirs of the *haw'iih*, they functioned also to distribute surpluses and special local products as "gifts" to the people invited to witness the claim being made. Their acceptance of these gifts acknowledged their acceptance of the claim.[87] Boas maintained that while the possession of wealth was considered admirable, the ability to hold great potlatches where wealth could be given away was even more admired: a chief's name "acquire[d] greater weight in the councils of his tribe and greater renown among the whole people" after each potlatch he held.[88]

Sociologist/anthropologist Marcel Mauss asserted that the motives behind gifting in potlatches were much more complex than early anthropologists and historians understood them to be. The principle of gift giving functioned within a highly intricate system of reciprocity governed by what Mauss described as "the

Cutting up a whale at Neah Bay, 1910. Photograph by Asahel Curtis; courtesy of Washington State Historical Society, Pullman.

concept of mana." Mana was the authority, honor, and prestige a chief derived by being known as a sophisticated and generous giver. A chief would constantly have to give gifts and have them reciprocated in order to keep and increase his mana. Problems could ensue if a gift was rejected or if a chief could not reciprocate.[89] In 1868, Gilbert Sproat noted that the collecting of property for the purpose of distribution was a constant aspiration of the Tseshaht people. One *haw'ilth* who held lavish potlatches to distribute his material goods was greatly admired; this was reflected in the name given to him by his village members, "strong heart."[90] Edward Sapir wrote that Sayach'apis became an honored member of his village and he and his family were respected throughout the West Coast because of the numerous potlatches he held in his lifetime.

The many feasts he [Sayach'apis] has given and the many ceremonial dances and displays he has had performed have all had their desired effect—they have shed luster on his sons and daughters and grandchildren, they have "put his family high" among the Ts'ishah'ath tribe, and they have even carried his name to other, distinct Nootka tribes, and to tribes on the east coast of the island.[91]

Sapir noted that Sayach'apis had such a large pile of blankets to give away at one of his elaborate potlatches that they poked through the roof of his longhouse. The potlatch goods were so heavy that the floor beneath them collapsed.[92]

The potlatch was central to the marriage ceremony of a whaling *haw'ilth* and a *haquum*. During the potlatch, skill-testing ceremonial games associated with whaling, which were part of the chief's *tuupaati* (ceremonial prerogatives), were executed by male guests to demonstrate their whaling prowess. This potlatch contest was recalled by Ahousaht elder Peter Webster:

Often the large potlatch, which could last all day, started with a game. One of these used a large board shaped like a whale. This had a red spot painted on it to represent the heart of the whale. One person at a time would be called upon to pretend to harpoon the whale by throwing at it the feather of an eagle or swan. This "spear" could be thrown from some distance and was, naturally, very hard to control. The winners would be those who either hit the bull's eye, the heart, or came closest to the target.[93]

After a whale was caught, it was divided among the tribal members, with the whaler keeping large quantities of whale oil and meat, which he used for trading purposes. Many chiefs became smart entrepreneurs and very wealthy by trading the whale oil and blubber to other tribes up and down the coast. Both the Makah and Nuu-chah-nulth established lucrative and beneficial trading networks along the coast, with whale oil being a major product in this trade.

One of the most important potlatches the *haw'iih* could hold was the *tlaqsit,* or whale-oil potlatch. Successful *haw'iih* who acquired a large quantity of whale oil from the whales they caught would give away this oil at a potlatch to show how wealthy they were. At the potlatch the host would dress up in his whaling regalia and act out his successful whale hunts, with his wife acting as the whale. Other whalers invited to the potlatch would also act out their whaling success stories. Occasionally, the whalers would act out whaling stories in which they were not successful. One such story focuses on a whaler who pretends he is sleeping. The point of his theatrical performance is to show how he overslept, which led to his not being successful in his whale hunting pursuits. This demonstrated the hunter's humility to the other whalers, and he was respected for his honesty.[94]

Wilson Parker, one of the Makah tribe's last whalers of the 1920s, told a story about a feast his father had held after he killed four whales in one season. The whales yielded an estimated five hundred gallons of oil and Wilson's father gave it all away at a whale-oil potlatch. All the great whaling *haw'iih* came decked out in their whaling regalia. The feast opened with a young dancer who shook his whaling rattle as he danced, imitating the actions of a whale. The whaling *haw'iih* sang their prayer songs, and after the dancer was finished, they, too, danced, imitating the motions of a whale.[95]

Participants sang a whale-oil song, which the chief had received from a whale he caught. The song signified how much wealth the whale brought to the chief, so much that he could afford to give away all the oil that was rendered. In the song, the whale questions the whaler's preparedness for all the people who would visit his village once they heard of his greatness as a whaler. The whale says to the whaler: "I have come to see how your house is. Is it prepared for large crowds?"[96]

When the whale-oil ceremonies were completed, a canoe was brought into the potlatch house and whale oil was poured into it. Young female dancers wrapped themselves in blankets and the host then poured oil over them. The oil was also poured lavishly onto the fire in the potlatch house. This demonstrated the chief's great wealth by his seeming disregard for an item of such great value. The rest of the oil was then distributed among the whaling chiefs, who brought containers with them to carry the oil back to their villages.[97]

While whaling elevated the status of the *haw'iih,* providing them with wealth that maintained their position within their societies, it also served an important societal function in maintaining social cohesion, communal sharing, and tribal unity. Distribution of the whale benefited all members of the village so that everyone had a stake in the whaling tradition. Even though only a few people actually hunted whales, the hunters relied on support labor from community members who helped process, preserve, and prepare the whale products.[98] The whaling *haw'iih* then acknowledged and thanked these people during the potlatch ceremony.

Haw'iih did not perform day-to-day activities such as gathering food and building houses because these jobs were done for them by the members of the village. Through the ceremonial distribution of food and material goods during a potlatch, the *haw'ilth* publicly acknowledged those who provided the labor. The laborers would then see rewards for their cooperation and would continue to support and serve the *haw'ilth.*

Consequently, while whaling potlatches helped raise and legitimize chiefs' status, the feasts and gifts were also mechanisms utilized by them to maintain a labor force and were a means of compensating the members of the village for their participation in the harvesting of the resources within the chief's territory. *Haw'iih* would strive to keep in good standing with all village members. Even though there seemed to be a power imbalance, with the chiefs having total dominance over the commoners, the relationship was in many ways reciprocal. The *maschimes* always had the ability to move to another local group or switch chiefs, and since to be successful the *haw'ilth* relied on the members of his village group, any tendency to exploit the *maschimes* could result in the loss of their support.[99]

In Nuu-chah-nulth territory, a successful whale hunt was also used to develop cordial relations with neighboring Nuu-chah-nulth tribes. Father Augustin Brabant was the first priest to reside among the Nuu-chah-nulth, from 1869 until his death in 1912. While living among the Hesquiaht people, he witnessed the seizure of a drift whale in 1875. He noted that "in the heat of their happiness" in acquiring the whale, the Hequiaht people invited the people from the neighboring Ahousaht village to join them in their celebration. The Ahousaht people were invited to the house of the whaling *haw'ilth,* where they were entertained with songs and dances. Following the ceremonies, the guests were given a meal of whale meat.[100] Nuu-chah-nulth *haw'ilth* Tom Mexsis Happynook says that the whale hunts strengthened and affirmed relationships and alliances within and beyond Nuu-chah-nulth territory. He says that when a whale was caught, people came from great distances to share in the processing of the whale and in the celebrations that followed. This not only strengthened relationships between families but also served to establish and reinforce intertribal alliances.[101]

Ahousaht *haw'ilth* Earl George remembered a story told to him about great whale hunters from his community that also provides evidence of the communal sharing aspects of whaling.[102] One particular whaler, Kista (Keesta) Atleo, would spend years preparing for a whale hunt. When a whale was captured, people from all the Nuu-chah-nulth nations were invited to feast on the whale meat and blubber. Ceremonies surrounded the distribution of the whale parts, George said, and "eventually, all the parts of the whale were given [to] all people of all parts of the coastline, [who] were rejoicing and feasting" on the whale.[103]

> People from all the Ahousaht Nation and farther away gathered to come and enjoy the celebration and feast of the killing of the whale. There were Kwaguilth people from the other end of the Island, Nimpkish Lake people came to attend the ceremony of the killing of the whale and enjoy the feast that was put on.

Also, people from Neah Bay, Washington, and the places near Neah Bay, Port Angelas and out to the outside areas, part of the Makah Nation which was also Nuu-chah-nulth. Of course there were famous whale hunters from all the Nuu-chah-nulth Nations that took part in that . . . famous hunters, who were well known for hunting and killing the giant whales. So, well over anywhere from 5,000 to 10,000 people came to take part in that ceremony which made Kista Atleo a very famous man.[104]

◆ ◆ ◆

Whaling did not just provide my ancestors with wealth, status, and food; it was the basis of Makah and Nuu-chah-nulth worldviews, identities, and cultures. Whales were seen as sacred gifts providing the Makah and Nuu-chah-nulth peoples with spiritual and nutritional sustenance. Following contact with non-Indians, the Makah and Nuu-chah-nulth people's lives began to change dramatically. Economic dislocation, commercial whaling, and federal assimilative policies challenged their cultural and spiritual association with whales, leading to the eventual demise of whaling practices.

2 / *Utla*

WORLDVIEWS COLLIDE

The Arrival of *Mamalhn'i* in Indian Territory

holism

T HE NUU-CHAH-NULTH HAVE A PHILOSOPHY OF *HISHUK ISH TSAWALK*, "everything is one." Our belief system includes the physical and metaphysical aspects of reality, with an understanding that everything in life is connected.[1] Since first coming in contact with *mamalhn'i* explorers and fur traders, and later when the newcomers began settling in Makah and Nuu-chah-nulth territory in the 1840s and 1850s, Native societies underwent significant political, economic, and spiritual transformations. *Mamalhn'i* brought with them diseases that ravaged our villages, a spiritual belief and value system that was the diametric opposite to our own worldviews, policies that forbade the use of our languages and the practice of our cultural traditions, and a new economy that destabilized our own. As a result, the interdependency of each aspect of our culture was challenged, causing a chain reaction that undermined the complex social, economic, religious, and subsistence network and ultimately led to the demise of Native whaling practices.

thesis of chapter

THE ARRIVAL OF THE *MAMALHN'I*

In the late 1700s, *mamalhn'i* began traveling along the west coast of North America through Makah and Nuu-chah-nulth marine space. Their first recorded contact with the Nuu-chah-nulth was in 1774, when Spanish explorer Juan Pérez sailed into Nootka Sound, looking for new lands for Spain.[2] The Mowachaht *haw'iih* paddled out to Pérez's ship and exchanged a few goods with the Spanish crewmen. Four years later, Captain Cook, under British employment, came to the Northwest Coast and anchored his two ships, the *Resolution* and the *Discov-*

ery, in a spot he named Friendly Cove,[3] which was in an area that was eventually named Nootka Sound. Cook stayed in the area for a month, trading otter, beaver, and other furs with the Mowachaht *haw'iih*. When he left the coast, he traveled to China, where he found that sea otter furs were highly prized. This discovery set off a major otter-fur trade market, and by 1795 the Northwest Coast was established as a commercial fur-trading center, attracting over fifty trading vessels from April to October for the next ten years.[4]

The marine fur trade caused a shift in indigenous social and economic systems. Native use of firearms that were introduced and traded to the coastal groups intensified tribal warfare, which modified tribal demographics. Depopulation through increased warfare weakened the less powerful groups, many of which were incorporated into the larger village units, triggering adjustments to political and social systems, which also altered resource and settlement patterns.[5] By 1795, the marine-based fur trade came to an end as a result of a serious decline in the sea otter population. For the next forty years, *mamalhn'i* rarely visited Makah and Nuu-chah-nulth territory.

White settlement of the Pacific Northwest began in the 1840s, initiated by the establishment of inland fur-trading centers along Canada's western coastline and in Washington's Puget Sound area. Settlement increased as more and more people from the East Coast moved to the region during this period of western expansion. By the 1850s, *mamalhn'i* settlement had increased enough to provoke tensions and escalate conflicts with the indigenous peoples. Disputes ensued over the land and resources. As these encounters became more violent, the territorial and colonial administrators overseeing the settlement of Washington Territory and the British colonies along the coast needed to find a way to quell or prevent these clashes and to free up indigenous territory for non-Indian settlement.

Indigenous leaders were frustrated by the *mamalhn'i* disregard for their territorial boundaries and by the increasing number of settlers moving onto their lands, and warfare continued. However, the escalation of violence combined with the introduction of *mamalhn'i* diseases weakened their populations, making it difficult to fight. In an attempt to protect their land, resources, and communities, some indigenous leaders met with territorial and colonial officials to negotiate agreements that would stop further non-Indian encroachment into their territories. In the east, the United States and Canada had adopted the policy of making treaties by which indigenous peoples ceded lands for settlement. That became a method for expanding their imperialist agenda over new lands in the West.

Through the treaty-signing process, Native peoples relinquished control over vast areas of their traditional territories in return for protection of smaller portions of their lands that were to be safeguarded from non-Indian settlement. The treaties stipulated that indigenous people would be provided with federal services such as health care and education, farming implements, and yearly payments for the land they ceded. The treaties were to protect their subsistence activities and allow them continued access to their traditional hunting, fishing, trapping, and gathering areas, both inside and outside the newly established reservations in the United States and reserves in Canada.[6]

Early Indian policy in British Columbia, however, did not follow the general lines established in other parts of Canada—or in the United States. In 1864, Joseph Trutch became chief commissioner of lands and works in the British colony that in 1871 became the province of British Columbia.[7] As chief commissioner, Trutch assumed control of Indian policy in the colony. While treaties were being signed in other parts of Canada during this time, Trutch refused to recognize Indian title to the lands and, therefore, never negotiated treaties with the indigenous peoples living in the colony. As a result, the Nuu-chah-nulth, along with other indigenous peoples in British Columbia, did not sign treaties.[8]

"HE WANTED THE SEA. THAT WAS HIS COUNTRY": THE MAKAH TREATY OF 1855

In 1854–55, the governor of Washington Territory negotiated a series of treaties with Indians throughout the area, including the Makah. In 1855, Governor Isaac Stevens appointed four Makah chiefs to negotiate, on behalf of all the Makah, the Treaty of Neah Bay.[9] The Makah, like the other indigenous groups along the coast, were facing the reality of non-Indian intrusion and eventual settlement on their lands. They listened to the territorial officials tell them what would be negotiated in the treaty. The Makah leaders understood that in signing the treaty, certain lands would be secured for their use and occupancy and their subsistence activities would be protected both inside their reservation boundaries and outside their reservations in the "usual and accustomed" areas.

In negotiating on behalf of all the Makah people, the designated *chah-chah-buht* (chiefs)[10] made it quite clear to the colonial administrators and to Governor Stevens not only how important their land base was to them but how important their marine space was as well. During the treaty negotiations, the designated head chief, Tse-kaw-wootl, told the governor and his men that "he wanted the sea. That was his country."[11] The Makah leaders explained how important fishing and sea mammal hunting were to them. Chief Klachote told Stevens that "he thought he ought to have the right to fish and to take whales and get food when he liked."[12]

The *chah-chah-buht* stressed the importance of their whaling tradition, making sure that Governor Stevens understood its significance to their societies and their economies. U.S. government officials were already aware of the Makah people's reputation as great hunters of whales. They also knew the Makah people's reputation as skillful traders in whale oil, trading to other indigenous groups along the coast and—following contact with non-Indians—developing this into a lucrative trading market with *mamalhn'i* as well.

During the three days of negotiations, the Makah leaders stayed firm in their insistence on having their subsistence rights, especially their right to whale, secured in the treaty. Governor Stevens could see that the Makah leaders would sign the treaty only if they were granted protection over their whale hunts. Stevens told the Makah *chah-chah-buht* that the "Great Father" (the U.S. government) understood what great whalers they were and how far they would go out to sea in pursuit of a whale. He assured the Makah leaders that their right to whale would be protected in the treaty. He told them that the federal government would also help them maintain their fishing, sealing, and whaling practices, providing them with whaling and fishing equipment. Knowing how important whale oil was to both their trade and their consumption, the governor stated that he would also provide the Makah people with barrels to hold their precious commodity.[13]

The Makah *chah-chah-buht*, on hearing Governor Stevens's promise to protect their whaling practices, signed the treaty.[14] Article 4 of the 1855 Treaty of Neah Bay guarantees to the Makah tribe the "right of taking fish and of whaling and sealing at usual and accustomed grounds and stations."[15] This is the only treaty signed between the United States government and the tribes that secures and protects the tribal right to whale.

Once the treaty was signed, the colonial administrators began their efforts to bring the Makah people under colonial control. Even though the right to whale was protected in the Makah Treaty, Washington Territory officials did not promote the continuance of whaling, as the Makah leaders were led to believe when they signed the treaty. Instead, colonial agents, missionaries, and teachers were sent to the reservation in Neah Bay to begin the process of dismantling the pre-contact societies, belief systems, and subsistence activities, with the ultimate goal of assimilating all Makah people into the emerging non-Indian society.

The Makah were urged to give up their subsistence lifestyle of fishing and sea mammal hunting and adopt a more sedentary economic base. There was a general assumption that an agricultural society was a sign of civilization; indigenous societies were encouraged to take up agriculture and farming implements were brought to the reservations. Turning Indians into farmers would also keep them confined to their reservations, making it easier to settle non-Indians on the lands that were ceded through the treaty process.[16]

"WE DO NOT WISH TO SELL OUR LAND OR OUR WATER": THE NUU-CHAH-NULTH AND *MAMALHN'I* SETTLEMENTS

The Nuu-chah-nulth, like their Makah relatives, were also concerned about the increasing number of *mamalhn'i* settling in their territory. Non-Indian settlement began in the 1850s as industries such as fishing and logging developed on Vancouver Island. One of the first *mamalhn'i* to come to the territory was Gilbert Malcolm Sproat, a Scottish businessman who was sent by a company in England to the Alberni inlet in 1860 to oversee the operation of a sawmill that was built that year. Sproat was also in charge of the developing township and of securing land from the indigenous groups for the non-Indian settlers moving into the area.[17] The Tseshaht *haw'iih* made it clear to the newcomers and to Sproat that the land they were settling on was their land, and if the *mamalhn'i* wanted to live there, they needed to purchase the land.

Sproat attempted to negotiate for land from the Tseshaht chiefs, but they declined to discuss any land transactions. Attempting to protect their ownership of both their land and marine spaces, the Tseshaht *haw'iih* told Sproat, "We do not wish to sell our land or our water."[18] This demonstrated the Tseshaht understanding of territorial ownership of both land and water. Sproat tried to ease the concerns of the Tseshaht leaders regarding the increase of non-Indians in their territory. He told them that the *mamalhn'i* settlement would actually benefit the Tseshaht people because the *mamalhn'i* would buy fish and whale oil from them and would pay them for labor in the growing township.[19]

The Tseshaht and the other Nuu-chah-nulth-aht fought to maintain control over their land and resources, but, like all other indigenous groups in Canada, they eventually came under federal authority. The fact that the Nuu-chah-nulth did not sign a treaty had little bearing on their keeping their autonomy and maintaining control over their land. In 1867, following Canadian confederation, the British North America (BNA) Act divided up federal and provincial powers, making "Indians" and "lands reserved for Indians" a federal responsibility. In the early 1880s, the Native groups in British Columbia, the Nuu-chah-nulth included, were granted "reserve" lands to live on.[20]

Both the United States and Canada developed federal policies specifically for their indigenous populations and set up departments to administer them. These policies represented an assimilationist approach, that is, indigenous peoples were encouraged and ultimately forced to give up their former lifestyles and adopt Euro-American and Euro-Canadian customs, values, and economic systems. The reserves in Canada and the reservations in the United States were staffed with Indian agents, schoolteachers, and missionaries who were stationed there to help in this assimilation process. The ultimate goal of these policies was to eradicate Native culture and transform the Native societies so they could be integrated into Canadian and U.S. society. Native people were taught how to read and write English, to understand and accept Christianity, and to develop the necessary skills to become small-scale farmers.

DISEASE AND THE LOSS OF KNOWLEDGE

A major consequence of early contact with *mamalhn'i* that initiated a serious transformation in tribal social systems was the introduction of diseases that indigenous peoples had no immunity to resist. *Mamalhn'i* visiting the Northwest Coast reported evidence of smallpox among the coastal indigenous groups as early as the late 1700s. Major disease epidemics swept through the region in 1781–82, 1801–2, 1824–25, 1836–37, 1852–53, and 1862. Disease epidemics were the major cause of population decline on the Northwest Coast. In the late 1700s, the Northwest Coast indigenous population has been estimated at around 180,000. A century later, that population was 35,000; over 80 percent of the indigenous population had been wiped out. Smallpox, the most devastating of the introduced diseases, is spread through direct human contact, thus having the ability to spread very quickly. Once an individual was infected, death usually occurred after one week of dreadful pain and suffering. Disease spread rapidly through the indigenous communities through continual contact made along the coastal trade routes and through the potlatch system that brought together large groups of people from different indigenous communities.[21] In many cases, these epidemics left villages with only a few members, who were then absorbed into the larger villages. In some cases, entire villages were wiped out along the coast.

The Makah and Nuu-chah-nulth societies faced drastic population declines as a result of these epidemics. In the latter part of the eighteenth century, the Makah population was estimated at about 1,500 to 2,000.[22] In 1862, Swan enumerated the Makah population at 654. By 1900, their numbers were estimated to be around 360.[23] These epidemics were as sudden as they were deadly, leaving indigenous communities in states of shock and despair. Samuel Hancock, a man who traded with the Makah, witnessed the devastation of the first smallpox outbreak in the village of Neah Bay in 1853. While living in Neah Bay, Hancock noted how quickly the disease spread through the village and how distrustful the Makah were of the *mamalhn'i* who were trying to vaccinate them. He learned that they believed these vaccinations were being used to make Makah women barren as a way to undermine their populations and take control of their land. Hancock said that within a few weeks of coming in contact with the disease, hundreds of Makah had died and that "the beach for a distance of eight miles was literally strewn with the dead bodies."[24]

The Nuu-chah-nulth population had also dropped dramatically as a result of these disease outbreaks. Historian Robert Boyd argues that the Nuu-chah-nulth appeared to have escaped the devastation of the disease epidemics that swept through the Northwest Coast in the mid-1800s, and this was mainly because of their relative isolation.[25] It is hard to believe that disease epidemics, which were sweeping through other villages along the coast, would bypass the Nuu-chah-nulth groups, especially since they were potlatching cultures and thus constantly in contact with neighboring groups. If one looks at the population documented by explorers traveling through the area and early settlers moving onto Nuu-chah-nulth lands, the decline in numbers suggests otherwise. It has been estimated that the Nuu-chah-nulth population before contact was around 20,000; by the late nineteenth century as many as half had died from disease.[26] In 1788, when Captain Cook visited Nootka Sound, he estimated the Mowachaht population to be 2,000. Ten years later, Meares assessed the population of all the Nuu-chah-nulth villages in the area to be between 3,000 and 4,000. When Sproat moved into Nuu-chah-nuilth territory in the 1860s, he noted the severe decline in the population, estimating only 600 members in all the Nootka Sound villages.[27]

Nuu-chah-nulth oral tradition documents the introduction of smallpox to Barkley Sound before 1875. In an interview conducted in 1962, elder Louis Clamhouse told how a ship came to the southwest coast of Vancouver Island with sailors who were sick with the smallpox disease. Clamhouse said that the Ohiaht people went to greet the ship and were invited on board by the captain. When they were on board, "they looked down the hatch . . . and they saw there was something wrong with many of the Whitemen, the sailors, for they were all groaning. It turned out that they were all sick, that they were sick with smallpox, the sailors. Said the Captain, 'For seven days you will be well. Then you will get that sickness.'"[28]

The southern Nuu-chah-nulth groups were the first in Canada to be struck by the smallpox epidemic. Hancock wrote that many Makah, after having their community of Neah Bay ravaged by the disease in 1853, fled in their canoes across the strait to the neighboring Nuu-chah-nulth group of Ditidaht. He said that "those who escaped became almost frantic with grief and fear, and conceived the idea of crossing the Strait and going to the Nitanat tribe living on Vancouver's Island. They crossed over to this place, carrying the infection with them, and soon nearly all those who fled from Neaah Bay [sic], besides a great many of the native tribe, became victims to the epidemic."[29]

Smallpox continued to spread through Nuu-chah-nulth territory. In 1858, Indian agent Bamfield wrote that warfare with the neighboring Coast Salish people and smallpox outbreaks had devastated the village of Pacheenaht. He said: "They were formerly much more numerous, but war with the Songish Indians has reduced this number in connection with smallpox, which ravaged them some 8 years since. They were at that time nearly annihilated."[30]

Reverend Augustin Brabant, who established a mission in the central Nuu-chah-nulth village of Hesquiaht, recorded a smallpox outbreak that struck this community in May 1875. It did not take long for the disease to spread through Nuu-chah-nulth territory, and by mid-1875, evidence of outbreaks was recorded in all the villages.[31]

A major consequence of depopulation was a change in how tribal knowledge was passed down from one generation to the next. The social structure was established so that traditions, ceremonies, and social position were passed to the younger generation through the potlatch system and through the knowledge of the elders. The *tuupaati* (ceremonial prerogatives) of the chiefs to names, songs, dances, rituals, and subsistence sites were inherited. If a line in this social structure was altered, it also changed how, or whether, knowledge and rights could be successfully transferred or handed down to the younger generation. Every indigenous community and, one could speculate, every family, had lost elders, leaders, fathers, mothers, and children to the diseases that swept through their societies. Many of these people were the bearers of the knowledge, the people whose position in the society was to pass down names, songs, and dances their families held and owned, as well as knowledge of ceremonies, rituals, and traditions. Because many of these knowledge-bearers died during the early-contact period, the chain of transmission was broken. If many people within one familial line died, then this family-owned knowledge was ultimately lost. Disease emptied ceremonial positions and left respected names unclaimed. As a result, some names were transferred to people without high rank and their social position was elevated.[32]

Another consequence of these disease epidemics was the undermining of indigenous spirituality. Native healers had no way of curing these diseases, and slowly faith in them began to fade. Members' faith was further weakened when their own healers succumbed to the diseases. Father Brabant noted that a Hesquiaht female healer had died in the smallpox outbreak of 1875. As smallpox spread through the Hesquiaht village, Father Brabant quickly began baptizing the sick and dying. He wrote:

> I went to his house and found the old man very sick, evidently with smallpox. He was lying in a corner of the room[,] in the other corner was his sister, an elderly woman, also in the last stages of the fatal disease. I baptized both of them, saw them well provided with food and water and went home convinced that a very trying time was before me. [33]

The missionaries took advantage of indigenous people's fear of these new diseases and, while they were in a weakened and confused state, worked in earnest to convert them.

MISSIONARIES AND THE FEDERAL INDIAN EDUCATION POLICY

Missionaries coming to the West Coast in the mid-1800s brought a belief system that challenged and undermined indigenous spirituality.[34] In many cases, religious conversion was linked to U.S. and Canadian government educational policies, and the schools that the governments built for the indigenous population were staffed by religious groups. In the process of extending political, economic, and social control over the indigenous populations, in the mid-1800s, the colonial and later federal governments began establishing day schools and industrial schools to teach Indians of all age groups subsistence farming and a range of trades. In the early years of these schools, the skills being taught to Native adults and youth were welcomed. Native people understood that to compete in the non-Indian society growing up around them, they needed to be proficient in certain skills and adapt to the changing economy.

Many of the day schools on the Northwest Coast were run by missionaries, who, together with the Indian agents, worked at undermining the coastal people's social structure.[35] They encouraged the younger members of the village to give up the multifamily houses and build nuclear-family dwellings based on the Euro-Canadian and Euro-American models. Eventually, the longhouses that housed the large extended families of a chief were torn down. Traditional clothing was replaced with what the agents and missionaries saw as more "civilized" attire.[36]

At the schools, the children were exposed to Christianity through attendance at church services and through the recitation of daily prayers. At the same time that they were being indoctrinated into Christianity their own worldviews were condemned. Following the establishment of an Indian agency on the Makah Reservation in 1863, a school was built to advance the federal government's assimilation efforts. Anthropologist Elizabeth Colson wrote that at the Makah school in Neah Bay, the teachers, many of them qualified missionaries, would combine religious training with education.

> At the same time as they were receiving this training, those in charge of the school attempted to wean them from their lingering belief in customs of their ancestors by a policy of ridicule. They were taught to regard their own elders as ignorant and superstitious barbarians whose advice should be ignored.[37]

By the late 1800s, both Canada and the United States had adopted a system of boarding schools that focused on the education of Native youth between the ages of five and fifteen years. School attendance was made compulsory in the United States in 1891,[38] and in Canada in 1920. Duncan Campbell Scott, Canadian superintendent general for Indian Affairs, summed up the reasoning behind the 1920 law: "Our object is not to quit until there is not one Indian left that has not been absorbed into the body politic."[39] Native people resisted the removal of their children and attempted to hide them from the authorities investigating their communities. When Makah parents refused to send their children to boarding school, the reservation agent often enlisted military troops to arrest the parents and place them in jail.[40]

Native youths were removed from their families and their communities and placed in residential schools, where they lived for ten months out of the year. When they first arrived at the schools, the children underwent physical transformations. Their hair was cut and their traditional clothing exchanged for uniforms and Western garments. They also underwent major psychological adjustments. While in the schools, they were taught English and indoctrinated into the American and Canadian value systems, with daily instruction based on individualism, competition, and a belief in the Christian faith. The youths spent little time on academic learning—the majority of their time was spent learning basic skills and embracing the values that would help them integrate into U.S. and Canadian societies by becoming economically self-sufficient. Young girls were taught how to cook, sew, knit, and clean. Young boys were taught farming, blacksmithing, and other work skills.[41]

The boarding school system of education tore at the very social fabric of Native communities. Native children were severed from daily contact with their families and were isolated from the influences of their elders and their cultures.

At school, the youths were prohibited from speaking their language and practicing their ceremonies and traditions. In 1863, an agent was assigned to administer the Makah village. The goal of the agency, according to the agent's report, was to "civilize and reclaim the Indians within our borders, and induce them to adopt the habit of civilization."[42]

The first boarding school for Makah children was established in 1874 and was located about a mile from the nearest village. The school's founder made his ultimate goal quite clear: "The Indian tongue must be put to silence and nothing but English allowed in all social intercourse. Meanwhile, habits of industry must be cultivated."[43] In order for the agency to carry out this difficult mission, the agents knew they would need to target the children and the language.

> The first step to be taken toward civilization, toward teaching the Indian the mischief and folly of continuing in their barbarous practices, is to teach them the English language. . . . If we expect to infuse into the rising generation the leaven of American citizenship, we must remove the stumbling-blocks of hereditary customs and manners, and of these languages is one of the most important elements."[44]

After years of living away from their cultures and traditions, Indian youths found it increasingly difficult to maintain a solid connection to their own belief system. With the children away for ten and sometimes twelve months out of the year, the parents, elders, and leaders lost the chance to pass on their knowledge to their children.

FORBIDDING THE CUSTOM OF *PA-CHITLE*

In the early 1880s, the missionaries began pressuring the colonial governments to legislate prohibitions on Native ceremonies, including the potlatch.[45] The missionaries hoped that if tribal members were forced to give up their customs, they would focus more attention on religious conversion. Federal Indian policy administrators viewed the potlatch as a worthless and wasteful custom that kept Native people from fully integrating into non-Indian life.[46] By the mid-1800s, the potlatches held by tribes in western Washington and Oregon had already gone through significant changes. Non-Indian settlement was more rapid and in many ways more devastating to Native cultures in these territories than in British Columbia. In 1850, geologist/ethnologist George Gibbs, who participated in Stevens's treaty negotiations, reported that for many of the tribes in western

Washington and Oregon the potlatch had already "fallen into disuse," because of these tribes' regular contact with non-Indians. However, with regard to the Makah, Gibbs noted that their isolated territory made contact with *mamalhn'i* limited and, as a result, there was not much change to their traditions.[47]

In 1872, Israel Wood Powell was appointed Indian superintendent to administer Indian legislation in British Columbia.[48] Two years later, Powell instructed Indian agent George Blenkinsop to visit with the Nuu-chah-nulth people to discuss issues related to the lands that were reserved to them. While there, Blenkinsop witnessed that the Nuu-chah-nulth spent much of their time feasting and giving away property, which he saw as impeding their pursuit of more industrious endeavors and interfering with their assimilation into Euro-Christian society. In his report to Powell, Blenkinsop said that until potlatches ended there was "little hope of elevating them from their present state of degradation."[49]

When Gilbert Sproat came to the British colony of Vancouver Island to acquire land for a sawmill, he met a Tseshaht chief, who told him that his people did not want to sell their land.[50] Sproat told the chief that if they did not sell, Britain would send people to take the land from them forcibly. Through coercion the Tseshaht sold the land for twenty pounds in goods and were forced out of their winter village. Sproat saw the ways in which contact with *mamalhn'i* had already affected the Nuu-chah-nulth people, with the introduction of diseases and alcohol causing high mortality rates.[51] According to Sproat, the only way indigenous people could survive was for the British to colonize them. In a book he published eight years after his visit, he wrote, "I would propose as follows: to teach the Indians any useful employments and arts that they were capable of learning; to improve their moral ideas, and to instruct them in Christian truth."[52] In 1876, Sproat was appointed to the Joint Indian Reserve Commission, which was formed to settle the question of Native reserve allocations in the newly formed province of British Columbia.[53] In October 1879, he sent a letter to the Canadian prime minister, Sir John A. McDonald, urging him to "lay an iron hand upon the shoulders of the [Native] people" in order to eradicate the potlatch, which "promoted habits inconsistent with progress."[54]

Canada legally outlawed the potlatch in 1884, and any indigenous nation caught conducting any kind of ceremony was subject to prosecution. The Canadian potlatch law stated that "any Indian or other person who engages in or assists in celebrating the Indian festival known as the "Potlach" . . . is guilty of a misdemeanor, and shall be liable to imprisonment."[55] Ceremonial masked dances and public giving of gifts became offenses punishable by fines and/or imprisonment.

Native people throughout British Columbia resisted the potlatch law and many chiefs sent petitions to Ottawa, Canada's capital, in protest. In their letters, they defended their ceremonies and elucidated how essential the potlatch was to their cultures and their societies. The chiefs explained that everyone in their communities benefited from the potlatch through the giving away of material goods and food, and when people could not find work or were too old to look after themselves, the potlatch would ensure that they were taken care of. They asserted that there was nothing "criminal" in their potlatches; in fact, the events were entertaining and were their "chief sources of pleasure and amusement."[56]

In October 1884, Indian agent Harry Guillod traveled through Nuu-chah-nulth territory informing the people of the new potlatch law. In his report, Guillod said that while the Nuu-chah-nulth were willing to give up some of their customs, such as gambling and use of their longhouses, they refused to stop potlatching, and many of the villages he visited openly defied the law. When Guillod tried to persuade the Tseshaht to stop, the *haw'iih* said to him:

> It is very hard to try and stop us; the white man gives feasts to his friends and goes to theatres; we have only our "potlachs" and dances for amusement; we work for our money and like to spend it as we please, in gathering our friends together and giving them food to eat and when we give blankets or money, we dance and sing and all are good friends together; now whenever we travel we find friends; the "potlach" does that.[57]

When Agent Guillod visited the Nuu-chah-nulth village of Mowachaht the following year, he met with the *haw'ilth*, Maquinna, and told him about the new law against potlatching. Maquinna brought out all his ceremonial regalia to show to Guillod and then gave a lengthy speech about the social, economic, and spiritual significance of potlatching to his people. He told Guillod how his village members had given up tribal feuding and stealing to please the agent, "but it was very hard to ask them to give up a custom which was intermixed with all their thoughts and feelings." Maquinna indicated that the potlatch had also benefited the "white man's trade in Victoria" and encouraged "friendly relations with other tribes." But, Maquinna told the agent, what was most important to him was how the potlatch brought him closer to his family members who had died, and when performing his sacred ceremonies, it was "as if his dead son came back to him."[58]

Anthropologists such as Franz Boas and Edward Sapir warned the Canadian officials of the hardships the coastal Native peoples would face if they were not allowed to practice their potlatch traditions. In a letter published in the Vancouver *Daily Province* newspaper on March 6, 1897, Boas wrote that non-Indians misunderstood the social and economic significance of the potlatch's redistributive function and that this sort of banking and credit system (his term for it) should be seen as "wise and worthy of praise."[59] Sapir was one of the most outspoken opponents of the potlatch law. In a letter he sent to the deputy superintendent general of Indian Affairs on February 11, 1915, Sapir wrote," It seems to me high time that white men realized that they are not doing the Indians much of a favour by converting them into inferior replicas of themselves."[60]

Although the ban on the potlatch had been initiated in 1884, it had been enforced only sporadically. In 1914, Canada's Indian Act was amended to strengthen the anti-potlatch law,[61] expanding on the definition of what tribal activities were prohibited, with the definition becoming so broad that it basically applied to any form of tribal organization, which made it much easier to enforce. In 1920, Indian agents and the Canadian police strengthened the enforcement of the law and instigated a major wave of potlatch arrests, charges, prosecutions, convictions, and imprisonment in British Columbia, adding pressure on the Native peoples to give up their former way of life.[62]

Although no formal law against the potlatch was initiated in the United States, the missionaries and the Indian agents exercised the same zeal in stopping it.[63] In 1887, an Indian agent for the Makah Reservation, working actively to suppress the potlatch, wrote in his report: "All heathenism and barbarous practices I have endeavoured to stop, and where possible prohibit altogether, such as the 'cloqually dance.' This dance, from what I have heard of it, must be a cross between the devil's dance and the can-can."[64]

The anti-potlatch law undermined one of the potlatch's most important social and economic functions: the ability to redistribute material goods and food to relatives and members of the village group, as well as to people from neighboring communities, and to have this generosity reciprocated. In his 1881 report, Indian agent Guillod observed that the potlatch was a "bond of union" among the Nuu-chah-nulth groups, a time when they could come together to share their food amidst songs, dances, and ceremonies. He maintained that while "there is some waste" at these potlatches, "the poorer Indians reap some benefit from it, and all carry away what they cannot eat."[65] In his research among the Coast Salish peoples, anthropologist Wayne Suttles suggested that the Coast Salish potlatch was a type of social insurance: a Native village would distribute food to neighboring villages during times when their resources were low, knowing that these villages would reciprocate when they had an abundant harvest. This method of sharing food through a system of distribution and reciprocation was maintained through kinship ties and marriages that reinforced bonds and obligations within and among village groups.[66] The inability to potlatch effectively destabilized this mutually beneficial arrangement.

Coastal Native peoples did not react to the potlatch ban in a unified way. The 1880s to the 1920s was a period of intense cultural change, and coastal peoples were attempting to adjust to the new lifestyles, new economies, and different religious systems being forced upon them. There were some who accepted these changes and the new way of life and changed their lives, giving up many of their traditions in an effort to adapt. Many of the Christianized Indians agreed with the ban, as they had already turned away from their ceremonies, and they publicly supported the outlawing of the potlatch.

Many people from the coastal villages continued to resist the potlatch prohibition and devised strategies to continue practicing their ceremonies. Potlatching went underground and coastal peoples began holding their ceremonies in secret locations or found innovative ways to conceal them. An Indian agent working among the Makah observed that by 1890, potlatching rarely took place in the village at Neah Bay but many people were holding potlatches on an island near Cape Flattery.[67] Makah elder Helen Peterson recounted the strategy they would use to hold a potlatch ceremony. "The agent used to come right into our house and lift the lid where we were cooking and say, 'Oh, you must be going to have a party. You can't do that.' So we'd go out to Tatoosh Island where he couldn't catch us. We'd say we were going fishing."[68]

Born in 1890, late Kwakwaka'wakw elder Agnes Alfred grew up during the prohibition. In her book *Paddling to Where I Stand*, Agnes wrote that her family devised a clever way to maintain their potlatch, or *pəsa*, tradition.

> We even did *pəsa* upstairs in our own houses! Moses had told his children that he had built an exercise room upstairs for them. It did have some gymnastic equipment, but, as they grew older, they found out that exercise was not the true purpose for this huge room. It was for *pəsa*. We were holding our *pəsa* upstairs, in secret. We would gather *pəsa* gifts and then take them and wrap them in Christmas wrapping. All *pəsa* were planned around Christmas time, for that is the one time of the year when the White people give gifts to each other. That is also the reason why so many couples married at this time of the year: so they would not arrest us for giving gifts.[68]

Colson described one Makah member's scheme to disguise the potlatch under the non-Indian Christmas tradition in order to keep practicing it.

After potlatches were forbidden, one member of the tribe who had some
acquaintance with European customs succeeded in giving a potlatch with the
agent's approval by quietly waiting until Christmas time, when he put up a
spruce tree, hung his goods upon this and then gave them away as Christmas
presents with the blessings of the agent and missionary.[70]

While these strategies for continuing the redistribution aspects of the potlatch
tradition were quite ingenious, the alterations that were made when the tradition
went underground did have an impact on its associated social and political functions. With potlatches being held in secret, it became increasingly difficult for
haw'iih to assert their status and to distribute wealth to maintain and reinforce
their social position. Thus, the community's public recognition and validation of
an individual's claims to status and rank were compromised.

Potlatches not only had to be held in secret but they also had to be shortened to lessen the time in hiding. Therefore, many of the ceremonies attached to
them had to be abridged versions of what they once were and ritual performances
that could take hours to complete had to be severely condensed.[71] By the 1940s,
the potlatch tradition had decreased dramatically among the Nuu-chah-nulth-
aht: the ceremonies became smaller, less dramatic and less elaborate, with fewer
people attending them.[72] Among the Makah, the continual pressure to stop the
practice of the potlatch and the internal changes to the tribe's social system from
disease epidemics, years of boarding school education, and missionary influence resulted in changes to the custom itself. Potlatches gradually moved away
from being public events where individuals would assert claims to social position
based on birthright and became more of an occasion for an individual to distribute goods for personal glory.[73]

DESTABILIZATION OF THE HAW'IIH

To help advance their goal of assimilation, both Canada and the United States
enacted legislation to eradicate indigenous political and governing systems. Federal Indian policy initiated the creation of band and tribal councils that eventually replaced existing indigenous political systems. These councils were modeled
after the Canadian and U.S. governing structures and were composed of officials
who were elected from the general tribal body and who then assumed the leader-
ship roles within their communities.[74]

After the Makah signed their treaty in 1855, an agency was established to
administer the reservation. All of the villages were placed under one jurisdic-

tion, with Neah Bay emerging as the main Makah village. Though the treaty was signed in 1855, changes did not take place immediately. In 1877, the Makah tribe held its first political elections to select its leaders. A tribal council was formed, which became the governing body of the tribe. Any Makah over the age of twenty-one, regardless of rank or status, could attend and vote at tribal meetings as well as run for political office. The Makah people were expected to accept this governmental body and abide by its decisions.[75]

In Canada, federal Indian policy, administered through the 1876 Indian Act, divided indigenous nations into separate political-administrative units known as bands. Bands came under the administrative supervision and control of the Department of Indian Affairs (DIA).[76] The Nuu-chah-nulth villages, which had already undergone numerous amalgamations before the arrival of *mamalhn'i*, were eventually restructured into fifteen bands that included a number of small reserves scattered throughout their traditional territory.[77] The first section of the Indian Act explained the procedure in the formation of band councils. Similar to the U.S. tribal council model, council members were to be elected from band populations and would have to be over twenty-five years of age.[78] The councils exercised municipal power delegated to them by the Canadian government.[79]

The new governing procedures initiated the development of a new body of laws about ownership and transmission of property that challenged the chiefs' authority and kinship roles and responsibilities. Formerly in coastal societies, social organization took precedence over political organization, as hereditary birthright, kinship, and rank determined one's social status and power (see chapter 1). A chief's authority came from his hereditary position and from the wealth he accumulated over his lifetime, which elevated his status and provided him with many privileges.

As political and social power began to shift to the elected governing councils, the chiefs' control over their land and marine space was challenged. Formerly, the ability to exploit or harvest resources came from the *haw'iih* overseeing the lineage groups. The chief's position included many social obligations; it had been up to each *haw'ilth* to make sure that his *ushtakimilh* was taken care of. The elected government system supplanted the hereditary chiefdom structure and, as a result, social obligations and a chief's authority were undermined.[80] The chiefs were still recognized as aristocracy and their lineage was respected. They were honored at potlatches and ceremonies, and their voices were heard by the governing councils. But official community business now rested in the hands of the elected officials, and these elected tribal and band councils were eventually accepted as the legitimate authority over all members of the community.

Under the new governing system, all people regardless of kinship ties, hereditary birthright, or social rank were considered equal. Social distinctions began to fade away, and people from all social ranks—chiefs, commoners, and slaves—had access to new economic opportunities for gaining wealth and moving up the social ladder.[81] Sapir noted that by about 1900, the Tseshaht people had already ceased seating their chiefs according to tradition because severe population declines from disease epidemics and the frequent extinguishing of the chiefs' descent lines made it difficult to determine the ranking of each chief.[82] The old lineage houses eventually disappeared and individual nuclear-family residences replaced them.[83] Harry Guillod, the first Indian agent to oversee Nuu-chah-nulth reserve lands, noticed that by the mid-1880s, some Nuu-chah-nulth people, especially the younger men of the villages, stopped living in the typical longhouse, multifamily residences, and began to build individual family houses fashioned after Anglo residences.[84]

SUBSISTENCE ACTIVITIES AND THE MARKET ECONOMY

The transforming of the Makah and Nuu-chah-nulth marine-based societies into agrarian land-based societies proved to be a difficult task for Indian agents supervising the reservations and reserves. For one, the reserved land was not conducive to a farming economy. The traditional lands were rocky, mountainous, and covered in forests. Indian agents objected to the aspect of federal Indian policy that focused on civilizing Native people by turning them into agriculturalists. Indian lands and social systems were so inhospitable to agriculture as a means of subsistence that some agents stationed at Neah Bay urged the Makah to enhance their subsistence systems by developing new methods of fishing and hunting, and they encouraged boatbuilding.[85] James Swan, who lived in Neah Bay in the late 1850s, noted how unsuitable both the Makah land and the coastal climate were to an agricultural economy. Instead of forcing the Makah to cultivate the land, Swan said, they should be "encouraged" to develop their fisheries into a commercial industry through the sale of fish and whale oil.[86]

Nuu-chah-nulth agent Harry Guillod commented, "The land, habits and mode of life of these Indians are against the use of necessity of agricultural pursuits."[87] The Makah and Nuu-chah-nulth societies had thrived on marine resources, with the majority of their subsistence coming from the sea. Trying to utilize a subsistence system they knew nothing about did not make sense to them, and, therefore, they resisted. The development of marine-based industries in the mid-1800s attracted Indian labor up and down the coast. Because the Makah and Nuu-chah-nulth made their living off the oceans and waterways where these industries were developing, it was quite easy for them to adapt to these new wage-labor activities while still maintaining their own subsistence activities. As non-Indians settled along the coast, industries developed that attracted both non-Native and Native labor. Newly emerging industries, such as commercial whaling, sealing, fishing, canning, logging, farming, and sawmills, required seasonal labor, which the coastal Native communities supplied. By the mid-1800s, the Native people living along the coast, including the Makah and Nuu-chah-nulth, were already being pulled into the larger market economy and had incorporated some form of cash income into their tribal economies.[88] The Makah and Nuu-chah-nulth were actually quite successful in adapting their marine-based activities to the marine-based industries of commercial whaling, whale and dogfish oil sales, sealing, and fishing that developed along the coast. As a result, their own subsistence systems were maintained and their economies supplemented with the money they derived from these seasonal industries.

As early as the 1840s, commercial whalers had been coming to the area in search of sperm and right whales. In the early days, the whalers were concerned only about the whale's oil, as there was a huge market for it on the East Coast. In the 1840s, whale oil was bringing $1.20 a gallon on the New York markets, which was a hefty profit.[89] Makah and Nuu-chah-nulth chiefs had been trading whale meat and oil to other Native groups up and down the coast for years. A lot of this oil was now being traded to the whaling ships coming into Makah and Nuu-chah-nulth territory, and the two groups benefited from this interaction in the early stages of commercial whaling. In his 1877 ethnographic survey of the western Washington tribes, George Gibbs noted that in one season alone the Makah traded as much as 30,000 gallons of whale oil.[90]

Beginning in 1868, commercial pelagic off-shore sealing grew into a major industry in the Pacific Northwest, peaking in 1896. Commercial sealing schooners hired Makah and Nuu-chah-nulth crewmen to accompany them to the northern sealing grounds in the Bering Sea. Makah and Nuu-chah-nulth were also involved in the local sealing activities in the Cape Flattery area, Strait of Juan de Fuca, and Barkley Sound. Because seal hunting was already a component of their subsistence activities, the Makah and Nuu-chah-nulth men easily modified their traditional techniques to fit the commercial sealing methods. Consequently, sealing became quite profitable for them and, during most of the peak years, was the major source of income for their families.[91]

Commercial sealing provided the groups and individuals with very good wages. Individual incomes were as high as $5,000 for a single season. By 1885, it was not uncommon for the Makah tribe as a whole to bring in an annual income of $20,000 to $30,000, just from sealing. Money made from sealing in 1892 allowed the Makah to purchase two food stores in Neah Bay, the local trading post, and one hotel.[92] By the late nineteenth century, some individual Makah and Nuu-chah-nulth members had become small-scale entrepreneurs. Nuu-chah-nulth sealers were finding ways to diversify their income, and by the late 1890s, five men had opened small stores in their communities.[93] As Makah incomes increased, the people began to purchase their own sealing schooners, which were also profitable. In 1883, the Makah head chief, Peter Brown, owned three sealing schooners, which at that time were worth $100,000. Native sealing businesses were so lucrative that the owners even hired non-Indian labor to operate them.[94]

By the 1890s, the commercial pelagic sealing industry collapsed because of unregulated harvesting, and many Makah and Nuu-chah-nulth members turned their attention to the emerging fishing industry. The fishing vessels provided seasonal employment for Makah and Nuu-chah-nulth men. By 1900, the average Makah fisherman was making $3 to $10 a day, which, at this time, was a very good income. Cape Flattery became a center for the halibut industry that grew up in the 1880s and lasted until the 1930s. The Makah were very involved in the halibut fishing industry, with the tribe making over $32,000 in profits in 1905.[95]

An offshoot of the fishing industry was the canning industry; canneries opened up and down the British Columbia coast. These canneries provided jobs for Nuu-chah-nulth women and men. But by the 1920s, the fishing and canning industries went into decline, and the Makah and Nuu-chah-nulth turned their attention to other sources of income from industries such as logging and tourism, which began to develop at this time. Women transformed their tradition of weaving cedar baskets into a viable business, selling their baskets to tourists and stores. Men also adapted their carving abilities for the cash economy by making small-scale canoes and other items and selling these for income. Ceremonial masks, rattles, and regalia were also being produced for museums and art collectors.[96]

COMMERCIAL WHALING AND THE
COLLAPSE OF THE WHALE POPULATIONS

Increased contact with non-Indians and pressure from federal agents to give up their cultural ways created dramatic changes in Makah and Nuu-chah-nulth societies. During this period of intense social, political, and spiritual change, they were able to adjust and modify their economies, adapting to the new maritime industries while at the same time staying connected to their whaling tradition. But, as the commercial whaling industry escalated, their ability to maintain their hunts was placed in peril.

Commercial whaling had developed in the Pacific Northwest in the early nineteenth century, when American whalers from the East Coast came to the area in search of the sperm whale and the slow-swimming and oil-rich right whale. At this time there was a market only for whale oil that was used for sawmills and lamps. Once the whales were killed, their oil was extracted and then the carcasses of the whales were discarded and left to rot along the ocean shores. By the 1850s, the right whale had been hunted to near extinction.[97]

In the 1840s, both off-shore whaling from sealing ships and shore-based whaling had developed along the California coastline. Humpback and gray whales were much sought after, as these whales are relatively slow swimmers and swim close to the shores. The whaling season lasted from the beginning of May until mid-September, when the whales were heading northward and feeding on herring and shrimp along their coastal route. Gray whales were hunted during the winter months, with a few whales taken in the summer in more northerly waters.[98] The whale oil that was extracted from the blubber and bone was the most important commodity. One whale could yield up to thirty barrels of oil (thirty gallons per barrel).

Whaling equipment in the early commercial whaling years limited the amount and types of whales caught. The ships were sail-powered and very slow moving, so only the slower-moving whales were sought. The harpoons were hand-held and the whales were processed on the boat, making the catching and harvesting of a whale a slow and very tedious process, which limited the number of whales that could be killed during an outing or during a season.[99]

By the late 1890s, new whaling technology made commercial whaling more economically viable. The new whaling ships were much larger than the previous vessels, up to 98 feet in length, and were powered by steam engines, making it easier to pursue the faster-swimming whales. Each ship was manned by a crew of eleven. The whale was killed with a muzzle-loaded harpoon gun that was mounted on the ship's bow. It fired a 100-pound harpoon with an exploding grenade head and a ring of barbs that opened inside the whale. Attached to the harpoon gun were 600 fathoms of rope. After the whale was harpooned and secured by the line, the crew then waited for it to tire out. Once the whale became weary, the crew moved in to kill it with additional harpoons. An air hose was inserted into the whale and compressed air pumped into it to keep it afloat. The whale was kept in this state while the ship moved along the coast in search of more whales.[100]

New whaling technology modernized the commercial whaling industry by making the killing and harvesting of the whales faster and more efficient. Because of the potential to make more profits from whaling operations, investors began pouring money into the establishment of permanent shore-based whaling stations in the Pacific Northwest. In the early 1900s, four permanent shore-based whaling stations opened along the British Columbia coast, and a fifth station opened in 1948. Two of these whaling stations, Sechart, which opened in 1905, and Kyuquot, which opened in 1907, were located in Nuu-chah-nulth marine space. In 1911, a whaling station was established in Bay City on Grays Harbor in Washington State and stayed in operation until 1925.[101]

As the commercial whale industry grew, a market began to develop for other whale parts. The meat was processed and sold for human consumption and for stock feed. The whale bones were ground up and made into fertilizer. The whale was also used to make edible products such as margarine and nonedible products such as fuel for lamps, lubricants for machinery, glue, soap, crayons, candles, lipstick, perfume, strings for tennis racquets, and tanned leather.[102]

All species of whales were sought: blue, fin, gray, humpback, minke, right, sei, and sperm. As one whale species was depleted, commercial whalers would focus on another species to hunt, continuing to exhaust all of the whale herds. From 1908 to 1967, when the last whaling stations closed on Vancouver Island, 24,427 whales had been killed by the stations in British Columbia.[103]

The commercial whaling industry was already beginning to die out by the 1940s as a result of the over-harvesting of the whale populations. It is difficult to estimate the exact population decline because, prior to commercial whaling, no statistics were kept on whale herds throughout the world. But, from the statistics on catches while commercial whaling was active in the Pacific Northwest, it is obvious that there was a rapid decrease in their numbers. For example, the Sechart whaling station, the first such station, caught a total of 250 whales in its third year, which was the first year that statistics on the annual catch were recorded. In 1911, it recorded its highest catch: 474 whales. Six years later, the annual catch had plummeted to only 90 whales. The second whaling station to open in 1908, the Kyuquot, recorded a catch of 319 whales in its first year of operation. In its last season of operation in 1925, the whale catch dropped to 80.[104]

Like commercial sealing and fishing, commercial whaling developed in the marine space where the Makah and Nuu-chah-nulth people traditionally whaled. But this was one ocean-based industry that they did not participate in. In fact, the commercial whaling industry attracted very little Makah and Nuu-chah-nulth labor. A few Nuu-chah-nulth men were employed as shoreworkers for the whaling companies at the Victoria Whaling Station, the two whaling stations located in their territories: the Kyuquot and the Sechart on Barkley Sound.[105] However, no Nuu-chah-nulth or Makah worked as crew on the whaling ships. This is interesting considering that they were quite actively involved in the other industries that developed on their lands and in their waters. Why did the Makah and Nuu-chah-nulth people not get involved in the commercial whaling industry? One reason could be that they were still whaling for themselves when commercial whaling was developing in their marine space along the Washington and British Columbia coast. And it could also demonstrate the importance of maintaining traditional hunts that held more than just economic significance.

The competition from the commercial whaling industry resulting in the continual decline in the whale populations had a serious effect on the Native whaling tradition. By the mid-1800s, the Makah and Nuu-chah-nulth people had already incorporated some form of wage-labor income into their economies and were involved in one way or another in the emerging coastal industries. However, they persisted in maintaining their traditional subsistence pursuits, using their cash incomes to supplement their traditional economies. Commercial whaling, like the other industries, would have supplied them with jobs and with another way to make an income. Even with competition from the commercial whalers and the continual decline in whales making it difficult for them to hunt, they still attempted to preserve their whaling practices.

To maintain their whale hunts, the Makah leaders began making requests to Governor Stevens as early as the late 1860s to live up to his treaty promise to provide them with more equipment for whaling. The Makah knew that they had to devise strategies to be able to compete with the commercial whalers. As the whaling industry became more technologically advanced, the Makah chiefs could see that their canoes and harpoons were no match for the modernized commercial whaling equipment. They appealed to Neah Bay agent Henry A. Webster, asking for steam-operated boats and harpoon-cannons similar to what the commercial whalers were starting to utilize. However, their petitions to modernize their whaling equipment fell on deaf ears.[106] In fact, little money was spent on the Makah tribe's marine-based economy as a whole, as the goal of the federal government was to put an end to their reliance on the sea and force them to put their attention on developing an agriculture-based economy.

The decline in whales resulting from the unregulated whaling industry made it extremely difficult for the Makah and Nuu-chah-nulth people to continue whaling. The gray whales, the species of whales the Makah most actively pursued, were the first to succumb to over-hunting. In 1856, the gray whale population was estimated at approximately 30,000. Twenty years later it had plummeted to between 8,000 and 10,000. From 1908 to 1943, when the four shore-based whaling stations in the Pacific Northwest were recording their annual whale catches, only one gray whale was caught. This was in 1912 at the Sechart whaling station (in Nuu-chah-nulth territory). These statistics demonstrate how quickly this whale population declined and how drastic the slaughter of this whale species was.[107]

The humpback whale was also being threatened. Before shore-based whaling developed in the Northwest, the humpback whale was believed to be the most numerous of all the whale species. Archaeological evidence shows that the humpback was the whale that the Nuu-chah-nulth most actively pursued because of its larger numbers, its high oil content, and the fact that it was available throughout most of the year. There was a resident humpback population in Barkley Sound before commercial whaling decimated it. Tseshaht elder Frank Williams told ethnologist Edward Sapir, when Sapir was conducting fieldwork with the Tseshaht in 1913, that there were so many humpback whales in Barkley Sound that when they were raking for herring they would have to beat the sides of their canoes to avoid colliding with them.[108]

The humpback, like the gray whale, is also a slow-swimming species and travels close to the shore, making it easy to catch. In 1911, the first year when statistics were kept for all four shore-based whaling stations, 1,022 humpback whales were captured, averaging 250 whales for each station. Between 1911 and 1925, the whaling station in Grays Harbor at Bay City, Washington, captured at least 1,933 humpbacks from the coasts of Oregon and Washington. The humpback whale population, like the gray whale population, also suffered a continual steady decline. After 1930, the two whaling stations still operating in Nuu-chah-nulth waters averaged only one to five humpback whales a year.[109]

Although commercial whaling intensified in Makah and Nuu-chah-nulth marine space, the Native people continued to hunt whales for subsistence. Between 1888 and 1897, the Makah were still able to harvest between two and twelve whales per year. In 1897, Indian agent Samuel G. Morse noted that whale oil was still a chief article of the Native diet. Early archaeological studies indicate that the food supplied by whales comprised over 80 percent of Makah precontact diets.[110] But as the gray and humpback whale herds disappeared, it became more and more difficult for the Makah to keep whale in their diets.[111]

Even though new foods were introduced into the Makah and Nuu-chah-nulth diets, whale meat, blubber, and oil were still highly valued by the community and were still being distributed to all the tribal members when a whale was caught. In the 1860s, whale oil was still a main staple in the Nuu-chah-nulth diet and was considered their most desirable food. Sproat observed that the Nuu-chah-nulth would rarely sell their whale oil. This could have been because many of the whale species were already declining and the people chose to keep the oil for themselves rather than trade or sell it.[112] As the whale disappeared from the Makah and Nuu-chah-nulth diets, new foods were introduced to compensate. By the 1940s, over 80 percent of the Makah diet was made up of nontraditional foods. Some families still relied heavily on fishing and attempted to maintain diets rich in their own food products, but many people also began to incorporate foods they bought from the local stores, such as meat, eggs, and milk, which became their staples.[113]

No more whales meant no more whale oil to trade, a reality that significantly affected Makah and Nuu-chah-nulth economies. The commercial whale-oil market had also collapsed by the 1860s, but whale oil was still highly prized as a trading item to other coastal groups.[114] But with so little oil being rendered, what was accumulated was used for consumption by the members of the chief's village and little was left for trade. With the decrease in whale oil, the whaling chiefs could no longer hold their once-prestigious whale-oil potlatches, where the oil was lavishly distributed among the invited guests. Accordingly, the rituals, songs, dances, and ceremonies that accompanied these whale-oil potlatches also went out of use.

Some whaling *haw'iih* persisted in maintaining their hunts, while others turned to other pursuits such as commercial sealing as a way to seek wealth and prestige. Formerly, it had been degrading for a chief to perform any labors other than those that had prestige significance (such as whaling). But with social distinctions diminishing, the old prejudices against labor began to fade away.[115] As whaling decreased, the ritual and spiritual elements that were central to the tradition also began to diminish. It took whaling *haw'iih* months, sometimes years, of physical and spiritual preparation to assure success in whaling. With many whaling chiefs now involved in the wage-labor economy, it became increasingly difficult for them to find time to prepare for a whale hunt. And, knowing that there was a great possibility that they would not catch a whale, many chiefs had to reconsider going through this arduous ritual and spiritual preparation, since it would keep them from engaging in other more reliable subsistence and economic activities that provided them with money and food needed for their families.

The loss of whaling also meant a weakening of the social elements that were integral to this tradition. Whaling had kept Makah and Nuu-chah-nulth communities together; strengthened the bonds between families, the local groups, and the village; and established alliances with other communities along the coast that were invited to share in the bounty of a captured whale. These bonds and alliances made through the sharing of the whale meat and oil were undermined as there were fewer and fewer whales to hunt. And, now, when a chief was able to successfully capture a whale, it was distributed only within his community. As the chiefs turned elsewhere for attaining wealth and prestige, whaling and the social mechanisms attached to this tradition began to disappear as well.

The *ushtakimilh* (lineage group) overseen by the *haw'ilth*, began to dissolve. In precontact and early-contact times, a village was structured around the chief and his *hahuulthi* (territory) and the resources that were derived from his land and marine space. All those within the *ushtakimilh* lived together in the big houses and worked together for the common good of the chief and the *ushtakimilh*. But the big house structures began to be dismantled as smaller, nuclear-family housing structures became more common, and the extended family social structure of living together and working together for the chief and for the common good of the *ushtakimilh* began to fade away.

For the whaling *haw'iih*, pulling together a whaling crew became ever more difficult as a result of the changes to the social structure. In pre- and early-contact times, only high-ranking chiefs had the undisputed privilege of acquiring and redistributing wealth. Population decrease and the beginning of alternative ways of obtaining wealth undermined control over the labor force and resources that a chief had formerly maintained.[116] In the new wage-labor market, whaling chiefs worked alongside other Makah and Nuu-chah-nulth members, regardless of previous social status, with all having access to the same labor and the same incomes. The *haw'iih* began to lose their control over resources and material goods as people who were from the commoner and slave social ranks now had the ability to support themselves and their nuclear families outside of the chief's sphere of influence.[117]

◆ ◆ ◆

Within Nuu-chah-nulth and Makah whaling cultures, the physical universe and the spiritual realm are intrinsically linked. In his book *Tsawalk*, Nuu-chah-nulth chief Umeek developed a theory of *tsawalk* (one) "that views the nature of existence as an integrated orderly whole" and sees an intrinsic relationship between the physical and spiritual realms, translating into *heshook-ish* (*hishuk ish*) *tsawalk*, "everything is one."

> I originally conceived of Tsawalk as a theory of context. In one respect, context defines recognizable units of existence, such as age group, gender, home, school, geographical region, society, and heritage, but Tsawalk, by comparison,

also refers to the non-physical and to unseen powers. Consequently, because the theory does not exclude any aspect of reality in its declaration of unity and, most important, because the concept of heshook-ish tsawalk demands the assumption that all variables must be related, associated or correlated, I now call this view of reality the theory of Tsawalk.[118]

Drawing from the many definitions of culture, it can be described as an integrated system of human knowledge, customary beliefs, values and laws, artistic expression, and social behavior and habits that are learned and transmitted to succeeding generations.[119] I have shown in this chapter how following contact with *mamalhn'i*, Makah and Nuu-chah-nulth societies underwent severe cultural change. Disease epidemics, colonial policies that undermined and suppressed cultural practices, entry into the global market economy, and the commercial over-harvesting of whales worked together in destabilizing the Native belief systems and dismantling the complex social, economic, and spiritual networks that were central to our whaling cultures.

Culture is not static; it encompasses both continuity and change, with change being influenced by both internal and external forces. Early contact with *mamalhn'i* introduced into Makah and Nuu-chah-nulth societies new material goods and technologies, which they adopted by adjusting their economies and subsistence activities. But as government officials began to pressure Native peoples to give up their traditional economic and social practices, change began to take place at such a rapid pace that social, political, and economic dislocation began to occur. This, in turn, had an impact on the way Makah and Nuu-chah-nulth interpreted the world around them, as change to the material aspects of their societies led to a weakening of the metaphysical association to whaling. Our whaling cultures had once flourished within a thriving maritime economy and were enmeshed in a system of rituals in which *haw'iih* had obligations to both the physical and spiritual worlds. Dramatic changes to social, political, and economic systems challenged and weakened the intimate spiritual relationship whalers had with whales and with the whale's spirit through *oo-simch*. The end of whaling signified a disconnect with the material aspects of our tradition and with the physical and spiritual connection to whales through whaling practices. But, as I will demonstrate in chapter 3, our whaling tradition remained integral to Makah and Nuu-chah-nulth identities and was maintained through songs, dances, ceremonies, and religious and artistic expressions.

3 / *Kutsa*

MAINTAINING THE CULTURAL LINK TO WHALING ANCESTORS

THROUGHOUT THE YEARS, NUU-CHAH-NULTH AND MAKAH SOCIETIES have undergone radical changes that significantly challenged their ability to maintain their cultures and traditions. By the late 1920s, whale hunts had ceased, but the people's emotional and spiritual relationship with this tradition continued, and the spirits of our whaling ancestors continue to walk in the world we live in today. In this chapter, I focus on my own family and community to demonstrate how the connection to our whaling tradition was maintained and how it continues to inform our lives. We still identify certain sacred areas in our land and marine spaces by the names given to them by our whaling ancestors. We hold personal names that directly tie us to our whaling lineage, and we carry these names with respect and pride.

Our whaling ancestors never left us—they breathe life into our rich whaling narratives, preserved and reinforced through oral traditions. They give power to our drums and nurture our voices as we sing the whaling songs, dance the dances, and perform the ceremonies. And they continue to guide the hands of our artists as they create the powerful images of the great Thunderbird and majestic Whale. Our whaling tradition is the heart and soul of our world.

THE PEOPLE OF TS'ISHAA

I am a member of the Tseshaht First Nation and grew up in my Native community. Tseshaht is a member group within the larger nation of Nuu-chah-nulth. We take our name from our principal village, Ts'ishaa, located on Benson Island, one

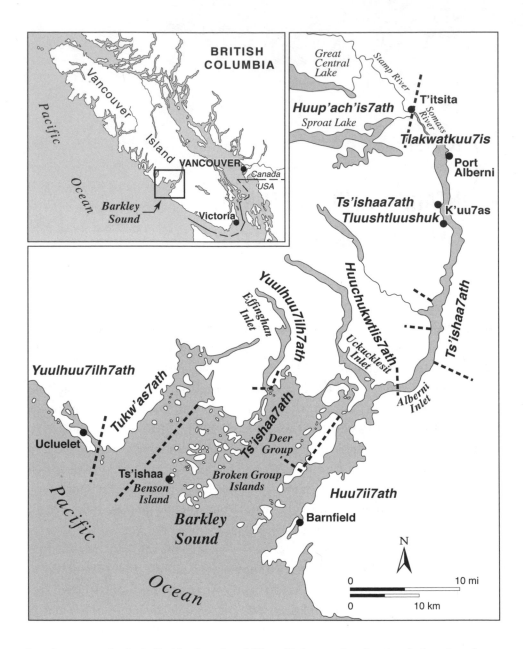

Local group territories in Barkley Sound and Alberni Inlet, ca. 1815, showing the location of Benson Island in the Broken Group. Adapted by Barry Levely from McMillan and St. Claire, *Ts'ishaa* (Burnaby, B.C.: Archaeology Press, 2005).

of the outer islands in the Broken Group in Barkley Sound. The name Tseshaht means "the people of Ts'ishaa."[1]

As the Tseshaht population grew, the community expanded into other areas of the island and eventually onto adjacent islands. Through tribal warfare and amalgamations, we seized and ultimately controlled territory from the Broken Group Islands up the Alberni Inlet and along the Somass River. Our main village, where we now reside, eventually shifted to the Alberni Valley, and by the early 1870s it had become our primary residence. We continued to use Hiikwis on Sechart Channel as a winter village, and our former principal village at Ts'ishaa became one of our main summer fishing and sea mammal sites.[2] Although we moved to a new village away from the Broken Group Islands, we continued to take advantage of the sea resources there and continued to whale in the waters off Barkley Sound.

In 1874, the newly appointed superintendent of Indian affairs, Dr. Israel Powell, sent George Blenkinsop to Barkley Sound to gather information on land use from the Nuu-chah-nulth groups living there. The reserve commissioner Peter O'Reilly visited the same groups in 1882 and began allocating reserves. He gave the Tseshaht a total of nine reserves, three in the Broken Group Islands, three on the upper shores of Barkley Sound, two on the Alberni Inlet, and one on the lower Somass River where most of Tseshaht resided. Our village at Ts'ishaa was not occupied at the time of the Blenkinsop and O'Reilly visits, and, as a result, this area was not included in the reserve allocations.[3]

HOW WE CAME TO BE

All societies have origin or creation stories that explain how their people and their world came to be. These stories have an explanatory and instructional function, and they usually contain guidelines for survival and proper moral conduct. Many of these stories provide a template of how to live and establish rules and principles for people to follow.[4] While growing up, I never really thought about our story of origin and never heard anyone talk about it. I remember that when I was a young girl, someone mentioned that we were created on one of the islands in the Broken Group, but I did not know much more than this. When, in the 1990s, I began research into our whaling traditions, I started by analyzing the written accounts of our creation story. I found three versions of the story that were similar in content. My cousin Anne Hunter, who has extensive knowledge of our history, told me that it is not surprising for the Tseshaht to have different versions of the creation story because of the various lineages that came together during the years of group amalgamations that eventually led to the community we have today.[5]

The three versions of the story that I found were recounted by my great-great-grandfather Sayach'apis and were recorded and translated into both Tseshaht and English by his grandson Alex Thomas, for the anthropologist and linguist Edward Sapir. The version I have included below is recorded in Edward Sapir and Morris Swadesh's *Native Accounts of Nootka Ethnography*.[6] I have included the characters' names from the earlier versions in parentheses along with an explanation in the chapter notes.

We Tsishaa people learned things because of the Day Chief [or Kapkimyis],[7] who created us at Hawkins Island [now called Benson Islands]. Because of this, we know for sure he is the chief in the sky. Yet we do not know his name.[8] He is an old man. She became aware, as though awakened from sleep, that there were two people, one an old man and one a shaman with bars painted across his eyes.[9] The young one who awoke there was a young woman. She realized she was a young woman. The old chief stood on a wide board and cut at the front of his thighs. The shaman scraped up the blood in his hand. He blew into it. He did that to the blood and it turned into a boy. The girl watched; they were doing this inside a house at the rear. Both the little girl and the little boy were growing rapidly.

"You shall be named Day-Down,"[10] they told the young boy. "You shall be named Sky-Day,"[11] they told the girl. Then the chief made a river. It became a real channel, the mouth at Village Island [now called Effingham Island]. The other side of the mouth would be Standing Point. The river formed a lake, well closed at the head of the canal near Rocky-Shore. Then they instructed the brother and sister as to the various things they would eat. They showed them all kinds of sea food. They mentioned bad things not to be eaten. They told them, "Use an instrument like this, tied along its shaft, for catching the big things of the sea." Because of that, sure enough, the whaling harpoon is tied along the shaft.

The two quarreled. The shaman became angry and scattered the river and channel everywhere. That is why the islands are scattered about now. What had been a lake went into the ground, which is why Water-on-Wall never dries up, for they say there is a lake inside Hawkins [Benson] island. That is why we have our seats at the rear end of the house. They were seated by the rear house post. It is because we were created there by my ancestor. The old man and the shaman left things so; before they went up to the sky, they finished instructing the two they created. "You must pray to me at times for I will always hear what you want," he told them before he left.

Many came from the two, being born of the womb, as a tribe which grew up fast. From the start they build a house, and that house has been copied. They came to have a canoe. Their adzing tool for felling trees was an elk bone. They got sea mammal spears. They started to hunt hairseal. They hunted porpoises. The spear line was made of hairseal guts. The tribe became numerous, reaching to the other end of the village on Hawkins Island. They hunted sea otter. They clothed themselves in sea otter skins.

The tribe was for a while called Cut Tribe (Ch'ichuu), derived from the fact that the girl saw the old chief cut the front of his thigh. Originating from that, they came to be called the Tsishaa Tribe. It became a big tribe. There were many sea otters all over the passes. There was a constant noise of kiikkiik as the sea otter broke up mussels. People would come home with five or six sea otters in a night when they went hunting. When Day-Dawn[12] was first created, he was given a war club with blood along its edge. He was told, "You will keep it on the beach and your tribe will never die out in future generations."[13]

Our creation story emerges as a powerful oral text providing important cultural associations and connections to the physical and spiritual worlds. The story discusses the creation of first woman and man at our former village site, Ts'ishaa. All Tseshaht believe that we are direct descendants of Naasayilhim (Sky-Day) and Naasiya atu (Day-Down), and their names continue to be passed down through family lineages. The story connects our creation to a specific place in our traditional territory, to mountains, rivers, lakes, streams, channels, islands, beaches, rocky bluffs—many of which are being created at the same moment as our creation. For example, in the story it says that when the shaman got angry with Naasayilhim and Naasiya atu, he "scattered the river and channel everywhere." This refers to the creation of the Broken Group Islands, where our principal village was located. These geographical landmarks provide orientation to and explanation of the nature of our existence.[14]

Kapkimyis provides the two people with a whaling harpoon and tells them how to use it. He says, "Use an instrument like this, tied along its shaft, for catching the big things of the sea." Hence, whaling is integral to our origin, and through the creation of the first man and woman, the Tseshaht are provided with the knowledge and tools to become great whalers.

Within our creation story is the unity of the physical and the spiritual, with the physical world being a manifestation of the spiritual world. These two worlds were experientially one, expressed through our principle of *hishuk ish tsawalk*, "everthing is one."[15] The story emphasizes the importance of spirituality and our connection to the spirit world. Day Chief tells the first woman and man, "You must pray to me at times for I will always hear what you want." Sayach'apis said this is why the Tseshaht people pray to Day Chief for all things: health, wealth, food, piety, and spiritual or shamanic powers.[16]

Sayach'apis said that the name for the Tseshaht was originally Ch'ichuu, which means Cut Tribe, referring to when Kapkimyis, or Day Chief, cut his thighs to create the first man. Ch'ichuu,

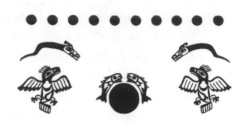

Thunderbird, Whale, and Lightning Serpent images painted on the head chief's house that once stood at Ts'ishaa, as described by Sayach'apis to Sapir in 1913. From McMillan and St. Claire, *Ts'ishaa* (Burnaby, B.C.: Archaeology Press, Simon Fraser University, 2005).

according to Sayach'apis, was eventually changed to Tsishaa. Tseshaht elders who have been asked about the meaning of our name said that Tseshaht means "People from an island that reeks of whale remains," which referred to the rancid smell of whales rotting on the beach at Ts'ishaa.[17] Sayach'apis told Sapir about a house that once stood at Ts'ishaa. Although these big houses were no longer on Benson Island when Sayach'apis was a young boy (in the 1850s),[18] he recalled stories about a house at Ts'ishaa that was located in the center of the village.[19] This house belonged to the Tseshaht *taayii haw'ilth* (head chief). Its architectural design clearly revealed that it was the home of a great whaling chief. On

Artist's interpretation of the inside of the head chief's house at Ts'ishaa as described by Sayach'apis to Sapir in 1913. From McMillan and St. Claire, *Ts'ishaa* (Burnaby, B.C.: Archaeology Press, Simon Fraser University, 2005).

the outside of the house, on the side facing the beach, were painted the images of two Thunderbirds, facing each other. Thunderbirds were known as the first great whalers. Above the Thunderbirds were painted two Lightning Serpents, which were utilized by the Thunderbirds as whaling harpoons. Inside the house, on the end wall, was a screen also painted with the images of pairs of Thunderbirds and Lightning Serpents. Each Thunderbird held a whale in its talons.[20]

On the inside of the house were carved figures that connected the Tseshaht to their creation story and to the tradition of hunting whales. A figure was carved on a post that held up the center beam of the house. This post was along the wall that faced the main doorway and was centered between the Thunderbird, Lightning Serpent, and Whale motifs. The figure was of a male, representing the first man of Ts'ishaa, Naasiya atu (Day-Down), holding a *ch'it'uul*, or whalebone war club. Another post located closer to the doorway of the house had a carved image of Kapkimyis (Day Chief), the creator of the first Tseshaht man and woman, holding a carved whale.[21]

IHINITSULHH, "WHERE THERE ARE MANY WHALE SKINS": THE CONNECTION OF PLACE-NAMES TO WHALING

Oral stories, ethnographic accounts, and archaeological evidence directly link the land and marine space around Ts'ishaa to our whaling tradition. The waters around Ts'ishaa were favored whaling locations because the gray whale's migration route ran directly along Benson Island.[22] The Tseshaht have names for numerous places within the Broken Group Islands, which are imbued with cultural and sacred meanings. These Tseshaht names have persisted throughout time, even after English became our working language. Within the context of colonization, these places and their continued use became even more significant. When explorers and later colonists arrived in this territory, they mapped and named the areas they visited, stamping their identities on the land. The symbolic colonization of the land began as colonizers used this naming process to bring the land under their sphere of control.[23] One strategy Native people utilized to resist domination and ensure survival of the culture and language has been the continual use of our own place-names rather than the new names mapped over these places by the dominant, white culture.

Native peoples gave names to places that were culturally significant, so, for example, there might be numerous names for important places on a mountain but no name for the mountain itself.[24] Place-names are more than just geographic descriptions; they and their translations distinguish meaningful spaces and are important in illustrating Native peoples' unique relationships with particular areas in their land- and seascapes.[25] The naming of land and marine space transforms these physical environments into "places" that become embedded within our histories and imbued with spiritual and cultural significance.[26] These names are, as anthropologist Keith Basso asserts, "the most highly charged and richly evocative symbols" that convey a wealth of information about the spaces they specify and the cultures they speak from.[27]

Anthropologist Thomas Thornton says that since "places are largely human constructions, then it should follow that, in order to understand people, one must know something of their places."[28] Place-names, he maintains, not only enlighten us about the structure and content of the physical environment, they also reveal how people perceived, conceptualized, classified, and utilized their environment.[29] Naming locations within areas provides a way to record the kinds of human experience that have occurred there. Hence, these place-names serve as a kind of archaeology of meanings, documenting aspects of the history of these areas that might otherwise be forgotten because the physical relationship to this land or marine space has changed over time.[30] In her research with Native elders in Canada's Yukon Territory, anthropologist Julie Cruikshank illustrated how place-names can indicate changes in the landscape and can be used to encode, enrich, and structure accounts of the past.[31] There is a place in the southern Yukon Territory that the Native elders refer to as Medzih E'ol, which means "place where caribou swim across in groups." Without these elders' stories to validate the cultural history of this area, Cruikshank maintains, the name would seem unusual because large caribou herds no longer pass through this land. Biologists are trying to reconstruct the history of these herd movements to find out why.[32]

Although the Tseshaht have not whaled in over seventy years, our names for former whaling sites continue to have cultural significance. For example, in our marine space, there is a pass between two islands (Benson Island and Clarke Island) that runs in front of our former Ts'ishaa village site. This pass is known by the Tseshaht as *hamuta*, which means "bones." Stories in our oral tradition say that after a whale was caught and divided up, our great whaling *haw'iih* would deposit the bones of the whales there as a monument and symbol of whaling successes. Sayach'apis told Sapir that there was such an abundant amount of whale bones deposited there that eventually the pass began to dry up.[33]

One of the islands (now named Gilbert Island) in the Broken Group chain is known by my people as *ihwitis*, "whale oil on it." The shoreline on another island (Dodd Island) is known as *ihinitsulhh*, "where there are many whale skins."[34] Some of these locations were well known as excellent whaling sites. One site is known as *tushumis*, "the place of shaking (tail) on the beach." This sandy waterway is where *maa'ak* (gray whales) would come to feed. While there, the whales would beat the sand with their flukes, causing the clams underneath to be exposed, which the whales would eat. This was considered one of the ideal sites for whaling because when the whales' heads were down in the sand feeding, they could not see the whaling canoes approaching, making it easier for the whaling crew to catch them.[35]

Place-names can serve many purposes. Basso says that both places themselves and place-names ground people in their environment and provide them with "symbolic reference points for the moral imagination and its practical bearing on the actualities of their lives." Thus, he posits, "the landscape in which the peoples dwell can be said to dwell in them."[36] Place-names are like pictures. They can also stimulate an enormous range of mental and emotional associations with time, space, history, events, people, and social activities. They have the capacity and power to evoke and consolidate the personal and cultural meanings attached to or instilled in a particular landscape.[37]

From these place-names we develop a sense of self. Basso says that this "sense of place roots individuals in the social and cultural soils from which they have sprung together, holding them in the grip of a shared identity."[38] A sense of place, embedded within land- and seascapes, serves as a peg on which people hang memories; these social memories and meanings become fixed within these land and marine spaces. Thus, a people's sense of self and place become intertwined.[39]

These land- and seascapes have spiritual significance, and our ancestors' spiritual powers are concentrated in the land, sea, rivers, streams, trees, and other material objects. These sites and the objects in these places become sacred, providing physical evidence of the spiritual energies that flow within them.[40] The spirits of our ancestors live on in the names and spaces allowing us to maintain an important connection to them, as expressed by Stó:lō cultural historian Albert (Sonny) McHalsie: "When I visit these places I feel an important connection to my ancestors. I sense their presence and I pray to them, asking them for strength, guidance, and protection in whatever I may be doing there."[41]

Our ancestors left supernatural powers on the land and waterways, which became transformed into part of the land- and seascapes. There is a rock at Ts'ishaa that sticks up on the beach. When whales were brought up on the beach, they were tied to this rock so that they would not float away. This rock is called Kapkimyis, after the creator of the first Tseshaht man and woman.[42] For the Tseshaht, this rock is a sign left by our ancestors and signifies the spiritual powers connected to this important cultural landmark.[43]

Indigenous histories are always narrated in relation to specific landscapes, waterscapes, and skyscapes. Native peoples make sense of their worlds by recounting events tied directly to their surroundings. These narratives both recognize and reinforce the webs of relationships that connect all entities of a community's special domain and then link that domain to their universe.[44] These Tseshaht place-names show how our whaling history is documented, preserved, and continually reinforced through the use of these words from one generation to the next. They keep our histories alive and my people connected to these places even when the places are no longer in use on a regular basis. The names frame the historical narrative, whereby our whaling history is something tangible and alive, grounded in the physical land and marine spaces.

ORAL TRADITIONS: NURTURING A COLLECTIVE MEMORY

In *Oral Tradition as History*, historian Jan Vansina writes: "No one in oral societies doubts that memories can be faithful repositories which contain the sum total of past human experience and explain the how and why of present day conditions. . . . Whether memory changes or not, culture is reproduced by remembrance put into words and deeds."[45] Oral traditions consist of all verbal testimonies or statements concerning the past that are transmitted from one person to another via the medium of language.[46] Indigenous oral traditions encompass a canon of narrative forms that include stories, legends, myths, histories, folklore, prayers, songs, music, performance, and ceremonies that are transmitted from generation to generation and, therefore, become widely known. The telling and performance of these narratives teach about morals, life lessons, history, spirituality, economics, politics, and the environment.[47] The continual passing on and performing of these narratives generate a collective memory. Accordingly, patterns of experience foster a group identity that serves to unite and hold communities together.[48] The stories, songs, and dances contained in oral traditions serve "to bind people to each other and to the social, physical, and spiritual worlds in which they are placed and where they interact with each other and with the non-human world."[49]

HIMWITSA HUMWIC'A (STORYTELLING)

Stories contained within the oral tradition provide a window into Native societies and cultures through which to define and understand their way of life. In his article "Decolonizing through Storytelling," Skokomish scholar Chi'XapKaid (Michael Pavel) says, "Before the introduction of written language, grandparents and gifted storytellers distributed all knowledge orally. It was through their living breath that the ancient tales of their ancestors were passed on and remembered."[50] The lived experiences of our ancestors are transformed into stories and legends that teach, document, and explain what is fundamental to our cultures. Through *himwitsa humwic'a* stories we learn who we are, how we should behave, what our history is, what should be important in our lives, how to stay connected to our spirituality—all that encompasses our worldview. Storytelling can be in the form of play or it can be serious. It can be fun, exciting, entertaining, and challenging to the intellect. Ultimately, stories serve to unite, joining people together in their past, present, and future—"an experience invoked by breathing the words of our ancestors."[51]

Passing on knowledge through storytelling has always been an important way to keep our traditions alive. In her book *Singing the Songs of My Ancestors,* Makah elder Helma Swan discusses growing up in a Makah family that was rich in the storytelling tradition. Born in 1918, she was raised during a time when the Makah people were experiencing intense cultural and societal transformations. As a way to cope with these changes, Helma's elders told her stories that kept her connected to the Makah culture. For Helma's family, storytelling took place in the evenings and a story sometimes lasted two or three nights. The people invited to the home of the storyteller would always bring food, maybe some dried or fresh fish to share with those gathered at the house. Thus, Makah storytelling not only passed on knowledge but also served to bring people together, reinforcing family and community bonds.

Helma Swan heard stories that were central to Makah culture, stories and legends about Kwaatie and Ishkus and about Snot Boy.[52] When she was a young girl, she heard many stories about whales and Makah whalers. At the time she was born, the Makah whale hunts had already been on the decline. She never witnessed a hunt, but she would hear the male Makah elders reciting stories about whaling. These stories that she heard during the evenings in Neah Bay kept Makah history and traditions alive for her.[53]

As a Nuu-chah-nulth person, I was raised in the *himwitsa humwic'a* tradition and came to understand my culture and my people's history through it. I grew up next door to my grandparents, in the community of Tseshaht, which I consider a cultural blessing. My grandparents, Hughie and Grace Watts, had a typical Nuu-chah-nulth home. Their door was always open, and their dinner table always had a place for an extra chair for anyone who dropped by. Their home was a central gathering place and was always filled with family, friends, people from our community, or people from other Nuu-chah-nulth communities who would stop by for a quick visit or spend endless hours being entertained by my grandparents' laughter, good spirits, and great stories.

I grew up with wonderful stories told to me by my mother, Evelyn, and my grandmother Grace, but it was my grandfather Hughie who was the real storyteller in my family. He was our family historian and passed down to his children, grandchildren, and great-grandchildren knowledge of family history, songs, and traditions. When I was a young girl, my nuclear family lived with my grandparents until our house was built on the lot next to theirs. My aunts, uncles, mother, and father referred to my grandfather and grandmother as Dad and Mom, and I grew up calling them Dad and Mom instead of Grandpa and Grandma. Dad (Grandpa) was born August 4, 1903, and grew up on the land on which he was born. He loved his home and made it into a wonderful welcoming space for his large family and many friends. As he got older, he began to devote a lot of time to cultivating his huge gardens, and he would spend hours in the evening weeding, watering, and nurturing his vegetable patch.

When he was not working or tending to his garden, he would be inside his house, sitting in the living room on his favorite Easy-Boy chair, waiting for someone to drop by so he could share his narratives. My grandfather always had a story to tell, whether it was about something current in our community, something that happened at the docks where he worked as a longshoreman, or something that provided the listener with insight into our culture. The storytelling did not stay in my grandparents' home. My grandfather would tell us stories in the warm summer mornings when all the grandchildren were packed in his station wagon, heading to the mountains for a day of berrypicking. Or he would tell us stories on hot summer days when we were helping him fish for salmon on the Somass River that flows behind our homes. But it was those stories he told to us during the chilly winter evenings that I loved the most, when all of us young ones gathered on my grandparents' living room floor for a night of storytelling.

My most vivid memories of my grandfather are of when he was sitting in his favorite chair, in his usual attire of a blue undershirt, black pants, and leather moccasin slippers, clicking his teeth and scratching his gray buzz-cut hair as he decided what tales he was going to tell us. He would begin the story, reciting it in both the Nuu-chah-nulth language and English. Sometimes he would pause and stare out of the large picture window, as many of these stories brought him back to his childhood and made him think of the stories he was told when he was a young boy. And then he would turn to us once again and complete the story. This would go on all evening, with my grandfather clicking his teeth and scratching his head, smiling and laughing, as we stared up at him with sheer delight on our faces.

My grandfather took great joy in telling us stories about our culture and traditions. He narrated stories about children not listening to their parents and the consequences of their disrespect; stories about humans turning into animals and animals turning into humans; stories about young girls and boys coming of age; stories about wolves; and, of course, stories about Thunderbird and Whale, and about whaling and our great whaling ancestors. There were also silly stories that he loved to recount, and as he told them, he would have a large, warm grin on his face. He told us stories about Kwatyat, the Nuu-chah-nulth trickster/transformer/creator, and about Pitch Woman stealing little children. We young ones did not realize it at the time, but my grandfather's stories were more than just entertainment. They were immersed in the Nuu-chah-nulth traditional form of *haahuupa* (teaching), passing on valuable knowledge through a narrative structure designed to both entertain and educate us. Anishinaabe (Chippewa) writer Gerald Vizenor says that "the teller of stories is an artist, a person of wit and imagination, who relumes the diverse memories of the visual past into the experiences and metaphors of the present."[54] Storytelling is an amazing art form, and as I grew older, I came to cherish the cultural knowledge I gained through my grandfather's creative, amusing, artistic, and always powerful narratives.

Native historian Angela Cavender Wilson (Tawapaha Tank Win) recounts how she grew up in the storytelling tradition and spent many cherished hours with her grandmother, listening to stories about Dakota life and history. Wilson says these stories are not only one of the most personal and powerful ways of passing on historical knowledge but are also necessary for cultural survival:

> The intimate hours I spent with my grandmother listening to her stories are reflections of more than a simple educational process. The stories handed down from grandmother to granddaughter are rooted in a deep sense of kinship responsibility, a responsibility that relays a culture, an identity, and a sense of belonging essential to my life. It is through the stories of my grandmother, my grandmother's grandmother, and my grandmother's grandmother's grandmother and their lives that I learned what it means to be a Dakota woman, and the responsibility, pain, and pride associated with such a role. These stories in the oral tradition, then, must be appreciated by historians not simply for the illumination they bring to the broader historical picture but also as an essential component in the survival of culture.[55]

Most of my grandfather's stories were those he heard when he was a boy, and he recounted them from memory. But he also used a book that was gifted to him and my grandmother from an anthropologist, Janice Irving, who lived with my grandparents in the early 1970s, when she was doing fieldwork in the Tseshaht community. The book, *Nootka Texts: Tales and Ethnological Narratives,* was written by anthropologist/linguist Edward Sapir and linguist Morris Swadesh and was published in 1939. *Nootka Texts* was a compilation of ethnographic data and stories Sapir collected when conducting fieldwork with Tseshaht elders between 1910 and 1923.

Starting in the early 1900s, linguists, anthropologists, and historians began extensive fieldwork in indigenous communities to record and collect information on Native cultures and traditions. A theory developed that Native cultures and traditions had been so severely undermined by non-Indian contact and threatened by government policies that they would eventually disappear through the processes of acculturation and assimilation. Scholars came to our communities to collect and record our histories, stories, and traditions. As a result, what was passed down through our oral traditions became part of the written record. Sapir compiled significant notes on Nuu-chah-nulth culture, history, and society. He interviewed many people in my community and worked extensively with my grandfather's grandfather, Sayach'apis. Sayach'apis would provide material to Sapir in the Nuu-chah-nulth language, and then his words were translated for Sapir by Sayach'apis's grandson, Alex (Alec) Thomas. Alex was away at boarding school the first time Sapir came to our community to conduct fieldwork in 1910. During Sapir's second visit in 1913, Alex was home on holiday, and he took great interest in watching Sapir record his material. Alex, who was around nineteen at the time, picked up Sapir's notation system and gradually became an expert ethnographer and linguist. For the next decade he worked for Sapir collecting, recording, and transcribing data, for 50 cents a page, and sending these to Ottawa.[56]

Sapir's notes were organized into a series of texts titled the *Sapir-Thomas Nootka Texts,* which were intended to provide a comprehensive ethnography of Nuu-chah-nulth cultural and social life. Between 1910 and 1925, Sapir worked as chief of anthropology at the Canadian National Museum (today the Canadian Museum of Civilization). Throughout the years, many of the *Sapir-Thomas Nootka Texts* were published: most recently, Part 10 in 2000, under the title *The Whaling Indians: Tales of Extraordinary Experience,* and Part 9 in 2004, titled *The Whaling Indians, Legendary Hunters.*

Sapir wanted the stories recorded and transcribed as closely as possible to the original way they were told to him. The interviews he conducted with Tseshaht elders were translated almost word for word from Nuu-chah-nulth into

My grandfather Hughie, ca. 1975, reading a story from Sapir's *Nootka Texts* to my cousins: (*from left*) Lisa, Gail, Hughie, and Lena. Photograph courtesy of Gail Gus.

English. In documenting the ethnographic material and stories in this way, Sapir was able to adhere to the Nuu-chah-nulth way of telling a story, which captured the linguistic and cultural nuances. Sapir's research contributed greatly to studies of indigenous languages and cultures.[57] *Nootka Texts* and other publications by Sapir have been invaluable to my people, as they have helped preserve our language and culture through the stories and ethnographic material that were recorded in the words of my ancestors.

My grandfather treasured his copy of *Nootka Texts* and took great pride in reading its stories to his grandchildren, thus validating how important the book was to him and to my family. The stories he read to us from *Nootka Texts* had their own unique flair and were informative, educational, humorous, sexually candid, and full of rich details of Nuu-chah-nulth life.[58] One story I still remember almost word for word today is a story about the marriage of Mink and how Mink got a chief's daughter pregnant by giving her chewing gum![59] Every now and then we would hear a yell from the kitchen from my mother, grandmother, or aunt, telling my grandfather in Nuu-chah-nulth to tone it down when they thought the stories were getting a little too racy. My grandfather is a great example of how his generation utilized and adapted to the changing way knowledge was passed down. Through the act of reading his own grandfather's stories to us, my grandfather retained their original narrative form.

Nootka Texts contained both the English and the Nuu-chah-nulth language, but my grandfather enjoyed teaching himself to read the Nuu-chah-nulth phonetics and would use both Tseshaht and English when he read the story. When he ran into pronunciation problems, he would ask for help from my mother, Evelyn, who was his oldest daughter. Evelyn was born March 29, 1928. She grew up speaking the Tseshaht dialect and was immersed in our culture. She never lost the language, because she attended boarding school for only two years when she was a young girl. She was born legally blind, and the teachers at the boarding school close to our home refused to teach her because of the extra effort it would take. My mother always said that not having eyesight was "a blessing in disguise," because she was not severed from our language and culture like other Native people who were forced to attend the boarding schools. When my grandparents went to work, my mother stayed with her grandmother, Laal (Eva Thomas), who would speak only Tseshaht to her. Thus, my mother grew up completely fluent in Tseshaht and could also understand all of the Nuu-chah-nulth dialects. So when my grandfather did not understand a word in *Nootka Texts*, or was unsure of the meaning of a particular word, he would turn to my mother for assistance.[60]

Memory is a powerful thing, and, through her ability to remember, my mother passed down to me many stories that helped frame my life as a Nuu-chah-nulth and Tseshaht person. Her stories were true to the oral storytelling tradition because of the simple fact that she did not have the eyesight to read. She learned by listening. Ballenger writes, "Memory is a place where cultural materials get put, usually in the form of stories that tell people who they are and who they have always been."[61] My mother's pedagogy was framed by the countless stories she heard growing up, which, passed on to me, taught me valuable lessons. For example, where I grew up, the Somass River literally runs through our backyard. One of my mother's stories was about the "lady who comes out at night" and searches for her child who had drowned in the river many years ago. Through this narrative, I learned that the river, while it sustained us, could also be dangerous, and so I should be cautious when swimming or playing close to it. Another story she told me was the tale of the hunchback lady, through which she taught me about respect and to not speak badly about people. When "hunchback lady" was a young girl, she would gossip about the people in our community. Throughout the years, she developed a curvature in her back. My mother said this was caused by her lack of respect for her community members. My mother's stories always connected me to our culture through her use of words in our language, place-names, personal names, songs, or certain aspects of our history, and her narratives have helped me maintain a powerful connection to my Tseshaht culture and identity. When a story is passed down to a Native person, we in turn must recognize our responsibility in repeating it so that these cultural threads through generations will not be broken. Dakota scholar Cavender Wilson (1999) writes,

> Because these stories are typically not told in the history texts, we also must recognize we are responsible for their repetition. The written archival records will not produce this information. These stories are not told by people who have been "conquered," but by people who have a great desire to survive as a nation, as Dakota people. Consequently, these are not merely interesting stories or even the simple dissemination of historical facts. They are, more important, transmissions of culture upon which our survival as a people depends. When our stories die, so will we.

My life was and still is filled with stories, each one serving to strengthen my knowledge of my people's history and culture, and as I pass them down to my younger relatives through both written and spoken narratives, they also serve to ensure that our Tseshaht culture will not die.

"STANDS-UP-HIGH-OVER-ALL": MY GREAT-GREAT-GRANDFATHER SAYACH'APIS

I have referred to Sayach'apis many times throughout this book. I came to know about him as a young girl, when I would hear stories about him from my family and community members. I heard stories about what a great man he was and that he had high status and a whaling lineage. I heard how he held huge potlatches at which he gave away many gifts to his guests. When I was a teenager, I learned that many of the stories my grandfather had read to me when I was younger were stories that Sayach'apis had told to the anthropologist Edward Sapir. And when my community came together to sing our songs, I learned that many of the songs that we sang and danced to had been passed down to us from Sayach'apis. There has not been a lot of material written about him, but what he has left us are wonderful songs, amazing stories, and rich cultural data that has helped maintain and preserve Tseshaht language and culture.

Much of the information I used to compile a history of Sayach'apis came from research that anthropologist Denis St. Claire conducted with and for the Tseshaht people for the last thirty years, and from the research Sapir conducted during his fieldwork in my community in the early 1900s.[62] In 2003, Denis compiled

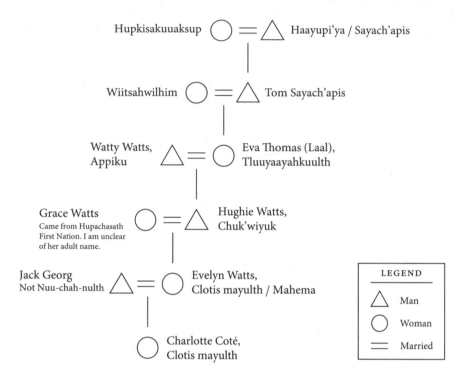

NOTE: Information is based on Sapir 1910–14, notebook 15, pp. 44, 44a. The chart is courtesy of Denis St. Claire and is based on the genealogy he prepared for the Thomas family in the unpublished document "Thomas Family History and Genealogy," 2003. I have changed some of the spelling to conform with the style used in this book.

a family history and genealogy for the Thomas family, who are also descendants of Sayach'apis. It is based on the accounts by Sayach'apis as told to Sapir in 1910 to 1914. This information is included in the unpublished document "Thomas Family History and Genealogy," which Denis provided to me to help with my genealogical research. I used the information he arranged in this document to compile my own family genealogy, showing how I am connected to Sayach'apis.

MY FAMILY GENEALOGY

Sayach'apis, also known as Tom Sayachapis, Big Tom, or Tom, was Sapir's principal informant. His name translates into English as "Stands-Up-High-Over-All." While conducting fieldwork in Alberni, Sapir spent many hours with

My great-great-grandfather Sayach'apis, with his wife Wiitsahwilhim (Wiitsah).
Photograph courtesy of Bob Soderlund.

Sayach'apis, recording his stories. These stories were then translated into English by Sayach'apis's grandson, Alex Thomas. In the first publication of the *Nootka Texts* in 1939, Sapir showed his gratitude to Sayach'apis for the endless hours he spent narrating. Sapir affectionately wrote that Sayach'apis was "a courteous and good-humored man" who was an inexhaustible source of wisdom; a man "steeped in the aboriginal past."[63]

Sayach'apis, "Stands-Up-High-Over-All," was born around 1843 and lived his early life in a traditional longhouse at the village of Hiikwis, which was located on the mainland in the Broken Group Island area in Barkley Sound. Hiikwis was one of the main Tseshaht villages and was most likely the main winter village until the mid-nineteenth century, when my people continued their territorial expansion and moved up the Alberni canal to our present-day village along the Somass River in the Alberni Valley. When Sapir sat down with Sayach'apis to record his stories, Sayach'apis was already quite elderly, blind and frail and in need of a cane to walk. Although he was by then physically weak, he was a man impressive in prestige and wealth.

Sayach'apis came from chiefs in both his father's and his mother's lineage. His

My great-grandmother Eva (Laal), ca. 1954. Photograph courtesy of Eileen Haggard.

My grandfather Hughie, ca. 1974. Photograph courtesy of Bob Soderlund.

father, Haayupi'ya, was a top-seated *haw'ilth* of the Mukw'aa'ath *ushḵimilh* (lineage group) of the Tseshaht (Ts'ishaa'ath). When Haayupi'ya died, Sayach'apis inherited his position. However, Sayach'apis chose not to accept the senior chief's position of the Mukw'aa'ath because he believed that both his great-grandfather and his father had been poisoned by people who were jealous of their high rank. He instead chose to take the Nash'as ath seat. His mother was from the Nash'as'ath *ushtaḵimilh*. Her father, Nuunup'itchmiik, came from chief's status. He did not have any sons. His oldest heir was a daughter, Hayuuhu'ulh, and she did not have any children, so the chieftainship was passed down through his second daughter, Suutahswuumtl, who was Sayach'apis's mother.[64]

Sayach'apis had three wives. First was Saaxtii'iwak, "Many Stones Are Rolled Together." She died before having any children. His second wife was Kiihnis (a name that refers to the flapping or thundering sound of Thunderbird's wings), and they did not have any children. His third wife was my great-great-grandmother, Wiitsahwilhim, and they had five children together. She came from high status, which was depicted in the names she received throughout her life.[65] Her first name was Hupalh'aks, which was changed to Hakum Maknit, which means

My mother, Evelyn, ca. 1980. Photograph
courtesy of Bob Soderlund.

"Always Chief Woman." Her next name was Yaatsuu'is'aks, "Woman Standing
on the Edge (Touching) a Big Chunk of Whale Blubber." This name was given to
a girl whose father was considered a great whaler. Her last name Wiitsahwilhim
(later shortened to Wiitsah), which means "Never Getting Poor," also shows that
she was a woman of wealth and status.[66]

My great-grandmother was Tluuyaa'yak'uulh (Laal, Eva); she was Sayach'apis
and Wiitsah's third child. Her first name, S'ishts'iya'utl, "Always Pouring Whale
Oil on the Fire," shows that she came from high status and wealth, as it was
only the successful whaling families who could pour whale oil on a fire at a potlatch. Her final name, Tluuyaa'yak'uulh, means "Making Rough Waters Calm."[67]
Tluuyaa'yak'uulh married Appiku' (Watty Watts), and they had eight children.
My grandfather Hiishtsukwatimiik (Hughie Watts) was their second child. He
married my grandmother, Grace Hamilton,[68] and they had twelve children. My
mother, Clotis Mayulth (Evelyn), was their first child. My Native name, Clotis
Mayulth, was my mother's last name and means "Woman Who Is Respected in
Her Community."

Although Sayach'apis chose not to inherit the top-seated chief's position of
Mukw'aa'ath *ushtakimilh*, he acquired a *haw'ilth* position among the Nash'as'ath
and was considered a man of chiefly status in his community.[69] His status was

enhanced by his trading skills and his impressive sea-mammal hunting ability. Although he had the birthright to hunt whales, he never pursued this vocation. He told Sapir that he "never ventured upon the more difficult and exhausting procedures required to make a successful whaler," even though he had the lineage to pursue such activities.[70] However, Sayach'apis became a man of great wealth and status by holding numerous potlatches. He was one of the first of his generation to seize the economic opportunities offered by the newly emerging cash economy and to exploit it to his advantage in traditional cultural activities such as potlatching.[71] He credited his long life and his ability to acquire goods and prestige to his commitment to prayer. He prayed every day to Day Chief: for health, he would pray, "Cause me to live, O Chief. Look after me, let me reach the top of my life"; for wealth, he would pray, "May only wealth keep traveling toward my house and stopping there. May I stir the minds of the chiefs in different tribes. May they want to give me wealth. . . . May they want to potlatch their goods to me."[72] Although he was not a *taayii haw'ilth*, he acquired immense status through trading and potlatching. He held a seat with the other Tseshaht chiefs and was considered a man of very high rank in his community.[73]

Sayach'apis was a great orator and passed on many stories to his children and grandchildren in the Nuu-chah-nulth language. At the heart of these stories was our whaling tradition. These stories were compiled by Edward Sapir into volumes under the heading *West Coast Legends and Stories* and have recently been published. In Part 10, *The Whaling Indians: Tales of Extraordinary Experience*, anthropologist Eugene Arima writes:

> Storytelling was a well developed West Coast art, and is often enthralling even in translation. Evocative atmospheres, dramatic moments, bold speech, and sometimes song enliven the account. When characters speak their individualities are sharply rendered, including idiosyncrasies. For the [Nuu-chah-nulth] these narratives tell of true events and are history. Their plots and histories reflect the native worldview, the cosmology structuring reality in terms of the supernatural and marvellous which through encounter bring prestigious power to individual and family.[74]

In narrating these stories to Sapir, Sayach'apis was able to leave to the following generations of Tseshaht, including my family, valuable and important stories, with such titles as "Owi:mln'I as a Whaler," "Tlan'iqol Becomes a Whaler," "Cha:kwa:siqmik Gets Whaling Power from the Sharks," and "The Rival Whalers."

One of the stories Sayach'apis narrated to Sapir in 1913 is excerpted here. It is a story about Na:we:i:k, who was Sayach'apis' great-great-grandfather. The story, "Na:we:i:k Relieves a Famine,"[75] centers on a great famine that struck the Tseshaht people. Fishermen and hunters continually went out in their quest for food but found nothing. Na:we:i:k's mother, He:ch'is, told her son that he must prepare himself to become a whaler, to catch a whale to relieve the famine that had overcome their village.

"NA:WE:ʔI:K RELIEVES A FAMINE"

There came a great famine among the Ts'isha:ʔath people, then at a land called Hots'atsswil. The best ocean fisherman and hunters repeatedly came in with nothing in their canoes. . . . And then the Ts'isha:ʔath people went out on a quest for food. . . .There were two whale hunters left, just the two of them left at home. All the Ts'isha:ʔath were gone. The name of one of the whalers was Na:we:ʔi:k: [Wake-Up], and the other whale hunter's name was Kwi:sa:hichi:l [Always-Turns-into-Something-to-Catch-Quarry]. . . . Na:we:ʔi:k told his mother . . . "you have never revealed to me your most potent ritual words.". . . "That is right, that's the way I am; I have never revealed [to] you the strongest, most potent of my words in relation to ritual ceremonies," said He:ch'is [Carrying-Thunder-Down-Woman], the mother of Na:we:ʔi:k, a woman of Hach'a. My father's name is Toto:t.sh [Thunderbird] as Head Chief of Hach'a."

He:ch'is got prepared, putting on ritual regalia, for what she was going to reveal to her son. "All right, now you just watch me. I am going to teach you to become what you will be, what you will do, what my father did to earn the name of Tl'a:tsmi:k [Getter-of-Whale-Fat]."

As soon as darkness fell upon the waters, Na:we:ʔi:k went out on the ocean. He went in the water and stayed in all night. He was sounding, imitating the whales, going around the island Hots'atsswil, drifting about on the rocks that had barnacle on them. . . . His wife was also going back and forth, up and down the beach bathing all night. Then He:ch'is, together with her daughter-in-law, took hold of her son by the arms, each under a shoulder, and dragged him up the beach. Na:we:ʔi:k could not walk because he was so cold. He:ch'is rubbed him with medicine for getting fat things [whales, seals] and also fed him . . . Na:we:ʔi:k lay down. . . .

He slept all day, then found himself sweating when he became conscious as he woke up. He noticed it was towards evening. After he woke up he sprang into action. He took his whaling harpoon head and put pitch in it. He put inside the harpoon head that which belonged in it, the medicine. He named his harpoon head Tl'a:tmik:k, the name which belonged to his grandfather. He had gotten it from the time he saw this mythical being that gave power to all to get whales. The stuff that was on the mythical being is the medicine that he jammed into his whale harpoon head. Thus he had his harpoon head prepared when he went to sleep again.

. . . There was a Humpback Whale! . . . "Wake up now, Na:we:ʔi:k" . . . he [the other whaler Kwi:sa:hichi:l] said. "You go get ready. Out there on the water is a Humpback."

. . . Na:we:ʔi:k and Kwi:sa:hichi:l brought their equipment down the beach. . . . The slaves were in the canoe. The one called Tsiqaʔo:ʔat sat next to the harpooner; he was Na:we:ʔi:k's slave. The slave called Taxokwaʔas belonged to Kwi:sa:hichi:l. There were women in front of the steersman because there were no men around, everyone being away getting littleneck clams. They went out from the beach towards where the Humpback was coming up out of the water. The whale went down and did not come up again. . . .

Tsiqaʔo:ʔat looked down in the water. It seemed as if the bottom of the ocean was coming up. Right away he punched his master on the back and pointed downwards into the sea. Na:we:ʔi:k ignored him, because he knew what was about to happen, for he was already made ready ritually: the whales would come to him, and he considered the whale already his own. He just looked back as his slave punched him on the back. He did not get excited.

There was a disturbance on the water where the whalers were. Just then a foreflipper on the whale appeared where Na:we:ʔi:k sat in the canoe. The whale hugged his canoe in the middle, floating on the water with the canoe between its flippers. The whale was lying on its back on the water; the crew were balancing the canoe with their paddles, trying to keep the canoe steady and upright. It just hugged the canoe, its flippers sticking up in the air on each side of the canoe where Na:we:ʔi:k sat. The flippers of the whale let go of the canoe; they sort of twisted off. The whale went down and turned around underwater, then it came up alongside, on the right side of the canoe. It was then he speared it on the side, as far in as the tied-on foreshaft would go. The whale dove with the whaling spear still imbedded in its side. It began to run, with the cedar withe rope paying out rapidly. All of the sealskin floats went overboard. The whale surfaced right in front of Tl'ihtl'ihʔa. The harpoon head was still in the whale. Na:we:ʔi:k strung the harpoon spear again. He did so himself for the crew.

"All right, you shall have the jawbone," he said to Kwi:sa:hichi:l. . . . Kwi:sa:hichi:l speared. He now shared in the killing of the whale. . . . The whale began then to run towards the ocean. . . .

Na:we:ʔi:k went back to the bow, grabbed his other harpoon and speared again. He started singing his medicine song. "Oh! This is my medicine I put in the harpoon. Oh! The bird of the spirit being . . ."

His song referred to a medicine charm that he put inside the harpoon head of the first spear he put into the whale. He speared even as the whale was already running real hard out towards the sea, and that is when he began to sing his medicine song. Just then the whale started shaking and stopped moving on the water. It was hardly breathing. Then it died.

Those who were camping out digging clams heard about it. They got ready and went out to help tow the Humpback that Na:we:ʔi:k caught. The women did not go with the men because they were afraid to cause ill luck to the hunters, as it was taboo for some women to go near whaling equipment. They started towing the Humpback and landed at ʔAqis a nice clear beach near M'oqwaʔa. The Hach'a:ʔath heard about it also. All the women from Hach'a:ʔath came to help butcher the whale. They brought dried butter clams and dried horse clams to trade for chunks of whale meat they cut off. And then all the canoes of each tribe were full of meat that Na:we:ʔi:k gave each one. . . .

They began to butcher, and the oil flowed out. The women caught the oil with buckets. One cut would fill a bucket, for it was so fat! . . . The Ts'isha:ʔath, Hach'a:ath and Ma:ktlʔi:ʔath thanked Na:we:ʔi:k. "You have done us a great favour. When we were hungry, it was as if you gave us back our lives." So they thanked him.

The story of Na:we:ʔi:k provides the reader with significant information about our whaling tradition. It discusses the importance of conducting the proper rituals and the diligence necessary in preparing for a hunt. If the whaler observed all the rituals and conducted them properly, he would obtain a strong spirit helper to provide him with the extraordinary strength needed to capture a whale. And if the whaler and his whaling crew had performed their prayers and songs to the whale and the whale's spirit with respect and reverence, then the whale would "give itself" to the whaler. This was evident when the whale came up out of the water and hugged Na:we:ʔi:k's canoe, cradling the canoe with its flippers, demonstrating how calm and comfortable the whale was in bestowing itself on Na:we:ʔi:k. We also learn about the importance of listening to parents and how knowledge passes from one generation to the next. We learn about the concept of sharing, when Na:we:ʔi:ik invites his friend into the whaling canoe and allows him the honor of also harpooning the whale. The concept of sharing is demonstrated in the distribution of the whale, with all members of the village getting a share of the whale.

Included in "Na:we:ʔi:k Relieves a Famine" are Nuu-chah-nulth names that are still used today to refer to specific locations in Tseshaht traditional territory. For example, in the story, Sayach'apis says that Na:we:ʔi:k's mother, He:ch'is, came from the village of Hach'a, or High Land, on the Alma Russell Islands next to the Broken Group Islands. The Hach'a'ath were once a separate group but eventually amalgamated with the Tseshaht (Ts'isha'aht). The village of Hikwis, where Sayach'apis was born, was in Hach'a'ath territory.[76] The story refers to He:ch'is's father, Totot'sh, who was the *taayii haw'ilth* (head chief) of the village. Because of his whaling prowess he earned the name "Tl'atsmik,' which translates as "Getter of Fat."[77] Including these references to actual people and specific locations makes the story more than a legend—it becomes an educational tool for understanding Tseshaht lineages and comprehending our people's connections to the land and water.

Keith Basso writes: "identifying the geographical locations at which events in the story unfold . . . your mind can travel to the place and really see it . . . the location of an event is an integral aspect of the event itself, and therefore identifying the event's location is essential to properly depicting—and effectively picturing—the event's occurrence."[78] Thus, narratives become "spatially anchored" to places in the land- and seascapes "with precise depictions of specific locations."[79] The primary spatial anchors are place-names.[80]

Storytelling provides a cultural framework for narrating the past and for establishing connections between the past and present and between people and place. Native histories are recorded in and transmitted through narratives, songs, place-names, and genealogies, all of which reflect worldviews.[81] Through their narrations, the storytellers provide valuable information and details of their peoples' cultural values, norms, and beliefs.[82] In *Life Lived Like a Story,* Julie Cruik-shank collaborated with three Yukon Native elders, Angela Sidney, Kitty Smith, and Annie Ned, to record their life histories, which include rich details of their lives, as well as provide a window into their communities during a time of social, cultural, and economic change. Their stories illustrate how people, stories, songs, and events are attached to places within their physical world. This is demonstrated through elder Kitty Smith's statement: "My roots grow in jackpine roots. . . . I grow here. I branch here. . . ."[83] Albert (Sonny) McHalsie (Stó:lō) demonstrates how place-names and stories connect:

The names speak of places of war and ambush and yet teach us the important principle of sharing intribal resources. Some names mark the places where people were punished for bad behaviour and then remind us of the virtues of good behaviour. . . . Some names show us where to gather herbs and plants for medi-cine and food . . . some names mark transportation routes through physical landscapes that are alive with the spirit of a transformed ancestor. The stories associated with these names use comedy, tragedy and irony as vehicles to com-municate important lessons of morality and acceptable behaviour. As a whole they transform our landscape from what some others consider as *terra nullus* ("empty land") into a place where our ancestors continue to live in spirit.[84]

Stories teach about relationships between people and relationships between people and their natural environment. "Place roots individuals in the social and cultural soils from which they have sprung together, holding them there in the grip of a shared identity."[85] Through the intersections of memory and place, Sayach'apis stayed connected to his physical environment through his stories. Place-names become "mnemonic codes for local stories and traditions recog-nized by and part of the shared memory of the local community."[86] Most of the stories Sayach'apis told to Sapir connected to his personal lineage through the people discussed, through the locations referred to, and through the themes of the stories.

"THE SOUND OF THE DRUMS IS THE VOICE OF OUR ANCESTORS"

While storytelling was the most common mode of communicating and pass-ing down knowledge from one generation to the next, other performances such as songs, dances, rituals, and ceremonies were also important in the preserva-tion and maintenance of our culture and traditions.[87] Songs and storytelling, Chi'XapKaid explains, are significant to the passing down of knowledge and are integral to our oral traditions:

> Songs help us to remember important teachings and events, and even help to identify who we are in the world. We often sing the most important concept of a story in compositions of four or fewer short lines. Before the invention of writing, singing and chanting allowed our ancestors to remember phenomenal amounts of information pertaining to our genealogy, family history, inherited rights, sacred ceremonies, and the great sagas of our ancestral heroes.[88]

Makah elder Helma Swan says that songs get more important the older they are because they have more history attached to them.[89] She reflects on the social value of owning a song: "If you own a song, it means you are an important person: it tells everybody where you're from, who your parents were, who your grandparents and great-grandparents were . . . a song is like a name. It's a hereditary thing and is greatly treasured."[90]

Music has always been an essential element in Nuu-chah-nulth and Makah societies and has supported our sociopolitical system. Our *nuukminh* (songs), along with our stories and ceremonies, maintained the social order and in precontact and early-contact times served specific functions: the most important function of Nuu-chah-nulth and Makah music was its use in ceremonies that served to uphold the power and position of our *haw'iih*. The chiefs and their families had rights to important songs, which were associated with specific dances, ceremonial masks and regalia, and ceremonies. The ownership of these songs and their performance during potlatches enhanced the chief and his family's social standing. When they sang and danced to one of his songs, this demonstrated his ownership and at the same time reaffirmed his rank, status, and power to those hearing the song and watching the dance performance. Commoners also had songs that they could sing. Commoners who developed skills such as fishing, hunting, canoe building, and basket making acquired songs that were specific to these activities.[91]

The fact that the chief and his family had the right to use and sing specific songs was the legal and historical proof of his lineage and status within his village. These songs served to reinforce both his material and his intangible wealth. Songs could be transferred as gifts through marriage dowries of high-ranking Nuu-chah-nulth and Makah people.[92] Sometimes chiefs would give away songs to chiefs in other villages. These songs would be presented to the new owner at a potlatch that was hosted by the former owner of the song. An announcement was made and then the song was sung. Guests who were invited to the song-transfer ceremony would be paid for their attendance, thus serving to legitimize and publicly acknowledge the transfer of a song.[93]

Every high-status family had a master singer or singers who could be male or female, or both. The master or lead singer was known as the *no no kwa tlokhisi*; that person would oversee the song and dance performances. If a child was observed by his or her parents to learn songs quite easily, that child was chosen to be trained as a master singer. The child was given medicines to help both voice and memory. Medicines and herbs were also given to the child so that his or her voice would not go hoarse. Alex Thomas noted that his family also had a breathing exercise they all performed before they sang: sticks were piled up and each person would have to say the word "pile" for each stick picked up without letting out a breath.[94]

Rules and proper protocol were and still are meticulously followed in the transfer of these songs. Even today, when a song is being passed on, a public ceremony is held by the family to announce the transfer. The guests are fed, and after the meal, the families from the visiting tribes are invited to perform their songs and dances. When these performances end, the host family performs its songs and dances. When this is completed, the host family announces the transfer of the song or songs.

In Nuu-chah-nulth and Makah culture, we have many kinds of *nuukminh*. Very formal songs like the *tsiiqaa* are sung for specific ceremonial and spiritual purposes. These songs are the *tuupaati* (ceremonial prerogatives) of the *haw'iih* and can be sung only by them or their family members. We have informal songs, such as the *kwiikwaatha*, which are fun songs that are used for light entertainment at social gatherings and can be sung by everyone. We have songs for the important times in our lives: songs for marriages and for coming-of-age, lullabies for newborn babies, doctoring or ritual songs, gambling songs, memorial songs to honor a deceased person, songs for our sacred wolf ritual, and, of course, songs for whaling, especially for success in whaling.

The *nuukminh* were and still are accompanied by hand-held drums covered in deer or elk hides, rattles carved out of wood, and whistles made by joining two hollow pieces of wood together. In precontact and early-contact times, we also utilized wooden plank drums and rattles made out of whale baleen. The music is still accompanied by specific dances that are associated with the songs and with the families who have the rights to sing them. Nuu-chah-nulth and Makah songs consist mostly of one melodic line sung solo or by a group. The songs usually have short choruses surrounded by syllables or vocals such as hu, hu, hu, which sustain the longer lines.[95] Each song usually contains a story, which the singers learn and in some cases recite before the song is sung. The verses, or choruses, usually describe or refer to a simple circumstance or occurrence that had some symbolic meaning. The significance of the words in the chorus depends on the knowledge of the legend, story, or event on which it was based.[96]

There is a wonderful story about a Makah whaler who received a song during a terrible hardship he experienced while whaling. The whaler was Helma Swan's great-great-grandfather, and she recounts the story of "The Song of Seven Daylights" (also called "The Spiritual Song") in the book she coauthored, *Singing the Songs of My Ancestors*.

> One time [he] went out, he speared a whale and got his leg caught in the rope.
> . . . When the whale dove under, he went right out with the whale because he

couldn't get his ankle all untied. The whale took him around in the ocean for quite a while. When the men in the canoe finally let the rope go, they thought the he had drowned, but they waited around for a while anyway. After he went under, he found enough strength within himself to untie himself even though the whale was pulling him around. He got all untied. When he came up, the guys saw him come up—they saw blood all around him (he had a terrible nose bleed from surfacing too fast). They couldn't believe he was alive! . . . He said to them, "I got a song when I went under. When I went under I saw seven day-lights" (seven changes in the light as he was dragged under). . . . So this is the song that he received after he came up from under the water . . . he got this song, which my mother used and now I use, from my great-great-grandfather.[97]

The song chorus translates into English as,

> *I went down as far as any human possibly can,*
> *To where the earth meets with the water,*
> *From daylight to dark,*
> *And came back up again.*

Helma said that the dance that accompanied this song has changed over the years. The song was sung by a male wearing a carved mask with small eyeholes; parts of the mask were painted green, like the color of the sea. The mask was painted with up-and-down swirls, which depicted the water spirit. "The Spiritual Song" has been passed down through Helma's family lineage and now belongs to her. Today the song is sung at potlatches, birthdays, weddings, and at the annual Makah Days celebrations.[98]

NUNUUK: "SINGING" THE SONGS OF OUR ANCESTORS
OUR WHALING NUUKMINH

Whaling *haw'iih* had many *nuukminh* that were sung during ritual preparations preceding a whale hunt, songs sung during the hunt, songs sung after the whale was caught and was being towed to shore, and songs sung to the whale spirit after the whale was beached. Chiefs obtained their whaling songs through a connection with whale spirits that they encountered in dreams or during a whale hunt. Once a connection was made with the whale spirit and the song was sung, the song became the property of the chief and was included in his *tuupaati*.[99] Some of these whaling songs were sung by the chiefs at potlatches, to demonstate their connection with a whale spirit and thus enhance their status.

Sayach'apis had many songs in his *tuupaati*, and many of these have been passed to my family. When Edward Sapir was conducting fieldwork in the early 1900s, he made a phonograph recording of sixty-seven songs that were sung by Tseshaht elders. Many of the songs were sung by Sayach'apis himself. Along with the songs, Sapir collected details about and a history of each. In the 1930s, additional information was obtained by ethnomusicologist Helen Roberts from Sayach'apis's grandson Alex Thomas. All of the songs collected were compiled into a phonemic orthography by linguist Morris Swadesh.[100]

Sapir collected ceremonial, gambling, lullaby, wolf ritual, and healing songs. Among these were songs that were connected to our whaling tradition, and some came from Tseshaht chiefs who derived the songs from encounters they had with the whales' spirits. These songs are called "spirit-communicating songs." Sayach'apis, who had many spirit-communicating songs in his *tuupaati*, sang six of them for Sapir. One song goes back to Sayach'apis's ancestor Makes-Oily (Tlatlaaqukwa'ap), who was known to be a great whaler and who caught many whales in his lifetime. This is the legend that goes with this song:

> When Makes-Oily was hunting he came upon a whale. He harpooned the whale, which then began towing him out to sea. The whale kept the chief out on the ocean water for four nights. On the third night at sea, Makes-Oily fell asleep and he dreamed he was in the house of whales. While in their house he could hear the whales singing lullabies. On the fourth night Makes-Oily once again fell asleep and once again dreamed he was in the whale's house. He heard the elder whales telling the young whale, which he harpooned, that they had kept Makes-Oily captive long enough. Then Makes-Oily heard the young whale sing a song. The following morning the young whale towed Makes-Oily and his whaling crew back to shore. All the while Makes-Oily was singing this song given to him by the young whale: "You will head for there, go to land. You will head for *Tsutsiit* where I have my ritual bathing place."[101]

The song was passed on to Makes-Oily's relatives and then to my great-great-grandfather. It was an honor to be given the right to sing a spirit-communicating song, and when Sayach'apis sang one of these powerful songs at a potlatch, it reinforced his and his family's spiritual connection to their whaling lineage.

The whaling *haw'iih* also had songs for drift whales that floated onto the village shores. They had rights to these whales, because it was understood that their whaling power had brought the whales to them. The chorus in the song would be used to affirm their status as whalers, beginning with "I have one drift whale," until the final chorus, "I have ten drift whales."[102] Many of the songs in Sayach'apis's *tuupaati* were whaling songs. One song goes back to Sayach'apis's ancestor Naasiya'atu, who was known as a great whaler. Naasiya'atu sang this song at a potlatch he held to display the five *chakwa'si* (dorsal fins) he had acquired from whaling.

The legend that goes with this song is as follows:

> Naasiya'atu was a great whaler and on one of his whaling excursions he had caught five whales. He held a feast to honor the spirits in the five *chakwa'si* that he removed from the whales. The chief's daughter danced when the song was song. She wore a decorated sea-otter blanket, with a thunderbird, lightning serpent, and a quarter moon painted on the back, a red cedar bark head ring and an eagle feather on each side of her hair. The feather signified her father's connection to ya'ii, who was a supernatural being that whalers obtained for luck in whaling. As Naasiya'atu sang his song his daughter swayed back and forth moving a few steps in each direction while holding her hands down at her sides. The chief sang the chorus of the song: "My dorsal-fins are insufficient in the house. My *yaatyaata* dance is always forgotten as I dance."[103]

While the chief's song seemed to display a humbleness about his impressive whale hunt, in a subtle way Naasiya'atu was boasting about his accomplishment in getting five whales. When Sayach'apis sang this song, it demonstrated his connection to this great whaling chief and reinforced his and his family's whaling identity.

When whaling ceased in the late 1920s, a lot of the songs associated with it began to fade away because the next generation did not have a direct connection to our whaling tradition through actual whaling. But some of our whaling songs did survive, and, today, my family and other Tseshaht members who descend from Sayach'apis proudly sing the songs passed down from him. Each time we sing one of his songs, we breathe life into his memory and into the great whaling heritage that we all are so proud to be a part of.

One of Sayach'apis's songs that we still sing at potlatches is a *haatshuuthla,* or wealth display song. This song was recorded by Sapir in the early 1900s.[104] The chorus of the song loosely translates as, "I have people gathered in my house. I have whale tied up on my beach. I have runaway slaves landing at my beach. I have many sea-otter skins stretched out on my beach." The text of the song focuses on the material wealth of Sayach'apis's ancestor. A whale on the beach would show how this chief could easily feed all the people gathered at his feast. Slaves who ran away from their chief to be with this one were a testament to his status and protective power. The sea-otter skins, which were considered an item of great prestige, were collected by the chief's family to give away.[105]

There is another *haatshuuthla* song that we sing at potlatches. The chorus roughly translates as, "My potlatch handle is carried around on the shoulder. My wealth is flying about; it seems to be seeking its equal in being wealthy."[106] Originally, this song was sung during a *pachaksma'aqa* (gift scramble), at which a *pacsaakum,* or potlatch handle, which was a piece of wood, was thrown out among the guests at the end of the song. The person who caught the handle would receive a gift. The more wealth the chief had, the more prestigious the gift. During one of Sayach'apis's potlatches, he gave to the winner of the scramble ten fathoms of dentalia shell, which was considered an expensive prize.[107] When we sing this song today, we acknowledge Sayach'apis's wealth and the status he proudly held coming from a long line of great whalers.

STAYING CONNECTED TO OUR WHALING IDENTITY THROUGH PERSONAL NAMES

Nuu-chah-nulth and Makah people received numerous names throughout their lifetimes that marked important periods or specific occasions. Names are obtained by inheritance and are still owned by the families. In precontact times, individuals could also obtain new names through dreams, visions, and supernatural encounters. These new names also follow the strict lines of descent and are only transferred to individuals connected through kinship. The head of the family oversees the family's collection of names. A name does not officially belong to a person until it has been announced and conferred at a public potlatch ceremony.[108] A potlatch is held to announce the recipient of the name and to transfer the name to this individual. A designated speaker announces to the guests the name that is being passed down and provides them with the history behind the name. The ownership of the name is traced back to its origin and to those who had carried it before, and honor is added to it each time it is handed down. It is up to the individual receiving the name to live up to the standards it has set and to carry it with great respect.

The names of individuals change throughout their lifetimes, marking their birth and their transition from child to young adult, to mature adult, and to elder. Therefore, an individual can receive four or more names during her or his life. In precontact times, high-ranking people had more names than people of lesser rank because of their wealth, which provided them with the ability to hold potlatches where names were conferred. But, more important, the kin connections embodied in a name were of more strategic value to people of higher rank. A name articulated an individual's status and rank and was a tangible symbol of that person's right to utilize privileges belonging to the *ushtakimilh*.[109]

The names of our *haw'iih* are considered a form of property that are linked to the associated ceremonial regalia, screens, prayers, songs, and dances that were part of their *tuupaati*. Each name embodies the cumulative honor of all the people who also held the name. For whaling *haw'iih*, prestige obtained from killing a large number of whales would continually pass on to the next chief in line for the name, thus staying with the name itself, which gained more and more prestige with every whale that was caught.[110] These names continue to be passed down within the Makah and Nuu-chah-nulth communities, forming a bridge from our former to our present-day traditions. Today, having a whale crest, story, song, dance, and/or name in one's *tuupaati* is still considered a great honor.[111]

Sayach'apis received many different names throughout his adult life that were connected to his whaling lineage. The earliest name he received was Tl'i'nitsawa, which means "Getting-Whale-Skin." The name came from Tseshaht whaling *haw'ilth* Hohenikwop. When Hohenikwop would bring his whales to the village shore, the young boys would run down to the beach for slices of whale skin. On watching these young boys, Hokeniwop made up the name "Getting-Whale-Skin" and gave it to his son. The name was passed down to Sayach'apis's grandfather and eventually to him.[112] The next name he received was Ha'wihlkumuktli, which means "Having-Chiefs-Behind." The name came from his paternal grandmother's grandfather. The chief received the name from a spirit whale that came to him in a dream. The name refers to the fact that the chief was having a lot of success in whaling and was becoming very wealthy and, because of this, was moving up the ranks, leaving other chiefs behind him. As a young man, Sayach'apis was also given the name Nawe'ik, meaning "Come-Here," which was a command given by a spirit whale to one of his ancestors.[113]

The last name my great-great-grandfather received was Sayach'apis, which means "Stands-Up-High-Over-All. It goes back eight generations through his mother's lineage to one of his whaling ancestors. The story behind the name is that the chief was conducting his whaling rituals for many days without taking time out to sleep. He began to get very tired and eventually fell into a heavy slumber. As he slept, Sky Chief appeared to him and asked, "Why are you sleeping? You are not really desirous of getting wealthy, are you? I was about to make you wealthy and to give you the name Stands-Up-High-Over-All." And so the chief came to have this name. The name was transferred to Sayach'apis at a coming-of-age potlatch he held for his oldest daughter.[114]

Although Sayach'apis did not himself go whaling, he received these high-status chiefly names because of his whaling lineage, through the prestige and wealth he attained through his economic pursuits, and by holding many potlatches. When Sayach'apis prayed to Day Chief, he would intone, "O Chief . . . May my chiefhood come to be foremost. May I be named by all people. May the different tribes hear of only me. May they know my name."[115] The names associated with whaling were among the most honored and could be passed on only by someone if they had the *tuupaati* or rights to do so.[116] My great-great-grandfather's achievements elevated his family to high-ranking positions within Tseshaht society. My family takes immense pride in being connected to his name and to this whaling history. The name Sayach'apis is still revered, and it is a great honor when one of my male relatives receives the name Sayach'apis, "Stands-Up-High-Over-All."

KEEPING ALIVE THE SPIRIT OF T'IICK'IN, IIḤTUUP, AND ITL'IK

Many of the early explorers who came in contact with Makah and Nuu-chah-nulth people noted in their journals the art forms they saw. Artistic expression was identified in the exterior and interior of our housing structures, in house posts, everyday clothing and ceremonial regalia, eating utensils, food-gathering items, and boxes used for storage. Ceremonial masks and rattles, combs, weapons, basketry, woven capes and hats, and various tools were finely designed and embellished far beyond mere functional needs.[117] The first contact with the Nuu-chah-nulth by white explorers was in 1778, when Captain James Cook visited the Mowachaht village of Yuquot. Accompanying Cook was artist James Webber, who constructed images of the places they visited. Webber's illustrations are the earliest images of Northwest Coast indigenous life and artistic expression. One of his drawings of the interior of a chief's house shows a man wearing a knob-topped conical hat with woven scenes of canoes and men carrying whale harpoons. Cook noted that this type of hat was worn by Chief Maquinna (see photograph on page 104). Situated on a platform alongside one of the house posts was a carved whale's dorsal fin similar to the one found at the former Makah village of Ozette in the 1970s.[118]

Some of the earliest art pieces found in Makah and Nuu-chah-nulth territory connect directly to our whaling tradition. For example, an object excavated at Yuquot, in the traditional territory of the Mowachaht people, was found to be a carved handle of a whalebone club dated at about 2,000 years old. The figure

The hat was similar to this one made by Jessie Webster (Ahousaht) in 1968. Photograph courtesy of the Burke Museum of Natural History and Culture.

carved on the club had a turned-down beak and featherlike projections on the back of its head, which had a clear resemblance to the Thunderbird image that has been found on more recently excavated whalebone clubs. Other excavations found pieces of whaling harpoons decorated with zigzag designs that represent Lightning Serpent and date back 1,200 years. The intricate designs carved onto the harpoon were believed to give it a magical or spiritual strength that enhanced a chief's whaling ability.[119] The excavation at the 2,000-year-old Makah village of Ozette uncovered many wooden items with the Thunderbird design drawn or painted on them. Planks recovered from the longhouses that once stood in the village revealed carved images of Thunderbirds and wolves. Other house planks that were uncovered revealed images of whales. One of the more elaborate ceremonial art pieces uncovered at the Ozette site was a large wooden effigy of a whale's dorsal fin carved out of red cedar. Inset into the effigy were approximately seven hundred sea-otter teeth, with some of these forming the images of Thunderbird and Lightning Serpent.[120]

Coastal indigenous art was connected to the spiritual world. It was understood that a person's ability to carve, weave, sculpt, and/or design came from spirit helpers or was inherited from an ancestor. The better their work, the more spirit power the artists had obtained.[121] Therefore, carvers, basket weavers, and tool and canoe makers were all revered in their communities. The art of a people reflects what is important to their culture and significant to their identity. Because Nuu-chah-nulth and Makah cultures changed considerably after contact with non-Indians, our traditions were altered or in some cases no longer utilized. Our artistic expression endured, however, and within our artistic designs, carvings, and images, our cultures and histories have been documented and affirmed.

The coastal potlatch ban, enforced from 1884 to the early 1930s in the United States and to the early 1950s in Canada, had a direct influence on Nuu-chah-nulth and Makah artistic expression. The ban not only made it difficult for chiefs to make public claims to their status, but many of the ceremonial items, masks, headdresses, drums, rattles, and family screens that they used to support their claims to status and wealth were taken away by Indian agents. On the other hand, as art historian Aldona Jonaitis points out, Northwest Coast Native artistic culture demonstrated impressive resilience. For example, as a way to resist the ban on potlatching, the Nuu-chah-nulth and Makah started making family history screens out of cloth instead of wood. This adaptation of wooden to cloth screens had a functional purpose and served as a resistance strategy. Cloth screens were much easier to carry and store away when not in use. Cloth was also much easier to hide from Indian agents.[122]

Following the potlatch ban, Northwest Coast art continued to be created, but it became less focused on ceremonialism and more focused on the tourist trade. Items that previously had a functional value, such as cedar woven baskets and hats, now became items to sell to tourists, art collectors, and museums.[123] While many of the women who produced these baskets and hats followed the conventional designs that were passed down through their families, some adopted designs made especially for the non-Indian market. One basket, woven by a Makah, for example, illustrates a twist on the whaling scene. A whale is being towed, not by a whaling canoe but by a motorized boat. On the lid of the basket are the woven designs of four anchors.[124]

There was reawakening of interest in artistic expression in the 1960s that was fueled by Native self-determination movements that reinvigorated and reinforced pride in one's culture and cultural traditions. Native artistic expression began to flourish and demand for Native art also increased. This in turn sparked a cultural revival as the myths, songs, dances, and ceremonies associated with the artwork were also rediscovered. New materials made it possible for Native artists to be more creative, and they were able to make more intricate and more detailed designs. Silk-screen printing was developed, which also expanded the market in coastal arts. Silk-screens prints were less expensive than hand-carved art, which helped make this art form popular. This innova-

Makah cedar basket, twentieth century. A motorized boat is towing the whale, which, in turn, tows the whalers in their canoe. Photograph courtesy of the Burke Museum of Natural History and Culture.

tive intertwining of new and old forms and styles is expressed in the art today.

Today, Nuu-chah-nulth and Makah artists continue to develop and stretch their art forms, with contemporary interpretations of traditional beings, personal visions, new ideas, and new materials, while still maintaining a connection with and respect for the oral traditions.[125] Art has become a means for Native peoples to showcase their histories and to demonstrate their connection to their lands and environment. In the precontact and early-contact periods, the art of the coastal peoples visually confirmed the social and spiritual order. The wearing of the Maquinna-style hat was a visible display of a chief's whaling status. The images that were and still are central to our artistic expression are T'iick'in (Thunderbird); the first whaler, Iiḥtuup (Whale); and Itl'ik (Lightning Serpent). These images on whaling chiefs' homes, as well as whaling scenes carved onto the exterior walls, showed the connection of the inhabitants to the whaling tradition, and they have been maintained in Nuu-chah-nulth and Makah art throughout our histories. Our artistic expressions complement our oral stories, and many of the figures and characters in these stories come alive in our art. In our artwork, the Thunderbird and Whale are usually depicted together, with Thunderbird holding Whale in its talons. Many pictures place Lightning Serpent alongside the

Art Thompson's Thunderbird, Whale, and Lightning Serpent print. Photograph courtesy of the Burke Museum of Natural History and Culture.

other two figures.[126] Ultimately, art has become a way to preserve and reinforce our whaling identity.

Silk-screen prints have become a new medium for creating whaling designs and scenes. However, these images have also been depicted in women's basketry and hat making. A family's historical connection to whaling continues to be displayed on family curtains at our twenty-first-century potlatches. Thunderbirds, Whales, and Lightning Serpents are designed, carved, and painted on masks, headdresses, and drums and are sewn or appliquéd onto dancing shawls. Nuu-

My cousin Hugh Braker performing our headdress dance with my mother and me at my niece and nephew's naming potlatch, 1982. Photograph courtesy of Bob Soderlund.

chah-nulth and Makah people are known for their headdresses, which are worn by male and female dancers and are painted and carved in the shapes of Thunderbird, Lightning Serpent, and Wolf.

ATSIC ("GOOD WITH HIS HANDS"): PAYING HOMAGE TO GAHNOS/TSAQWASSUP

My brother-in-law Art (Gahnos/Tsaqwassup) Thompson opened my eyes to our artistic expression and how it informed our whaling tradition.[127] Art, who passed away in 2003, was an internationally renowned artist and a historian who carried with him years of knowledge obtained from his parents and grandparents. When I began working on my dissertation in the late 1990s, I spent many hours with Art, either on the phone or during visits with him and my sister in the summer months. When I told Art that I was going to write a book, he was very excited and very supportive of my writing. He told me how proud he was that I, a Nuu-chah-nulth woman, was writing our history. During the summers, I would come back home and stay with Art and Charlene in Victoria. I would sit for hours watching

Art while he carved and painted, and, while there, I would listen to his amazing stories about our culture and whaling history.

Art was born in 1948 in the Ditidaht village of Whyac, an isolated village located on the western end of Nitinaht Lake. He had both Nuu-chah-nulth and Coast Salish roots; his father was Ditidaht and his mother was Cowichan. When he was twelve years old, he was initiated into the Tluukwana, the sacred wolf society of the Nuu-chah-nulth people. As a young man, Art faced many challenges. When he was three years old, he contracted tuberculosis and spent three years in the hospital, and most of that time he was in a full-body cast. In 1955, at the young age of six, he was placed in the Alberni Indian Residential School. While there, he faced physical and sexual abuse at the hands of the school administrators. These abuses left him with serious emotional scars, and for many years he turned to alcohol and drugs to mask his inner turmoil and deep-rooted pain.

Art credits his eighty-three-year-old grandmother, Helen, for leading him away from the self-destructive path he was on. When he was living on the streets in Vancouver's slum neighborhoods, she took a bus from her home on Vancouver Island to rescue her grandson. She told Art that he was a better person than what alcohol and drugs had made him become. She said that "he needed to put on another face, another set of warrior clothes." She then told him a story about when he was a small baby. His great-grandfather would take Art's hands and rub them between his own. As he was doing this, he told his great-grandson how *atsic* he was going to be, meaning that "he was going to be good with his hands." This story helped Art understand that he had a purpose in life.[128]

Helen took Art away from the Vancouver slums and brought him to a stream on Vancouver Island. They stayed there for a month, where they would *oo-simch* together. While they were cleansing themselves in the stream, Helen sang songs to Art. She told him, "We're going to make you a better man." His grandmother knew it would take great spiritual power to help Art change, so she invoked the power of their *na-na-nikx-soo* (ancestors) to help physically, emotionally, and spiritually cleanse her grandson. Helen would *ahapta* (as he called it), whereby she would constantly talk to him, teaching him, telling him about his family and reinforcing in him his history and his culture.

To develop in him a sense of cultural pride, Helen told him that he had powerful blood running through his veins and that he came from chiefs' lineages in both his mother's and his father's lines. She reinforced in him his connection to his whaling culture, telling Art stories about his great-grandfather Chester, who was a whaler. And, as they continued to *oo-simch*, Art's grandmother sang songs that his great-grandfather used to sing when he would *oo-simch* in preparation

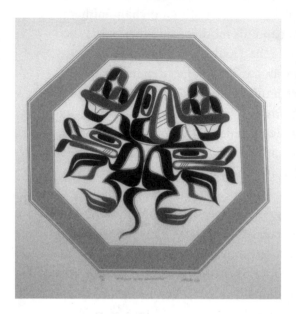

Art Thompson's print dedicated to his grand-mother. Photograph courtesy of the Burke Museum of Natural History and Culture.

Art Thompson's Pook-ubs print. Photograph courtesy of the Burke Museum of Natural History and Culture.

for his whale hunts. During the many conversations that I had with Art, he also told me stories about his great-grandfather, the whaler. Art's grandfather had kept one of Chester's whaling harpoons in his home, and Art told me that this material remnant of the whaling tradition became a focal point for many family stories. Art recited a story about a whaler in his family, who was given one of the most important and most dangerous tasks during a whale hunt. This task was performed by the one in the whaling canoe who, following the capture of the whale, jumped into the frigid water and sewed the whale's mouth shut.[129]

The stories that Helen told to her grandson and the songs she sang to him during their cleansing ritual raised him up out of his self-destructive ways and put him on a path to healing. Her determination to change Art's life for the better and the power he received from *oo-simch* provided him with spiritual strength and opened his heart and mind to develop his artistic talents. Art's grandmother told him that being an artist was the best warrior he could ever be and was a way to keep Nuu-chah-nulth culture alive. She said, "If you don't want to do anything

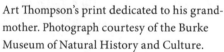

One of Art Thompson's Thunderbird and Whale prints. Photograph courtesy of the Burke Museum of Natural History and Culture.

resilrance

else with your hands, do your art, because that's what is going to tell people that we haven't died, and prove that they're not going to be able to kill us. As long as you're alive and doing your arts, people will know that we're not going away."[130] And, as a result of his grandmother's teachings, Art learned to channel his negative emotions into a positive and promising artistic future.

Having completed only a sixth-grade formal education, Art first got his GED (the equivalent of a high-school diploma) and then enrolled in art school. As he developed his artistic abilities, much of the inner turmoil that constantly stood in the way of his moving forward in life was pacified. As his inner demons began to fade, his artistic abilities flourished. Art began to visit museums to view and research Nuu-chah-nulth art forms and designs. He read books about his people's culture and history and began sitting with his elders to learn more about his Indian identity. He used this knowledge and utilized the art pieces he saw in the museums and in books as models for his own artwork, creating art through his personal lens. Art became an accomplished artist and developed his skill in various media, such as wood carving, drawing, painting, and jewelry engraving.

Today, his artwork can be found in museums, homes, and offices, and on university and college campuses throughout the world. Art never forgot about how his grandmother, Helen, had saved him from his self-destructive path, and when he became an accomplished artist, he created a print and dedicated it to her to show his respect and to honor her for guiding him along his artistic pathway.

Art's pride in our whaling culture was clearly expressed through his artwork. He told me that when he was a young boy, his elders would tell him that the Thunderbird headdresses used in our ceremonial dances were our most important cultural items. He said that every time we dance with these headdresses we invoke the spirit of Thunderbird. Thunderbird, Lightning Serpent, and Whale are represented in many of his artworks. One of his favorite figures was Pook-ubs, the whaler who had been transformed into a spirit.[131]

What is important in Art's story is not only that he helped revitalize Nuu-chah-nulth artistic expression, but that he was also instrumental in using artwork to educate others, including people in our own communities, about our art, our history, and our culture. Once he became an accomplished artist, he began designing ceremonial art for community members. He researched ceremonial items that were connected to Nuu-chah-nulth families, and then he would carve or paint regalia for the family members to use during their potlatches. He also designed silk-screen prints for them to give away as gifts.

My sister, Charlene, said that it gave her husband great pride to see his Thunderbird, Lightning Serpent, and Wolf headdresses, modeled on our ancestors' designs, being brought out and danced with during our ceremonies. He would see the smiles on the Nuu-chah-nulth women's faces as they danced with regalia embellished with his designs, and this would give him great delight. It gave our people strength, Art said, to see that "their old treasures had come back."[132] Art was a very generous person, and throughout the years he gifted a lot of art to his family members. Hanging on the walls of my home and my family members' homes are numerous silk-screen prints designed by Art, which he gave to us over the years. In our jewelry boxes are necklaces, earrings, bracelets, and rings, which were also his gifts. Most of these art pieces are embellished with images of Thunderbird and Whale. More important, these beautiful artistic expressions provide us with a lasting memory of Art Thompson, which we keep alive in our hearts.

Art also gave away numerous designs to educational institutions, organizations, government offices, and businesses, sharing his artwork with many different communities. Each piece of art that he created and each piece he gave away kept alive the stories of T'iick'in and Iiḥtuup and maintained, affirmed, and preserved our whaling tradition. When Art's youngest daughter, Evelyn, was

Art and his daughter, Evelyn, showing his art to Evelyn's grade-two classmates (1993).
Photograph courtesy of Evelyn Thompson.

in grade school, during Native Studies month, her teachers would invite Art to the school to share his knowledge of Nuu-chah-nulth culture, history, and art. Evelyn said, "Dad loved coming to my class, and he would bring his artwork to explain our history and to show how important art was to our culture. He also brought his carving tools to show us how he carved masks."[133] Art was a gifted storyteller, and Evelyn said he would have her classmates mesmerized with his tales of Thunderbird, Whale, and Lightning Serpent.

On September 8, 1999, a Conference on Indigenous Whaling was held at the University of Victoria, and Art Thompson was invited to be on one of the panels. Art told the audience about the "invisible history" of Canada's First Nations and how many people did not know the tragic and painful history of boarding schools, a history that he and many other Native people experienced. Our experiences were hidden, he said, and at the same time the federal government, its institutions, and its policies worked at undermining and destroying our cultures. But, he told the audience, "First Nations nurtured their history and kept it alive." And through it all, Art added, the Nuu-chah-nulth people never forgot "their treasured whaling heritage, even as outside influences sought to destroy the very fabric of [our] lives."[134]

When I moved to the San Francisco Bay area in the fall of 1994, Art, Charlene, and their family flew there to share with me my first Christmas away from home. They gave me a book about Northwest Coast art titled *Indian Artists at Work*. Inside the book, my brother-in-law made an inscription telling me to stay close to my heritage while I was living away from home to attend university. The inscription reads: "Always remember the proud heritage that we respectively hung on to, sometimes I'm sure by the finest of threads. But, be proud, look at the strength of all the fibers that make up the Nuu-chah-nulth peoples." Art's artwork is one of these important cultural fibers that will always keep us connected to our traditions, and although he is no longer with us, his legacy and his spirit live on in the magnificent artwork he left us.

◆　◆　◆

When we utter the Nuu-chah-nulth names of our land and marine space that were once significant to our whaling pursuits, we maintain a physical connection with our whaling tradition. When our parents and grandparents narrate to us stories about our ancestors and tell us what great whalers they were, these stories keep us connected to our whaling identity. When we pass on a name to a young boy or girl that was passed down from our ancestors, we transmit our whaling tradition to the next generation. Art Thompson, Gahnos/Tsaqwassup, said that when we speak our language, when we go to potlatches and sing our songs, we are connecting to and breathing the same air as our ancestors, our *na-na-nikx-soo*.[135] The designs we sew on our dancing shawls of Thunderbirds and Lightning Serpents and our Thunderbird and Lightning Serpent headdresses visibly display our whaling tradition. When we sing and beat our drums we continue to breathe life into our traditions and our connection to our whaling identity is thus reinforced and preserved.

4 / *Muu*

THE MAKAH HARVEST A WHALE

REVIVING THE MAKAH AND NUU-CHAH-NULTH WHALING TRADITION is part of a larger cultural revitalization and self-determination movement that Native peoples began in the 1960s in both the United States and Canada. The strengthening of a political consciousness went hand in hand with the resurgence of traditions and customs that were central to the nation-building process that was unfolding. As Native people became more politicized, they sought a reinvigorated identity, spirituality, and community. Here in the Pacific Northwest, we renewed the potlatch, the longhouse, and the canoe traditions. A return to whaling has also become a powerful way for us to connect once again with the spirits of our whaling ancestors.

FIGHTING FOR OUR RIGHTS

Native peoples in the United States and Canada have a long history of asserting their rights to land and resources through protests, petitions, litigation, and negotiation. With new political awareness, Native nations began exerting legal and political pressure to have their rights upheld by the federal, state, and provincial governments. Throughout the years, both the Makah and the Nuu-chah-nulth Nations have engaged in numerous legal and political battles to secure rights to their land and marine space and the resources these held.

Beginning as early as the late 1800s, the Makah, as well as other tribes in the Pacific Northwest, began bringing lawsuits to fight for their treaty rights to fish; they have continued ever since to engage in legal skirmishes with the state of Washington, which has a record of attempting to prevent tribes from exercising these rights.[1] Fishing was central to the coastal tribes' economic and cultural survival. Their subsistence was dependent on the return of the migrating salmon, and ceremonies and prayers were conducted during the first salmon run to show reverence for the spirit of the salmon. In 1930 Boas recorded a Kwakwaka'wakw prayer offered to the salmon spirit:

> We have come to meet alive, Swimmer. Do not feel wrong about what I have done to you, friend Swimmer, for that is the reason why you come, that I may spear you, that I may eat you, Supernatural One, you, Long-Life-Giver, you, Swimmer. Now protect us, me and my wife, that we may keep well, that nothing may be difficult for us that we wish to get from you, Rich-Maker-Woman. Now call after your father and your mother and uncles and aunts and elder brothers and sisters to come to me also, you, Swimmer, you Satiater.[2]

If proper rituals were conducted during the First Salmon Ceremony, the salmon would see that as respect and would continue to return year after year.[3] When negotiating treaties with Isaac Stevens in the 1850s, the western Washington tribes were unyielding in making sure that their salmon resource would be guaranteed to them. All the treaties signed by these tribes contained similar language regarding fishing rights: "The right of taking fish at all usual and accustomed grounds and stations is further secured to said Indians in common with all citizens of the Territory."[4] However, as soon as Washington became a state in 1889, its officials ignored the Stevens treaties and began enacting legislation to regulate rivers and waterways in the name of conservation, regardless of whether these areas were treaty-protected fishing grounds. Native people attempted to harvest the fish, but faced arrests and fines for fishing without state licenses or for fishing out of season.[5]

Washington State's obstruction of tribal fishing rights was challenged in the courts, and the legal decisions, in most cases, upheld the treaty rights. In 1905 the court ruled in *U.S. v. Winans* that tribal members had the right to cross privately owned lands to access their usual and accustomed fishing grounds outside of the reservation boundaries. The court acknowledged that the treaties needed to be flexible enough to accommodate the newly arriving non-Indian settlers yet not undermine the tribes' treaty rights. The court ruled that "the treaty was not a grant of rights to the Indians, but a grant of rights from them." Thus, through the treaty, the tribes retained a property right that functioned as a legal right-of-way to their usual and accustomed fishing areas.[6] In 1942, in *Tulee v. Washington*, the court ruled that Washington State could not limit the exercise of treaty fishing rights by imposing a license on tribal fishers, and it upheld tribal treaty rights to fish free of obstruction.[7] The Makah were thrust into the middle of these legal challenges, and in the 1950s the tribe brought forward a court case seeking to lift state restrictions on its fishing activities. The state of Washington prevented the tribal members from exercising their treaty right to fish at their off-reservation fishing grounds on the Hoko River, arguing that this was necessary for conservation.[8] The tribe lost in District Court but won a reversal in the Ninth Circuit. In *Makah Indian Tribe et al. v. Schoettler* (1951), the court ruled that "Washington could not limit Indian fishing on the Hoko River . . . because it had not sustained the burden of proving that such regulation was necessary for the conservation of fish."[9]

Although the courts continued to uphold treaty fishing rights, the state disregarded these judicial rulings and enacted laws and regulations that prohibited tribal members from exercising their right to fish. As the conflicts grew, tribal challenges became more than just a fight over fish; they initiated a political movement against all state regulations and federal policies that undermined Native rights and cultures throughout the United States. Northwest Coast tribes connected their struggles to the emerging civil rights movement and were joined by other militant Native groups to openly defy state laws. In actions similar to the sit-ins in the South, they began staging "fish-ins" to draw media attention to their grievances and to publicize their treaty rights.[10] Many people, Native and non-Native, activists and actors, began arriving in the Pacific Northwest to lend their support to the tribes.[11] By the 1960s the region had become a political hotbed for tribal protest, and it emerged as the moral center of the national Indian sovereignty and self-determination movement.[12] Historian Alexandra Harmon wrote:

> Those who wanted to resist state limitations on their fishing found encouragement in the victories of the civil rights movement and in the general surge of ethnic pride during the 1960s. . . . To various Indians and their supporters, the fishing rights dispute was a reminder of Indians' need for recognition and respect as a distinct people, the sanctity of American promises to Indians, the need to conserve ancient cultures, the value or indestructibility of cultural differences, and even the imperialist American subordination of the Third World.[13]

Nisqually elder Billy Frank Jr. rose to become one of the leading tribal fishing rights activists and today continues in his role as the chair of the Northwest Indian Fisheries Commission. His family's territory, known as Frank's Landing, became the focal point of the fishing rights struggle and was targeted by state game wardens during the "fish wars" of the 1960s. Frank's first encounter with state officials began in 1945, when he was fourteen and was arrested by two game wardens. This began three decades of activism and more than fifty arrests that he endured while attempting to fish. In Charles Wilkinson's book *Messages from Frank's Landing*, Billy Frank recounts one conflict with state officials in 1964, at the height of the tribal fishing rights struggle in the Pacific Northwest.

> At the beginning these guys [game wardens] had no idea how to run a boat on this river. . . . But they got real serious about this. And this was the time of Selma; there was a lot of unrest in the nation. Congress had funded some big law-enforcement programs and they got all kinds of training and riot gear— shields, helmets, everything. And they got fancy new boats. So all of a sudden this boat was coming at me and Bridges like a bat out of hell. . . . Those bastards rammed us at full speed and knocked us clean over. We had our hip boots on and it was harder'n hell to swim. I honestly thought I was going to drown. We finally got to shore and other guys were waiting for us. "Stop or we'll shoot." These guys had a budget. This was a war.[14]

While the courts have in general upheld tribal treaty rights to fish in "usual and accustomed" places outside of the reservations, a case came forward that countered these earlier rulings and said that tribal off-reservation fishing was subject to state laws and regulations. In *Puyallup Tribe v. The Department of Game et al.* (1968), the court upheld the Nisqually and Puyallup's right to fish off-reservation but ruled that the state could regulate fishing in the interest of conservation. Following the ruling, Washington State immediately imposed a ban on all Native net fishing of steelhead trout, while still allowing sportfishers to catch this fish.[15] Needless to say, tribal members were both furious and bitter over this legal decision that threatened their treaty fishing rights.

In 1962 the tribes in western Washington united to form the Indian Fisheries Association (IFA) in an effort to assert their views on the cultural and subsistence importance of salmon. Throughout the 1960s, hearings were conducted in the state that examined the commercial fishing resource. Many tribal members testified at these hearings, explaining how their lives depended on their salmon resource. For the coastal Native peoples, preservation of the salmon stocks was fundamental to their cultures, and they had always understood that conservation was important to making sure the salmon runs would return each year.[16] This was explicit in the IFA constitution, which reads:

We, the Indians of Western Washington, recognize that our fisheries are a basic and important natural resource and of vital concern to the Indians of the state and that conservation of this resource is dependent upon effective and progressive management thereof. We further believe that by unity of action we can best accomplish these things, not only for the benefit of our own people, but for all of the people of the Pacific Northwest.[17]

Thus, they felt that not only should they, as sovereign governments, be able to fish free of state regulation, but they should also be included in the management of these resources and that they had a sovereign and cultural right to harvest a "substantial amount" of the fish stocks. The Makah tribe had estimated at this time that the Native fishermen were catching only 5 percent or less of the total harvestable catch of salmon.[18]

In 1968 a test case came forward focusing on the treaty fishing rights issue, which became a major breakthrough for the tribes. A Yakima fisherman, Richard Sohappy, and his uncle, David Sohappy, openly defied state fishing regulations and were arrested for fishing with gill nets. The case was filed in the U.S. District Court as *Sohappy v. Smith*. The repeated prosecution of treaty fishermen forced the federal government to take action, and the Sohappy case and other fishing rights cases were consolidated into one case in 1969 as *United States v. Oregon*. Judge Belloni upheld Indian treaty rights, ruling not only that treaties were valid but that they guaranteed the exercise of tribal treaty rights outside of state law. The court also ruled that tribes had the right to an allocation of the fish resource and that this portion should be a "fair share" of the harvestable salmon.[19] But what was considered a substantial allocation or fair share of fish? This legal ruling led to one of the most significant court cases in Washington State history, *U.S. v. Washington*, also known as the "Boldt Decision."

After years of staying out of the fishing controversy, the federal government began putting its support behind the western Washington tribes, and in 1970, a U.S. attorney for western Washington, Stanley Pitkin, filed a complaint against the state for interfering with tribal treaty fishing rights. On behalf of the Makah and thirteen other tribes, the government attorney brought forward lawyers, historians, anthropologists, and biologists to conduct research and to testify on circumstances surrounding the Stevens Treaties. The state defense was led by the Washington State attorney general (and future U.S. senator) Slade Gorton. Commercial and sportfishing groups also submitted friend-of-the-court briefs opposing treaty fishing rights. Later, the State Department of Fisheries (Fisheries) and the State Game Commission (Game), their respective directors, and the

Washington Reef Net Owners Association (Reef Net Owners) were included as defendants.[20]

The court case was assigned to Judge George H. Boldt, known as a tough but fair judge.[21] The trial began on August 27, 1973. Judge Boldt held court six days a week, including Labor Day. Forty-nine experts and tribal members testified. On February 12, 1974, Boldt handed down his decision.[22]

In *U.S. v. Washington*, Judge Boldt noted that the tribes' marine resources were an integral aspect of their cultures and were significant to their diets and religious practices and had been important for trade. He ruled that the Stevens Treaties "expressly reserved the right to fish at off-reservation usual and accustomed fishing places."[23] The treaties stipulate that the tribes have the right to fish "in common" with other citizens. The state argued that this meant that the tribal fishing could be regulated by state laws, the same as other people living in the state. Boldt disagreed, asserting that "there is no indication that the Indians intended or understood the language 'in common with all citizens of the Territory' to limit their right to fish in any way." Quoting the *Winans* decision, Boldt reiterated that a treaty "was not a grant of rights to the Indians but a grant of right from them—a reservation of those not granted."[24] Therefore, he ruled, Washington State was forbidden from regulating Indian fishing without adequately showing that no other measures would preserve the fish and, if measures were taken, that they were "reasonable and necessary for conservation."[25] Boldt interpreted the "in common" clause to mean that the tribes would "equally" share their fishing resource with non-Indians; this, he asserted, entitled the tribes to 50 percent of the harvestable fish that passed through their usual and accustomed fishing areas.[26] Boldt also acknowledged the tribes' right to manage their fish resources and ordered Washington State and the tribes to work together to establish a co-management regime.

This case was not just a legal victory for the tribes but it also affirmed their economic, spiritual, and cultural connections to their marine space. With respect to the Makah, Boldt stated:

Makah wealth, power and maintenance of Northwest Coast culture patterns were achieved by and dependent upon a thriving commercial maritime economy which was well established prior to 1855. . . . Most of their subsistence came from the sea where they fished for salmon, halibut and other fish, and hunted for whale and seal. . . . The treaty commissioners were aware of the commercial nature and value of the Makah maritime economy and promised the Makah that the government would assist them in developing their maritime industry.

. . . Salmon is a staple food of the Makah Tribe today and is used for all ceremonies and potlatches. In addition to personal use, the Makah depend upon their commercial take of salmon . . . for economic survival.[27]

For the Makah and the other thirteen western Washington tribes, the Boldt Decision was a major victory and a legal affirmation of the rights protected in their treaties.[28] And, more importantly, the ruling demonstrated to them that their treaty rights were still valid and could be exercised regardless of state laws and regulations.

PROTECTING OUR SACRED TREES:
THE NUU-CHAH-NULTH FIGHT FOR MEARES ISLAND

During the 1960s, while the Makah people were battling over their right to fish, the Nuu-chah-nulth-aht were also fighting for rights of ownerships to lands and resources. Following Britain's policy on dealing with indigenous peoples, set forth in the British Royal Proclamation of 1763, Canada negotiated more than five hundred treaties with the indigenous nations across what eventually became the Canadian nation. The British Proclamation implied recognition of Native title to the land by establishing a treaty-signing process whereby indigenous peoples would be dealt with as nations.[29] Nonetheless, British Columbia refused to recognize Native title and landownership, and First Nations peoples living within the province have actively pursued political and legal recognition of their rights.[30]

Although First Nations throughout Canada have organized politically since being forced under colonial and Canadian administration, it was during the 1960s that their political activism became a major force. In 1969 Canada released its "Statement of the Government of Canada on Indian Policy," better known as the "White Paper," which called for the abolishment of the Indian Act and the Department of Indian Affairs. After the White Paper announcement, Prime Minister Pierre Trudeau made it quite clear that Canada's new policy would continue the denial of Native rights. In his public address in August 1969, Trudeau stated:

. . . aboriginal rights, this really means, "we were here before you. You came
and you took the land from us and perhaps you cheated us by giving us some
worthless things in return for vast expanses of land and we want you to re-open
this question. We want you to preserve our aboriginal rights and restore them
to us." And our answer—it may not be the right one and may not be one which
is accepted . . . our answer is no.[31]

The White Paper policy, Native activist Harold Cardinal argued, was "a thinly disguised programme of extermination through assimilation," as it would effectively strip Native people of legal Indian status.[32] The release of the White Paper generated a wave of protest from First Nations, and Native leaders came together to formulate a formal response in their "Red Paper," titled "Citizens Plus."[33] The document charged that instead of Canada living up to its treaty obligations to Native peoples, it was attempting to get rid of them by calling Natives "ordinary citizens," thus ignoring the special status that set them apart from mainstream society.[34] After harsh criticism by both Native and non-Native people, the Canadian government retracted the White Paper. (Thirteen years later, for the first time in its history, the government of Canada recognized aboriginal rights in its constitution.)[35]

The White Paper was a major wake-up call for Native people, who realized that they must become more politically active to hold onto the rights they had and to challenge Canadian policies that undermined these rights. Fueled by the civil rights and American Indian movements in the United States, First Nations generated their own "Red Power" movement, fostering political mobilization across the country. Native people united in their political struggles and continued to lobby Canada for recognition of their rights. These political contests moved into Canada's courts, with land claims, aboriginal rights, and the right to self-determination the focuses of the judicial challenges.

The Nisga'a, who had been fighting for recognition of their land rights since the 1880s, brought forward a lawsuit in the 1960s that led to one of the most important legal cases involving Native title to land in British Columbia. The hereditary chief of the Nisga'a Nation, Frank Calder, advanced the case on behalf of all Nisga'a, arguing that the Nisga'a held aboriginal title to their ancestral lands in the Nass Valley prior to the assertion of British sovereignty and that this title had never been negated. The Calder case made its way to the Supreme Court of Canada in 1973. In a surprising decision, six of the seven justices found that the Nisga'a held title to their lands before the assertion of British sovereignty. However, in determining if they still held title to those lands, the court was split; three justices held that title still existed and three held that title, though it had existed, had been extinguished by the assertion of British sovereignty over Nisga'a lands. The seventh justice, who ignored the substantive issues, dismissed the case, not because of anything to do with aboriginal title but because of a technicality in how the Nisga'a filed their suit.[36] Nevertheless, this was a major case in Canadian Indian history because of the court's recognition of aboriginal title, and it opened the door for other First Nations to bring forward legal cases dealing with aboriginal title and rights.

In British Columbia, Native groups began uniting as early as the 1900s to form political lobbying organizations to fight for their land rights. In 1958 the Nuu-chah-nulth groups came together to form a collective political body called the West Coast Allied Tribes, which later changed its name to the West Coast District Council.[37] The Nuu-chah-nulth, although connected through language, culture, and kinship, remained socially and economically independent and were administered separately by the federal government through a band system established under the Indian Act. In 1978 this group changed its name to the Nuu-chah-nulth Tribal Council (NTC).

The formation of tribal councils in itself was a political act. These councils were not formed by the Canadian government but were created by the Native people themselves, to meet their own political, social, and economic objectives.[38] The councils enabled the smaller bands to achieve higher levels of political authority than they would not have been able to attain at the local level. The NTC emphasized customary political authority that acknowledged hereditary chiefs and elders.[39] So, while it served as a mechanism for intergovernmental relations and administrative control, as well as provided its members with a strong political voice, it functioned within a culturally responsive environment that supported the maintenance of Nuu-chah-nulth traditions.

During the 1960s and 1970s, the politically united Nuu-chah-nulth became active in developing initiatives to improve their community's socioeconomic conditions. Council members pressured the Department of Indian Affairs to transfer to them control over the tribes' affairs so that they could increase their own policy-setting power. Through their political body, the Nuu-chah-nulth began a process of decolonization by assuming more administrative authority over their lands and communities. As lawyer Hugh Braker, asserted, it "was one further step on a long road to self-government."[40]

George Watts (Wahmeesh) was the president of the NTC from 1970 to 1993. He devoted his life to advancing the social, economic, and political conditions of our people and worked in the national and international arenas advocating for indigenous rights.[41] He was always optimistic that the Nuu-chah-nulth would become a self-determining nation. At a forum on Native rights, he told the audience that the only way this would take place would be by removing ourselves from the grip of the federal government.

> I come from a strong culture. When one of our oldtimers in a conference says:
> "You know what self-government is? Self-government is teaching your children
> to survive." Well, I want to tell the Canadian people we're going to survive.

We're going to survive and teach our kids to be tougher than us. . . . My two
little boys and my daughter are going to survive, and they're going to survive
as Nuu-chah-nulth. And, I don't want to get personal with the people at the
Department of Indian Affairs, but you better not be around when my kids grow
up because they're not going to put up with you. They're not going to put up
with the colonialist government running our lives.[42] *based*

Watts was a visionary leader. Under his direction the NTC grew to be one
of the most influential Native political bodies in Canada; it not only fought for
local control but was active in fighting for the primary goal of all Native people
in B.C.: recognition of Native title and a land claims settlement.[43] One of our first
significant land issue battles took place in the 1980s, when Nuu-chah-nulth leaders effectively blocked logging access to our lands until the question of aboriginal
title had been settled by the provincial and federal governments. In 1980 a logging company was given a tree farm license to cut trees on Meares Island, which
enraged my people and moved them to action. Determined to fight for our land,
in the same year the NTC filed a formal land claim with Ottawa in an attempt to
negotiate control over our lands before they were decimated by developers.[44]

At the heart of this issue was the island named Meares, which was sacred
land of the Ahousaht and Tla-o-qui-aht peoples. Their physical connection to the
land was demonstrated through the dozens of archaeological sites, shell middens,
burial and village sites, and fish weirs contained on the island. Meares is home
to some of the largest western red cedar trees in the world. Western red cedars
played a vital role in the lives of the Northwest Coast Native peoples and formed
the material backbone of our cultures.[45] Many of these ancient trees on Meares
Island had been culturally modified, meaning they were intentionally altered by
the indigenous peoples in the area who participated in traditional uses of the forest.[46] Research conducted on the trees showed that approximately 2,000–4,000
trees had bark and planks stripped from them, dating back to 1692.[47] In precontact times, cedar bark was used to make clothing, blankets, and baskets; it was
also pounded to become soft enough to use for babies' diapers. Cedar planks
were used for the siding and roofs of the longhouses. They were also used as
ceremonial planks, which were painted with family designs and displayed at potlatches.[48] The fact that thousands of these modified trees were found on Meares
Island validated the Ahousaht and Tla-o-qui-aht claim to having a historical and
spiritual connection to this land.[49]

The Nuu-chah-nulth united with environmental groups and set up physical
blockades to bar loggers from the island. This action led to major media coverage

and put the Meares Island land claims issue in the national spotlight. In November 1984, the logging company sought and was issued an injunction to prohibit the protesters from interfering with the logging operations on the island. The Nuu-chah-nulth countered this action by filing a legal claim arguing that they had never ceded title to this land through treaty or by any other means, and, therefore, they still had rights to their trees.[50]

The B.C. Supreme Court ruled against the Nuu-chah-nulth, claiming that halting logging on Meares Island would have "disastrous consequences" on the forestry industry in the province.[51] The case moved up to the B.C Court of Appeals, which made a rather unexpected and unprecedented decision. The court took note of the Nuu-chah-nulth people's historical relationships to the land in question, which was evident in the numerous culturally modified trees on Meares Island. The court saw this as proof that the Ahousaht and Tla-o-qui-aht had a legitimate claim to this land, and therefore, the court ruled, the lands in dispute must not be logged until the issue of title was dealt with. Justice Seaton stated that it was necessary to protect this area, arguing that it would be impossible for a Native right to be "exercised on lands that have been recently logged,"[52] or, in this case, clear-cut. He added that it would also be pointless for Native people to negotiate for their land if then, when the issue was finally resolved, "their property is gone." After hearing the ruling, an emotional George Watts wept. This ruling, he said, was "a victory of David over Goliath."[53] The Meares Island ruling became a symbolic victory for the Nuu-chah-nulth and set the stage for us to move forward with our self-determination efforts.[54]

THE OCEAN IS OUR GARDEN

Throughout the years, the Nuu-chah-nulth-aht continued their legal battles over land and water rights and resources.[55] In the twenty-first century, we are once again defending our rights to our fish resources. On June 19, 2003, eight Nuu-chah-nulth First Nations initiated a landmark lawsuit against the Canadian and B.C. governments asserting the right not only to harvest our fish resources but also to trade, barter, and sell these resources. The lawsuit came about after years of frustrating and unproductive fisheries negotiations with the federal and provincial governments, which were prohibiting our right to sell our fish.[56]

The trial began on April 24, 2006, with more than 120 Nuu-chah-nulth First Nations leaders and Natives and non-Natives gathered outside the courthouse to show their support.[57] Nuu-chah-nulth elders and leaders, as well as non-Native anthropologists and historians, testified at the trial. Nuu-chah-nulth leader

Lillian Howard told the court that First Nations have a right to earn a living from their ocean and freshwater resources: "We are an ocean people. Our lives as a people were totally dependent on the ocean. We're more connected to the ocean than to the land base . . . because that was our primary resource extraction area."[58] Elders provided evidence of how they have always sustained their communities through both subsistence and commercial use of the fish resource. They discussed how we were and still are dependent on our marine space for survival. And many of the people who testified told the court that this case was not just about commercial fishing rights; as Nuu-chah-nulth leader Barney Williams Jr. asserted, "Fishing is in my blood. It's something I was born with."[59]

In June 2008 the witnesses concluded their testimonies. In the second stage of the trial, Canada entered evidence and presented witnesses to testify. The trial resumed in March 2009, with all parties giving oral submissions. On November 3, 2009, the court affirmed the right of Native people to sell the seafood they harvest. In a lengthy written decision, Justice Nicole Garson upheld their right to both harvest and sell the fish in their territory, concluding that Canada's fishing regulatory regime excluded Native people and infringed on their rights. Many Nuu-chah-nulth were deeply moved by the decision. Tseshaht chief councilor Les Sam grew up fishing on the Somass River with his late father, Chuck. In the 1980s the Tseshaht experienced our own fish wars similar to the one that took place in Washington State in the 1960s. Because of Canada's laws restricting and prohibiting Native people from exercising their fishing rights, Tseshaht were threatened and charged at gunpoint by federal fisheries officers when they attempted to harvest and sell their fish. Numerous time Sam witnessed a gun pointed at his father's face by fisheries officers who tried to stop him from fishing

Filled with emotion, Sam said, "Now [they] can't pull their guns on us . . . and threaten Tseshaht people and say we can't do it, because we won today. . . . I feel proud for the fight that we continued on for my late father. I feel good about that."[60]

Cliff Atleo Sr., president of the NTC, said, "Today this decision confirms what we've known all along. We have been stewards of our ocean resources for hundreds of generations, and the Government of Canada was wrong to push us aside in their attempts to prohibit our access to the sea resources our people depend on."[61] Sam sees the victory as providing leverage for Tseshaht's treaty negotiations. "I think this is a solid win. . . . You have a court affirming [your] right to sell fish. Now [the Department of Fisheries and Ocean] has got to come to the table and negotiate."[62]

"A GIFT FROM THE PAST": CULTURAL REVITALIZATION AND THE OZETTE EXCAVATION

In 1970 a severe storm uncovered a Makah village that had been buried by a mudslide over five hundred years earlier. For the next ten years a massive archaeological excavation was conducted at the site, uncovering more than 55,000 precontact Makah artifacts. During excavation, many whalebones and implements that were utilized for whaling were uncovered, leading archaeologists to believe that this was not only a major Makah whaling village but may also have been the leading whale- and seal-hunting region along the entire west coast south of the Aleutian Islands. More than 1,900 whalebones were recovered from the site, which clearly established that whaling was these people's most important subsistence activity.[63]

Large panels from housing structures were found at the site. The largest panel unearthed measured nearly twenty-three feet long and three feet wide and had carved into it an image of a whale. Another housing plank was decorated with designs of two Thunderbirds and two wolves. Whalebones were utilized for bark shredders and spindle whorls. They were also used for water diversion, drainage, and stabilization of the banks behind the housing structures. Besides the wooden effigy of a whale's dorsal fin, discussed in chapter 3, numerous items associated with whale hunting were also uncovered. Whale-hunting tools, pieces of harpoons, and other items used for whaling were found. A mussel-shell blade was discovered still embedded in whalebone.[64]

The large quantity of whalebones at the site also proved how important whales were to the Ozette economy. The whalebones indicated that at least 931 tons of edible food were represented in the midden, which was a large quantity of food and affirmed the importance of whale oil, meat, and blubber to the Ozette people's diet. The calculations of proportional amounts of food represented by all faunal remains found at the site indicated that whale products made up as much as 80 percent of all animal products consumed.[65]

The Ozette discovery sparked a cultural renaissance among Makah members and reinvigorated and strengthened their ties to their whaling tradition. Uncovering their ancestral village gave tribal members tangible evidence of their whaling history and sparked an interest in learning more about their whaling culture. One Makah member exclaimed that the Ozette archaeological site was like "a telescope that reaches back to life before European contact."[66] Throughout the excavation, Makah members came to the site to find out what had been unearthed on that particular day. Makah students were invited to participate in summer field schools at the site. Elders were invited to share their knowledge and assist the archaeologists in identifying the artifacts and how they were utilized in precontact Makah society.[67] In many ways, the Makah members' participation in the Ozette excavation "unlocked their memories" of their whaling history.[68] One Makah elder explained the interesting process of identifying the pieces being brought to the elders for examination: "That was very unique; you get a bunch of oldtimers talking in Makah, shaking their heads 'no' [that the name was not right], then one would, all of a sudden, say the right word, and they would all shake their heads 'yes, yes, that's it.'"[69]

At the onset of the excavation, the Makah tribe oversaw all the activities, controlling the procedures for stabilizing the banks and storing the artifacts. As the excavation progressed, the tribal leaders realized that they would need a permanent facility to house, protect, and display these culturally valuable objects. Construction of a facility was initiated, and in 1979 the Makah Cultural and Research Center (MCRC) opened its doors.[70] The MCRC was a way for the Makah to showcase these precious objects and reaffirm to the outside world their whaling history. As news of this archaeological gold mine spread, people began making the trek out to the Makah Reservation to view the objects that were unearthed. As a result, tourism became one of the main industries in Neah Bay. The significance and centrality of the Makah's whaling tradition was captured in the text that was written to accompany the first exhibit case in the main gallery of the Center.

> While the Makah were noted for their ability as fishermen and seal hunters, they were probably most noted for their exploits as whale hunters. More than anything else, whale hunting utilized almost every technical skill possessed by the Makahs from the building of the canoes, to the development of the equipment, the intense physical training, the fulfillment of spiritual preparations for the hunt, and extraordinary knowledge of the ocean . . . the whale hunt represented the ultimate in both physical and spiritual preparedness and the wealth of the Makah Indian culture.[71]

Following the establishment of the MCRC, there was a resurgence of interest in Makah culture and history among tribal members. A Makah language program was implemented and work began on creating a written cultural dictionary. Programs were implemented to teach tribal members traditional skills such as basket making and wood carving. Elders were invited to the Center to record their oral stories and to teach the Makah language to the younger members of the tribe. For the Makah, the Ozette discovery not only strengthened their connection to their whaling tradition but also invigorated their community with renewed interest in their culture and language and provided a way to link the knowledge of the elders to the education of the younger Makah members.[72]

THE MAKAH REVIVE THEIR WHALE HUNTS: MY VISIT TO NEAH BAY

I was unable to leave my academic studies at UC Berkeley during May 1999 when the Makah tribe's whale hunt took place. So the following summer, I decided to go to Neah Bay to meet with Makah tribal members and talk to them about the whale hunt. I packed up my vehicle and began the long drive north. It was a beautiful sunny morning as I entered the Olympic Peninsula and meandered along the precarious road to Neah Bay. As I followed the ocean shore, I thought about our whaling culture and about Makah whalers: how physically, mentally, and spiritually strong they must have been to battle this unforgiving cold and restless sea in search of a whale. I thought about the contemporary hunt and about the young Makah men who were chosen to be members of the whaling crew. How pleased they must have felt to be following in their ancestors' footsteps, and how delighted they must have been to be given the opportunity to revitalize a fundamental Makah tradition.

I arrived late in Neah Bay, and after a quick drive around the reservation, I retired to my hotel room. The following morning I drove over to my cousin Anne Hunter's house. Anne and her husband, Keith, graciously offered their home as a place to hold my interviews. Anne made a pot of tea, and as I sat at her kitchen table sipping my tea, she began phoning Makah members to let them know I was in town and to set up interviews for me for the week. Not that Anne needed to tell anyone I was there. The Neah Bay community is quite small—about 1,800 residents—with around 1,400 of the little over 2,300 Makah tribal members living on the reservation.[73] The main village consists of a few streets established in a grid pattern that follows along the ocean bank. When Anne made her phone calls, most of the community members already knew that a "stranger" in a silver Firebird had been cruising around their community.

I wanted to make sure that I followed protocol while in Neah Bay, so the first thing I did was meet with the Makah Tribal Council to let them know who I was and why I was there, and to seek their support and consent. I explained that I was a member of the Nuu-chah-nulth Nation and told them who my family was and also that I had family members living in Neah Bay. I told them that I was conducting research and that I wanted to interview tribal members about their successful whale hunt the previous year. The tribal councilmen were gracious hosts and gave me their support. They provided me with written materials to help me with my research, and George Bowechop filled me in on details of the hunt. Keith Johnson, the president of the Makah Whaling Commission, told me that it was good to see a Nuu-chah-nulth person writing about our whaling history and welcomed me into their community.

One of the first Makah members I interviewed was Micah McCarty. Micah was one of the original members of the whaling crew.[74] He later decided to take himself off the crew but stayed actively involved in the tribe's preparation for their first contemporary hunt. Anne greeted Micah and his dog at the front door and then introduced me. Micah is one who leaves a strong impression in your mind. He is very articulate, very knowledgeable, and a genuinely nice guy. He also has a natural gift as a speaker; after nine hours, two meals, and many cups of tea, we were still absorbed in a wonderful and engaging conversation about whales, the environment, environmentalists, tribal politics, the Makah community, and, most important, the 1999 whale hunt.

Micah told me that he did not grow up on the Makah Reservation but had remained connected to his cultural roots by returning to the reservation each summer. He made a permanent move to Neah Bay in 1990. He was raised with the understanding that he came from a whaling lineage. His great-grandfather was Hishka (hishkoop shah nulthshe), whose name means "He Who Makes the Whale Blow on the Beach." Hishka was a great whaler and held the prestigious position of harpooner. Micah was told that his great-grandfather was one of the Makah's last whalers. Micah's own Makah name is Klaowus, "One Who Is Waiting," which implies that he is in line for a hereditary name linking him to his whaling ancestry.[75]

Micah was very knowledgeable about the whaling history in the Pacific Northwest, and as we sat at Anne's kitchen table, he told me how the Makah came to the decision to revive their whale hunts. Because of the devastation to the whale population caused by the commercial whaling industry, many of the various species of whales were hunted to near extinction. The gray whale, the whale most commonly hunted by the Makah people, was one of these. International rules and regulations were established to prohibit more depletion of the whale stocks, but the gray whale stocks continued to decline and because of the threat to its population, it was placed on the Endangered Species list in 1973. By the 1960s the gray whale stocks had begun to recover from serious depletion, and by 1994 the gray whale population had recovered sufficiently to have it removed from the list. The delisting of the gray whale opened the door to making a Makah contemporary whale hunt a reality and provided an opportunity for the tribe to exercise its treaty right to whale.

In July 1995, two months after the Makah tribe announced its intention to revive its whaling practices, a Makah fisherman accidentally caught a gray whale in his net. Whales had gotten entangled in Makah nets before and were always confiscated by the federal government. This time the government allowed the Makah to keep the whale. The whale had been dead for over twenty-four hours and some of it had already gone bad. But a large part of the carcass was still edible and some fifty people from the Makah community took part in processing the meat and blubber. By the end of the day, 300–400 people had traveled down to the beach to check out the unusual find and to offer a helping hand. All the Makah members were offered a piece of the whale and many of them welcomed the opportunity to feast on whale meat and blubber. Maria Pascua, researcher, curator, and linguist at the MCRC, boiled some of the blubber and took a plate of smoked whale blubber over to the Center to share with the other staff members. The staff found the blubber to be soft and chewy, similar to salmon jerky, and tasting like pork rind but not as fatty. Eating the whale kindled an excitement in the Makah tribal members over the possibility that whale could, in the very near future, become a regular meal.[76]

Micah said there was a constant buzz in the Makah community as tribal members contemplated reinstituting the whale hunts. While the majority of the Makah tribal members were in favor of reviving their whaling practices, there were some members who questioned the decision. According to Micah, some of the Makah, including his aunt, were hesitant because they were unsure about reviving a tradition that they had lived without for so long. Some Makah were worried, as well, about the repercussions a return to whaling would have on their community, as the anti-whaling forces had begun to verbally attack the Makah following the tribal council's announcement.[77]

The Makah Tribal Council wanted to make sure that the Makah members supported the hunt, so in 1995 they held a referendum; over 76 percent of tribal members voted in favor of reviving whaling practices. Subsequent opinion polls indicated a continual increase in tribal members' support.[78] Micah and his father, John McCarty, were part of the Makah majority who wanted to see a whale hunt happen. One day Micah and his father visited Dan Greene, the Makah tribe's director of fisheries at around the time the gray whale was delisted, who talked to them about the idea that the Makah could actually whale in the near future. Micah told me,

> My dad had been a fish buyer and a fisherman and he's been around fisher-
> ies and has been politically active. So, me and my father walked into the office

one day and I noticed on one of the drawing boards they had a whole list of sea mammals, marine mammals, and the gray whales were on the top of the list and humpbacks and minke whales. The first thing Dan said was, "Oh, how would you like to go whaling, John?" My dad paused for a long time, and he was really excited . . . my dad had a lot going through his head and he said to me, this would be a big circle for me, to come full circle and to get a whale before his time was over. And things just started to happen.[79]

Keith Johnson, who was appointed the president of the Makah Whaling Commission, shared the excitement. He also came from a whaling family, and stories of whales and whaling had been passed down to him through his family's oral tradition. His great-grandfather Andrew Johnson was a whaler who had caught his last whale in 1907. His grandfather Sam Johnson was a young boy of six when the whale was caught, and he told Keith how he had played on the whale's tail after it was brought to shore.[80] Although whaling ended during Keith's father's generation, Keith was still taught the spiritual rituals associated with whaling, which allowed him to maintain both a connection to and a deep respect for his whaling heritage.

I lived with my grandfather for sixteen years and heard his stories about our whaling tradition and the stories of family whaling told by my father, Percy, and my uncle, Clifford. When I was a teenager I was initiated into Makah whaling rituals by Uncle Clifford. While I cannot divulge the details of these rituals, which are sacred, they involve isolation, bathing in icy waters and other forms of ritual cleansing. . . . When the idea of resuming whaling first spread through our village, I was intensely excited, and so was my whole family. In fact, I can say I was ecstatic about the idea of resuming the hunt; [it was] something my grandfather was never able to do. I am proud to carry on my family legacy and my father is overjoyed because he is going to see this in his lifetime.[81]

Although the Makah have the right to hunt whales protected in their 1855 treaty, the Makah Tribal Council decided to act within the international legal arena and follow the rules and regulations attached to contemporary whaling. Tribal leaders approached the U.S. government to seek permission from the International Whaling Commission to hunt gray whales for food and ceremonial use.[82] In May 1995, the Makah tribe sent their whaling proposal to the federal government, explaining why they felt it was important to reestablish their whaling practices. The proposal provided details of the social and health issues that plagued the Makah community. The tribe had an unemployment rate of over 50 percent; many Makah youths were battling drug and alcohol addictions; community members faced many health problems. The proposal maintained that "reestablishing a ceremonial and subsistence hunt would be a catalyst which would allow us to instill in our young people the traditional values that have held our people together over the centuries. In addition, whale oil, meat and blubber would be a welcome addition to our diet."[83]

Some Makah members did not feel that the Makah tribe needed to negotiate with the federal government or with the IWC. John McCarty, who was appointed as first executive director of the Makah Whaling Commission, said: "Many of us on the commission [MWC] consider it a birthright. We don't feel we have to ask a commission [IWC] to hunt. We feel we have to ask the fathers."[84] Although the tribe always maintained that the IWC had no legal jurisdiction over their right to whale, they finally agreed to the international process.[85]

The IWC was established in 1946 and became the regulatory body of contemporary whaling. Its main purposes were articulated in its founding document, the International Convention for the Regulation of Whaling (ICRW): to regulate the worldwide whaling industry and to protect and conserve threatened whale stocks.[86] Membership in the IWC is open to any country that adheres to the 1946 convention.[87] In 1982 the IWC members voted to end commercial whaling, and by 1987 the commission imposed a worldwide moratorium on all commercial whaling activities. However, it exempted whaling that was conducted for scientific purposes and for Native communities who whaled for subsistence purposes. The IWC established a definition of Native subsistence whaling as follows:

> Aboriginal subsistence means whaling, for purposes of local aboriginal consumption carried out by or on behalf of aboriginal, indigenous or native peoples who share strong community, familial, social, and cultural ties related to a continuing traditional dependence on whaling and on the use of whales.[88]

With respect to aboriginal subsistence whaling, the IWC listed as one of its main objectives: "To enable aboriginal people to harvest whales in perpetuity at levels appropriate to their cultural and nutritional requirements, subject to their objectives." The commission also determined that the whale products would be consumed only by the local community to meet its "nutritional, subsistence and cultural requirements." And, finally, that there would be no commercial aspects to the hunts.[89]

In order to continue their whaling activities, Native whaling groups needed to obtain a whale quota from the IWC. This was given after the country, representing its Native whaling communities, demonstrated these groups' "continuing" tradition of both hunting and eating whales. Once this was proven, the IWC granted the quota.[90] At the 1996 IWC annual meeting, the United States submitted a proposal on behalf of the Makah tribe. As Micah informed me, it was obvious that the United States could not demonstrate the continuity in Makah whaling practices as the Makah had not whaled or eaten whale products they harvested since the late 1920s. And, because of this, the United States had a difficult time convincing some of the IWC members that the planned Makah whale hunt should be sanctioned. The United States noted that the Makah whaling practices were preserved in their 1855 treaty. It outlined the 1,500-year-long tradition of subsistence whaling by the Makah and how the exploitation of gray whales by commercial whalers in the late 1800s led to the tribe having to give up its whaling practices. It also emphasized that even though Makah had stopped whaling, the tradition still continued in their community through their oral traditions and ceremonies and, therefore, was still central to Makah culture and identity.[91]

But these arguments did not persuade some commissioners to accept the Makah proposal. France and the Netherlands were concerned about the Makah's seventy-year hiatus from whaling and wondered how the tribe could still be recognized as having a "continuing tradition" of whaling. Some commissioners also felt that this long period of no whaling suggested that the Makah no longer had a dependence on whales. Micah attended the IWC meeting. The key issue among IWC members, he said, was continuity in the Makah's whaling practices, and whether continuity in the whaling tradition through their oral tradition could be recognized under the present IWC definition of aboriginal subsistence whaling. What was also interesting, Micah told me, was the lack of attention by the IWC commissioners to the Makah 1855 treaty, which protects the tribe's right to whale. Even though the Makah did not whale for more than seventy years, Micah argued, "case law clearly establishes that the absence of practicing a treaty right in no way extinguishes that right."[92]

Following these discussions, the United States decided to withdraw the Makah whaling plan and present it at the IWC meeting the following year. In 1997 the IWC amended its Schedule, which contains the rules governing whaling to establish a broader definition that would include the Makah.[93] The section defining the provisions for taking gray whales was amended as follows:

The taking of gray whales . . . is permitted, but only by aborigines or a Contracting Party on behalf of the aborigines, and then only when the meat and products of such whales are to be used exclusively for local consumption by the *aborigines whose traditional aboriginal subsistence and cultural needs have been recognized.*[94]

The Makah still had to deal with the fact that the IWC did not want to hand out any more whale quotas. So, Micah said, compromises were made, and Russia and the United States agreed to submit a joint request for a quota. The Russian Chukchi people in Chukotka gave up part of their gray whale quota so that they could receive a bowhead whale quota, which they shared with the Eskimos whalers in Alaska and Russia. The Makah ended up getting part of the Russian quota, with a combined total of 124 whales per year, 120 going to the Chukchi people and 4 to the Makah. At the time, the gray whale population was estimated at around 26,000. What this meant, Micah said, was that the Makah quota was not removing any more gray whales from the general population, because the whales granted to the Makah would have been caught under the Russian quota anyway. The IWC determined that the Makah would harvest 20 whales over a five-year period, from 1998 through 2002.[95]

STAYING TRUE TO TRADITION WHILE REARTICULATING THE HUNT

As the Makah began to work through the legal process of getting a whale hunt established, the tribal council also began to look internally at how they would manage and conduct future whale hunts. It formed the Makah Whaling Commission (MWC), which consisted of representatives of twenty-three traditional whaling families who would manage, oversee, and implement the whale hunts. The MWC consulted with community members on how to move forward with the hunt. It was decided following these community meetings that the first whale hunt would be a community hunt rather than a family hunt and that the whaling crew would be chosen from various Makah families. Following these consultations, in 1997 the MWC adopted a gray whale hunting management plan that was accepted by the Makah community and was also in compliance with IWC regulations.[96] The plan was finalized in an agreement with the National Marine Fisheries Service, which monitored the hunt.[97]

The MWC wanted the whale hunt to stay true to tradition by retaining the same ritual, ceremonial, and spiritual elements of former hunts. It selected a whaling crew and established rules for the crew members to follow to make sure they were physically, mentally, and spiritually ready for this hunt. These rules were specific to the contemporary environment in which this hunt was being conducted, and the whaling crew was asked to abstain from drinking alcohol, smoking, and using drugs. The crew members faced significant physical and emotional challenges, but the MWC president, Keith Johnson, said they all understood the cultural importance of what they were preparing for:

> I can tell you that all of the Makah whalers are deeply stirred by the prospect of whaling. We are undergoing a process of mental and physical toughening now. I feel the cultural connection of whaling in my blood. I feel it is honoring my blood to go whaling. We are committed to this because it our connection to our Tribal culture and because it is a treaty right—not because we see the prospect of money. . . . We are willing to risk our lives. . . . The only reward we will receive will be the spiritual satisfaction of hunting and dispatching the whale and bringing it back to our people to be distributed as food and exercising our treaty right.[98]

◆　◆　◆

While in Neah Bay, I had the opportunity to spend the afternoon with one of the whaling crew members, Theron Parker. Theron was also the person who had the most important position in the canoe—the harpooner. As Theron and I talked, I could see that this experience had had a profound effect on him. And, even a year after the hunt, speaking about it elicited in Theron such pride and excitement that it was as if the hunt had happened yesterday. Theron told me that he descended from a long line of Makah whalers—that whaling was in his blood. He said his great-grandfather was Quanah Parker, known as a great Makah whaler.[99]

Theron was proud to be part of the historic whale hunt that took place on May 17, 1999. He said that ever since he was a young boy he had heard stories from family members about great Makah whalers, which always made him think about how these men must have felt when they caught a whale. Like many Makah members, Theron's thoughts about his whaling culture had been reinforced by the archaeological discovery at Ozette. And even though he was just a young boy when the excavation took place, it left a huge impression on him, especially the unearthing of artifacts that linked his people to their whaling culture. Little did he know then that he would someday reconnect to his whaling culture in such a profound way and that he would be holding the same whaling implements that his whaling ancestors had held:

> We say that our culture has never been dead or put aside, it's always been a living, breathing culture. It's always been a part of my life. As a young boy I had

a paper route (that's when the Ozette digs were going on) and I used to deliver papers to a lot of people who stored the artifacts so that I became friends with those people. And then, as I became friends, they let me in the lab and showed me the preserving techniques that they used and I got to learn a lot about the stuff that was coming out of there. And, I saw harpoons and I got to see paddles and bits and pieces of everything that came in and out of that place. . . . They brought in a backbone of a whale and it had a mussel-shell harpoon tip embedded in it. I thought, that must have been one powerful man to do such a feat. I used to think about this when I was a kid. And then they brought in the saddle, the whale saddle, the trophy piece, that the harpooner gets. I always wondered, wouldn't it be great to be that guy to get all those honors, and now here I am, that guy.[100]

Being physically, emotionally, and spiritually ready to whale was a prerequisite for the whaling crew members. The MWC established a certification process for all the members who participated in the hunt to ensure that each member received sufficient training to perform his assigned role.[101] Theron said the whaling crew followed the spiritual guidelines that were established by their ancestors; they all underwent months of rigorous training, spiritual cleansing, sacred rituals, purification ceremonies, and prayer. Although the young men who made up the whaling crew had never hunted whales before, they did fish and hunt, and as Theron explained, they incorporated many of their fishing and hunting rituals into their preparation for the whale hunt. The spiritual preparation was personally very important to Theron, who spent months conducting the proper rituals and purification ceremonies. He told me that "to take such a creature you must be clean in your heart, mind, body, and soul."[102]

Darrell Markishtum was one of the first men selected to be a crew member. For eighteen months, he closely followed all the rules of physical preparation and training. It was the religious aspect of the training, being spiritually clean, that was the most important, Darrell said. "Cleansing your spirit and making sure your heart and your soul were ready" were crucial for the culturally important mission that they were about to carry out.[103] While the Makah whaling crew conducted the same spiritual rituals and physical preparations that their whaling ancestors followed, they also adopted purification rituals from other indigenous cultures, traditions such as cleansing through sweat and sage ceremonies. As Theron explained, incorporating these non-Makah cleansing traditions into their daily purification regime "helped my heart, and that's what counts."[104]

The MWC wanted to conduct a hunt that maintained the cultural integrity of the whaling ancestors, but at the same time, they knew that changes would have to be made to ensure that this contemporary hunt would be safe, efficient, and humane.[105] The hunt still utilized a traditional canoe manned by a crew that had been spiritually and physically conditioned. The harpooner still used a traditional harpoon to make the first strike on the whale. Formerly, when a whale was harpooned it could take days before it would eventually tire and finally die; during that time the whaling crew would be dragged around by the whale. To overcome this, the Commission, with guidance from the IWC, elected to use a high-caliber rifle to swiftly kill the whale after it was harpooned. The rifle was specifically designed by a veterinarian, Dr. Allen Ingling, a specialist in the humane killing of animals who worked with the University of Maryland.[106] Shooting the whale after it was harpooned made the hunt more humane by allowing the whale to die almost instantly and, at the same time, lessened the danger to the whaling crew.[107] Also, as a precaution, motorized boats bearing members of the Makah tribe followed the traditional canoe; these nonhunters were on the water to watch over the crew and make sure they were safe and to assist them if the canoe capsized.[108]

A SIH-XWAH-WIX GIVES ITS LIFE TO THE KWIH-DICH-CHUH-AHTX

Months of praying, fasting, cleansing, and physical preparation finally paid off for the Makah whaling crew members on May 17, 1999. They had already spent a couple of days out on the cold, choppy ocean waters without landing a whale. But on the evening of May 16, the crew could feel that the time was right. They had been conducting their rituals and prayers carefully and diligently, and now with even more fervor. Their spirituality was so thick and so strong, Theron said, that the people around them could feel it.[109] So the next day, the whaling crew got in the *Hummingbird* and swiftly paddled out to sea; as they propelled their canoe through the frigid waters, they all knew in their hearts that this time they were not going to go home empty-handed, that this time they were going to make history.

As they paddled through the water, the *Hummingbird* suddenly crossed the path of a whale. Theron slowly pulled his paddle out of the water and carefully picked up his harpoon. He quickly looked behind him to make sure the lines and the floats were in order. Then he stood in the front of the canoe and waited. As the gray whale moved in front of the canoe, Theron braced himself, leaned back, and hurled the harpoon. The harpoon struck the whale. The crew began paddling backward, and as they did, the whale slapped its tail on the surface, causing

The gray whale being cut up. Photograph courtesy of Debbie Preston, Northwest Indian Fisheries Commission.

a loud crash and a wave. And then it began to sink. The other Makah members steered the chase boats close to the whale so they could utilize the high-powered rifle to expedite the whale's death. The first attempt was thwarted by a media boat that got in their way. They were finally able to get close enough to the whale to shoot it, but missed. Another harpoon was launched and hit the whale. And finally the fatal bullet was shot.[110]

When the whaling crew realized that the whale was dead, the magnitude of what they had done began to sink in, and they put their paddles on their knees and prayed.[111] Theron told me that at first, he had an overwhelming feeling of happiness, but at the same time, he was filled with a sense of remorse. "You feel sad," he told me. "You have to. You've taken a pretty big life there." But he also knew that their hearts were pure—they would have to be for the whale to have allowed itself to be taken—so his confidence remained high and his heart was comfortable. At that moment, Theron knew that they had done everything right in bringing the whale to their canoe and that their spirituality was "so in tune" that when they asked the whale's spirit to come home with them, it did.[112] After a period of more than seventy years, a *sih-xwah-wiX* gave its life to feed the Makah people. This time, it was a thirty-foot, female gray whale that gave itself to the Makah at 6:54 A.M., May 17, 1999. With that one heave of the harpoon, the Makah people had made history and revitalized a tradition central to their culture and identity.

One of the crew members, Donnie, dove into the icy water and pulled a rope over the whale's tail. The rope was attached to a hydraulic winch on one of the Makah's support boats, and the whale was towed to shore. The crew took the long six-hour ride back on the support boat, which wound around the cape and through the choppy waters to Neah Bay. As they neared the community, the whale was fastened to the *Hummingbird* and the whaling crew got back into their canoe and paddled ashore, pulling their treasured prize behind them. The crowd that lined the shores cheered and applauded as the canoe came closer. The Makah people carried drums and sang songs in honor of the whale and to show it respect as it was brought to shore. When the whale was beached, Theron raised his hand high in triumph. He then ceremoniously sprinkled the whale with eagle down.[113] As he did so, he realized his dream of one day being the whaler who would bring home the cherished whale to his community, the person who was honored with the prized dorsal fin.

REVITALIZING "COMMUNITY"

According to Makah tradition, the whale was cut up and distributed among tribal members. The whalers also saved meat and blubber to serve at the potlatch they were holding that weekend to honor the historic event. The potlatch attracted more than 3,000 people to Neah Bay to join the Makah in celebrating their successful hunt. Throughout the evening, songs were sung to pay respect to the whale's spirit, which had given itself to the Makah people. As the evening progressed, the Makah made announcements to their guests that "the whale's spirit is with us, among us . . . it is happy." Elders and chiefs paid tribute to the members of the whaling crew, thanking them for bringing the whale to their community. Stories were told about the significance of the whaling tradition to the Makah people and how this hunt validated and reaffirmed their whaling identity. A sense of pride permeated the air in the celebration hall. Young children proudly wore buttons that read "my grandfather was a whaler."[114]

When the Makah first began discussing the possibility of reviving their whale hunts, the tribal leaders analyzed how it would impact the community. Many of them focused on the social issues that were prevalent and how reviving such an important tradition would revitalize in tribal members, especially the youth, a sense of cultural pride through the strengthening of their whaling identity. Keith Johnson had stated that he believed the whale hunts would give the youth something tangible to link their lives with the lives of their ancestors. He said that seeing the crew members physically, mentally, and spiritually preparing for the hunt would teach the young people about discipline and self-respect.[115] As preparation for the hunt progressed, tribal elders encouraged the youth to think about how the hunt involved self-purification and abstinence from alcohol and tobacco. The tribal chair, Hubert Markishtum, stated that it was not that the Makah believed that a whale hunt would "solve" these issues of youth alcoholism and drug abuse, but that they thought it would teach the young about discipline, cooperation, and spirituality.[116]

I asked both Micah and Theron, as well as other tribal members I met while in Neah Bay, if the hunt had had a positive impact on the Makah community, and they all strongly agreed that it had. As far as the children go, Theron told me, "their lives will never be the same."[117] He said that when the whaling crew was out on the hunt, a group of young girls from the Neah Bay school went to their teacher and asked if they could take ten minutes to lie still and be quiet and pray while the hunt was taking place, because they had been told that that was historically what young women in the community did.[118]

Some of the youth participated in the hunt by helping to bring the whale to the shore, where it was divided up among all Makah members and visitors. Seventeen-year-old Patrick DePoe remarked on how "humongous" the whale was as he helped haul it to the beach. Patrick, like the other Makah youth, was excited about participating in his first whale hunt and said that he "just wanted to be a part of it. It was an adrenaline rush."[119]

It was "amazing," Theron said, how the youth began to take such a strong interest in their culture. Young children "began speaking their language a lot more, more and more each day. . . . And, regardless of what people say, I attribute that to our whaling. It's built pride in them."[120] Theron remembers how, when he was a boy, he would hear stories about whalers. Now, here are the young Makah not just hearing the stories but actually witnessing a whale hunt—an experience that will be forever in their memories. "It's in their lives, for the rest of their lives. They'll never forget."[121] And a year later, Theron said he could still see the community changing as a result of the hunt; the interest in Makah culture and traditions continued. Theron told me that the grade-school children began putting on song and dance performances. They danced and gave narrations about what the dances were and where they came from. Their interest, said Theron, was "boiling over."[122]

The Chukchi people in Russia provide a good example of how revitalizing their whaling tradition in turn reinvigorated their communities. In 1954 the Russian Federation banned indigenous, community-based whaling in Chukotka and replaced it with state-run whaling. Whales were caught and processed by state whale-catcher boats, and then the meat was delivered to the indigenous whaling communities, where it was individually sold. While the connection to and the consumption of whale oil, meat, and blubber were maintained by the Chukchi people, the social, spiritual, and cultural significance of whaling was taken away. In the 1990s, after state-run whaling ended, the Chukchi people undertook a revival of their community-based whale hunts. As Chukchi whaler Alexander Omrypkir noted, revitalizing their whaling tradition served to revitalize their culture and reconnect them to their environment.

> The preservation of whaling knowledge, the teaching of children the skills of whaling and associated traditional knowledge, all of which are vital for the revival of the traditional mode of life, for national identity, and for harmonizing the life of the indigenous residents of Chukotka with their environment. . . . The knowledge of whales and whaling is necessary for all residents of Chukotka.[123]

Once whale hunting resumed, the Chukchi people noticed almost immediately the cultural effects on their communities. Community members started to recall traditional methods of hunting and local ecological knowledge central to this tradition. Whalers recalled the whaling rituals and the rules that governed a whaler's behavior. And, most important, they recalled and revived mutual assistance and sharing between villages.[124]

Micah said he also saw overwhelming changes taking place within the Makah community. Not only was there renewed interest among the Makah in their culture and traditions, but there was also a tribal unity that developed as preparation for the whale hunt continued. What was ironic, Micah told me, was that the anti-whaling protesters actually helped bring the community together in support of whaling. Everyone, including the Makah youth, experienced the opposition to the whale hunts. They saw the negative portrayals of the Makah whalers on the Internet and on television. And many of them even faced personal harassment in the towns close to Neah Bay. This opposition, Micah said, provoked a common bond among the Makah, especially among the children, reinforcing in them a sense of cultural pride.[125]

When the Makah began to discuss the possibility of reviving their hunts, many tribal members contacted their relatives in the Nuu-chah-nulth communities to let them know what was being planned. My brother-in-law, Art Thompson, phoned to let me know the news and told me how excited he and his famly were about the possibility that they would actually witness a whale hunt. I received calls from other family members in the Tseshaht community as well, who said that the news about the Makah was causing quite a stir among tribal members.

Nuu-chah-nulth leaders began looking at the possibility of reviving our own whaling practices and began holding workshops throughout the Nuu-chah-nulth communities to talk about our whaling tradition and to discuss how a contemporary whale hunt could be initiated. One of the groups had already begun the process of reconnecting to their whaling tradition as a way to revitalize their culture. In 1983 the Mowachaht people began discussions about building a museum in which to repatriate a sacred whaling shrine that had been removed from their community in 1905 and taken to the Natural History Museum in New York. The whaling shrines, also called whalers' washing houses, held great spiritual significance and were utilized exclusively by the whaling chiefs for their purification rituals. The more elaborate shrines were used by whalers to entice dead whales to shore during their drift whale rituals. The Mowachaht leaders believed that the return of this particular shrine was crucial to their cultural revitalization efforts, and as late Mowachaht chief Jerry Jack asserted, "It's got to go back where it belongs. It was a part of the Mowachaht nation. It represented our *haw'iih*, it represented our *ha-houlthee* [land], it represented our strength."[126]

In the early 1990s, Mowachaht delegations traveled to New York to visit the American Museum of Natural History, where, for the first time, tribal members got to see the shrine. The journey had a profound effect on those who viewed and touched the shrine's sacred objects. The members could feel the strength of the shrine, and prayers were sung to honor the objects. For Mowachaht member Max Savey, it was a life-changing experience.

> That New York trip was something else to me. Right away I could feel the power that was there. I never experienced anything like it in my life. They had this shrine laid out for us on the table. . . . All the figures were there. For some reason, I don't know what made me do it, I started to pray. I'm not a very religious person but then and there I started to pray in my own language, inside of me, deep within. I asked for the strength these people had that used that shrine. I

asked for their knowledge, the self-sacrifice and all the things that go with it, all the things these people had to do in order to get that whale out there. I noticed something strange was happening to me. I feel, I used to shrink away from problems . . . today I have a hard time keeping quiet. . . . Now I want to learn all there is to know about my culture.[127]

At first, some Mowachaht members were concerned about bringing home such a powerful object and were worried that they would not be able to control its power. But as discussions continued, the members became unified, understanding that bringing their whaling shrine home would provide them an opportunity to learn more about their whaling culture, which could help restore pride in their community.[128] The Mowachaht people are still carrying on their efforts to have this sacred object returned to them and plan to build a cultural center to display and protect the shrine.

On December 4–5, 1998, the Nuu-chah-nulth Tribal Council brought elders together to discuss issues ranging from traditional whaling practices and their accompanying social prerogatives to how a management scheme could be established that would allow for the sustainable utilization of whales. Elder Edgar Charlie talked about the history of trading whale oil up and down the West Coast. Elder Stanley Sam talked about the strength a whaler needed to catch a whale and the sacrifices a whaler had to make through fasting and spiritual preparation in order to be ritually purified for a whale hunt. He also talked about how much of this knowledge had been lost because of our inability to continue our whaling practices. Elder Robert Peters discussed *oo-simch* rituals and talked about how Nuu-chah-nulth youth were taught at a young age about ocean tides and to watch the moon at certain times of the month, which helped guide the whaler. Elder Earl George said that when he was a young boy he heard about a whaler who used an area for his cleansing rituals that he was not supposed to use, and, because of this, he died during a hunt. These discussions continued throughout the two days and generated excitement among the elders who attended.[129]

When I returned home in the summer of 2000, I traveled throughout the Tseshaht community speaking to our leaders and elders about our whaling tradition and about what reviving the whaling practices would mean to our people. I spent an afternoon talking with NTC co-chair Nelson Keitlah about our position on whaling. Nelson told me that

the time is coming where whaling will be realized by our communities. We see our cousins down south, the Makah, successful in getting a gray whale . . . when we heard that, it generated much excitement here. . . . The meaning of whaling and the significance to our people has not disappeared by any stretch of the imagination. . . . Whaling is still important to us.[130]

There have been many challenges placed on our cultures, Nelson told me, such as the laws initiated to ban our potlatches and the schools established to destroy our languages—a system, he said, "that was out to destroy us." But it never destroyed our whaling tradition, and now that we have the opportunity to revive our hunts, Nelson maintained, there was no way the Canadian government was going to take this away.[131] Following the Makah hunt, the Nuu-chah-nulth leaders began to seek protection of whaling practices through the contemporary treaty process.[132] Native peoples in Canada have a constitutionally protected right to hunt whales for nutritional and cultural purposes.[133] My people are currently (2010) in treaty negotiations with the Canadian and B.C. governments.

One evening I visited with one of the elders, Stanley Sam, from the Ahousaht Nation, with whom I had a wonderful, informative, and candid conversation about whaling. Stanley told me he came from a whaling lineage on his mother's side, and he learned most of his family's whaling history from her. He recounted many whaling stories throughout the evening, many of them silly and full of sexual innuendo. He had me laughing so hard that I had to tell him to quit. I told him that many of the stories were so "raunchy" that I would not be able to use them in the research I was conducting at that time.[134]

I asked Stanley what he thought about our people reviving our whaling practices. He said that this was a very exciting time for us because our whaling tradition is the most important expression of our culture. He was glad to hear that many young people in our communities wanted to whale. But, he said, the young people who say they want to whale needed to be prepared and should not rush into something that is so sacred and so powerful.

We had a whaling meeting and the young people told us they were going whaling. My friend spoke up and said, "Are you prepared for this whaling? What are you talking about? Are you ready for it? Where's your medicine? Where's your canoe? Where's your harpoon, all the equipment you use for whaling? You can't just say you are going whaling. You need to get your family together, your elders together, to help and support you with all the traditional ways of whaling."
"Can you support me?" a whaler would say. He couldn't feed his family anymore when he was getting ready to whale. His family had to feed them. A whaler is not by himself, he's with his family.[135]

I ended the evening by asking Stanley what he thought about the current opposition to reviving the whale hunts. He told me that many people outside of the Nuu-chah-nulth community think this is just about killing a whale, but it is more than that. Reviving our whaling practices, Stanley told me, is about "connecting to our spirituality" and revitalizing our whaling tradition is tied directly to self-government because it would demonstrate to the Canadian government and to the outside world "that whaling is still important to us and that we have kept our whaling culture alive."[136]

In March 2005, Nuu-chah-nulth chief Tom Mexsis Happynook was invited to the University of Washington to give a talk, titled "Food, Health and Traditional Values." I listened to Chief Mexsis as he discussed how the return to whaling is connected to spirituality, land, and identity.

> As indigenous people rise from the ashes of colonialism and oppression, shed the shackles of despair and dependency, secure our right to live, create a safe environment to live in, revive our identities, restore our languages, assert our right to our customary foods, return to our belief systems, utilize our accumulated ancient wisdom, rebuild our local economies, revitalize our natural resources, and restructure our respective traditional governments to be effective in the twenty-first century—then, and only then, can we look in the face of genocide with self-determination.[137]

THE RIGHT TO WHALE AND NUU-CHAH-NULTH TREATY NEGOTIATIONS

Today the Nuu-chah-nulth First Nations are in tripartite treaty/land-claims negotiations with the Canadian government and the province of British Columbia to settle long-standing land claims issues and regain control over lands, resources, and lives.[138] We initially began our negotiations in 1973 as one large group, and in March 2001, we signed an agreement-in-principle that covered concepts of ownership and governing authority over negotiated lands, recognition of Native rights and interests on these lands, and financial compensation for the historic loss of and access to our resources.[139] However, some of the groups, such as mine, the Tseshaht First Nation, felt that we were not yet ready to move forward in our negotiations, so we moved away from the treaty table.

Five northern Nuu-chah-nulth groups—Huu-ay-aht, Uchucklesaht, Toquaht, Ucluelet, and Ka:' yu:'k'th/Che:k'tles7et'h—came together in joint treaty negotiations under the name Maa-Nulth First Nations, and in December 2006, they initialed their final agreement. The agreement covers 24,459 hectares of land and has a cash settlement of $62.6 million to be paid to the consortium by the provincial and federal governments. All the rights negotiated into the agreement are protected under the Canadian Constitution of 1982, which removes them from administration under the Indian Act.[140] The Final Agreement recognizes the Maa-nulth First Nations' right to hunt whales.[141] But a side agreement was negotiated whereby the Maa-nulth agreed to "not harvest grey [gray] and sei whales for a period of twenty-five years."[142]

Canada is one of the largest whaling nations in the world and was one of the founding members of the International Whaling Commission. It left the IWC after a moratorium was placed on whaling in 1982. The Inuit in the eastern and western Arctic regions annually harvest beluga, narwhal, and bowhead whales.[143] Whaling in Canada's North is managed under three separate land claims agreements.[144] All three agreements recognize the rights of the Inuit to hunt whales for subsistence purposes; these rights are protected under Canada's constitution and through acts of Parliament.[145]

In a conversation I had with Tom Mexsis Happynook, Nuu-chah-nulth council president and Huu-ay-aht treaty negotiator, he mentioned that when negotiations began in the late 1990s, the controversy surrounding the Makah whale hunt caused some pretty intense discussions at the treaty table. The Canadian and B.C. governments were concerned that the environmental and animal rights groups would turn their attention across the border and try to interfere with their treaty discussions. Mexsis said,

It became a political decision. The federal and provincial negotiators were having difficulty with the whaling right. There was a lot of political maneuvering—but the Maa-nulth were not going to give up our right to whale. But we needed to find a way to include it so that it wouldn't cause an uproar, like what happened with the Makah when they exercised their right to whale.[146]

Rather than have the treaty talks stalled or undermined by anti-whaling groups, they sought a compromise and agreed to place a moratorium on hunting the gray and sei whales. Mexsis said that the federal and provincial governments were most concerned about the gray whale, since it was the whale caught by the Makah in 1999 and was at the heart of the whaling debates. There was so much concern over the political fallout that could happen over their right to whale that the people decided not even to put the word "whale" in the treaty agreement and instead incorporated it under the right to "fish," which is defined in the agreement as including the right to hunt sea animals.[147]

Mexsis made it quite clear to me that accepting this side agreement did not mean that they would not hunt whales. The right to hunt whales is in their treaty and is constitutionally protected, meaning it can never be taken away. This means that the Maa-nulth First Nations can still harvest whales that are not endangered. Besides, according to Mexsis, the whale that the Maa-nulth are most interested in is the humpback, which is integral to their cultures. Historically, it was the whale of choice for the Nuu-chah-nulth-aht and the one most frequently hunted. This is documented in our oral traditions and is supported by archaeological excavations in Nuu-chah-nulth territory that show humpback whale bones comprising over 80 percent of all the bones found at some sites.[148]

The Canadian government will provide the Maa-nulth with funding to conduct research on whales. In coming years, the Maa-nulth First Nations will be monitoring the population levels of the humpback whales, and, Mexsis told me, when their stocks rise to a healthy level and they are no longer considered threatened, the Maa-nulth will hunt them. But this will happen only after they conduct extensive research that shows that these whales can be sustainably harvested without negative impacts on their population growth.[149] The Maa-nulth will also look at other opportunities, Mexsis said, especially conducting research on the health benefits to their communities of hunting both whales and seals: "We want to reintroduce these valuable and healthy food sources into our diets, but for now, we are focusing on finalizing the treaty process."[150]

The Maa-nulth treaty process provides a good example of the complexities of negotiating treaties in a modern world. Many different problems, needs, and desires necessitate complex dialogues, leading to years of negotiating. Many of the approximately two thousand Maa-nulth rely heavily on the tourism industry, which provides a good income for individuals, as well as revenue for their communities. Mexsis said, "The Maa-nulth leaders really had to look at the bigger picture and consider the whole treaty agreement."[151] Some members were concerned about the anti-whaling groups interfering with economies that depend highly on continual visits from tourists. They felt that initiating their whale hunts now, when the political climate is still so volatile, could keep the tourists away. Chief Mexsis emphasized that this side agreement did not mean that they do not feel strongly about their whaling heritage: "Whaling will always be central to our lives, our cultures, and our spirituality and will remain central to our songs, dances, ceremonies, and artistic expressions."[152]

Four of the five groups, as well as the federal and provincial governments, have ratified the final agreement.[153] The Huu-ay-aht First Nation has not yet ratified the treaty and is waiting until the current Nuu-chah-nulth fishing litigation is settled, which will have an impact on their treaty fishing rights.[154] The Tseshaht have always maintained that when we do move forward with our treaty negotiations, we will let the federal and provincial governments understand that the right to whale will not be on the bargaining table.[155]

◆ ◆ ◆

Within the Makah and Nuu-chah-nulth communities, we are witnessing a cultural renaissance. The Makah people's successful whale hunt has become a symbol of our cultural survival. After the whale hunt, after all the prayers were conducted and ceremonies were performed to the whale and to its spirit for giving its life to feed their community, the physical remains were taken away and carefully cleaned and preserved. For six years, as part of a high school project in the Neah Bay school, the whale's 700-pound, 30-foot-long skeleton was meticulously reassembled by the Makah students. The students spent hours each day cleaning, scrubbing, and tagging the bones. Many of the students wore sweatshirts and T-shirts with the words "May 17, 1999, 6:54 a.m," signifying a special moment in their lifetimes that will never be forgotten.[156]

In the shed behind the Neah Bay school, the students worked at putting the whalebones back together. One of the students working on the project, sixteen-year-old Eddy McCarty, said it felt kind of "weird" to be working on "something that used to be living." But, he added, "it isn't all that strange, because we're assembling something we're proud of. It's about going back to our tradition, learning more about our culture. I thought it was really cool."[157]

In December 2005, six years from the day the Makah people made history by reviving their sacred whale hunts, the skeleton of the famous whale, the whale that gave itself to them, was proudly hung in the Makah Cultural and Research Center. One of the whaling crew members, Andy Noel, who came to the Center to view the prize, said it was great to see all the bones reassembled but "we need more bones to add to them." Janine Bowechop, executive director of the Center, said that the new exhibit demonstrates to the world how important whaling was and still is to the Makah people. The skeleton, Janine asserted, "is a tangible representation of the success of our resumption of whaling." My niece Jeannie Thompson was one of the Makah students who supervised the project. When she saw the final reward for all the hours she worked putting the prize whale skeleton together, Jeannie had only one word to describe it, "awesome."[158]

5 / *Sucha*

CHALLENGES TO OUR RIGHT TO WHALE

THE MAKAH AND NUU-CHAH-NULTH DECISIONS TO REVIVE TRADI-
tional whaling practices were met with overwhelming support from people
of all races, ethnicities, and ages within the United States and Canada, as
well as from people from other countries throughout the world. Nonetheless,
there were some who opposed the decisions and banded together to organize an
anti-whaling campaign. The anti-whaling protesters effectively initiated a discourse that regenerated ethnocentric notions of Native people and Native culture, which was, for the most part, racist. The whaling opponents utilized images
of the "Indian as noble," "Indian as savage," and "Indian as environmentalist" to
create a rhetoric founded on misconceptions, stereotypes, and myths.

"WE KNOW WHO THE 'REAL INDIANS' ARE"

The anti-whaling activists comprised a loose coalition of marine conservation-
ists, animal rights activists, people from the whale-watching tourism industry,
and people opposed to the Indian treaties. The Sea Shepherd Conservation Society (headed by its president, Paul Watson) was the most vocal of the anti-whaling groups, and it spearheaded the campaign to stop the Makah hunt.[1] Other
well-known environmental groups stayed out of the debates.[2] In response to the
Makah tribe's decision to hunt gray whales, Greenpeace representatives said they
would not get involved because they did not see the hunt as a threat to gray whale
stocks.[3] The World Wildlife Fund also chose to stay out of the dispute. WWF vice
president Ginetter Hemley said that her group was not "happy" with the Makah
whale hunt but did not see it as a major conservation issue.[4]

One of the first attempts by whaling opponents to undermine the Makah whale hunt was their challenge to its cultural authenticity. The Makah, after publicly announcing the revival of the hunts, met with officials from the National Oceanic and Atmospheric Administration (NOAA) to formulate a plan to manage them, one that would be acceptable to their tribal members and would fulfill the guidelines of the International Convention for the Regulation of Whaling (ICRW) and the International Whaling Commission (IWC). A Makah Whaling Commission (MWC) was established to oversee the hunts. The MWC formulated a plan that established guidelines for contemporary actions. Within the plan were also rules and a certification process for the whaling crew, who had to undergo months of physical preparation, spiritual cleansing, and training, accompanied by hours spent with their elders who supervised the training.

The MWC wanted to conduct a hunt that adhered to the cultural practices of the whaling ancestors, while at the same time incorporating into it modern technology and equipment to ensure the safety of the whaling crew and to assure that the hunt would be efficient and humane. For the Makah, this did not make their hunt less "traditional," because they understand culture to be something dynamic and adaptive. The whaling plan established that the crew would utilize a canoe to conduct the hunt and a harpoon to strike the whale. The canoe would be accompanied by other canoes and motorized boats to make sure that the crew was safe at all times.[5]

With guidance from the IWC, the Makah agreed to incorporate a high-powered rifle into the hunt so that once the whale was struck by the harpoon, a bullet from the rifle would swiftly kill it.[6] The rifle was designed and tested by Dr. Allen Ingling, a veterinarian with the University of Maryland.[7] In precontact and early-contact times, a harpooned whale could take days to die, which prolonged its agony and placed the whaling crew in a dangerous position as they were dragged around for a lengthy period of time and were sometimes pulled out into the crashing waves of the sea. During the 1999 hunt, the whale was shot immediately after it was struck by the harpooner, and it died almost instantly.[8] A line was attached to the whale, which was then secured to a motorized boat so it could be towed to shore as quickly as possible, thus lessening the chance of spoiled meat or blubber. Just before they reached the shore, the Makah whaling crew took over the towline and pulled the dead whale onto shore with their canoe, just as their whaling ancestors had done before them (see also chapter 4).

When the Makah Whaling Commission released its whaling plan, opponents immediately condemned it. Rather than focus on the tribe's effort to conduct a hunt that was humane, ethical, and safe, members of the Sea Shepherd Society attacked the whaling plan, arguing that there was not a trace of "ceremonial aboriginal whaling" in it.[9] Other people who opposed the hunt came forward with the same argument—that the hunt was not traditional or culturally authentic. One person wrote a letter to the editor of the *Oregonian* questioning how the Makah could say that their hunt was following their "ancient culture" when the whaling crew was using "high-powered rifles, motorized chase boats, cellular phones and high-tech tracking devices to chase and kill a whale." The reader wrote: "While I would be against this kill under any circumstances, I could at least respect their culture a bit more if they were being true to their ancient cultural ways."[10]

These ideas of Native culture are based on problematic images constructed by non-Natives at their first encounters with indigenous peoples, which have persisted throughout U.S. and Canadian history. When *mamalhn'i* came to this land, they encountered diverse and distinct indigenous cultures with separate languages, traditions, governments, and laws. But the realities of indigenous peoples were ignored and they were flattened into one general category, "Indian," which contained two contradictory images: the "noble Indian" and the "savage Indian."

In his book *The White Man's Indian*, Robert Berkhofer examines the term "Indian" as a conception of non-Indian society and demonstrates how its fundamental meaning was maintained through imagery, which was perpetuated with little or no change over the decades. The image that was emphasized, whether it was the noble or the savage, was always antithetical to the view non-Indian people had of themselves and their cultures. The "real Indian" became identified as the Indian encountered at the time of contact, locking indigenous cultures in the past, unable to progress into modernity. Berkhofer writes,

> Since Whites primarily understood the Indian as an antithesis to themselves, then civilization and Indianness as they defined them would be forever opposites. Only civilization had history and dynamics in this view, so therefore Indianness must be conceived of as ahistorical and static. If the Indian changed through the adoption of civilization as defined by Whites, then he was no longer truly Indian according to the image, because the Indian was judged by what Whites were not. Change toward what Whites were made him ipso facto less Indian.[11]

For non-Indians, the image of the Indian as the "Other" was integral to this process of self-identification. "Indian" stood for everything Euro-Americans and Euro-Canadians were not, and thus served as a marker to distinguish "them" from "us." In his book *The Imaginary Indian*, Daniel Francis explores how Native peoples were imagined in the minds of Canadians and how these imaginings became manufactured as real representations of Native people and then were reaffirmed in Canadian literature and popular culture. There is no such thing as a "modern Indian," Francis asserts, because this is a contradiction in terms. A "traditional" Indian was always "a relic of the past." As a result, the image that was constructed and perpetuated was an ahistorical one, in which real or traditional Native people existed only in bygone years. If Native peoples or their cultures changed, they were perceived as less Native, something "not Indian," and their cultures less than pure. Therefore, as Francis explains, the "imaginary Indian could never become modern."[12] Consequently, the inability by non-Indians to accept change, adaptation, or modernization of Native cultures ultimately denies Native peoples their history.

Cultures are dynamic and fluid; they change and transform according to internal and external forces, adaptations, and the introduction of new ideas, skills, knowledge, and technologies. However, non-Native society has consistently attempted to lock Native society and culture into a specific time. What is completely ignored in this line of reasoning is the fact that indigenous societies had already undergone significant changes and modifications to their cultures long before non-Indians came to our lands. In Nuu-chah-nulth oral traditions, we have stories of tribal warfare that caused a series of amalgamations to occur that literally transformed Nuu-chah-nulth villages. Archaeological data support this.[13] Fixing our cultures at the time of contact disregards the social, political, and economic changes that had already taken place.

When *mamalhn'i* came to our territories, the Nuu-chah-nulth and Makah began adapting non-Indian items, technologies, and food into their cultural systems. In fact, as I noted in chapter 2, one of the reasons the Makah people signed their 1855 treaty was because the U.S. government guaranteed that it would provide the Makah with technologically advanced equipment and boats for their marine hunting and fishing practices.[14] By the early 1900s, the Makah had already incorporated motorized tugboats and rifles into their whale- and seal-hunting activities. By the 1920s, seals, like the whales, were also hunted to near extinction and a ban was placed on commercial pelagic sealing. The U.S. and Canadian governments allowed the Makah and Nuu-chah-nulth peoples to continue their sealing activities. But, because government officials viewed Native culture through their own distorted lens, we were allowed to hunt seals using only "traditional" canoes and harpoons, not the motorized boats and rifles that we had already adapted to our cultures.[15]

Other ethnic and racial groups have taken advantage of technological changes and adapted these into their societies. However, it seemed this fundamental opportunity to balance tradition with modernization was denied the Makah and Nuu-chah-nulth based solely on their identities as indigenous people. In pointing to technological advancement as a sign that the Makah whale hunt was not traditional or culturally authentic, the whaling opponents utilized old ethnocentric notions concerning assimilation and "progress." Their argument reflects misconceived notions of culture change by assuming that any technological innovation used during the hunt, or within Makah society for that matter, demonstrated the group's cultural assimilation.[16] When the Makah were preparing for their whale hunt, the Progressive Animal Welfare Society (PAWS) distributed a brochure insinuating that the Makah people were not authentic Indians because they had lost their cultural ways and their need to whale by adapting to a modern lifestyle. As evidence of their assimilation, the brochure cited the tribe's lighted tennis courts and the fact that Federal Express makes deliveries to the reservation. Former MWC chair Keith Johnson called PAWS's attack on Makah culture outright foolish.

The fact that Federal Express makes deliveries to our reservation . . . does that mean that we have lost our culture? . . . No one can seriously question who we are; we are a small Native American tribe whose members were the whalers of the American continent. We retain our whaling tradition today. It resonates through all of our people from the youngest to the oldest, and we don't take kindly to other people trying to tell us what our culture is or should be.[17]

Janine Bowechop, director of the Makah Cultural and Research Center, says that her people have always taken advantage of technological developments and improvements, just as they did in their whale hunt, to make their lives a little easier and safer. But, says Bowechop, this does not make them any less Indian than their ancestors.

For some reason some people like to freeze us in the past. If you're not doing something the way it was done prior to contact, than you're not doing it right—you're not doing it in the Native way. We allow other cultures to make changes. One of my friends said, "I'm a White American but I don't make my butter in a butter churn anymore, and I'm not criticized for that.". . . Folks don't ride around in covered wagons anymore, but we don't turn around and say, "Gee, you're not a real American. . . . But, unfortunately, we're continually criticized if we do anything different from the way we did it 500 years ago.[18]

Anthropologist Michael Harkin agrees that this assumption that cultural practices must be static to be authentic is applied only to indigenous societies.[19] The separate standards for Indians and non-Indians were quite obvious when, during their physical attempts to stop the Makah whale hunt, the Sea Shepherd Society utilized high-powered boats and equipment, even while they attacked the Makah for using the same equipment. Harkin says, if one applied these standards of authenticity to Western institutions, almost nothing would be considered legitimate—for example, the Catholic Church, the French legal system, and the American university system have undergone radical changes over many decades.[20] In many ways, false assumptions concerning Native "traditional" practices disempower Native people by denying them the right to advance technologically.

◆　◆　◆

Who has the right to decide what is traditional or culturally authentic? The whaling opponents had their own preconceived notions and concluded that Western society has some kind of right to make these determinations for the Makah and Nuu-chah-nulth peoples. Anthropologist Patricia Pierce Erickson argues that at the heart of the whaling controversy were the processes of authenticating and discrediting Makah identity, with the anti-whalers attempting to control the expression of Makah culture and identity—both its legitimacy and its legality.[21] In his master's thesis "'We Know Who the Real Indians Are': Animal-Rights Groups, Racial Stereotyping, and Racism in Rhetoric and Action in the Makah Whaling Controversy," Native scholar Michael Two Horses examines the ethnocentric notion that non-Native society "knows" who the "real Indians" are. This same rhetoric surfaced in the anti-whaling discourse during the Makah whale hunt and was manipulated by protesters and the animal-rights groups to challenge the validity of Makah culture, beliefs, traditions, spirituality, and sovereignty. Two Horses writes:

> These Makah, these contemporary whalers, are not *real* Indians because
> anti-whalers *know* who "real" Indians are. "Real" Indians are only symbols
> of a bygone, naturalist childhood of man, not participants in the present-day
> world. A "real" Indian appears in a television commercial, a tear running down
> his cheek as he sits astride a pony in traditional Northern Plains dress, look-
> ing down upon a garbage dump, his confusion and heartbreak at the wanton
> pollution of contemporary society writ large on his lined and noble face. . . .

"Real" Indians would hunt whales (if anti-whalers permit them to do so, which, of course, in a "civilized" world, they cannot) with "traditional" harpoons of yew, alder and mussel shell. . . . *"Real" Indians play the parts that the colonizing society has created for them and instructed them to play, and these Makah are not behaving in a way that qualifies them as "real" for that society's purpose; they are therefore not "real" Indians.*[22]

THE "NOBLE" AND "SAVAGE" INDIAN IMAGES IN ANTI-WHALING RHETORIC

Non-Indians constructed the "real Indian" from two diametrically opposed views of Native peoples: the noble Indian and the savage Indian. French philosopher Jean-Jacques Rousseau has been cited as the inventor of the "Noble Savage" image of indigenous peoples throughout the world. The noble Indian was an individual living in a "pure state of nature," a gentle and wise person, uncorrupted by the vices of civilization.[23] The Indian as noble, the one who was friendly, courteous, and hospitable to non-Indians, was an image that was established during the "discovery" and settlement period of the United States and Canada. During the Makah whale hunt, the whaling opponents utilized the "noble Indian" image to contrast with their opposite view of the Makah. In a letter to the *Cornell Daily Sun*, a reader wrote:

Contrary to the patronizing views of many white liberals, however, not all native people can be lumped under one *noble* banner. Some Native Americans are just as conniving, barbaric, savage and capitalistic as their European counterparts. . . . Gray whales, and all of nature by extension, are facing threats not only from obvious corporate killers like Mitsubishi, but also from more insidious evildoers masquerading under the guise of "cultural rights."[24]

Hence, if the Makah and Nuu-chah-nulth were not "noble" Indians, this left only one other identification, "savage" Indians. Roy Harvey Pearce argues that non-Indians, from 1750 to 1850, constructed the image of the Indian as savage in order to justify their policies of extinction and assimilation. The Indian was seen as an impediment to western migration and settlement, a fierce figure that stood in the path of civilization.[25] The concept of the Indian changed according to the needs of Euro-Americans and Euro-Canadians. The noble and good image served to attract settlers, missionaries, and financial investors to lands where they saw the easy and peaceful exploitation of indigenous peoples and their territories. The construction and perpetuation of the savage and bad image served to rationalize European conquest, to strengthen religious conversion efforts, and to justify the culturally destructive policies implemented by the U.S. and Canadian governments, which effectively brought indigenous peoples under federal control and administration.[26] As Native people showed aggression to the colonizers and fought for their lands, the image of the wicked, bloodthirsty, savage Indian intensified. The Indian began to represent to the non-Indian imagination everything that was evil and to stand as a symbol of uncivilized savagery.[27]

The whaling opponents built their anti-whaling campaign on the image of the "Indian as savage" calling the Makah whale hunt "barbaric."[28] When the Makah began preparing for their first hunt in 1998, the whaling opponents brought their protest to Neah Bay and stationed themselves on the Makah Reservation. During their demonstration, one of the protesters, holding a sign that read "There is no honor in killing whales," got into a confrontation with a Makah police officer. She yelled at all the tribal members who were watching, "You're not spiritual in any way. You're evil—evil as hell!"[29] When the Makah whaling crew attempted to carry out their hunt, they endured constant physical obstruction by the protesters. During the hunt, members of the Sea Defense Alliance were accused of spraying chemical fire extinguishers into the faces of the whaling crew, shooting flares over the bow of their canoe, and threatening their lives.[30]

When the Makah finally succeeded in capturing and killing a whale in 1999, the visual image of its capture and death was transmitted throughout the United States and Canada and to many parts of the world. In their media campaign, the whaling opponents anthropomorphized the whale, describing it as a defenseless victim, while the Makah whalers were portrayed as bloodthirsty murderers carrying out a brutal and barbaric act. Responding to a CBC editorial, a person from Canada wrote:

> Personally, I think it is a stupid, senseless, and needless slaughter by a bunch of jerks. They didn't go out in their canoe's as their forefathers had done, with spears, etc., no they went out with a motor driven craft, armed with high caliber rifles and took unfair advantage of a creature that was not bothering them. . . . [W]ho do they think they are? It's time their special status ended and they were treated like any other citizen. . . . Take them off the welfare rolls, and give them something to do besides killing whales. They still appear to be ruthless savages.[31]

The fact that the Makah were reviving an aspect of a tradition that was central to their spirituality and their identity was scorned by anti-whalers, who could see the hunt only through their ethnocentric vision of Native cultures. In a letter to the *Seattle Times*, a person from Pebble Beach, California, wrote: "I am anxious to know where I may apply for a license to kill Indians. My forefathers helped settle the west and it was their tradition to kill every Redskin they saw. 'The only good Indian is a dead Indian,' they believed. I also want to keep faith with my ancestors."[32]

Longtime opponents of Indian treaty rights, U.S. Representative Jack Metcalf and former state and U.S. Senator Slade Gorton, both Republicans, joined in the anti-whaling campaign. Metcalf circulated a petition against the hunt in which he reinforced the concept that "all" Native people came from a state of savagery. He said, "I thought we were beyond the point of slaughtering the buffalo for their hides or the whales for their body parts."[33] Gorton called the Makah whale hunt "an aggressive effort orchestrated by the tribe to show they can avoid the laws that govern the rest of us." Gorton's response to the Makah whale hunt reiterated what he had espoused while serving as Washington's attorney general, when he advocated forcing Native nations to give up their treaty-guaranteed rights so that tribal sovereignty could be done away with: "I am more convinced today than ever before that we must bring common sense back to the relationship between this country, our laws and Native American tribes. All Americans should be subject to the same laws."[34]

THE "ECOLOGICAL INDIAN" IN ENVIRONMENTAL AND ANIMAL RIGHTS RHETORIC

Historically, Native peoples have often been romanticized as the "original environmentalists" who lived harmoniously with nature, having the utmost reverence for the land and all living things. Native people were admired for their innate knowledge of the environment and for their understanding of environmental sustainability long before the concept was established in the minds of non-Indians. Native people did have an intrinsic understanding of the world around them; however, non-Indians constructed the image of the "ecological Indian" to serve a specific purpose. The environmental movement emerged in the late 1800s during a time when many non-Indians became frustrated with their society's lack of respect for the environment and were concerned about the rise in water and air pollution because of negligence. The construction of Native people as noble environmentalists provided mainstream society with an example of environmental intuitiveness that they could follow in changing their own self-destructive path.[35]

Chief Seattle and the famous speech attributed to him serve as a perfect example of how environmentalists tried to fit Native people into their social agenda. When the territorial governor, Isaac Stevens, came to Puget Sound in the 1850s to begin treaty negotiations with tribes in the area, he met with the various leaders of the tribal nations. One of the leaders was Sealth, who later became known as Chief Seattle. During his meeting with Stevens in 1854, Chief Seattle was said to have delivered a speech in which he lamented the changes taking place in his culture and the destruction of his people's land since the arrival of non-Indian settlers. Many versions of this speech have appeared throughout the years, and there is debate as to whether Chief Seattle even wrote the original speech. Nonetheless, one version, rewritten by a teacher in the early 1970s, combined the images and ideals of the "noble Indian" with the principles that formed the core of the environmental movement; this version served as an ecological wake-up call to non-Indian society.

> Every part of the earth is sacred to my people. . . . We are part of the earth and the earth is part of us. . . . If we sell you land, you must remember that it is sacred, and you must teach your children that it is sacred . . . . We know that the white man does not understand our ways. One portion of land is the same to him as the next, for he is a stranger who comes in the night and takes from the land whatever he needs. The earth is not his brother, but his enemy, and when he has conquered, he moves on. . . . Our ways our different from yours. . . . The earth does not belong to man; man belongs to the earth. This we know. All things are connected like the blood which unites one family. . . . Man did not weave the web of life: he is merely a strand in it.[36]

Using Native people's historical relationship with the land, Chief Seattle's revised speech offered non-Indian environmentalists an emotionally powerful manifesto for understanding and taking care of the land, linking all people in one nature-loving family.[37]

In the 1960s a campaign was designed to promote environmental awareness. The Keep America Beautiful campaign created a poster with the face of a Native man and a caption that read "Get Involved Now. Pollution Hurts All of Us." The face on the poster belonged to Native actor Iron Eyes Cody, who was also featured in a televised public service announcement (PSA).

In the PSA, Cody is dressed in Plains Indian regalia and his hair is braided with one feather tucked into the back. He paddles a canoe down a river, passing factories spewing toxic clouds into the air and garbage floating in the water. Western-film-genre, Indian-themed music plays in the background. Cody pulls his canoe up onto a beach that is littered with garbage. He walks to a nearby highway, and as he watches the vehicles speeding by, a non-Native woman in the passenger seat of a car throws out garbage, which lands at his feet. The film pans to Cody's face, and as he turns away from the highway, a tear forms and falls from his eye. The music cuts away to a voice that says, "Some people have a deep abiding respect for the natural beauty that was once this country, and some people don't. People start pollution, people can stop it."[38] The advertising campaign utilized the image of the Indian as one who respects nature and who has an intrinsic or natural sense of ecology. In the poster, Cody is brought to tears over non-Indian societies' disregard for the environment.[39]

Following the television debut of the PSA, questions were raised regarding Iron Eyes Cody's ethnicity and whether he was really Native American. Some people claimed that Cody was actually Italian American. His ethnicity really did not matter for the purpose of the PSA, since it was what Cody represented that was important: he symbolized Native people's lament over non-Indian society's destruction of "Mother Earth." Since the 1960s, Native people have been constructed as both environmental and spiritual gurus. The New Age Movement celebrated and, at the same time, appropriated the spiritual and healing powers of Native elders and shamans. Non-Native society's fascination with Native ecological and spiritual knowledge may have resulted from non-Native people feeling an absence of the sacred in their own lives and looking to the Native people and their cultures for values they found lacking in their own.[40]

Environmentalism emerged as a grassroots political movement in the 1960s; its followers joined with people involved in the conservation and preservation efforts initiated by Gifford Pinchot and John Muir in the late 1800s.[41] Out of this developed two forms of environmentalism characterized as the "shallow ecology" movement and the "deep ecology" movement, terms coined by Norwegian philosopher Arne Naess in 1972. Naess described "shallow ecology" as seeking a single objective: "the health and affluence of people in developing countries." Shallow ecology is human-centered, focusing on the health and well-being of man and the implementation of policies that directly benefit humankind.[42]

The philosophy of the "deep ecology" movement was based on "biospherical egalitarianism" and the recognition that all living things have an inherent value. Deep ecologists believe nonhuman elements of nature have their own intrinsic worth and that all living things, human and nonhuman, have the right to live and flourish.[43] The rights of animals and marine mammals became entwined in the deep ecology movement that developed in the 1970s. The movement's underlying philosophy is that nature is independent of and does not exist for the benefit of humans, and animals, because they are intricately linked to nature, do not exist for the benefit of humans either. The core principle of the deep ecology movement—that nature had value in its own right apart from the interests of humans—appealed to people like Tom Regan, a leader of the animal rights movement.[44]

In his book *Defending Animal Rights*, Regan refutes the notion that human beings are superior to animals, which justifies the exploitation of animals for the benefit of humans. He defends and supports the deep ecology movement's belief that humans and animals have inherent value and both have the right to life.[45] The rights of animals have been questioned and debated for over two hundred years. In 1789 Jeremy Bentham posed the question "Can animals suffer?" which has been the driving force of the animal rights movement.[46] The animal rights question evolved into a movement in the 1970s through the philosophical investigations of Peter Singer and with the attention placed on sealing practices in Canada's Arctic during that period. The efforts of a coalition of environmental and animal welfare activists to halt sealing brought attention to this issue and to moral considerations of animal suffering. The movement is founded on utilitarianism and the idea that, because animals are sentient beings, they have the right to live free from human mistreatment and exploitation. Singer argues that animal rights and human rights should be given equal consideration and both animals and humans should have the liberty to live lives free from pain.[47]

In its early inception, the deep ecology movement idealized the environmental ethos of indigenous people, who were praised for their inherent understanding of the ecosystem. However, this image of the "ecological Indian" is exploited only when the Indians are doing what the ecologists and animal rights activists want them to do. This was clearly evident during the sealing protests in the 1970s and carried over into the whaling protests that arose in opposition to the whale hunt in 1999.

During the 1970s, Greenpeace carried out an effective campaign against the hunting of seal pups in northern Canada, which seriously undermined the traditional seal hunts of the Arctic Inuit peoples. The activists knew that their campaign was having a damaging effect on the Inuit seal hunters, but they claimed that the "traditionalism of the hunt" was corrupted by the fact that the Inuit also hunted commercially. The Greenpeace campaign undermined the Inuit ecology and drastically destabilized their culture. In fact, as anthropologist George Wenzel argues, their protests seemed "to contradict the organic view of deep ecology regarding Native people. . . . The protest movement, while it cast aside species-ist attitudes, was unable to categorize Inuit seal hunting other than through its own ethnocentrically derived universalist perceptions of animal rights and values."[48]

During their anti-whaling campaign, animal rights activists suggested to the Makah that instead of actually killing a whale, they should just go out into the ocean and touch it, to "count coup" such as the Plains Indian used to do. Counting coup was a non-violent demonstration of bravery and consisted of a warrior touching an enemy warrior. If the warrior could do this and leave unscathed, this was seen as a sign of his being a successful and fearless warrior.[49] Makah artist Greg Colfax, who is also a Makah whaling commissioner, said that this suggestion demonstrated the environmentalists' and animal rights people's lack of understanding of the cultural and spiritual significance of the hunts. Colfax explains,

> Many of the folks who offered this idea said this is what they did in the Plains— counting coup. I know nothing of counting coup. I've not heard this in anything I've experienced. But, from the folks I have talked to about it, it was an act committed between one warrior and another. We are not at war with the whales.

The whaling opponents continually challenged the environmental intuitiveness of the Makah and Nuu-chah-nulth peoples in regard to their whale hunting plans. The ecological image of Native peoples was completely set aside by the anti-whalers, who reinvented the Makah and Nuu-chah-nulth as people who were disconnected from their cultural knowledge of nature. The whaling opponents also ignored the fact that when commercial whalers had hunted the gray whale to near extinction, both the Makah and the Nuu-chah-nulth ended their hunts for the sake of the whale population; we had foreseen what was happening to the whale stocks, and, although our cultures are enmeshed in whaling traditions, we stopped the hunts. Subsequently, the Makah and Nuu-chah-nulth people would have a more legitimate claim to a "conservation ethic" than non-Indian society, which, years later, finally established a moratorium on commercial whaling.[50]

The Makah people and my own people have lived alongside whales and have had a relationship with them for thousands of years, one that is sacred and respectful. But, deep inside our cultures, we also have a belief and understanding that killing animals for sustenance is acceptable and necessary to our survival. And no matter what we say or do, there will always be people who will not accept that we hunt and kill whales, because they do not believe any animal should be hunted and killed. The group People for the Ethical Treatment of Animals (PETA) opposes killing animals for any reason. PETA's slogan is "animals are not ours to eat, wear, experiment on, or use for entertainment."[51] PETA promotes a vegan lifestyle and has on its Web site a "vegetarian starter kit" that provides vegan recipes, nutritional facts on a vegetarian diet, information on the inhumane way animals are raised for food, and testimonials from famous vegans, like actors Pamela Anderson and Alec Baldwin.[52]

This vegan lifestyle is one that some people throughout the world have chosen to embrace, but it is ultimately a personal choice. We Native people do not want people who choose to live that way imposing their dietary rules on us, as this is just another form of cultural imperialism and food hegemony. Ecologist Russell Barsh writes,

> The public discourse over the acceptability of killing and eating marine mammals has been couched in moral and legal terms, but the real issue is relative power. Privileged societies have acquired the power to determine what the world eats and to impose their own symbolic and aesthetic food taboos on others. Placed in proper historical context, contemporary efforts to abolish whaling and sealing are exposed as the flip side of Western European domination of world food supplies. . . . Moral indignation, rather than conservation, has driven the anti-harvesting campaigns for the last twenty-five years.[53]

We are all part of the natural world, and predation is also part of life and integral to the world we live in. Orca whales attack and eat gray whales and their calves, for instance, as well as seals and fish. There is a reason that some whales are called "killer" whales, but this side of their nature is ignored by whale watchers who often romanticize the whale.[54] Native people see their relationship with the environment as mutually dependent. In a document published by the Nuu-chah-nulth Tribal Council, we outline our position on sustainable resource development.

> One of the most important teachings, a lesson learned by each successive generation, was that everything was connected. To unduly harm one natural resource meant the almost certain ruin of another. For thousands of years, Nuu-chah-nulth people lived in harmony with the natural world. They treated the forest with respect, because they knew that the forest protected the streams that the salmon spawned in. And they treated the returning salmon with respect because they knew that wiping out individual salmon stocks would irreparably harm the intricate web of animal and plant life in the surrounding forest. Millennia before the words "sustainable development" gained vogue,

Nuu-chah-nulth people had fully embraced the concept. They had to. It's what kept them alive.[55]

When the gray whale was placed on the Endangered Species list in 1973, its population was around 1,500. When the Makah began negotiations with the IWC in the mid-1990s for a gray whale hunting quota, the whale population had grown to 26,000. Throughout the years the IWC scientific committee has monitored the growing gray whale population and determined that 484 whales could be taken out of its stocks without having any negative effects on its population growth.[56] Other scientific studies on gray whales provide evidence that the revival of Makah and Nuu-chah-nulth whaling may, in fact, benefit the existing gray whale population. The highest number of gray whale deaths in twenty-four years was recorded in the winter of 1998–99. Sixty-five grays were found dead along Mexico's Baja Peninsula coast and another twenty-five washed up on California's shores in the spring of 1999. Environmental groups blamed ocean temperature changes and pollution, but biologists point toward a more natural explanation than human-induced factors. The deaths may have resulted from the strain on the whales' feeding areas. Gray whales are bottom-feeders and, according to biologists, "may have reached the carrying capacity of their feeding grounds."[57]

Director of the Makah Natural Resources Department David Sones says that the core values of the Makah and the environmental and animal rights groups are basically the same. That is, they all want to bring the whale populations back up to healthy levels. But where their ideas differ is in regard to sustainability: the Makah want to introduce gray whales back into their culture through the sustainable use of the whale as a resource; the environmental and animal rights people want to protect them at all cost. But, Sones maintains, humans are also part of the ecosystem and have a role to play in helping to balance its resources. When humans are prohibited from utilizing certain resources, such as harbor seals, this can have a negative impact on other resources—for example, fish populations have been threatened because of the overpopulation of seals.[58]

In my culture, we have an understanding that we all exist—humans, animals, plants, etc.—in a shared environment in which everything is equal. Our cultures thrived in a world of reciprocity between us and our environment. Our relationship with animals has always been one based on respect and gratitude, and there is a sense of sacredness attached to the spirit of the animal for giving itself to us for sustenance. Within this symbiotic relationship was the understanding that death is ultimately integrated into life.[59] The anti-whaling groups saw the death of the whale through a Western cultural lens and thus ignored the spiritual and sacred elements attached to the Makah and Nuu-chah-nulth whaling tradition.

◆ ◆ ◆

Throughout the last five hundred years, for most non-Native people "the Indian" of imagination and ideology has been viewed as real, perhaps more real than the Native peoples of actual existence and contact in the United States and Canada.[60] Former Makah Whaling Commission chairman Keith Johnson explains that "too often these days Native people are being judged by a dominant culture that fails to understand us or our cultures."[61] The whaling opponents generated a discourse against Makah and Nuu-chah-nulth whaling that overlooked and ultimately, and probably intentionally, discredited the cultural significance of our decision to revive our whaling practices. Cultures must be examined within their own ethnohistorical, contemporary, and societal contexts to understand the reasons why people act in certain ways or make decisions based on their own cultural understanding.

6 / *Nupu*

LEGAL IMPEDIMENTS SPARK
A 2007 WHALE HUNT

LTHOUGH THE MAKAH PEOPLE HAD SUCCESSFULLY HARVESTED A gray whale in 1999, the tribe has been tied up in lawsuits ever since, which has prevented it from fully exercising its treaty right to whale. On September 9, 2007, five Makah men, frustrated by the legal hassles and their inability to proceed with their rightful hunting, harpooned and then shot a gray whale in the waters off Neah Bay. The hunt was a surprise to people both inside and outside the Makah community. The men had not received permission from the Makah tribe to hunt a whale, and their actions challenged a 2002 legal ruling that placed a moratorium on whaling. In this chapter, I will analyze the events that sparked these men's defiance and what motivated them to disregard the law. Their actions have added fuel to a dialogue that developed during the legal cases, one that questions the future not only of the Makah tribe's whaling right but of all tribal treaty rights.

THE IWC AND THE MAKAH TRIBE'S REQUEST TO WHALE

The Makah people's right to whale is guaranteed in the 1855 Treaty of Neah Bay.[1] In 1994, when the Makah tribe realized that the gray whale population had once again reached healthy levels, it approached the federal government to seek an International Whaling Commission whaling quota on their behalf (see chapter 4) and agreed to conduct a hunt within the international rules and regulations established under the IWC. The IWC administers the International Convention for the Regulation of Whaling (ICRW), which regulates the global whaling industry and protects and conserves threatened whale stocks.[2] In 1987 the IWC imposed a worldwide moratorium on all commercial whaling activities but exempted whaling for scientific and aboriginal subsistence and cultural purposes.

In May 1995, members of the Makah tribe sent a detailed whaling proposal to the federal government that outlined the cultural significance of their whaling tradition, stressing that reviving the hunts would revitalize and strengthen their culture and reconnect them to their whaling identity. The proposal also showed how reintroducing whale oil to their diets could help alleviate some of the health issues plaguing the Makah community.[3] In 1996 the federal government submitted a proposal to the IWC for Makah whaling. One of the stipulations of the IWC is that a member state bringing forward a proposal must demonstrate the Native group's "continuing" tradition of both hunting and eating whales. The United States could not show a "continuing" tradition or a "dependence" on whaling, because the Makah tribe had not whaled since the early 1900s, when the gray whale stocks were almost wiped out from unregulated commercial whaling. After much debate with IWC members, the United States decided to withdraw the Makah plan until the following year. In 1997 the IWC amended its schedule, which contains the rules governing whaling, with a broader definition that would include Makah whaling.[4] The amended section reads:

> The taking of gray whales . . . is permitted, but only by aborigines or a Contracting Party on behalf of the aborigines, and then only when the meat and products of such whales are to be used exclusively for local consumption by the *aborigines whose traditional aboriginal subsistence and cultural needs have been recognized.*[5]

In 1997 the IWC issued the Makah a whaling quota.

A STRANGE ALLIANCE: ENVIRONMENTALISTS AND ANTI-INDIAN/ANTI-TREATY/RIGHT-WING POLITICIANS

Immediately after the Makah tribe announced its whaling plan, environmental and animal rights groups began to organize in opposition. Nongovernmental organizations (NGOs) from around the world signed a letter that was sent to the Makah asking them not to whale. The "Open Letter to the Makah Nation" stated: "The undersigned groups respectfully appeal to the Makah Nation to refrain from the resumption of whaling. People from many cultures worldwide hold whales to be sacred and consider each species a sovereign nation unto itself, worthy of respect and protection."[6]

Two well-known politicians, Slade Gorton and Jack Metcalf, moved into the spotlight during the Makah whaling rights debate. Throughout their years in office, both Gorton and Metcalf initiated and supported campaigns against tribes and tribal treaty rights. Former Makah Tribal Council chair Ben Johnson Jr. said that Native people call Gorton an "Indian fighter," because he has led a personal campaign to abolish the treaties between the federal government and the tribes.[7] Micah McCarty says that the "whole legal mess" stifling the Makah tribe's right to whale began by anti–treaty rights people such as Gorton and Metcalf allying with NGOs such as the Fund for Animals, the Humane Society of the United States, and the West Coast Anti-Whaling Society, which led to a strange alliance of right-wing politicians and left-wing environmentalists. Together, McCarty says, they "manipulated the system by holding the federal trust hostage because of culturally biased thinking about whaling."[8] As a result, "the system has been abused to deprive us of our treaty rights."[9]

Republican Slade Gorton's political career spans more than fifty years. He began as a Washington State senator in 1959 and then served as the state's attorney general from 1969 until 1981 and as a U.S. senator from 1989 to 2001.[10] Gorton was the attorney general who represented the state of Washington in the 1974 treaty fishing rights case, *United States v. State of Washington*, also known as the Boldt Decision. His family had ties to the fishing industry; in the 1970s, they ran a wholesale fish distribution firm in Boston called Slade Gorton and Co., Inc.[11]

Gorton was an outspoken opponent of Indian rights who crusaded against Indian treaty fishing rights in Washington State. In fact, the anti–treaty rights movement began in the 1960s and grew out of the opposition to tribal fishing rights claims in the Puget Sound area.[12] During the 1960s and 1970s, in his position as a state senator and then attorney general, Gorton continually brought legal challenges against the Washington State tribes' treaty rights to fish.[13] Washington State's campaign against Native rights came at a time when African Americans were fighting for social equality. One tribal fisheries manager compared the two struggles, stating that Washington State's resistance to Indian treaty fishing was analogous to the Southern segregationists who blocked the entry of black children into white schools. But, in this case, Washington was standing in the schoolhouse door.[14]

In the years leading up to the Boldt Decision, Gorton argued that treaty rights made Native people "supercitizens," affected the civil rights of non-Indians, and was "inconsistent with a drive toward equal treatment of all citizens under the same system of laws."[15] After Judge Boldt handed down his ruling in 1974 affirming tribes' treaty rights to fish, Gorton contended that his decision was unjust and awarded "special rights" to Native treaty fishers, which went against the U.S. tradition of equal rights. He said:

> Thus this state . . . now has two completely unequal classes of citizens: treaty Indians and everyone else. Such an unjust resolution cries out for change, for a solution which restores equality of treatment for all citizens, Indian and non-Indian, in the fisheries resources of the state. The Boldt decision is both unjust and contrary to our basic values as a national society. A policy under which one class of citizens is entitled to special rights in perpetuity by reason of race or, more precisely, by reason of a combination of race and the luck of an ancestral treaty, is both wrong and destructive of social peace.[16]

Following the Boldt Decision, the anti–treaty rights movement intensified, with Attorney General Gorton in the forefront of an attempt to have the decision overturned. The case was appealed to the Ninth Circuit Court of Appeals, which affirmed the lower court's decision. Gorton then appealed the ruling to the U.S. Supreme Court, which refused to hear the case, thus endorsing Boldt.[17]

In 1981 Gorton introduced legislation to prohibit tribal steelhead fishing in Washington State. His proposed *Steelhead Trout Protection Act* sought to de-commercialize steelhead trout and make all state laws regarding this species of fish also applicable to tribal treaty fishers. The bill died.[18] Ten years later, he publically denounced an exhibit at the Smithsonian Institution that described as genocide the treatment of Indians during America's westward expansion. Gorton said the exhibit "depicts a terribly distorted, negative, and untrue statement about the settlement of the west."[19] In 1994 he proposed a bill to Congress to over-turn tribal sovereign immunity. Sovereign immunity is granted to governments (tribal and non-tribal) to provide protection from lawsuits.[20] With respect to the Makah hunt, Gorton was a vocal opponent and disparaged the tribe's treaty right to whale, revisiting his "supercitizens" argument used during the 1960s fishing rights struggles to argue that the Makah should not be allowed "special" rights to whale and should be subject to the same laws as every other citizen in the United States.[21]

Republican Congressman Jack Metcalf from Washington State is also a well-known anti-Indian activist, who for over two decades has campaigned against Indian treaty rights. Metcalf was a member of the Washington State House of Representatives from 1960 until he was defeated in 1964. In 1966 he was elected to the Washington State Senate and served until 1974 and then served again from 1980 to 1992. In 1995 he was elected to the U.S. House of Representatives and served until 2001.[22] Like Gorton, Metcalf also had ties to the fishing industry and was a former commercial fisherman. After Judge Boldt gave his decision in *United States v. State of Washington*, Metcalf was involved in coordinating a coalition of sportsfishing groups, Steelhead-Salmon Protection Action for Washington Now (s/SPAWN), to pressure the state not to comply with the court order. The group circulated a petition, initiated by Metcalf, that stated that no citizen should be denied access to natural resources based on sex, origin, or cultural heritage.[23]

When s/SPAWN disbanded, Metcalf became involved in a similar group, United Property Owners of Washington (UPOW), which for years has crusaded against tribes' off-reservation treaty fishing rights.[24] In the 1980s, this group lobbied (unsuccessfully) to have a congressional commission study the effects of federal Indian policies on non-Indian American citizens.[25] As a state senator, Metcalf, in 1983, introduced a bill calling for the abrogation of all existing treaties and a return of the management of the state fishery back to Washington State.[26] In Congress he served on the Native American and Insular Affairs Subcommittee and in 1996 sponsored legislation (HR 2997) to make it more difficult for unrecognized tribes to petition for federal recognition.[27]

Metcalf's alliance with the environmental and animal rights groups seemed unusual considering his anti-environment and pro-hunting and pro-fishing stands. He had been actively involved in the anti-environmental movement through his participation with the wise-use movement. The wise-use movement was founded in 1988 and is a grassroots component of the national anti-environmental movement. Wise-use members, many of whom are ranchers, farmers, and miners, advocate for the rights of property owners to develop and use their private lands, mainly for hunting and fishing. They have lobbied Congress to open up and/or privatize federal lands for timber and mining development. They have actively lobbied Congress to terminate environmental laws that prevent them from exploiting the land.[28] The movement views Native treaties as an impediment to moving forward with its mission. Metcalf has been rated by environmental groups as having one of the worst green voting records in Congress.[29]

In 1996 Metcalf introduced a resolution in Congress condemning the Makah hunt.[30] He headed the emerging anti-whaling alliance, calling on the U.S. government to withdraw its request to the IWC for a Makah whaling quota. In June 1996 he was able to get a resolution passed unanimously in the House of Representatives Committee on Resources that expressed opposition to the Makah whale hunt. A contingent of anti-whaling NGOs, which included two Makah members, attended the IWC meeting, where they appealed to the IWC members not to issue the Makah a whale quota.[31] Makah leaders believed that Metcalf's actions caused the IWC to shy away from issuing a quota in 1996, when it was first proposed by the United States.[32] When the Makah tribe began to prepare for its hunt in May 1999, Metcalf addressed the House of Representatives, saying: "Mr. Speaker, the day we have all dreaded has arrived. After years of U.S. policy in opposition to commercial whaling, the Clinton-Gore administration is reopening whaling. This is a tragic day, and we will regret that this has happened."[33]

In 1997 the environmental group the Sea Shepherd Society began urging its members to contact Metcalf to let him know that they supported his efforts to stop the Makah from hunting whales. In November 13, 1997, the Sea Shepherd Action Alert newsletter reported that the society's Northwest Pacific coordinator, Michael Kundu, said that they had contacted Metcalf in January "to [brief] him on the potential economic and ecological consequences of a Makah whale kill."[34] In June 1999, during a Seattle Town Hall panel discussion on Makah whaling, members of Sea Shepherd called Metcalf a "stellar leader" and a "great public servant.[35]

There were skeptics who believed that Metcalf's actions had more to do with his opposition to Indian tribes than to any fondness for cetaceans. Bill Watson, member of the Seattle-based NGO Northwest Coalition, says, "I don't believe for a minute that Jack Metcalf cares about whales. . . . It's a way to go after the tribe. It's a way to extend his anti-whaling campaign. Believe me, if it was someone else doing the whaling, he wouldn't mind at all."[36]

BUILDING A CASE AGAINST MAKAH WHALING

After the IWC issued a quota to the Makah tribe in 1997, NGOs sent letters to the federal agencies that oversee the Makah whaling plan, the National Oceanic and Atmospheric Administration (NOAA) and the National Marine Fisheries Service (NMFS), alleging that the government had breached many of its own environmental statutes when it gave its support to the Makah tribe to whale.[37] In particular, the anti-whalers argued that the federal government had violated the National Environmental Policy Act (NEPA) because it prepared no environmental assessment of the whale hunts.

NEPA, established in 1969, was one of the first laws to create a national framework for protecting the environment. NEPA's basic policy is to assure that all branches of government give proper consideration to the environment prior to undertaking any major action that could significantly affect it.[38] Agencies must also conduct an environmental review early in the planning for any proposed actions.[39]

After the United States submitted its initial whaling proposal to the IWC in 1996, the government circulated a draft environmental assessment (EA) for public comment in August 1997. In October of that year, NOAA and the Makah tribe entered into a new agreement, which was similar to the one signed in 1996.[40] Four days after signing the new agreement, NOOA/NMFS issued a final EA and a finding of no significant impact (FONSI) to the environment from the Makah's proposed whale hunt. The day after the final EA was issued, the U.S. government again submitted the Makah whaling proposal to the IWC, and this time their whaling proposal was approved. The whale quota established that the Makah could take twenty gray whales over a five-year period.[41] In April 1998, NOAA issued a federal notice stating that the Makah subsistence and cultural needs had been recognized by the United States and the IWC, allowing the tribe to whale legally pursuant to the federal Whaling Convention Act.[42] On May 17, 1999, the Makah harvested a thirty-foot California gray whale.

When the federal government issued the new EA in April 1998, the anti-whaling coalition, led by Jack Metcalf, filed a suit in district court on the same day accusing the federal government of violating NEPA because of the way the environmental assessment was carried out.[43] The plaintiffs argued that in granting the Makah authorization to resume whaling, the federal defendants violated NEPA by (1) preparing an EA that was both untimely and inadequate, and (2) declining to prepare the more stringent EIS (environmental impact statement) as required under NEPA. The lower courts disagreed. Judge Franklin Burgess rejected the plaintiff's arguments and denied the motion, thereby upholding the federal EA and the Makah whaling proposal. Burgess granted the federal defendants and the Makah tribe's motion for summary judgment.[44] The plaintiffs appealed the decision and the case went to the Court of Appeals.

In *Metcalf v. Daley* (June 9, 2000),[45] the Ninth Circuit Court of Appeals overturned the early court decision and suspended federal approval of the Makah whale hunt, ordering that a new environmental study be conducted. In a 2–1 decision, the court ruled that the NMFS had violated the law by failing to conduct a review that was timely or in good faith. It said that even though the federal agencies did prepare an environmental assessment, they did so after already signing agreements that bound them to the Makah's whaling proposal.[46]

The court said that the review should have been completed before the NMFS and the tribe signed the agreement. Because the management agreement was completed before the study was concluded, the court said this created the appearance that the assessment's result was predetermined. NEPA procedures require that an assessment be "prepared early enough" so that it can be utilized during the decision-making process.[47] The court ruled that the improper timing of this EA did not allow this to take place.

These events demonstrate that the agency did not comply with NEPA's require-ments concerning the timing of their environmental analysis, thereby seriously impeding the degree to which their planning and decisions could reflect envi-ronmental values. . . . This Agreement was signed four days before the final EA in this case was issued. . . . This is strong evidence that NOAA and other agencies made the decision to support the Tribe's proposal in 1996, before the EA process began and without considering the environmental consequences thereof.[48]

The court held that the NMFS failed to take a "hard look" at the environmental impact of the proposed whale hunt and violated environmental laws in its rush to grant the Makah tribe the authorization to hunt whales.[49]

The court considered the second issue of whether an environmental impact statement (rather than another environmental assessment) should be prepared. Under NEPA regulations, an EA must first be prepared to determine whether a more detailed EIS is required. The EA considers the impacts of the proposed action and alternatives and then recommends moving forward with the prepa-ration of an EIS or with a finding of no significant impact (FONSI). An EIS is conducted if the EA determines that federal action will cause a significant impact on the environment.[50] A federal agency can prepare an EA as long as it also deter-mines whether an action will have a "finding of no significant impact" on the environment and studies the short- and long-terms effects on the environment.[51] The responsibility for determining whether an EIS is necessary rests on the fed-eral agency proposing the action.[52] The court decided "that it is appropriate only to require a new EA" and that a FONSI would be prepared. It required that the new EA "be done under circumstances that ensure an objective evaluation free of the previous taint."[53] In sum, the court ordered the NMFS to establish a new NEPA process and conduct another environmental assessment of Makah whaling.[54]

Following the court ruling, the NMFS agreement with the Makah was dis-solved and a new EA review process began. On January 12, 2001, the NMFS completed the environmental assessment process and released its draft EA. The draft reexamined the environmental consequences of issuing an IWC quota to the Makah tribe to hunt gray whales for ceremonial and subsistence purposes. It outlined four alternatives: Alternative 1 would grant the Makah tribe an IWC quota of five whales a year with limits on the time, place, and manner of the hunt, similar to those placed on the 1999 hunt. The hunt would be restricted to migrat-ing whales from either the northward or the southward migration. Alternative 2 would also grant the Makah tribe the IWC quota of five whales a year but with fewer time and place restrictions. It also opened the hunt to the Pacific Coast Feeding Aggregation (PCFA). The PCFA was the name the EA used to describe the portion of the eastern North Pacific gray whale population that stays along the Pacific coast to feed rather than migrating to the Bering Sea.[55] Alternative 3 would allow the Makah an IWC quota of five whales a year and their hunt would be free of any time or area restrictions; Alternative 4 would not allow a whale hunt and no whaling quota would be issued to the Makah tribe.[56]

A thirty-day public comment period was established following the release of the draft EA, and the NMFS began conducting public hearings in Seattle, Washington. The process provided forums for heated debates between pro- and anti-whaling people.[57] Members of the anti-whaling coalition were upset over the fact that some of the alternatives loosened the restrictions that had previously been placed on the Makah, allowing the tribe to hunt any time of the year and in the more sheltered area in the Strait of Juan de Fuca, as well as off the beaches of the north Olympic coast. The anti-whalers were also surprised and angry that the hunts might target the PCFA, a group of whales they described as "local" or "resident" whales. Members of these groups argued that gray whales feeding in Pacific Northwest waters are genetically different from the whales that migrate along the coast to Alaska and that they had also grown friendly to people. Therefore, they believed these whales should be protected.[58]

The previous EA had excluded the PCFA whales from the Makah hunt until further studies had been conducted on this group. Scientific studies had not yet determined why a portion of the 26,000 gray whales that migrate to feeding grounds in the Bering Sea leave the larger group and spend part or all of the summer and early fall feeding in waters from northern California to the southeastern Alaska coastline. However, recent photo-identification studies showed that these whales, while they remain along the Pacific coast in the summer and fall, move widely in the area to feed and were not always observed in the same area each year. Therefore, Micah McCarty (former Makah Tribal Council chair) says that the designation "resident" or "summer resident" is a misnomer.[59]

Also, scientific studies showed that the PCFA was not a subgroup of the eastern North Pacific whales and the whales were genetically the same as all the whales in the larger population.[60] The inclusion of the PCFA in the proposed alternatives was based on extensive scientific studies and this new photo-identification research, which showed that a limited hunt on this group of whales would pose no risk to its population. Understanding the issues that could develop with the inclusion of the PCFA, NOAA dealt with this group as a separate management unit and evaluated the impact of a hunt and strikes on this group separately from the larger whale stock using a potential biological removal (PBR) framework. The PBR is the maximum number of animals, not including natural mortalities, that can be removed from a marine mammal stock and still allow that stock to reach or maintain its optimum sustainable population.[61] The PBR studies showed that a range of two to six whales a year could be removed from the PCFA without any significant effect.[62]

Micah McCarty maintains that there is no such thing as a resident or non-migrating whale, because all whales, including the PCFA, eventually join the migrating population. McCarty believed that the anti-whaling groups focused on the PCFA, calling them local or resident whales, simply to interfere with the EA process and stop the whale hunts.[63] As for the anti-whaling activists' claim that the resident whales had grown friendly to people and become accustomed to their boats, research biologist John Calambokidis refuted this statement. These whales, said Calambokidis, are "unconscious" of people and boats in the area when they are eating.[64] The whales stick around the area to eat, not to hang out with the locals.

The EA was completed on July 12, 2001, and released the following week. In the final EA, a FONSI was once again issued, concluding that the Makah whale hunt posed no threat to the eastern North Pacific gray whale population, which at the time was approximately 26,000 animals.[65] NOAA's choice of alternatives was based on extensive current and past scientific research, drawing on a considerable body of scientific information and scholarly studies. Alternative 1 in the final EA was the preferred action and was also the alternative most in line with the Makah Management Plan, which had been revised following the public review process and prior to the finalization of the EA.[66] Under the proposed action, NOAA would grant the Makah tribe the IWC quota of five whales a year for ceremonial and subsistence purposes.[67] NOAA would lessen the time restrictions on the hunt, allowing hunts in September and October and in the summer months when the weather conditions allowed for a much safer hunt. The Makah tribe would also be allowed a limited hunt on the Pacific Coast Feeding Aggregation. Taking into account the PBR, NOAA took a conservative approach that allowed the tribe only five strikes (in a two-year period) in the PCFA area; once this was met, they would have to focus their hunts on whales migrating between December 1 and May 31. No hunts were allowed within 200 yards of Tatoosh Island, Washington, or White Rock, British Columbia, between May and September.[68]

The method requirements were the same as the requirements in the 1997 agreement—methods the Makah tribe utilized in their 1999 hunt. They would use a canoe and harpoon and would follow up with a high-caliber rifle to kill the whale.[69]

Once again, the anti-whaling alliance brought the issue back to the courts. They filed suit in U.S. District Court on January 10, 2002, alleging federal violations of both NEPA and the Marine Mammal Protection Act (MMPA) of 1972. MMPA bans the hunting and killing of whales and most other marine mammals and is the principal federal law guiding marine mammal conservation. Alaska Natives are exempted from the MMPA.[70] The Act reads:

> The Act does not apply to the taking of marine mammals by an Indian, Aleut, or Eskimo who resides in Alaska and dwells on the North Pacific Ocean or Arctic Ocean, if the taking is done in a nonwasteful manner and is for subsistence purposes or for creating and selling authentic native handicrafts and clothing. These takings may be regulated by the Secretary, however, if the marine mammal is depleted.[71]

The anti-whaling coalition charged that the NMFS had ignored the federal permitting process required by the MMPA because it had not issued a waiver to the Makah tribe. The coalition once again alleged that the government failed to study adequately the ways in which the Makah whale hunt could harm the environment, as required under NEPA. They also claimed that the PCFA should not be included in the Makah whale hunts.[72] The District Court denied the plaintiffs' motion for a preliminary injunction and granted summary judgment in favor of the federal defendants. Judge Burgess concluded that "the federal agencies had taken the requisite 'hard look' at the risks associated with the whale hunt" and determined that the plaintiffs' arguments were unfounded.[73] The plaintiffs appealed the case to the Ninth Circuit.

UNDERMINING THE WHALE HUNTS: *ANDERSON V. EVANS*

On December 20, 2002, a three-judge panel of the Ninth Circuit Court of Appeals overturned the District Court ruling and rejected the federal environmental assessment that showed that Makah whaling would cause no significant environmental impact. The court ruled in *Anderson v. Evans* that the National Marine Fisheries Service must conduct a more stringent environmental impact statement under the National Environmental Policy Act, and until one was completed the Makah tribe's annual whale hunt must stop. Whereas the judges in *Metcalf v. Daley* felt that the EA was adequate, the judges in *Anderson v. Evans* did not. The Court ruled "that the federal defendants did not satisfy NEPA when they issued a finding of no significant impact as a result of an environmental assessment: For the reasons set forth . . . it is necessary that the federal actions be reviewed in an environmental impact statement (EIS)."[74]

NOAA analyzed the long- and short-term effects that Makah whaling would have on the environment and, in its 2001 EA, concluded that a Makah whale hunt of up to five whales a year would not significantly affect the environment; therefore, an EIS was not required.[75] The court stated, "There is no disagreement in this case concerning the EA's conclusion that the impact of the Makah Tribe's hunt on the overall California gray whale population will not be significant. What is in hot dispute is the possible impact on the PCFA whale population in the area where the Tribe wants to hunt."[76] This, the judges argued, needed to be analyzed through an EIS.

As noted earlier, the inclusion of the PCFA in the proposed alternatives for the Makah whaling quota was based on extensive detailed scientific studies and new photo-identification research, which showed that a limited hunt on this group of whales would pose no risk to its population. And, even though the scientific evidence established that the PCFA was not biologically different from the migrating whale population, NOAA took into consideration the anti-whaling groups concerns and evaluated the PCFA as a separate management group and established conservative whaling regulations in the EA alternatives that would cause the least impact to this group of whales.[77] Even with all the evidence presented in these detailed studies and extensive research, the judges were not convinced and still questioned whether opening the whale hunt to the PCFA could pose a substantial risk to this population of gray whales.[78] Therefore, the court ruled, the new EIS must demonstrate that a hunt which included the PCFA would "not threaten the role of [these] gray whales as functioning elements of the marine ecosystem."[79]

The court determined that the Marine Mammal Protection Act did in fact apply to the Makah and that the tribe's treaty right to whale did not exempt them from the scrutiny of this Act. Therefore, the court held "that both the federal defendants and the Tribe did not satisfy the permit or waiver requirements of the MMPA" and that they must do so before NOAA can authorize a Makah whaling quota.[80]

According to the court, NOAA's issuance of a gray whale quota to the Makah tribe without compliance with the MMPA violated federal law. Alaska Natives have an MMPA exemption that allows them to hunt whales and marine mammals for subsistence.[81] The U.S. government did not issue to the Makah an MMPA exemption because of the recognized fundamental legal principle that Indian treaty rights were exempt from its provisions.

Although the Makah tribe has a treaty right to whale, the federal defendants also pointed out to the courts that the tribe received international approval for their whale hunts from the International Whaling Commission. The IWC, which was set up under the International Convention for the Regulation of Whaling, regulates the global whaling industry and protects and conserves threatened whale stocks.[82] The IWC definition of aboriginal subsistence is whaling that is conducted for local aboriginal consumption and is carried out by indigenous peoples who have "strong community, familial, social, and cultural ties" related to their whaling traditions and have "a dependence on whaling."[83] The IWC amended its schedule, which contains the rules governing whaling, to establish a broader definition that would include the Makah.[84] The 1946 ICRW grants the IWC the power to amend the Schedule by adopting subsequent regulations, which include quotas. In 1997 the Makah tribe received an IWC quota to hunt whales.

In court, the federal defendants for the Makah tribe argued that the 1946 ICRW entitled the Makah tribe to whale outside of the MMPA regulations. Section 1372 (a)(2) of the MMPA exempts international treaties that predate the MMPA. The defendants asserted that since the IWC was given the power to adopt quotas in 1946, the Makah tribe's 1997 quota was a right under the 1946 Convention and, therefore, predated the MMPA. The court disagreed.[85] The court ignored the ICRW and looked at the fact that the 1997 Schedule, which recognized the Makah tribe's right to hunt whales, was adopted twenty-four years after the MMPA came into effect. Although section 1372 (a)(2) of the MMPA exempts international treaties that predate the MMPA, the court argued that this did not include their amendments. Thus, the court reasoned, "if Congress wanted to exempt subsequent amendments, then Congress could have done so explicitly. But Congress did not do so."[86] Therefore, the court asserted, Makah whaling can be preempted by MMPA even though the tribe has IWC approval to hunt whales.

The court utilized a test it established in *United States v. Fryberg* (1980) to determine when conservation statutes impinge on Indian treaty rights.[87] The test has three prongs: (1) the sovereign has jurisdiction in the area where activity occurs, (2) the statute is nondiscriminatory, and (3) the application of the statute to treaty rights is necessary to achieve conservation purpose. The court concluded that the test applied to the Makah whale hunt because the United States had jurisdiction where whaling occurs, the MMPA applied to both treaty and nontreaty people, and the application of the statute to regulate treaty rights was necessary to achieve its conservation purpose.[88] The court concluded that Makah whaling needed to be sensitive to the MMPA's major objective, which is to ensure that whales continue to be "significant functioning element[s] in the ecosystem." Again, they referred to the PCFA, which was open to tribal hunts.[89]

Scientific studies conducted in the late 1990s revealed that the gray whale was nearing its carrying capacity, reaching the largest population that could be supported by an ecosystem.[90] In 1997, when the federal government approached the IWC for a Makah quota to hunt gray whales, its scientific committee found that up to 482 gray whales could be taken out of the present population each year, and this would not have a detrimental impact on its overall growth and sustainability. In fact, the committee found that "removing these whales would likely allow the population to stabilize above the maximum sustainable yield level."[91] The IWC issued scientific committee reports in the following years that revealed the same results, concluding that this number of whales could be taken out of the gray population and it would continue to grow at healthy levels.[92]

In 1999 a study was conducted on the unusually high number of gray whale deaths occurring among the eastern North Pacific gray whale population. Over sixty whales washed up along the Mexican and Pacific coasts.[93] Biologist John Calambokidis, who analyzed the whales that had washed ashore, said that they had thin layers of blubber and were clearly underweight.[94] Gray whale populations have risen dramatically over the last fifty years, from a few thousand whales in the mid-1940s to over 26,000 in 1999. Dr. Bruce Mate said that a "possibility for the gray whale mortalities might be that they are not getting enough to eat during the summer."[95] The large population of whales could be putting a strain on the Alaskan feeding grounds, and, Mate speculated, the whales may have reached the carrying capacity of these feeding areas.[96] The Ninth Circuit Court, however, discounted these scientific conclusions or any other evidence that did not support its interpretation of the MMPA. Thus, it seems that the court's mandate that Makah treaty rights conform with the MMPA in essence undermined the Act's own definition of conservation, which is to maintain an "optimum *sustainable* population" of gray whales.[97]

In its interpretation of the Makah tribe's 1885 treaty, the Ninth Circuit Court seemed to ignore the canons of construction that were developed by the federal courts to recognize the federal-tribal trust relationship and to rectify the inequality in federal treaty negotiations and the unfair bargaining position of the tribes at that time. These canons are that ambiguous expressions must be resolved in favor of the Indian parties concerned, that Indian treaties must be interpreted as the Indians themselves would have understood them, and that Indian treaties must be liberally construed in favor of the Indians.[98] The canons also recognized that a treaty is not a grant of rights to the tribes but were a grant of rights from them.[99] Treaties "reserved" rights that the tribes already had, such as rights to hunt, fish, trap, and, in the Makah tribe's case, to whale. This was reinforced in the 1974 case *United States v. State of Washington*, now well known as the Boldt Decision. Judge Boldt interpreted Indian treaty rights as distinct from and superior to the rights of state citizens. In the Stevens treaties, the tribes were guaranteed a right to fish "in common" with citizens. This right, said Judge Boldt, was not *granted* to the tribes but was a right they extended to and shared with non-Indians [italic added].[100]

The Makah tribe ceded to the United States most of their traditional lands, with the understanding that their marine-based lifestyle would be protected in their treaty. While the Makah people were willing to negotiate the sale of their land, they made sure that their connection to the sea and its resources would not be interrupted, because, as they told Governor Stevens, who negotiated their treaty, the sea was their "country."[101] During the three days of negotiations with Stevens, the Makah *chah-chah-buht* (chiefs) were adamant that their fishing and sea mammal hunting be safeguarded in the treaty. The fact that the Makah leaders refused to sign the treaty until the governor assured them that these rights would be secured demonstrates how vital whaling was to the Makah people's economy and culture. Chief Klachote told Stevens that "he thought he ought to have the right to fish, and to take whales and get food when he liked."[102]

U.S. government officials told the Makah leaders that they knew about the Makah people's reputation as great whale hunters and skillful traders in whale oil. Stevens assured the Makah chiefs that the government would help them maintain their fishing, sealing, and whaling practices and would supply them with equipment so that they could continue these practices. Understanding the importance of whale oil for both their trade and their consumption, Governor Stevens told the leaders that he would provide them with barrels to hold their prized commodity.[103]

In their treaty, the Makah retained the right to whale "in common" with U.S. citizens, believing that this would mean that they could continue to whale for eternity. No one could have foreseen at the time that the whale population would be decimated by commercial whalers and that measures would be taken to ban whaling altogether. Nowhere in the treaty does it indicate that the U.S. government would penalize the Makah for decreasing whale stocks or that it would deny them their whaling right.[104]

Again, the *Anderson* case failed to read the Makah treaty in the same manner that the *chah-chah-buht* would have understood it at the time they signed. The judges noted that the Treaty of Neah Bay did not limit the tribe to a particular method of hunting and that the tribe could "use evolving technology to facilitate more efficient hunting."[105] Even though the tribe has maintained that their hunts would always respect the environment, the judges were not convinced this would be the case. They said, "But if a treaty right is presented, it is not necessarily limited to the approvals of the IWC or the Tribe's Gray Whale Management Plan. The intent of Congress cannot be hostage to the goodwill or good judgment or good sense of the particular leaders empowered by the Tribe at present."[106] Whereas the Canons of Construction established that Indian treaties must be liberally construed in favor of the Indians, the judges' analysis in *Anderson* was anything but "liberal." It appeared that the court was using worst-case scenarios to guide its decision.

As I have demonstrated in previous chapters, Native whaling tradition was and still is integral to our cultures. During the last half of the nineteenth century, whaling was an important aspect of the U.S. economy, which was reflected in the "in common" clause of the Makah treaty. Whaling, however, is *not* integral to U.S. culture. Using its *Fryberg* test, the Ninth Circuit Court of Appeals argued that the MMPA extended to "any person subject to the jurisdiction of the United States" and that the Act did not "discriminate between treaty and non-treaty persons because members of the Tribe are not singled out any more than non-treaty people."[107] The court overlooked the cultural significance of whaling to the Makah people and ignored the fact that preserving whaling rights was an essential element of the treaty negotiation process. The Treaty of Neah Bay was to secure and "protect" the Makah people's whaling right. Courts must uphold these treaty rights and interpret them liberally to safeguard tribal culture and traditions. The Ninth Circuit Court failed to uphold the treaty's protective purpose and thus undermined the third and fourth canons of construction by failing to interpret the treaty in a way that would be favorable to the tribe and by neglecting its protective purpose.[108]

With respect to Native people, the 1972 MMPA text mentions exemptions only for Alaska Natives. Alaska Natives did not sign treaties with the United States. A 1981 House Report for Amendments states that "the native exemption . . . does not apply to Indians, Aleuts or Eskimos" who reside in states other than Alaska.[109] Because Alaska Natives did not sign treaties and, therefore, do not have a treaty-protected right to hunt marine mammals, Congress needed to provide them with an MMPA exemption in order to recognize Alaska Natives' subsistence hunting practices. Therefore, the statute did not contain any mention of tribes that have treaty rights to hunt marine mammals. Because the Makah tribe had a treaty right to hunt whales, it was unnecessary for Congress to give them an exemption from the Act.[110] In 1994 the MMPA was amended to clarify the statute's objective with respect to Indian treaties: "Nothing in this Act . . . alters or is intended to alter any treaty between the United States and one or more Indian tribes."[111] The amendment is explicit in demonstrating that the federal government's objective was *not* to impact, modify, or abrogate Indian treaties through the MMPA.

The Makah and the U.S. government petitioned to have the *Anderson v. Evans* case reheard. The courts reviewed the case and on June 7, 2004, gave its ruling. The Ninth Circuit Court of Appeals refused to reconsider its decision.[112]

STARTING OVER

The Makah were frustrated over the complications of the legal system, which now put a judicial hold on their treaty right to whale. Following the *Evans v. Anderson* ruling, the Makah tribe was placed in a difficult position. They could ignore the ruling and assert their right to whale, which meant they would have to face legal repercussions. They could push the issue into the Supreme Court, which at the time *Anderson* was decided was a very conservative court and could further undermine their treaty rights. Or they could abide by the decision. They chose the last alternative. Eight months after the Court of Appeals declined to review its earlier ruling, the tribe submitted a letter to NOAA in February 2005, requesting a waiver of the MMPA to hunt whales for ceremonial and subsistence purposes:

> The Tribe strongly disagrees with the Court's holding but is filing this application to provide a legal framework that will allow for long-term exercise of its treaty whaling rights consistent with the needs of the gray whale. Approval of this waiver request is needed to meet the Tribe's cultural and subsistence needs and to fulfill the United States government's Treaty and trust obligations to the Tribe.[113]

In its application, the tribe proposed whaling regulations with severe restrictions on where and when whales could be hunted. The regulations were sensitive to the Pacific Coast Feeding Aggregation. As a way to place the least impact on the PCFA, the regulations prohibited hunts between June 1 and November 30. The waiver application stated that the purpose of this seasonal restriction was "to prevent the intentional harvest of whales that may be part of the Pacific Coast Feeding Aggregation."[114] The regulations provided that the tribe would conduct detailed photographic monitoring of all landed whales and compare these photos with NOAA's National Marine Mammal Laboratory photo-identification catalogue for the PCFA to determine if the whale caught was from this group.[115]

Following *Anderson v. Evans*, NOAA initiated the EIS process and began holding public meetings to solicit Washington State residents' comments and advice on the Makah whale hunts. These meetings were similar to the meetings held for the EA and were part of a review process under NEPA that would provide public input for the EIS. According to Micah McCarty, the EIS was way behind schedule by the summer of 2008, and many of the tribal members were becoming frustrated with the process.[116]

"I'M NOT ASHAMED": THE 2007 WHALE HUNT

On September 9, 2007, almost five years after *Anderson v. Evans* banned the Makah tribe from hunting whales legally, five male members of the Makah tribe, frustrated with the inability to exercise their right to whale and irritated by what they saw as the federal government's sluggish pace in formulating an EIS and working through the MMPA waiver process, decided that they had had enough. At around 6:30 A.M., Wayne Johnson, Frankie Gonzales, Andrew Noel, Theron Parker, and William Secor Sr. headed out to the open seas in two motorized boats, just east of Neah Bay.[117] Around three hours later, they came upon a forty-foot gray whale, which surfaced alongside the two boats. Johnson later told reporters that the whale had come to them, that "it chose [them]."[118] The men first harpooned the whale and then shot it. They then attached buoys to it to keep the whale afloat so they could bring it back to Neah Bay.[119]

Immediately after hearing the shots, the Coast Guard dispatched a boat to the area and placed the men in custody, confiscating their gun and boats. The whale had a harpoon line still attached to it. The Coast Guard cut the line and the whale, which was mortally wounded, was left to die. The whole process took close to eleven hours. The Makah tribal members heard about what had happened. While many of them had conflicting feelings about the hunt, they all mourned the slow death of the whale and could not understand why the Coast Guard had left the whale to die on its own. "Why waste it like that?" one tribal member asked. "Now it really has died for no purpose."[120] Makah members went out to see the whale and performed sacred songs over its dying body. One of the men, tribal spiritual leader Joe McGimpsey, said, "It wouldn't have been right to let the whale die alone."[121]

This hunt was not authorized by the Makah Tribal Council, nor did it receive federal government approval. The following day the council issued a statement, which was printed in the *Seattle Times,* condemning the hunt:

> The Makah Tribal Council denounces the actions of those who took it upon themselves to hunt a whale without the authority from the Makah Tribal Coun-

cil or the Makah Whaling Commission. Their action was a blatant violation of our law and they will be prosecuted to the fullest extent of the law. . . . The tribe has demonstrated extraordinary patience in waiting for the legal process to be completed in order to receive our permit to conduct a whale hunt. We are a law-abiding people and we will not tolerate lawless conduct by any of our members. We hope the public does not permit the actions of five irresponsible persons to be used to harm the image of the entire Makah tribe.[122]

When tribal chairman Micah McCarty heard what had happened, he felt torn.[123] He told me that, on the one hand, he could understand the frustration of these men, whose right to whale had been tied up in lawsuits for many years, but, he added, the men should have waited until the waiver process was completed and should have gotten permission from the Makah Tribal Council and the Whaling Commission. Even more important, he said, "they should have thought about their community and the negative impact their unauthorized hunt would have on the Makah people."[124]

Immediately after the hunt, one of the men involved, Wayne Johnson, told the media that he had no regrets and that he was tired of spending the last eight years battling in the courts over permission to do what he felt was his birthright.[125] Johnson, who was also the captain of the 1999 Makah hunt, said he conducted this whale hunt to keep the Makah whaling culture alive. "I'm not ashamed," he told the media. "I come from a whaling family. . . . It's in the blood."[126] He later told the media, "The five of us did this to protect the kids," adding that if they do not exercise their treaty right, "we don't have one."[127]

In October 2007, a federal grand jury indicted Johnson and the other four men on charges of conspiracy, violations of the International Convention for the Regulation of Whaling, and violation of the Marine Mammal Protection Act. All are misdemeanor charges punishable by up to a year in jail and a $100,000 fine on each count. In a courtroom filled with supporters from their Neah Bay community, all five men entered pleas of not guilty. Outside the federal courthouse, Makah elders held signs that read: "Broken trust." One elder, Gail Adams, said they were there to support their young people and that "they shouldn't have to pay a fine" or "go to jail."[128]

This hunt, like the one the Makah conducted in 1999, also generated considerable discourse around the Makah Nation's treaty right to hunt whales. Immediately following the media announcement that the Makah had conducted what was defined as a "rogue" whale hunt, a fisherman in Bellingham put a sign on his truck stating his support for the Makah's right to hunt whales.[129] Others were not so supportive. One reader from Tacoma wrote to the *Seattle Times*, saying that the Makah need to adhere to the laws like everyone else in the United States. The reader was also disturbed by the fact that this whaling crew used a motorized boat and a gun in their hunt. "If they did it the way they used to do it, with the harpoon and canoe, it'd probably be fine with me."[130]

The day after the hunt, the *Seattle Times* set up a Reader Feedback Web site with the caption: "Five Makah Nation members harpooned and shot a gray whale east of Neah Bay yesterday morning, shocking environmentalists and tribal leaders alike. What are your thoughts on the hunt?" In two days the newspaper received over ninety comments from readers whose opinions on the hunt ranged from support to opposition to uncertainty. One person sympathized with the Makah Nation, commenting that these men's actions might negatively impact the tribe. At the same time, the reader questioned the men's use of "nontraditional" equipment in their hunt: "This is a very sad time for the Makah Nation. These 5 people are ruining it for the rest of the tribe. And a note on this type of whaling . . . since when do machine guns and motorized boats preserve a culture?"[131] A Native man wrote about his repugnance at the hatred and racism shown Native people when they exercised traditions that non-Native society did not agree with:

> I try to balance everything I think about, good vs bad, right vs wrong etc. I am proud to be native. I am also an animal lover. I was at the celebration back when the first whale was caught a few years back to support my heritage. I was appalled and scared at the same time by people, media and protesters calling us savages and killers, and what this latest incident will cause again. Thinking about history up to the present, what nerve people have to throw such judgment, hatred and accusation, why not raise such uproar and [be] quick to convict farmers, hunters and so-called animal "caregivers" who abuse, neglect, harm and torture animals. . . . Please throw hatred their way and convict them to the fullest extent (there are many more than the 5 "rogue" killers that people are condemning with this incident). My family and my heritage deal enough with hatred, racism, judgment and shun from society and the media.[132]

Another reader from Lynnwood wrote about the Makah men's use of "tradition" to justify the killing of a whale:

> I am saddened by this act of cruelty. We need to start realizing these are intelligent, nurturing, caring creatures. I hope this leads to the end of this practice. As a non-native American, my own ancestors did many cruel things too, to both

animal and human alike. No one accepts these practices anymore and we have no right to do those things in our day and age. We have no right to say, "but this is our tradition!" Because hopefully we as a species are growing past all those things. We need to stop killing animals altogether.[133]

A lawyer from Lacey wrote:

> The Makah Nation was granted the right to hunt whales under the 1855 treaty. They were granted that right as consideration for giving up tribal land. If we do not allow them to hunt whales then we should be required to give them the land they traded in the treaty back.[134]

Even the Makah tribal members themselves were at odds in their responses to their fellow tribal members' actions. Arnie Hunter, vice chairman of the Makah Whaling Commission, felt that these men did nothing wrong and were simply exercising a right that was secured in their treaty. The whaling tradition, he said, "is something we grew up with. It's our songs. It's our dances. It's who we are. We are whale hunters, and our forefathers reserved that for us in the treaty."[135] But Ed Claplanhoo, who is also a member of the commission, worried about the legal repercussions for the Makah from this unlawful hunt. "We are a law-abiding people," he said. "This . . . puts kind of a black eye on us. I thought it was wrong."[136]

Micah McCarty said that many people in the Makah community were discouraged over the slow and lengthy federal process to secure an MMPA waiver and for NOAA to complete the EIS. "A lot of our people have become disillusioned with the system," Micah said. "People have become frustrated at these challenges to our way of life. Some people turn to chemical dependency as a way of self-medicating their frustrations. . . . But the strongest medicine is always our cultural values and cultural practices," which, he felt, is why the Makah were trying to revitalize their whaling culture.[137]

Darrell Markishtum, one of the 1999 whaling crew members, said that the frustration goes beyond the current whaling issue. The *Seattle Post-Intelligencer* newspaper conducted a study a few years ago that examined the Pacific Coast salmon industry. The study found that sportsfishermen, on average, were catching over three times the limit placed on the sport salmon fishery. However, Markishtum said, the Makah and other Native tribes are continually monitored to make sure that they adhere to the salmon quota established for them. He asserts that the Makah tribe has carefully managed its fisheries, as well as other resources, continually looking at ways to protect both the salmon stocks and their habitat.

The Makah "are making every attempt to work within the legal system, yet, as soon as they do something that non-Indians see as wrong, they get attacked."[138] Most people within the Makah community are ambivalent about the recent Makah whale hunt, but, he adds, even though they are not happy with these men conducting an unauthorized hunt, "they do support their right to whale."[139]

In March 2008, three of the men—Frankie Gonzales, Theron Parker, and William Secor Sr.—entered guilty pleas in federal court to one misdemeanor charge of taking a whale in violation of the Marine Mammal Protection Act.[140] Their plea was part of an agreement that was offered to all five men the month before: if the men pled guilty to the MMPA violation charge, Judge J. Kelley Arnold would drop the other charges. The judge dismissed the conspiracy charge and ruled that the language of the Whaling Convention Act on criminal violations was too vague to apply to this case. He also dropped the charge of conducting a whale hunt that contravened the Makah tribe's Whale Management Plan because the plan had expired before the hunt took place.[141]

The other two men, Wayne Johnson and Andy Noel, did not take the plea agreement and chose to stand trial. They were found guilty of the same charges as the other men, of taking a whale in violation of the MMPA.[142] Johnson and Noel had considered the plea agreement but decided they would go forward with a trial when the judge told them there was a possibility that they would have to forfeit their right to whale during their probation period. Although the federal prosecutors decided not to impose this stipulation, the two men said they had lost their trust in the government and were reluctant to accept the plea deal for fear that the prosecutors would still put "conditions" on their probation.[143] And, the two men said, they were going to stand trial as a matter of principle. They understood that pleading guilty implied that they had done something illegal and that they were accepting that the MMPA applied to the Treaty of Neah Bay. The men believed that they were just exercising a right to whale guaranteed to them under their 1855 treaty.[144]

Johnson and Noel also waived their right to a jury trial so they could appeal their convictions to the Ninth Circuit Court of Appeals.[145] Jack Fiander, the attorney representing Andy Noel, intended to use religious freedom as a defense, because the federal government's slow pace in dealing with the MMPA permit process and EIS was interfering with these men's exercise of their religious liberty, which is protected by the First Amendment. Fiander said that denying these men the right to whale was "like telling you that you can't go to church."[146] But, during Judge Arnold's pretrial ruling, he barred a defense based on religious freedom, saying that this was a "protest hunt" and was not based on these men's religious beliefs. Fiander retorted that the judge had no right to make this ruling and that there would be no reason to go through a jury trial if the men would not even be allowed to present their defense.[147] So Noel and Johnson submitted a document to the court that admitted they hunted a whale, and the judge found them guilty. According to Fiander, this is what Noel and Johnson wanted so that they could appeal their case to a District Court judge.[148]

On June 30 Judge Arnold handed down his sentence for the five men. He sentenced Wayne Johnson to five months in jail and Andy Noel to ninety days. They were also to serve one year's probation and perform community service. The other three men (Secor, Parker, and Gonzales) received two years' probation and were ordered to perform 100 to 150 hours of community service. In his sentencing, Judge Arnold stated: "They decided to take the law into their own hands. They defied their own community and the laws of this country, which they well knew."[149]

Johnson's and Noel's decision to appeal the case had some Makah tribal members concerned. Many felt that the ruling in *Anderson v. Evans* undermined their treaty rights, and some Makah members were worried that another legal opinion could further erode these rights, especially if the ruling determined that the federal authorities could regulate their treaty whaling right without Congress's authorization.[150]

"TRUSTING" THE FEDERAL TRUST RESPONSIBILITY

Johnson, who spent three months in federal custody awaiting his court appeal, feared that the Makah's 1855 treaty was becoming another symbol on the long trail of broken federal promises, claiming that "the government has dwindled our treaty down to nothing" by allowing lawsuits and bureaucracy to impede their treaty right to whale.[151] Between 1787 and 1871 the United States entered into nearly four hundred treaties with the indigenous nations. In these treaties the tribes ceded vast portions of their traditional territories. In return, the United States set aside reservation lands, which it held in trust for the Indian nations. The United States also guaranteed to respect and honor the tribes' sovereignty and to protect the rights that the tribes reserved in their treaties.[152] The federal government's trust obligation to tribes is rooted in the treaty process.

The trust responsibility is one of the most important principles in federal Indian law and was developed into a doctrine that originated from Chief Justice John Marshall's opinions in two seminal Supreme Court cases, *Cherokee Nation v. Georgia* (1831) and *Worcester v. Georgia* (1832).[153] In these cases, the court acknowledged that tribes were nations with their own governments, their own laws, and their own customs. A tribe was, as Justice Marshall asserted, "a distinct political society, separated from others, capable of managing its own affairs and governing itself."[154] Justice Marshall stated that all "the rights secured to these Indians, under the treaties made with them, remain unimpaired." But, Marshall noted, when tribes signed treaties, they placed themselves "under the protection of the United States.[155] He described the relationship that developed between the United States and the tribes as one that "resembles that of a ward to his guardian" because the tribes look to the federal government for protection. Therefore, he defined tribes as "domestic dependant nations."[156]

The Marshall decisions created the notion that Congress, the judiciary, and the executive branch each have a fiduciary obligation to Native Americans that governs the federal government's standards of conduct toward tribal lands, resources, and culture. Tribes envision the trust principle as entailing four inter-related components:

> that the federal government—or its agents—was pledged to protect tribal property and sovereignty and would not move for or against tribes without first secur-ing tribal consent; that the United States would act with the utmost integrity in its legal and political commitments to Indian peoples as outlined in treaties or governmental policies (e.g., provide health care, educational support, housing assistance); that the United States would act in a moral manner regarding tribal rights, as the Judeo-Christian nation it historically professed to be in its dealing with tribes; and that the United States would continue to support any additional duties and responsibilities in its self-assumed role as the Indian's "protectors."[157]

When tribes signed treaties, they trusted that the federal government would protect the rights that were reserved in these agreements. Only after their right to whale was written into the treaty did the *chah-chah-buht* agree to have their names added. Micah McCarty believes that the federal government has not upheld its trust responsibility to the Makah tribe. "We have a cultural right to whale," Micah asserts. "The federal government needs to step up and take responsibility and honor its trust responsibility to us."[158]

THE DRAFT EIS IS RELEASED

On May 9, 2008, five and a half years after *Anderson v. Evans* ordered NOAA to conduct an environmental impact review, the NMFS completed its 900-page draft

EIS and released it for public comment. To establish a wide range of alternatives, the NMFS examined closely the following components of whaling: the area where whaling would occur; the annual and five-year limits on the number of whales harvested, struck, and struck and lost; termination of whale hunting if a predetermined number of identified whales were harvested (this includes the Pacific Coast Feeding Aggregation); and the method of whaling. Based on these factors, the NMFS came up with seven options for issuing a quota to the Makah tribe to hunt gray whale:

Alternative 1 does not allow a whale hunt.

Alternative 2 allows a harvest of four gray whales per year (with a maximum of five in one year) and up to twenty whales in a five-year period. Hunting would begin December 1 and end May 31 and would take place in the Makah tribe's usual and accustomed whaling areas. Hunting would be forbidden within 200 yards of Tatoosh Island and White Rock. Seven whales could be struck in one year with a maximum of thirty-five whales over the five-year period. Three whales could be struck and lost in one year with a maximum of fifteen in the five-year period.

Alternative 3 is the same as Alternative 2, but it removes the timing, killing, and landing restrictions.

Alternative 4 is the same as Alternative 2, but it prohibits Makah, protest, media, and law-enforcement vessels from entering the 200-yard exclusionary zone established by the U.S. Fish and Wildlife Service in the Washington Islands National Wildlife Refuges area.

Alternative 5 includes the same hunting area as Alternative 2, but it eliminates the timing and landing restrictions and imposes additional restrictions on the number of whales harvested, struck, and struck and lost.

Alternative 6 is the same as Alternative 3, except that it lifts the hunting area restrictions. It also removes the timing restrictions and harvest limitations.[159]

Out of the six alternatives studied in the draft EIS, the NMFS recommended Alternative 2, which placed the most severe restrictions on the Makah whale hunt and included many prohibitions that were not included in the environmental assessments. Alternative 2 was also the one that corresponded with the Makah tribe's proposed regulations set out in their 2005/6 waiver requests. It prohibited hunts from June 1 to November 30, which would "avoid any intentional harvest of gray whales that have been identified within the PCFA survey area outside of times that coincide with the summer feeding period."[160] The EIS states that the Makah tribe "could use both traditional and modern methods of hunting whales to balance the preservation of traditional cultural methods, safety, and the need for increased efficiency." Similar to the EA, the EIS states that there would be no commercial aspects to the whale hunt but the tribal members could utilize whale products for artwork, which could be sold. As well, all tribal members involved in the hunt would have to go through a training and certification process and spiritual preparation (also requirements for the 1999 hunt).[161]

According to McCarty, a whale hunt under this proposed alternative would take place under the worst conditions because of the restrictions placed on the time when a hunt could be conducted. The weather and water are more severe during this time. And the whales are migrating north to south during this time, so they travel farther away from the shores because they are not feeding, which makes the hunts more dangerous for the whaling crew. However, McCarty said, the Makah Whaling Commission could revise its whaling plan to include hunts with motorized boats to accommodate the hunts that would be farther out in the open sea and extremely difficult to conduct in a canoe.[162]

The tribe also would revise its whaling plan to limit the hunting of nonmigrating whales. If a nonmigrating whale was landed, the hunt would end, without completing the four-whale quota. According to McCarty, they decided to take this more restrictive approach to their hunts in order to demonstrate their commitment to ensuring that their hunts would not damage the ecosystem and would not jeopardize the Pacific Coast Feeding Aggregation.[163]

Once the Makah tribe fulfills the requirements established in *Anderson v. Evans*, an administrative law judge will look over all the documents and determine if they are in compliance with the MMPA and NEPA. This will take place before an MMPA waiver is even considered. This is an open process and people from both sides of the whaling issue will be allowed to submit briefs to the judge. Once this process is completed, the judge will make a recommended decision, which the Ninth Circuit Court will accept or reject.[164]

◆ ◆ ◆

Will the anti-whaling groups and the courts accept the exhaustive studies contained within the comprehensive 900-page draft EIS that shows that Makah whale hunts will pose no risk to the gray whale population, including the ones they call resident whales? Or will they continue to base their argument against Makah whaling on moral grounds and ignore the fact that more than 480 whales can be removed from the eastern North Pacific gray whale population and it will still retain a healthy sustainable growth. Is this a clash between the Makah tribe's cultural rights and the rights of animals? Or is this a clash between cultures?

There are many definitions for the term "culture." A dictionary definition refers to "culture" as "patterns of human activity and the symbolic structures that give such activities significance and importance."[165] Drawing on these many definitions, culture can be viewed as a system of shared beliefs, values, customs, behaviors, and art that the members of a society use to make sense of their world—these are passed on from generation to generation.[166] A problem arises when other societies do not respect or understand your culture and, as a result, look to find ways to suppress it and/or destroy it. Native professor and lawyer Robert Miller writes,

> The dominant American society reflects its religious and cultural values. American citizens are so accustomed to these activities that few people question the right of the dominant society to honor and observe its cultural and religious values. It is another issue, however, when a minority religion or culture wants to follow its traditional precepts but they conflict with majority interests.[167]

Why are Native people denied the same rights to preserve and practice their cultures and traditions as granted to other people in the world? Anti-whaling protestors led a successful legal campaign to stop the Makah from exercising their cultural right to whale. These groups imposed their own belief and value systems on the Makah people, which can be viewed as cultural imperialism. President of the Makah Whaling Commission Keith Johnson says that scientific studies demonstrate that the gray whale population is healthy. Johnson asks: Are the people who are attempting to stop their hunts basing their reasoning on science, law, and treaty rights? Or are they basing their decisions on "their own personal point of view"?

The people who oppose hunting whales argue that there is an environmental risk to whaling and that allowing Native peoples to exercise traditions could lead other groups around the world to claim their cultural or subsistence rights and thus pose a potential risk to the environment. Were Native peoples the ones who decimated the whale populations in the first place? No. We have always lived in harmony with the whale and with nature, and our sustainable use of our resources and our utilization of the environment has always been conducted with respect. Why should our culture and traditions be sacrificed upon the altar of the non-Indian conscience to pay for the environmental sins of the dominant culture?[168]

7 / *Atlpu*

RESTORING *NANASH AQTL* COMMUNITIES

ALTHOUGH THE MAKAH AND NUU-CHAH-NULTH PEOPLES NO LONGER need to whale for subsistence, introducing whale products back into our diets is important for our well-being and community health. The whale's nutritional value could help to alleviate some of the health problems that plague our communities. And because our traditional foods have cultural, social, and spiritual significance, the harvesting and sharing of these foods unite our communities while putting *nanash'aqtl* (healthy) food on our dinner tables. The revival of the prayers, songs, ceremonies, and stories that are integral to our whaling tradition have the power to reinvigorate in us a sense of sacredness and gratitude for being given the spiritual gift of whale as food.

HEALTH AND DISEASE IN NATIVE COMMUNITIES

In numerous studies conducted on indigenous peoples globally, it has been found that indigenous communities have the worst health and nutrition in all countries worldwide.[1] Today, Native peoples in Canada and the United States suffer from chronic, debilitating, and life-threatening illnesses, such as heart disease, diabetes, rheumatoid arthritis, autoimmune diseases, and obesity. In many of these communities, these diseases are on the increase and are much higher than in the general Canadian and American populations.[2]

Data gathered from Statistics Canada census and surveys and Health Canada and Indian and Northern Affairs Canada databases and research studies show that Native peoples in Canada have disproportionately higher rates of chronic diseases and lower life expectancy rates than the overall general Canadian population.[3] Prior to the 1940s, diabetes was virtually unknown among Native people in Canada.[4] Today, studies in Canada show that the incidence of type-2 diabetes is three to five times higher than in the general population.[5] In some First Nations communities, diabetes has doubled in the last twenty years;[6] in some, over 55 percent of the population has been diagnosed with the disease.[7] One study in British Columbia showed that Native communities suffer from higher rates of mortality from diabetes than any other race of people in the general population.[8] In the United States, diabetes among Native Americans and Alaska Natives has also continued to increase over the last sixty years and in some communities is in epidemic proportions. The highest occurrence of diabetes in the world has been found among the Pima Indians in Arizona.[9]

Diabetes has become a serious problem in my own community, as well as in other Nuu-chah-nulth communities. Elder Trudy Frank, from the village of Ahousaht, is actively involved with her community's Tee Cha Chitl (Getting Well Again) group, a family-centered program that teaches Nuu-chah-nulth people to understand and manage diabetes in their families. "We are eating too much sugared stuff now, that's why we have an uprise in diabetes," Trudy says. She points a finger at the federal government's boarding school system and the introduction of nonnutritious foods into Nuu-chah-nulth communities. The foods offered in these schools were mostly high in both fat and sugar.

> When we got to residential school we were supposed to eat what was put in front of us. And it was none of our type of food. They'd make fun of us if we wanted to have some boiled fish heads or something like that. They used to call us savages because we ate all this . . . natural foods. If we were hungry [for traditional foods] they used to say, "Oh, the savage in you is coming out." You know, we learned to eat processed food, we learned to eat sweetened food. So, we had no choice in what we had to eat.[10]

Chief Simon Lucas sees the rise in diabetes and other diseases in Nuu-chah-nulth communities as a direct result of a change in eating patterns. Growing up in the 1940s, Simon said, everyday meals in the small isolated village of Hesquiaht consisted of foods from the marine-based economy: "There was smoked fish, canned fish, and fresh fish, clams, and sea urchins, all the foods that surrounded us; that was part of my life."[11] But when his family moved to an urban area, they began to accept processed foods and ultimately began to turn away from their more nutritious traditional foods. In 1980 he noticed his first symptom associated with diabetes, which was a tingling in his fingertips. The symptoms progressed throughout the years, leading to the full development of the disease.[12]

While type-2 diabetes has been a significant health problem for Native adult men and women for over forty years, recent studies reveal that it is becoming a serious health issue for Native children, adolescents, and young adults as well. One U.S. study showed that between 1990 and 1998, type-2 diabetes increased among American Indians and Alaska Natives under age thirty-five by 46 percent. This was over 35 percent higher than in the general U.S population under forty-five years, among whom the increase in this disease was 14 percent.[13] A 2004 study conducted by the Indian Health Service (IHS) on Native Americans and Alaskan Natives under the age of thirty-five found that diabetes had doubled in this age group in a ten-year period. At the start of the study in 1994, a little over 6,000 Native people thirty-five and younger had diabetes. Ten years later, this number was over 12,000. The study also found that the risk of contracting diabetes increased with age and incidents were higher among females.[14]

Diabetes leads to other illnesses and health concerns, such as cardiovascular disease, kidney failure, blindness, lower-extremity amputation, disability, and a decreased quality of life. The risk of developing type-2 diabetes increases with obesity and physical inactivity.[15] Community studies conducted in Canada on obesity in First Nations children and youth reveal serious childhood obesity problems.[16] It was found that in some First Nations communities close to 50 percent of the children were clinically obese.[17] Childhood obesity causes high blood pressure, high levels of fat and insulin in the blood, increased blood clotting, joint problems, gall stones, and sleep apnea. Many of these health issues lead to heart disease and diabetes when the children get older.[18]

As diabetes continues to rise within Native communities, cardiovascular disease has become a major concern for Native populations and is the leading cause of death in both Canada and the United States.[19] In the States, cardiovascular disease accounts for 30 percent of all Native American deaths.[20] In the 1990s the risk of mortality from heart disease in Native populations in both countries was considerably lower than in any other population group. Today, the rates have climbed dramatically and a Native person's risk of death from heart disease is becoming higher than in the non-Indian population.[21] In Canada, First Nations people living in reserve communities have rates of heart disease 16 percent higher than the general population.[22] Overall, the presence of heart disease in First Nations people is three times more than in the general Canadian population.[23]

Research studies have shown that diet plays a huge role in the development of many illnesses, including diabetes and cardiovascular disease.[24] Simon Lucas says that many people do not understand the psychological effects of diseases on individuals and on whole Native communities: "People don't understand that when you're sick your spirituality is affected, your mentality." He worries that Native people are moving away from the teachings of their elders. "We got to take back these great teachings," Simon says, in order for our Nuu-chah-nulth communities to become healthy again.[25]

MAKING OUR COMMUNITIES *NANASH AQTL* (HEALTHY) AGAIN

Dietary changes from traditional foods to processed foods high in saturated fat and sugar, along with more sedentary lifestyles, led to the rise in many diseases in Native communities today. As a way to overcome these major health problems in both Canada and the United States, Native people are starting to look at ways to reincorporate traditional foods into their diets and to restore cultural food practices. Before the arrival of *mamalhn'i*, the indigenous peoples of the Northwest Coast lived in natural environments that were rich in resources. Marine-based economies provided them with wholesome food that not only sustained their communities but were rich in vitamins and minerals. For the Makah and Nuu-chah-nulth, whaling was the foundation of the economic structure. Our societies maintained optimum health by consuming large quantities of meat, fat, and oil from whales and other sea mammals, which provided health-promoting nourishment and an overall sense of well-being.[26] Federal policies and the commercial over-harvesting of whales severed us from this nutritious food source. Today, Makah and Nuu-chah-nulth health is a long way from that of our ancestors, and our communities, as well as other indigenous communities worldwide, suffer from chronic, debilitating, and life-threatening diseases, largely because of dietary changes.[27]

Recent studies conducted among the indigenous groups in northern Canada and Alaska are discovering the health benefits of sea mammal meat, blubber, and fat. Clinical trials being conducted on indigenous whaling peoples throughout the world found that a traditional diet rich in sea mammal oil dramatically decreased the risk of death from heart disease, reduced symptoms of diabetes, and helped alleviate symptoms of arthritis and other chronic diseases.[28] A study in the mid- and late 1990s of marine-based Native peoples living in northern Canada found that their traditional diets high in sea mammal fats provide essential nutrients that promote healthy lifestyles. The study found that beluga and narwhal whale oil, meat, blubber, and *mattak* (or *muktuk*; a whale's outer layer of skin and fat) are high in the essential vitamins A, E, and D. Diets that are low in vitamin D have been linked to diabetes and autoimmune diseases.[29]

Studies with indigenous people whose traditional diets are high in n-3 fatty acids have shown that essential fatty acids derived from fish and sea mammal oils improve metabolic health, decrease cardiovascular disease, and reduce the risk of developing type-2 diabetes.[30] The traditional diet of the Inuit of Nunavik in northern Canada, which consists mainly of beluga whale, seal, fish, and caribou, rich in n-3 fatty acids, has been directly linked to low rates of heart disease. In the 1950s, the Inuit briefly moved away from their marine-based diet as they became more reliant on market and store-based food products. As a result, they experienced an increase in high blood pressure, diabetes, and obesity.[31] In the 1970s, the trend toward market foods began to change, and the Inuit turned back to their traditional foods to alleviate some of their health concerns. Further studies conducted on the same people in the 1990s showed that as they began to incorporate more traditional foods, especially marine mammals and fish, back into their diets, the incidence of disease went down.[32] A 2001 study has also shown that a diet of marine mammals and fish continues to be popular among the Inuit, and benefits to their health continue to accrue with their ongoing use of traditional foods.[33]

Medical experts have now begun to look at ways to treat diseases such as high blood pressure and diabetes through a prescribed diet and supplements that are high in n-3 fatty acids. Initial studies on the Inuit people living in Greenland showed a correlation between a low prevalence of coronary heart disease and a diet high in sea mammals and fish. Additional research with groups in Japan, Alaska, and the Faroe Islands produced the same results. Patients with type-1 and type-2 diabetes have an increased risk of heart disease. Dietary n-3 fatty acids lower blood pressure and thus reduce the risk of this disease.[34]

As Northern Native peoples continue to focus their attention on increasing the amount of sea mammal oil, blubber, and meat in their diets, there is a growing concern about exposure to toxic mercury. Studies conducted on the beluga whale, the whale most heavily consumed by the people in northern Canada and Alaska, have shown that those whales often exhibit high levels of mercury contamination. Mercury is a naturally occurring element that is released into the environment through degassing of the earth's surface, volcanic eruptions, mineral deposits, forest fires, and emissions from water surfaces. It is also a product of human activity, such as metal production, chlor-alkali and pulp industries, waste treatment, and wood burning. Because mercury is naturally occurring, it has always been present in the Inuit diet. In fact, a 2006 study showed that although higher levels of mercury have been found in modern beluga whales, historic Inuit populations had higher concentrations of mercury in their diets because they consumed more whales than today's population. The study concluded that more research needed to be done on mercury health risks in diets rich in marine mammals.[35]

Dr. Jim Berner, director of community health with the Alaska Native Tribal Health Consortium, has been analyzing the studies that look at whether industrial contaminants and heavy metals that concentrate in the tissues and muscles of marine mammals make them too risky to eat. He says it is true that marine mammals have been found to have increasing levels of mercury in recent years, but these sea mammals, especially whales, also have elevated levels of the mineral selenium and vitamin E that could counteract the effects of the mercury.[36] Selenium is an antioxidant and anticarcinogen that may exert an antagonistic effect on mercury toxicity. This could explain why mercury toxicity is absent among Native people even though they have high concentrations of mercury in their blood from diets rich in sea mammals and fish.[37] And because whale meat is high in iron and the blubber contains fat that has been found to reduce heart disease and boost immune systems, Dr. Berner argues that the benefits of eating whale meat considerably outweigh the risks.[38]

Other studies have found high levels of mercury concentrations in fish and marine mammals. But the threat of overexposure appears to be low, and avoidance of traditional foods could cause other health risks, such as the obesity, diabetes, and cardiovascular disease associated with a more Westernized diet.[39] The conclusion from all of the studies is that increasing n-3 fatty acids derived from sea mammal oil in diets can alleviate many chronic illnesses that are prevalent in Native communities today.

"I AM WHAT I AM BECAUSE OF WHAT I EAT": THE CULTURAL IMPORTANCE AND PSYCHOLOGICAL SIGNIFICANCE OF EATING TRADITIONAL FOODS

While there are studies that show that a return to traditional foods will promote health and wellness, Native people are also returning to these foods for cultural reasons. For Native people, traditional food is sacred and has a spiritual connection to the world we live in. At their first annual Indigenous Food Sovereignty conference, First Nations groups from the interior of British Columbia came together to discuss ways to control and secure access to their traditional foods. Like indigenous people throughout the world, the Ktunaxa, Nlaka'pamux, Secwepemc, St'at'imc, Syilx, and Ts'ilqotin peoples believe that they and their land, language, and food are one in an interconnected web of life.

The underlying eco-philosophy and worldview embedded in our Interior Salishan languages and tribal social structures emphasize good relationships between all of creation. Therefore, our relationship with the land, plants, and animals that make up our food systems embodies a deep and profound gratitude and spiritual understanding of the sacredness of the gift of food.[40]

Studies of the indigenous whaling nations in the Arctic demonstrate how traditional foods, especially whales, have social, cultural, spiritual, and psychological value. As stated by the Inuit, "I am what I am because of what I eat."[41] A high value is placed on whales because they are a healthy food source and contribute a large quantity of food for Inuit subsistence. However, whale hunts also maintain community solidarity and collective security through communal hunting, processing, distributing, and consuming of whale products by the community members.[42] Whaling is at the center of Inuit life and "serves to link Inuit symbolically and spiritually to their cultural heritage."[43] Not only are the oil of *mattak/muktuk* and meat consumed for their nutritional benefits, but they also satisfy emotional and psychological needs. The widespread sharing among relatives and the community, as well as with other Inuit communities, serves to create and sustain the bonds that remain the basis of Inuit social and economic relationships in the Arctic regions; bonds that are critical to Inuit cultural survival.[44] Don Long, an Inuit whaler from the Alaskan Eskimo community of Barrow, describes how the sharing of the whale instills in his people a sense of community through the wide sharing of the prized *mattak* and whale meat and oil.

> Why did I become a whaling captain? Because of the opportunity to feed the community. . . . The whale basically to me is a community whale. I get my share like everyone else, but you have the honour of feeding your community after a whale is caught. And the sharing . . . is where the attributes of culture haven't changed. . . . It's not that we go whaling for individual gain; it's for community gain.[45]

Wales is a small Inupiat community in northwest Alaska. The people in Wales have maintained their marine-based economy and continue to hunt bowhead whales, seals, and walrus. They also rely on land-based foods, such as caribou, for their survival. The Inupiat villages revolve around family networks of sharing. Each family group harvests, processes, and shares their subsistence foods. These networks harvest an annual average of 2,268 pounds of food per household (744 pounds per person). Thus, the concept of sharing not only works to unite the communities and maintain strong kinship lines but also assures that everyone in the community gets a significant portion of the harvested food.[46]

The Yupik people living in the whaling community of Gambell (Sivuqaq), Alaska, still derive most of their subsistence from their marine space. Their traditional foods occupy a central space in their cultures and are referred to as *neqepik*, which means "real food." The Yupik are whalers and have maintained an unbroken link to their whaling tradition. The whale, particularly the bowhead, is at the heart of Yupik culture and identity. Community members rely on whale oil, meat, and blubber for a healthy source of food. The taking of a bowhead whale is also a major cultural event, and when one is captured, all community members share in its distribution. Older men continue to pass on the knowledge of whaling to the younger men. These young men are taught the underlying principles of generosity and are educated about the importance of sharing with everyone in their community. Whaling reinforces and strengthens Yupik kinship and community ties. Eating *neqepik*, especially bowhead whales, is integral to Yupik identity and to their sense of belonging. To go without it, the Yupik say, "is to lose part of one's being."[47]

The bowhead is also the most culturally significant resource for the Inupiat Eskimos living in the North Slope Borough of Alaska. The 7,000 people who live in the North Slope Borough rely heavily on marine mammals for subsistence and have hunted whales for thousands of years. Knowledge of whaling continues to be passed down to the youth, who are taught how to prepare the *umiaq* (the traditional hunting boat) and how to navigate the treacherous, ice-laden sea to their whaling camps. Inupiat whaling captain Harry Brower Jr. stresses that "passing on this knowledge helps to assure the continuation and survival of the Inupiat culture. It is important to teach the skills and knowledge needed so the younger generation is able to subsist and maintain our cultural existence. Subsistence whaling is a physical, emotional, and spiritual experience which gives our people self confidence and unites our communities."[48]

Sharing their subsistence resources is central to the Inupiat culture, and various events take place throughout the year to celebrate their whaling tradition. After a whale has been killed, it is brought to shore and divided according to tradition. The day after the harvest, the captain of the hunt hosts a feast at his home and invites all the community members for *uunaalik* (boiled skin and the underlying blubber), which is an Inupiat delicacy. When the whaling season ends, each successful whaling crew will host an *apugauti*, a feast that is prepared by the whalers' wives and is held on the beach to honor the whalers' safe return home. Each June the Inupiat hold a Nalukataq, a whaling festival where friends and relatives from elsewhere are invited to come to their community to celebrate their whaling culture and to share with them the whale meat, blubber, and oil they have obtained from their hunts.[49]

A survey conducted among the Inuit in northern Canada in the mid-1990s found that their traditional marine-based foods have retained their cultural and social importance even though there is now a reliance on market and store-bought foods. Out of the 102 households that were surveyed, a preference for traditional foods remained high among all respondents regardless of age. Out of all the favorite foods identified by adults, seal meat and beluga *muktuk* were at the top of the list.[50] Preferred foods for both adults and young people (ages six to sixteen) were dried fish, goose, beluga *muktuk*, and reindeer meat. The reasons given for liking these foods included their taste and texture and their health-giving quality. Adults also noted the cultural and social significance of these foods and associated them with pleasurable events and times when the foods were harvested. They believed that traditional foods were needed for health, and they linked bodily warmth and strength with the consumption of traditional foods. The respondents found that when they did not eat these foods, they felt tired, cold, and weak.[51] Sheena Machmer from the Inuit whaling community of Pangnirtung in Nunavut said that Inuit elders, like her mother, are especially receptive to the health-promoting properties of whale oil, blubber, and meat.

> When it's been a long time since (my mother) had Inuit food she gets weak, and she only gets better when she eats Inuit food. A lot of Inuit are like my mother. They need their type of food to keep their strength. We depend on whales and other marine mammals for strength.[52]

According to Nuu-chah-nulth chief Earl George, the reintroduction of whale products to our diet would reaffirm our spiritual connection to the great Thunderbird and would serve an important social function in bringing our people together.

> Tiskin [Thunderbird] was here before life was formed. He was here before the creation of humankind. Tiskin is sacred, he holds the world in his wings. We are not fooled because he is invisible, because we know his spirit is in all areas that are moving on the face of the earth: the weather, the four seasons. The song of the Thunderbird is what gives us success. . . . We learned from Tiskin the value of being a strong person, gaining strength from the abundant foods we ate. . . . He is happy when everyone is included in the feast of the giant whale.[53]

After the Makah tribe successfully harvested a gray whale on May 17, 1999, they followed the tradition of their whaling ancestors. Tribal members held a huge potlatch in honor of the historic event and to thank the people who had supported them. On May 22, more than 3,000 people came to the small Makah village of Neah Bay to share in the celebration. There were people from the local Native and non-Native communities, people from tribes across the United States and from the First Nations communities in Canada, and people from around the world, as far away as Africa.

The Makah people sang and danced for their guests to honor the return of the whale to their community. Living up to their Makah name, "generous with food," they served their guests heaping plates of salmon, halibut, steamed clams, and oysters. And, for the first time in more than seventy years, whale was the main food on the menu. The whale meat was baked, roasted, and broiled. The blubber was served both cooked and raw. Many people from neighboring Nuu-chah-nulth communities attended the celebration and partook in the tasting of whale for the very first time. Denise Ambrose said that sharing in this feast made her feel proud to be a Nuu-chah-nulth.

> This was the first time that I would taste whale meat, a food that I, as a Nuu-chah-nulth person, should have been brought up on. The meat looked somewhat like dark chicken meat. To me, it smelled and tasted like corned beef. It is hard to describe my feelings after tasting the roasted meat. I was proud to be Nuu-chah-nulth-aht. . . . So many other [Nuu-chah-nulth] people have passed on without having the opportunity to share in what was the most integral part of our culture; the whale. I felt honoured. . . . I cannot thank the Makah people enough for allowing me to share in the "Back to Tradition" feast. They have given me treasured memories and renewed pride in being a Nuu-chah-nulth person. Kleco, Kleco [thank you, thank you]![54]

Two years after the Makah tribe's 1999 whale hunt, the Makah Cultural and Research Center administered a survey of Makah households to clarify and quantify the reactions of Makah tribal members to the revival of their whaling practices. The results of the Makah Household Whaling survey were overwhelmingly positive, with over 95 percent of the respondents indicating full support for restoring the whale hunts. The survey also indicated an eagerness of all Makah members to incorporate more traditions and cultural practices into their daily lives.[55]

A second Makah Household Whaling Survey was conducted in 2006 to see

Bruce Gonzales, a whaling crew member, eats blubber from the first whale harvested by the Makah Tribe in seventy years, May 17, 1999. Photograph courtesy of Debbie Preston, Northwest Indian Fisheries Commission.

if the Makah people still supported continuing their whale hunts. The responses were overwhelmingly positive for whaling. Over 88 percent of the Makah people surveyed believed that revitalizing their whaling tradition was a positive move, especially for its cultural value and political importance. The respondents noted how the revival of whaling had unified their community and had a beneficial effect on Makah youth. More than 70 percent of respondents supported the revival of whaling for ceremonial reasons and for maintaining Makah treaty rights.[56] The Makah have continued eating traditional foods such as salmon, halibut, and shellfish, and the majority of Makah households welcomed the opportunity to incorporate whale products back into their diets. The respondents were asked if they would eat whale meat on a regular basis; 71.1 percent said they would. They were also asked if they would incorporate whale oil in their diets, and 67.1 percent said they would use it on a regular basis. Eating whale blubber received a lower score, and only 47.4 percent of the respondents said they would eat it on a regular basis. This is not surprising, since many of the respondents would not have had the opportunity to taste blubber, other than what they sampled from the whale caught in 1999. When asked if they had ever eaten whale products, 57.9 percent said they had. The respondents indicated a strong interest in learning how to render oil and prepare and cook whale meat and blubber.[57]

After the 1999 Makah hunt, tribal members took pieces of whale meat home and, for the first time, served whale at their dinner tables. Some households utilized old secret recipes that had been passed down through their families, while others adapted recipes for cooking seal and fish. All in all, eating whale is something the Makah people want to experience again.

CULTURAL AND CULINARY IMPERIALISM: CHALLENGES TO OUR RIGHT TO EAT WHALE

Having access to and control over our traditional marine mammal food products continues to be a challenge. The International Whaling Commission enforces restrictions on indigenous whaling, setting stringent quotas on how many whales can be caught per year. And wealthy Western states and international NGOs continue to influence what is acceptable as food, as well as what animals or mammals should or should not be eaten.[58]

When the Makah tribe began preparing for their contemporary hunt, the anti-whaling coalition argued that this whale hunt had no "cultural relevance" and that there was no "need" for them, or the Nuu-chah-nulth, to hunt whales because we had all the food we needed, that is, all the food that was determined to be correct for our societies. After colonization, indigenous people around the world have had to struggle to control access to and production of their food products. Imperialism was a central theme as empires not only appropriated the foods of indigenous, colonized peoples but also decided what foods these peoples would produce and eat.[59] As the Nuu-chah-nulth and Makah people came under colonial rule, government agents actively forced on them an agrarian system and at the same time attempted to turn them away from marine-based economies and subsistence. As Robert Friedheim argues: Native nations "do not want to give up distinctive features of their cultures in order to be consistent with the postmodernist values of metropolitan societies."[60] Yet the history of Western hegemony over food production and consumption continues, as demonstrated through the attacks on the revival of whale hunts, perpetuating a form of cultural and/or culinary imperialism.

Native people did not, and do not, make the same distinctions about animals that have become familiar and fixed categories in the media discourse on whaling. The First Species Ceremonies of my people, for example, is a sacred event that affirms the "personhood" of these animals and mammals and honors them for giving themselves to feed us. The Nuu-chah-nulth and Makah, and other Native peoples, have a belief that "all living things—both plants and animals—have a reciprocal relationship to humans and elicit a certain reverence."[61] There is a sense of sacredness and gratitude attached to the spirit of the animal or plant that gives itself to humans. The songs and prayers sung during First Salmon ceremonies, and, more importantly, the songs and prayers that were conducted during and following the Makah whale hunt, demonstrate the continued cultural importance of honoring the spirit of the animal.

Anti-whalers argued that whales should not be eaten because they are intelligent and conscious beings. But the fact that whales are conscious beings is exactly why we revere them, and why we show the utmost respect for all life that gives itself to us. Chief Tom Mexsis Happynook says that the Nuu-chah-nulth see whales, and all other elements of nature, as our equals. He asks: "Is this not the ultimate expression of what has been called 'animal rights'? To address them as equals, to honour and respect them for their contribution to our health, our cultures, societies and economies?"[62] As Chief Mexsis asserts, our principle of *isaak* (respect) relates to all life forms:

> Our principle of respect was not born from a longing for mere sustenance, but instead in gratitude for the cornucopia found within our territories. Indigenous peoples subsist enmeshed in the pattern of relationships with nature, the environment and the ecosystems. This pattern of relationships is not merely to survive, but to thrive; it includes everything; the plants, the fish, the sea-mammals, the land mammals, the mountains, trees, water, and even the winds which change with the seasons. Everything is deemed worthy of our respect, and consideration.[63]

Respect for all people and all living things is at the foundation of Nuu-chah-nulth existence. The environment, the ecosystems, the animal world, all interconnect with our world, and as Chief Mexsis asserts, "unite us into the web of life."[64] It is difficult for non-Indians to comprehend indigenous people's relationship to the natural world because it is so different from their own. Our language, our oral traditions, our worldview, our ethics, our education, and our epistemology evolved from our marine and land space, from the atmosphere, and from the plant and animals that surround us. Therefore, indigenous culture "is a manifestation in human terms of the environment that has been its sustaining foundation."[65]

The public discourse over the acceptability of killing and eating whales is couched in moral and legal terms, but the larger issue is one of power: the power to determine what we eat. Indigenous nations continue to have people outside our cultures impose their own symbolic and aesthetic food values on our societies. In 1948 the UN General Assembly adopted the Universal Declaration of Human Rights. Article 25 states: "Everyone had the right to a standard of living adequate for the health and well-being of himself and his family, including food." More important, Article 1 of the Declaration states that all people have the right to self-determination and that "in no case may a people be deprived of its own means of subsistence."[66]

Whales are special. And they are wonderful and beautiful. My people do not deny this. And they have remained in our lives and cultures as sacred and respected animals, but they were also once an important food source.

◆   ◆   ◆

Our whaling tradition was and continues to be at the heart of our cultures, our spirituality, and our identities. Makah chief Arnie Hunter says the whale hunt has brought their tribe back "full circle" and "restores a missing link in [their] heritage."[67] Following the Makah contemporary whale hunt, a little Makah boy asked his father what the whale was. His father replied, "That's a whale. That's for our Indian tradition. That's for our rights."[68] As former Makah Whaling Commission chair Keith Johnson declared: "It's who we are."[69]

In 1996 I attended a meeting held in Berkeley, California, that led to the formation of the World Council of Whalers organization the following year. The meeting was initiated by the Nuu-chah-nulth chief Tom Mexsis Happynook, who formed the organization to provide a forum for indigenous whaling people around the world. Many of my Nuu-chah-nulth leaders attended this meeting, along with representatives from other whaling communities throughout the world. At the end of the meeting, all the participants were gifted a cookbook from Japanese restaurant owner Mrs. Mutsuko Ohnishi. Mrs Ohnishi owns a whale cuisine restaurant in Osaka, Japan. I laughed when I received the book, thinking how funny it was to receive a book about how to cook whale meat. At that time, I never thought that I would have the chance to eat whale, or that I would ever witness a hunt by my people. Now, after my Makah relatives successfully harvested a whale, I am optimistic that I will witness a Nuu-chah-nulth hunt. I now cherish this book that sits on my bookshelf with all my other cookbooks, and I look forward to the day that I can try out Mrs. Ohnishi's recipes. When I do, I will know that our philosophy of *hishuk'ish tsawalk*—everything is one—has been fulfilled and that our whaling tradition is whole once again. And when that day comes, when we do harvest a whale, we will not only restore this missing link in our tradition but we will truly be honoring the spirits of our whaling ancestors.

Notes

INTRODUCTION

1   In Makah, the word for the gray whale
    is *sih-xwah-wiX*.

2   Taiaiake Alfred, *Peace, Power, Righ-
    teousness: An Indigenous Manifesto*
    (New York: Oxford University Press,
    1999), 80–82.

3   Taiaiake Alfred, *Wasáse: Indigenous
    Pathways of Action and Freedom* (Peter-
    borough, Ont.: Broadview Press, 2005),
    29.

4   Keith Johnson, president of the Makah
    Whaling Commission, in the film *The
    Makah Nation: A Whaling People*, pro-
    duced by the Makah Tribal Council.

5   The village of Ts'ishaa was located on
    Benson Island, which is one of the outer
    islands of the Broken Group in Barkley
    Sound. It eventually became a summer
    fishing and sea mammal hunt site as we
    moved our main village to the Alberni
    Valley. Alan McMillan and Denis St.
    Claire, *Ts'ishaa* (Burnaby, B.C.: Simon
    Fraser University Archaeology Press,
    2005), 10–11. Susan Golla, "Legendary
    History of the Tsisha'ath," in *Nuu-chah-
    nulth Voices,* ed. Alan L. Hoover, 140–41
    (Victoria: British Royal Museum, 2000).

6   Julie Cruikshank, "Getting the Words

Right: Perspectives on Naming and
Places in Athapaskan Oral History,"
Arctic Anthropology 27, no. 1 (1990):
52–65, 63.

7   Angela Cavender Wilson, "American
    Indian History or Non-Indian Percep-
    tions of American Indian History?" in
    *Natives and Academics: Researching and
    Writing about American Indians*, ed.
    Devon A. Mihesuah (Lincoln: Univer-
    sity of Nebraska Press, 1999), 24.

8   Janice Acoose, "Post Halfbreed: Indig
    enous Writers as Authors of Their Own
    Realities," in *Looking at the Words of Our
    People: First Nations Analysis of Litera-
    ture*, ed. Jeanette Armstrong (Penticton,
    B.C.: Theytus Books, 1993), 330.

9   See Donald L. Fixico, "Ethics and
    Responsibilities in Writing Amercan
    Indian History," in *Natives and Academ-
    ics*, ed. Devon A. Mihesuah (Lincoln:
    University of Nebraska Press, 1999).

10 Ibid., 86.

11 Devon A. Mihesuah, "Introduction," to
    Natives and Academics, 2, 3.

12 Duane Champagne, "American Indian
    Studies Is for Everyone," in *Natives and
    Academics,* 182–83.

13   Linda Tuhiwai Smith, *Decolonizing Methodologies: Research and Indigenous Peoples* (New York: St. Martin's Press, 1999), 137–40.

14   Winona Wheeler, "Social Relations of Indigenous Oral Histories," in *Walking a Tightrope: Aboriginal People and Their Representation* (Waterloo, Ont.: Wilfrid Laurier University Press, 2005), 191.

15   Ibid.

16   Richard E. Atleo, *Tsawalk: A Nuu-chah-nulth Worldview* (Vancouver: UBC Press, 2004), 130.

1 / TSAWALK

1   This is the version of the story I grew up with. The Thunderbird, Whale, and Lightning Serpent were also significant to our precontact material culture and were depicted on longhouse interior walls and on cedar woven hats and baskets. Contemporary Nuu-chah-nulth and Makah artwork continues to be inspired by these important cultural beings that are illustrated on silk-screen prints and cedar-carved and woven art. For versions of the Thunderbird and Whale story, see James Swan, *The Indians of Cape Flattery* (Washington, D.C.: Smithsonian Institution, 1870), 7–8; Alan D. McMillan, *Since the Time of the Transformers: The Ancient Heritage of the Nuu-chah-nulth, Ditidaht, and Makah* (Vancouver: UBC Press, 1999); Aldona Jonaitis, *The Yuquot Whaler's Shrine* (Seattle: University of Washington Press, 1999), 89, 181.

2   This version of the story was told to me by my brother-in-law, Nuu-chah-nulth artist Art Thompson. The story is also recited by Makah language and cultural educator Maria Pascua in "Ozette: A Makah Village in 1491," *National Geographic* 180, no. 4 (October 1991): 50.

3   Alice B. Kehoe, *North American Indians: A Comprehensive Account* (Engle-wood Cliffs, N.J.: Prentice-Hall, 1981), 403–6.

4   The Nootkan language has three dialectic divisions: Nootka proper, spoken from Cape Cook to the east shore of Barkley Sound; Nitinat, used by the groups of Pacheena and Nitinat Lake; and Makah, spoken by the Cape Flattery people. These dialects seem to differ through a few fairly simple and consistent phonetic shifts, so that although at first the forms are mutually unintelligible, a person who speaks one form can soon understand the others and make herself understood. Philip Drucker, *Indians of the Northwest Coast* (New York: Natural History Press, 1955), 16. George Gibbs, "Tribes of Western Washington and Northwestern Oregon," *Contributions to North American Ethnology* 1 (Washington, D.C.: U.S. Department of the Interior, 1877), 226. Herbert C. Taylor Jr., "Anthropological Investigation of the Makah Indians," in *American Indian Ethnohistory: Indians of the Northwest*, ed. David A. Horr (New York: Garland Publishing, 1974), 37.

5   James Swan was the first teacher in Neah Bay; in the early 1860s, he conducted extensive ethnographic research among the Makah. Swan, *Indians of Cape Flattery*, 57.

6   McMillan, *Since the Time of the Transformers*, 87. Eugene Arima, *The West Coast (Nootka) People* (Victoria: British Columbia Provincial Museum, 1983), 2.

7   The Makah people were also called Klas-set/Classet (which means "Cape People" or "Outside People"), a name given to them by neighboring tribes. Swan, *Indians of Cape Flattery*, 1, and Taylor, "Anthropological Investigation," 6.

8   Philip Drucker, "Rank, Wealth, and Kinship in Northwest Coast Society," *American Anthropologist* 41 (1939):

58. Alan D. McMillan and Denis E. St. Claire, *Ts'ishaa: Archaeology and Ethnography of a Nuu-chah-nulth Origin Site in Barkley Sound* (Burnaby, B.C.: Archaeology Press, Simon Fraser University, 2005), 9. The current spelling of these groups are Ahousaht, Ehattesaht, Hesquiaht, Huu-ay-aht, Hupacasaht, Kyuquot/Cheklesahht, Mowachaht/Muchalaht, Nutchatlaht, Tla-o-qui-aht, Toquaht, Tseshaht, Uchucklesaht, Ucluelet, and Pacheedaht (a group that has remained outside of the Nuu-chah-nulth political body). Although the Dididaht are politically and culturally related to the other "aht" groups, they are usually referred to separately.

9 Gilbert M. Sproat, *Scenes and Studies of Savage Life* (London: Smith, Elder and Co., 1868), 20.

10 W. J. Langlois, ed., *Nutka: Captain Cook and the Spanish Explorers on the Coast*, *Sound Heritage* 11, no. 1: 54 (Victoria: Provincial Archives of British Columbia, 1978).

11 Gregory G. Monks, Alan D. McMillan, and Denis E. St. Claire, "Nuu-chah-nulth Whaling: Archaeological Insights into Antiquity, Species Preferences, and Cultural Importance," *Arctic Anthropology* 38, no. 1 (2001): 65. Data collected from the Ozette excavation site in the 1970s show that whale procurement among the Makah remained basically unchanged for 2,000 years. David R. Huelsbeck, "The Utilization of Whales at Ozette," in *Ozette Archaeological Project Reports*, ed. Stephen R. Samuels and Richard D.Daugherty (Washington State University, Pullman, and the National Park Service, 1994), 2: 267. An archaeological site in Tseshaht territory uncovered a whale skull with a mussel-shell harpoon blade still embedded in it. This skull was dated to be over five hundred years old. The whale skull and numerous whalebones at the site show

that the Tseshaht were actively whaling by this time. Alan D. McMillan and Denis E. St. Claire, *Ts'ishaa: Archaeology and Ethnography of a Nuu-chah-nulth Origin Site in Barkley Sound* (Burnaby, B.C.: Archaeology Press, Simon Fraser University, 2005), 92.

12 Monks et al., "Nuu-chah-nulth Whaling," 75–76; Huelsbeck, "Utilization of Whales," 267.

13 David R. Huelsbeck, "Whaling in the Precontact Economy of the Central Northwest Coast," *Arctic Anthropology* 25, no. 1 (1998): 10. Cary C. Collins, "Subsistence and Survival: The Makah Indian Reservation, 1855–1933," *Pacific Northwest Quarterly* 87 (Fall 1996): 183; E. Y. Arima, *West Coast (Nootka) People*, 44; McMillan and St. Claire, *Ts'ishaa*, 25–26.

14 Huelsbeck, "Utilization of Whales," 284–89; McMillan and St. Claire, *Ts'ishaa*, 71–81.

15 Travis Reaveley, "Nuuchahnulth Whaling and Its Significance for Social and Economic Reproduction," *Chicago Anthropology Exchange Graduate Journal of Anthropology* 28 (Spring 1998):23–40; reprinted on Native Americans and the Environment Web site, http://www.ncseonline.org/nac/docs/reaveley.html, 3.

16 Philip Drucker, *Cultures of the North Pacific Coast* (Scranton, Pa.: Chandler Publishing Co., 1965), 46.

17 Individuals of high rank were related to individuals of lower rank. Individuals from all ranks lived in the same house, with the chief having authority over his house group within the village. Drucker, *Cultures of the North Pacific Coast*, 46.

18 Ibid., 52.

19 Arima, *West Coast (Nootka) People*, 59–60; McMillan and St. Claire, *Ts'ishaa*, 8–10.

20 McMillan and St. Claire, *Ts'ishaa*, 8–10. St. Claire, pers. comm., October 18, 2007.

21 McMillan and St. Claire, *Ts'ishaa*, 25–27.

22 Charlotte Coté, "Whaling, Religious and Cultural Implications," in *American Indian Religious Traditions: An Encyclopedia*, ed. Suzanne J. Crawford and Dennis F. Kelly (Santa Barbara: ABC-CLIO, 2005), 1141–53.

23 Suzanne Crawford, "Guardian Spirit Complex," in Crawford and Kelly, *American Indian Religious Traditions*, 355–59.

24 Crawford and Kelly, *American Indian Religious Traditions*, 355–56.

25 Variations on the phonetic spelling are *oosumich*, *uusimch*, and *uusimich*.

26 Richard E. Atleo, *Tsawalk: A Nuu-chah-nulth Worldview* (Vancouver: UBC Press, 2004), 74.

27 Ibid.

28 Peter Webster, *As Far As I Know: Reminiscences of an Ahousaht Elder* (Campbell River, B.C.: Campbell River Museum and Archives, 1983), 23.

29 Philip Drucker provides a detailed discussion of Nuu-chah-nulth puberty ceremonies in *The Northern and Central Nootkan Tribes* (Washington, D.C.: Smithsonian Institution, 1951), 137–44.

30 The *haahuupa* of the young girl during the puberty rites ceremony was very important, and it was usually the girl's *ne'iiqsu* (aunts) or her *naniiqsu* (grandparents) who were given this role.

31 Edward Sapir and Morris Swadesh, *Native Accounts of Nootka Ethnography* (Bloomington: Indiana University Press, 1955), 308–11. Edward Sapir, "Sayach'apis, A Nootka Trader," in *American Indian Life*, ed. Elsie Clews Parsons (Lincoln: University of Nebraska Press, 1922), 301. Philip Drucker, *Northern and Central Nootkan Tribes*, 152.

32 Coté, "Whaling, Religious and Cultural Implications," 1144.

33 Webster, *As Far As I Know*, 24.

34 Ahousaht is one of the Nuu-chah-nulth northern groups.

35 Atleo, *Tsawalk*, 93.

36 Ibid, 94.

37 Ibid.

38 Nuu-chah-nulth Elder Stanley Sam, Nuu-chah-nulth Elders' Whaling Workshop, December 4–5, 2000; audiotape held at the Nuu-chah-nulth Tribal Council Office.

39 Edward Sapir and Morris Swadesh, *Nootka Texts: Tales and Ethnological Narratives, with Grammatical Notes and Lexical Materials* (Philadelphia: Linguistic Society of America, 1939), 115; Sapir and Swadesh, *Native Accounts*, 177–79; Arima, *West Coast (Nootka) People*, 40–41.

40 T. T. Waterman, *The Whaling Equipment of the Makah Indians*, University of Washington Publications in Anthropology (1920), 39; Arima, *West Coast (Nootka) People*, 40.

41 Waterman, *Whaling Equipment*, 39.

42 Sapir and Swadesh, *Nootka Texts*, 115. Drucker, *Northern and Central Nootkan Tribes*, 177. Erna Gunther, "Reminiscences of a Whaler's Wife," *Pacific Northwest Quarterly* 1, no. 1 (January 1942): 67, 68. Drucker, "Diffusion in Northwest Coast Culture Growth in the Light of Some Distributions," Ph.D.diss., University of California, Berkeley (1936), 24.

43 *Nootka*. Provincial Archives, British Columbia Heritage Series, 5 (Victoria: Province of British Columbia, Provincial Museum, 1966), 35.

44 Drucker, *Northern and Central Nootkan Tribes*, 170–71.

45 The word *tciyasam* is also used by Drucker to refer to the shrines used by chiefs to attract dead whales to the shores. Ibid. *Haw'ilth* Jerry Jack discusses the importance of *cheesum* in the film *The Washing of Tears* (National Sound and Picture Company, Inc./

National Film Board of Canada, 1994). Aldona Jonaitis, *The Yuquot Whalers' Shrine* (Seattle: University of Washington Press, 1999), 8, 45.

46 Drucker, *Cultures of the North Pacific Coast*, 156.

47 *The Washing of Tears* (film).

48 In 1905 the whaling shrine was removed from the northern Nuu-chah-nulth village of Mowachaht, the same area where Cook landed 127 years earlier, and was transported to the American Museum of Natural History, where it remains today. The shrine was purchased from Mowachaht *haw'iih* in 1903 by anthropologist Franz Boas, who was working for the museum at the time. Boas had commissioned a Tlingit-English man, George Hunt, who grew up among the Kwakw<u>a</u>ka'wakw (Kwakiutl) people, to buy the shrine from the Mowachaht people. This shrine was no longer being used as a special cleansing site, and after much bargaining, Hunt was able to purchase the shrine and had it taken apart and brought to the Natural History Museum in New York. It was believed that this shrine had been utilized for rituals concerning the procurement of drift whales and was where the *haw'iih* who had owned it conducted their secret rituals in order to obtain the power needed to entice dead whales to shore. Jonaitis, *The Yuquot Whaler's Shrine*, 54–55.

49 Aldona Jonaitis, *Art of the Northwest Coast* (Seattle: University of Washington Press, 2006), 124, 125.

50 Jonaitis, *The Yuquot Whalers' Shrine*, 193.

51 Sapir, "Sayach'apis, a Nootka Trader," 309.

52 Frances Densmore, *Nootka and Quileute Music* (Washington, D.C.: Smithsonian Institution, 1939), 53.

53 Sapir, "Sayach'apis, a Nootka Trader," 309–10.

54 This is a version of a story that has been passed down through the Huu-ay-aht oral tradition. Huu-ay-aht is one of the Nuu-chah-nulth southern groups. This story was told to author Kathryn Bridge, who was given permission to print it in her book *Extraordinary Accounts of Native Life on the West Coast: Words from Huu-ay-aht Ancestors* (Canmore, Alberta: Altitude Publishing, 2004), 99–104.

55 Ibid., 103–4.

56 Swan, *Indians of Cape Flattery*, 7–8.

57 David Spalding, *Whales of the West Coast* (Madeira Park, B.C.: Harbour Publishing, 1998), 56–68. Huelsbeck, *Whaling in the Precontact Economy of the Central Northwest Coast*, (1998), 1; Monks et al., "Nuu-chah-nulth Whaling," 65; McMillan and St. Claire, *Ts'ishaa*, 197.

58 Huelsbeck, "The Utilization of Whales at Ozette," 271–78; Huelsbeck, *Whaling in the Precontact Economy*, 4–5.

59 Huelsbeck, "Utilization," 271–78; Huelsbeck, *Whaling in the Precontact Economy*, 4–5; McMillan and St. Claire, *Ts'ishaa*, 26.

60 Makah linguist Maria Pascua, pers. comm., October 31, 2007. In Swan's notes on the various whale species important to the Makah, he wrote the name for gray whale as *chet-a-puk*, which he said was also the generic name for whale. Swan, *Indians of Cape Flattery*, 19.

61 Jose Mariano Moziño, *Noticias de Nutka: An Account of Nootka Sound in 1792*, trans. and ed. Iris H. Wilson Engstrand (Seattle: University of Washington Press, 1970), 48.

62 Ibid., 47.

63 Swan, *Indians of Cape Flattery*, 4.

64 Waterman, *Whaling Equipment of the Makah Indians*, 10–29. Eugene Arima, "Thoughts on the Nuu-chah-nulth Canoe," *Huupak anum Tupaat: Nuu-*

chah-nulth Voices, Histories, Objects and Journeys, ed. Alan D. Hoover (Victoria: Royal British Columbia Museum, 2000), 310.

65 Waterman, *Whaling Equipment of the Makah Indians,* 29–31.

66 Densmore, *Nootka and Quileute Music,* 47.

67 Waterman, *Whaling Equipment of the Makah Indians,* 39.

68 Drucker, *Northern and Central Nootkan Tribes,* 52; Waterman, *Whaling Equipment of the Makah Indians,* 39. Philip Drucker, "Nootka Whaling," in McFeat, *Indians of the North Pacific Coast,* 22.

69 Quoted in Martha Black, *Huupukwanum Tupaat, Out of the Mist: Treasures of the Nuu-chah-nulth Chiefs* (Victoria: Royal British Columbia Museum, 1999), 33.

70 Maria Parker Pascua, "Ozette: A Makah Village in 1491," *National Geographic* (October 1991).

71 Drucker, *Northern and Central Nootkan Tribes,* 54–55.

72 Also spelled *tsakwassi.* McMillan and St. Claire, *Ts'ishaa,* 14.

73 Jonaitis, *Yuquot Whalers' Shrine,* 9.

74 McMillan and St. Claire, *Ts'ishaa,* 25.

75 Helen H. Roberts and Morris Swadesh, *Songs of the Nootka Indians of Western Vancouver Island* (Philadelphia: The American Philosophical Society, 1955), 316.

76 McMillan and St. Claire, *Ts'ishaa,* 25–26.

77 Ibid., 26.

78 For analysis of the Nuu-chah-nulth potlatch, see Philip Drucker, *Indians of the Northwest Coast* (Ottawa: Carleton University Press, 1955, 1963), 131–44; H. G. Barnett, "The Nature of the Potlatch," *American Anthropologist* 40 (July–September 1938): 349–57, reprinted in McFeat, *Indians of the North Pacific Coast,* 81– 91; Drucker, *Northern and Central Nootkan Tribes,*

376–444; Drucker, *Cultures of the North Pacific Coast,* 46–47; Edward Sapir and Morris Swadesh, *Native Accounts of Nootka Ethnography,* Indiana University Research Center in Anthropology, Folklore, and Linguistics Publications, no. 1 (1955): 230–332 . For a general analysis of the potlatch and specific attributes of the Kwakwaka'wakw (Kwakiutl) potlatch, see Franz Boas, "The Potlatch," in *The Social Organization and Secret Societies of the Kwakiutl Indians,* Report of the United States National Museum (Washington, D.C., 1895): 341–55, reprinted in McFeat, *Indians of the North Pacific Coast,* 72–80; Helen Codere, *Fighting with Property: A Study of Kwakiutl Potlatching and Warfare, 1792–1930* (New York: American Ethnological Society, 1950). For an analysis of the religious and political dimensions of the Tlingit mortuary potlatch, see Sergei Kan, *Symbolic Immortality: Nineteenth-Century Tlingit Potlatch* (Washington, D.C.: Smithsonian Institution, 1989). For an analysis and comparison of Northwest Coast peoples' potlatches, see Abraham Rosman and Paula G. Rubel, *Feasting with Mine Enemy: Rank and Exchange among Northwest Coast Societies* (Long Grove, Ill.: Waveland Press, 1986 and 2001).

79 *Pa-chuck* is the noun meaning "to be given." Both words would be used during a potlatch. George Clutesi, *Potlatch* (Sidney, B.C.: Gray's Publishing, 1969 and 1973), 10.

80 Drucker, *Northern and Central Nootkan Tribes,* 377–82, Drucker, *Indians of the Northwest Coast,* 131–32; Douglas Cole and Ira Chaikin, *An Iron Hand Upon the People: The Law against the Potlatch on the Northwest Coast* (Vancouver, B.C.: Douglas and McIntyre, 1990), 8–10.

81 Susan M. Golla, "He Has a Name: History and Social Structure among the Indians of Western Vancouver Island,"

Ph.D. diss., Columbia University, 1987, 94.

82 There are a variety of spellings for these words.

83 Alice Henson Ernst, *Wolf Ritual of the Northwest Coast* (Eugene: University of Oregon Press, 1952 and 2001). See also Richard E.Atleo, *Tsawalk*, 105–7. Sapir and Swadesh, *Native Accounts of Nootka Ethnography*, 89–120.

84 McMillan, *Since the Time of the Transformers*, 22–23.

85 Clutesi, *Potlatch*, 10–11.

86 In Christopher Bracken, *The Potlatch Papers: A Colonial Case History* (Chicago: University of Chicago Press, 1997), 141.

87 Drucker, *Northern and Central Nootkan Tribes*, 377–79. Drucker, *Indians of the Northwest Coast* (1955), 132–37; Rosman and Rubel, *Feasting with Mine Enemy*, 87–106.

88 Boas, reprinted in McFeat, *Indians of the Northwest Coast*, 74–75.

89 Marcel Mauss, *The Gift: The Form and Reason for Exchange in Archaic Societies*, trans. W. D. Halls (London: Routledge, 1990), 8–13.

90 Sproat, *Scenes and Studies of Savage Life*, 112–13.

91 Edward Sapir, *Sayach'apis. A Nootka Trader* (Lincoln: University of Nebraska Press, 1922; reprinted in *American Indian Life*, ed. Elsie Clews Parsons [Lincoln: Bison Books, 1991], 297). See also, Sapir and Swadesh, *Native Accounts of Nootka Ethnography*, 304–6.

92 Sapir and Swadesh, *Native Accounts of Nootka Ethnography*, 305.

93 Webster, *As Far As I Know*, 27.

94 Densmore, *Nootka and Quileute Music*, 69.

95 Ibid., 67.

96 Ibid., 68.

97 Ibid., 72.

98 Ann Renker, "Whale Hunting and the Makah Tribe: A Needs Statement."

Paper presented to the International Whaling Commission, Aboriginal Subsistence Working Group, April 2007, http://www.iwcoffice.org/_documents/commission/IWC59docs/59-ASW%209.pdf.

99 Arima, *West Coast (Nootka) People*, 70.

100 Lillard, *Mission to Nootka, 1874–1900* (Sidney, B.C.: Gray's Publishing, 1977), 49.

101 Tom Mexsis Happynook, "Securing Nuu chah nulth Food, Health and Traditional Values through the Sustainable Use of Marine Mammals," *World Council of Whalers Report* (Brentwood Bay, B.C, 2001).

102 Chief Earl George passed away in April 2006.

103 Chief Earl George, "Living on the Edge: Nuu-chah-nulth History from an Ahousaht Chief's Perspective," 28, master's thesis, University of Victoria, 1994.

104 Ibid., 27–28.

2 / UTLA

1   Chief Umeek developed a theory of *tsawalk* that "assumes reality to be one network of relationship." Richard E. (Umeek) Atleo, *Tsawalk: A Nuu-chah-nulth Worldview* (Vancouver: UBC Press, 2004), 118.

2   John Meares was the first person to visit Makah territory in 1788, when he anchored off Tatoosh Island. Richard I. Inglis and James C. Haggarty, "Provisions or Prestige: A Re-evaluation of the Economic Importance of Nootka Whaling" (Victoria: British Columbia Museum, 1983), 204.

3   The name was given to the Nuu-chah-nulth people by Cook because of their reputation as "peaceable and willing to supply the vessels with fresh foods and other supplies." Inglis and Haggarty, "Provisions or Prestige," 3.

4   Ibid.

5   Alan D. McMillan, *Since the Time of the Transformers: The Ancient Heritage of the Nuu-chah-nulth, Ditidaht, and Makah* (Vancouver: UBC Press, 1999), 195.

6   Jill St. Germain, *Indian Treaty-Making Policy in the United States and Canada, 1867–1877* (Lincoln: University of Nebraska Press, 2001).

7   This area, along with Vancouver Island, was previously a separate British colony. The two colonies were joined in 1864 and in 1871 became the province of British Columbia. Native land title in British Columbia was not legally recognized until 1973, and today the Nuu-chah-nulth groups are currently in tri-partite treaty/land-claims negotiations with the Canadian government and the province of British Columbia. Tony Penikett, *Reconciliation: First Nations Treaty-Making in British Columbia* (Toronto: Douglas and McIntire, 2006).

8   While treaties were being signed in other parts of Canada, the majority of the indigenous groups in the province of British Columbia remained without treaties. A few treaties were negotiated with tribes in the Victoria area in 1849, when the British colony of Vancouver Island was administered by Governor James Douglas. Paul Tennant, *Aboriginal Peoples and Politics: The Indian Land Question in British Columbia, 1849–1989* (Vancouver: UBC Press, 1990), 39–52. Robin Fisher, *Contact and Conflict: Indian-European Relations in British Columbia, 1774–1890* (Vancouver: UBC Press; Seattle: University of Washington Press, 1977), 160–61. Olive Patricia Dickason, *Canada's First Nations: A History of Founding Peoples from Earliest Times* (Toronto: McClelland and Stewart, 1992), 261–62; Penikett, *Reconciliation.*

9   Carroll L. Riley, "The Makah Indians: A Study of Political and Economic Organization," *Ethnohistory* 15 (1968):

64.   Anne Renker and Erna Gunther, "Makah," in *Handbook of North American Indians,* vol. 7: *The Northwest Coast,* ed. Wayne Suttles (Washington, D.C.: Smithsonian Institution, 1990), 427.

10   The Makah word for "chief" is similar to the Nu-chah-nulth word, *haw'ilth.*

11   The Makah treaty proceedings were documented in the journal of George Gibbs who accompanied Governor Stevens during the negotiations with western Washington tribes in the 1850s. George Gibbs, "Treaty of Neah Bay," transcript of *Journal Proceedings,* microcopy no. T-494, roll 5 (National Archives, Washington, D.C.), 3.

12   Ibid., 2.

13   The Makah Indian Tribe and Whaling Fact Sheet, Makah Tribal Council, http://ncseonline.org/nae/docs/makahfaq.html.

14   Ibid.

15   Gibbs, "Treaty of Neah Bay."

16   The five autonomous Makah villages were incorporated as a single political unit and were assigned one main reservation. In 1882, a smaller reservation was created for the Makah living farther away at Ozette, but this was sold after the last inhabitant moved to Neah Bay in the early twentieth century. This land was officially returned to the Makah in 1970. McMillan, *Since the Time of the Transformers,* 216, 217.

17   Charles Lillard, *Gilbert M. Sproat: The Nootka: Scenes and Studies of Savage Life* (annotated and edited edition of the original Sproat publication, *Scenes and Studies of Savage Life* [1868]) (Victoria, B.C.: Sono Nis Press, 1987), xiv.

18   Gilbert Malcolm Sproat, *Scenes and Studies of Savage Life* (London: Smith, Elder and Co., 1868), 4.

19   Ibid.

20   Dickason, *Canada's First Nations,* 262. Tennant, *Aboriginal Peoples and Politics,* 41–52.

21 Robert Boyd, *The Coming of the Spirit of Pestilence: Introduced Infectious Diseases and Population Decline among Northwest Coast Indians, 1774–1874* (Seattle: University of Washington Press; Vancouver: UBC Press, 1999). James R. Gibson, "Smallpox on the Northwest Coast, 1835–1838," *BC Studies* 56 (Winter 1982–83): 66–67.

22 The 1889 measles and 1890 typhoid epidemics also caused a major decline in the Makah population. Riley, *Aboriginal Peoples and Politics*, 63.

23 Alix Jane Gillis, "The History of the Neah Bay Agency," in *American Indian Ethnohistory: Indians of the Northwest: Coast Salish and Washington Indians,* ed. David E. Horr (New York: Garland Publishing, 1974), 15.

24 Ruth Kirk, *Tradition and Change on the Northwest Coast: The Makah, Nuu-chah-nulth, Southern Kwakiutl, and Nuxalk* (Seattle: University of Washington Press, 226); Boyd, *Coming of the Spirit of Pestilence*, 167.

25 Boyd, *Coming of the Spirit of Pestilence,* Appendix 4, 302.

26 Kirk, *Tradition and Change,* 226.

27 Sproat, *Scenes and Studies of Savage Life,* 275; Kirk, *Tradition and Change,* 225.

28 E. Y. Arima et al., *Between Ports Alberni and Renfrew: Notes on West Coast Peoples* (Ottawa: Canadian Museum of Civilization, 1991), 211–12. Boyd, *Coming of the Spirit of Pestilence,* 302.

29 Quoted in Boyd, *Coming of the Spirit of Pestilence,* 168.

30 Quoted in Arima et al., *Between Ports Alberni and Renfrew,* 295.

31 Kirk, *Tradition and Change,* 226.

32 Ibid., 233.

33 Brabant in Charles Lillard, ed., *Mission to Nootka, 1874–1900* (Sidney, B.C.: Gray's Publishing, 1977), 37–39.

34 Robin Fisher, *Contact and Conflict: Indian-European Relations in British Columbia, 1774–1890* (Vancouver: UBC Press, 1977, 1987), 119–45.

35 The United States eventually took over the administration of the schools, but Canada continued the policy of funding schools administered by churches. J. R. Miller, *Shingwuak's Vision: A History of Native Residential Schools* (Toronto: University of Toronto Press, 1996), 121–49.

36 Elizabeth Colson, *The Makah Indians: A Study of an Indian Tribe in Modern American Society* (Minneapolis: University of Minnesota Press, 1953), 14–16; J. E. Michael Kew, "History of Coastal British Columbia since 1846," 162; Cesare Marino, "History of Western Washington since 1846," *in Handbook of North American Indians*, vol 7: *Northwest Coast*, 173, 174.

37 Colson, *The Makah Indians,* 20.

38 David W. Adams, *Education for Extinction: American Indians and the Boarding School Experience, 1875–1928* (Lawrence: University of Kansas Press, 1995), 63–64.

39 *Indian Residential Schools: The Nuu-chah-nulth Experience* (Nuu-chah-nulth Tribal Council, 1996), 193.

40 Colson, *The Makah Indians,* 10.

41 Adams, *Education for Extinction;* Celia Haig-Brown, *Resistance and Renewal: Surviving the Indian Residential School* (Vancouver, B.C.: Arsenal Pulp Press, 1988); J. R. Miller, *Shingwuak's Vision: A History of Native Residential Schools* (Toronto: University of Toronto Press, 1996); Jean Barman et al., *Indian Education in Canada*, vol. 1: *The Legacy* (Vancouver: UBC Press, 1986); Jon Reyner and Jeanne Eder, *American Indian Education: A History* (Norman: University of Oklahoma Press, 2004).

42 From the 1863 Report of the Commissioner of Indian Affairs, quoted in Colson, *The Makah Indians,* 11.

43 Ibid., 19.

44 From the 1887 Report of the Commissioner of Indian Affairs, quoted in Colson, *The Makah Indians,* 11.

45 McMillan, *Since the Time of the Trans-formers*, 215.

46 E. Brian Titley, *A Narrow Vision: Duncan Campbell Scott and the Administration of Indian Affairs in Canada* (Vancouver: UBC Press, 1986), 15, 166.

47 George Gibbs, "Treaty of Neah Bay," 173, 205.

48 Dickason, *Canada's First Nations*, 262–63.

49 Douglas Cole and Ira Chaikin, *An Iron Hand Upon the People: The Law Against the Potlatch on the Northwest Coast* (Vancouver, B.C.: Douglas and McIntyre; Seattle: University of Washington Press, 1990), 15.

50 The land Sproat was to acquire was within my ancestors' important winter village site. This area and the surrounding region became known as the Alberni Valley.

51 Jan Peterson, *The Albernis, 1860–1922* (Lantzville, B.C.: Oolichan Books, 1992), 28–34.

52 Sproat, *Scenes and Studies of Savage Life*, 292.

53 British Columbia joined Canada in 1871. For information on Sproat, see Bracken, *The Potlatch Papers*, 40–41.

54 Quoted in Cole and Chaikin, *Iron Hand Upon the People*, 15.

55 Quoted in F. E. LaViolette, *The Struggle for Survival: Indian Cultures and the Protestant Ethic in B.C* (Ottawa: University of Toronto Press, 1973), 43.

56 Cole and Chaikin, *Iron Hand Upon the People*, 128.

57 Guillod, *Annual Report of the Department of Indian Affairs* (West Coast Agency) (Ottawa: Maclean, Roger and Co. [October 1, 1884]).

58 Ibid., and *Annual Report of the Department of Indian Affairs* (West Coast Agency) (Ottawa: Maclean, Roger and Co. [August 13, 1885]).

59 LaViolette, *Struggle for Survival*, 74.

60 Quoted in Cole and Chaikin, *Iron Hand Upon the People*, 131.

61 In 1876, all laws affecting Native people in Canada were combined by the federal government under one piece of legislation known as the Indian Act. This statute set forth a complex system for registering Native peoples, administering and controlling their lands, and regulating every aspect of their lives. The ultimate goal of the Act was the complete assimilation of the indigenous population into Euro-Canadian society. Dickason, *Canada's First Nations*, 258–60, 283–86.

62 Tennant, *Aboriginal Peoples and Politics*, 101.

63 The potlatch ban was lifted in the United States with the passage of the Indian Reorganization Act in 1934. In 1951, the Canadian government amended the Indian Act and basically removed the section that banned the potlatch. The law was never rescinded or repealed.

64 From the 1887 Report of the Commissioner of Indian Affairs, quoted in Colson, *The Makah Indians*, 17.

65 Harry Guillod, Annual Report of the Deputy Superintendent-General, Indian Affairs (West Coast Agency) (September 22, 1881), 6.

66 Wayne Suttles, "Affinal Ties, Subsistence, and Prestige among the Coast Salish," *American Anthropologist*, n.s., 62 (April 1960); Suttles, "Coping with Abundance: Subsistence on the Northwest Coast," in *Coast Salish Essays*, ed. Suttles (Vancouver: Talon Books, 1987), 60–63.

67 Goodman and Swan, *Singing the Songs of My Ancestors*, 35.

68 Kirk, *Tradition and Change*, 32.

69 Agnes said potlatches are called *pəsa*, which means flatten gift containers. *Paddling to Where I Stand* (Vancouver: UBC Press, 2004), 123–24.

70 Colson, *The Makah Indians*, 17.

71 Ronald P. Rohner and Evelyn C. Rohner, *The Kwakiutl Indians of British Columbia* (New York: Holt, Rinehart and Winston, 1970), 110.

72 Cole and Chaikin, *Iron Hand Upon the People*, 165, 166.

73 Colson, *The Makah Indians*, 81.

74 Dickason, *Canada's First Nations*, 284–86.

75 Colson, *The Makah Indians*, 107.

76 In the United States, tribes are administered by the Bureau of Indian Affairs. Indian Act, c.29, s.1 (Ottawa: Queen's Printer and Controller, 1951 and 1968), 2–3.

77 The total area encompassed is a little more than 12,000 acres, about half the size of the Makah Reservation. In McMillan, *Since the Time of the Transformers*, 216.

78 Indian Act (1968), 1.

79 Donna Lea Hawley, *The Indian Act Annotated* (Calgary: The Carswell Company Ltd., 1984), 3–4.

80 Eric R. Wolf, *Envisioning Power:Ideologies of Dominance and Crisis* (Berkeley: University of California Press, 1999), 123–31. Wolf examines the impact contact with non-Indians had on chiefs' powers among the Kwakwaka'wakw.

81 Ibid., 128–29.

82 Denis St. Claire, "Tseshaht Traditional Chieftainship," prepared for Tseshaht First Nation, Coast Heritage Consulting, 2007. Also Denis St. Claire, pers. comm., October 18, 2007.

83 Colson, *The Makah Indians*, 81.

84 *Annual Report of the Department of Indian Affairs* (Ottawa: Mclean, Roger and Co., August 13, 1885).

85 Colson, *The Makah Indians*, 18.

86 James Swan, *Indians of Cape Flattery* (Washington, D.C.: Smithsonian Institution, 1870), 33.

87 Agent Harry Guillod, *Annual Report of the Department of Indian Affairs* (West Coast Agency) (Ottawa: Maclean, Roger and Co., October 16, 1882).

88 Rolf Knight, *Indians at Work: An Informal History of Native Labour in British Columbia, 1858*–1930 (Vancouver, B.C.: New Star Books, 1996); John Lutz, "After the Fur Trade: The Aboriginal Labouring Class of British Columbia, 1849–1890," *Journal of the Canadian Historical Association* 3, no. 1 (1992).

89 T. W. Paterson, "Foreign Competition, Too Much Hunting Threat to Whalers," *The Daily Colonist*, July 4, 1965, 6.

90 George Gibbs, "Tribes of Western Washington and Northwestern Oregon," *Contributions to North American Ethnology* 1 (Washington, D.C.: Government Printing Office, 1877), 175.

91 Elizabeth Crawford Cairn, "Nuu-chah-nulth Labour Relations in the Pelagic Sealing Industry, 1868–1911," master's thesis, University of Victoria, 2006; Knight, *Indians at Work*, 217–30.

92 From the 1885 Makah Agent Annual Report. In Cary C. Collins, "Subsistence and Survival: The Makah Indian Reservation, 1855-1933," *Pacific Northwest Quarterly* 87, no. 4 (Fall 1996): 184.

93 Knight, *Indians at Work*, 163.

94 Collins, "Subsistence and Survival," 185.

95 Ibid., 189.

96 Knight, *Indians at Work*, 152–57.

97 Ibid., 214.

98 Scott Richardson, "Washington State Status Report for the Gray Whale" (Washington Department of Fisheries and Oceans, 1997), 4.

99 Richard I. Inglis and James C. Haggerty, "Humpback Off Port Bow," *Wildlife Review* (Spring 1985): 25; Nichol et al., *British Columbia Whaling Catch Data 1908 to 1967: A Detailed Description of the B.C. Historical Whaling Database*, Canadian Technical Report of Fisheries and Aquatic Sciences 2396 (2002), 2.

100 Robert Lloyd Webb, *On the Northwest: Commercial Whaling in the Pacific*

Northwest, 1790–1967 (Vancouver: UBC Press, 1988), 135–45. New regulations established that whales would have to be processed within twenty-four hours after being killed. Paterson, "Foreign Competition," 7.

101 The whaling station in Gray's Harbor predominantly hunted the humpback whale. John Calambokidis, Gretchen Steiger, and David Ellifrit, *Distribution and Abundance of Humpback Whales and Other Mammals off the Northwestern Washington Coast*, National Oceanic and Atmospheric Administration Fishery Bulletin 102, no. 4 (2004), 563. Nichol et al., *British Columbia Whaling Catch*, 11–17.

102 Inglis and Haggarty, "Humpback Off Port Bow," 26; Webb, *On the Northwest*, 143, 224–25.

103 The first whaling station to open was Sechart in 1905, followed by Kyuquot in 1907, both in Barkley Sound. The third station opened in 1907 at Page's Lagoon near Nanaimo and was in operation for only two years. Two more stations opened in the Queen Charlotte Islands, one in Rose Harbour in 1910 and one in Naden Harbour the following year. The final station opened in Coal Harbour in 1948 and stayed in operation until 1967. A small shore-based station had opened in 1868 in Saanich Inlet. It later moved to Cortez Island and then Whaletown on Hornby Island, where it went bankrupt five years later. No data were kept during the first three years of operation of these five whaling stations. Nichol et al., *British Columbia Whaling Catch*, 11–17.

104 Ibid., 9–10.

105 Webb, *On the Northwest*, 206–7; Knight, *Indians at Work*, 216.

106 As recorded in the Makah Indian agent annual reports. Collins, "Subsistence and Survival," 183.

107 Earl Swanson, "Nootka and the Cali-fornia Gray Whale," *Pacific Northwest Quarterly* 47, no. 2 (1956): 52–56. Inglis and Haggarty, "Humpback Off Port Bow," 26, 27; Nichol et al., *British Columbia Whaling Catch*, 10.

108 Edward Sapir et al., *The Whaling Indians: Legendary Hunters* (Ganiteau, B.C.: Canadian Museum of Civilization, 2004), xix; Alan D. McMillan and Denis E. St. Claire, *Ts'ishaa: Archaeology and Ethnography of a Nuu-chah-nulth Origin Site in Barkley Sound* (Burnaby: Archaeology Press, Simon Fraser University, 2005), 26–27.

109 In 1943, a new whaling station opened in Coal Harbour and stayed in operation until 1967. Nichol et al., *British Columbia Whaling Catch*, 9–10. Edward J. Gregr et al., "Migration and Population Structure of Northeastern Pacific Whales of Coastal British Columbia: An Analysis of Commercial Whaling Records from 1908–1967," *Marine Mammal Science* 16 (2002): 699–720.

110 David R. Huelsbeck,"Whaling in the Precontact Economy of the Central Northwest Coast," *Arctic Anthropology* 25, no. 1 (1988): 8. Ann Renker, "Whale Hunting and the Makah Tribe: A Needs Statement," International Whaling Commission, Aboriginal Subsistence Working Group, April 2007, 21; www.iwcoffice.org/document/commission/iwc59docs/59-ASW%209.pdf.

111 Collins, "Subsistence and Survival," 183.

112 Sproat, *Scenes and Studies of Savage Life*, 61.

113 Colson, *The Makah Indians*, 154–56.

114 Webb, *On the Northwest*, 116.

115 Swan, *The Indians of Cape Flattery*, 11.

116 Wolf, *Envisioning Power*, 128.

117 Denis St. Claire, "Tseshaht Traditional Chieftainship," prepared for the Tseshaht First Nation, Coast Heritage Consulting, Victoria, B.C., 77–80. Also Denis St. Claire, pers. comm., October 18, 2007.

118 Atleo, *Tsawalk*, 117, 135.

119   For the classic anthropological definitions of culture, see Edward B. Tylor, who describes it as the "complex whole which includes knowledge, belief, art, morals, law, custom, and any other capabilities and habits acquired by man" in *Primitive Culture: Researches into the Development of Mythology, Philosophy, Religion, Art, and Custom* (London: Murray, 1881); Franz Boas, *The Mind of Primitive Man* (New York: Macmillan, 1911); Ruth Benedict, *Patterns of Culture* (Boston: Houghton Mifflin, 1934); Alfred L. Kroeber, *The Nature of Culture* (Chicago: University of Chicago Press, 1952); Alfred Kroeber, Clyde Klukhohn, et al., *Culture: A Critical Review of Concepts and Definitions* (Cambridge, Mass.: Peabody Museum, 1952); Clifford Geertz, *The Interpretation of Cultures: Selected Essays* (New York: Basic Books, 1973).

3 / KUTSA

1   Alan D. McMillan and Denis E. St. Claire, *Ts'ishaa: Archaeology and Ethnography of a Nuu-chah-nulth Origin Site in Barkley Sound* (Burnaby, B.C.: Archaeology Press, Simon Fraser University, 2005), 8.
2   Ibid., 35.
3   Ibid.
4   Jan Vansina, *Oral Tradition as History* (Madison: University of Wisconsin Press, 1985), 21–27; David Adams Leeming, "Creation," in *Storytelling Encyclopedia: Historical, Cultural, and Multiethnic Approaches to Oral Traditions around the World* (Phoenix: Oryx Press, 1997), 125; Veronica Strang, *Uncommon Ground: Cultural Landscapes and Environmental Values* (New York: Oxford University Press, 1997), 242–46.
5   Anne Hunter, pers. com., August 27, 2008.
6   Edward Sapir and Morris Swadesh, *Native Accounts of Nootka Ethnography* (Bloomington: Indiana University Press, 1955), 52–53. The story is included in the chapter titled "Beliefs."
7   Anthropologist Susan Golla said her informants told her that the person who created the Tseshaht was Haw'ilth N'as, which means Chief in the Sky. In the late 1970s, Susan Golla conducted fieldwork with the Tseshaht and the Huupachasaht Nuu-chah-nulth Nations in Port Alberni. She worked with elders on translating some of Sapir's *Nootka Texts*. She includes an English translation of the 1910 version in her chapter "Legendary History of the Tsisha'ath: A Working Translation," in *Nuu-chah-nulth Voices: Histories, Objects and Journeys,* ed. Alan L. Hoover (Victoria: British Royal Museum, 2000), 133–70.
8   In the 1910 version of this story, Sayach'apis said the old man's name was Kapkimyis and he was either the son or the brother of Kwatya't, the Nuu-chah-nulth trickster-transformer-creator. Susan Golla includes an English translation of the 1910 version in "Legendary History of the Tsisha'ath," 138–40. Archaeologists Alan D. McMillan and Denis E. St. Claire, who also conducted extensive research with the Tseshaht, included translations of the 1922 version in their book *Ts'ishaa: Archaeology and Ethnography of a Nuu-chah-nulth Origin Site in Barkley Sound* (Burnaby, B.C.: Archaeology Press, Simon Fraser University, 2005), 8–9.
9   The 1910 and 1939 versions have only one man present at the Creation, Kapkimyis, who is also called a shaman. The 1910 version of the story is translated by Golla in "Legendary History of the Tsisha'ath," 138–40. For the 1939 version, see Sapir and Swadesh, *Nootka Texts: Tales of Ethnological Narratives* (Philadelphia: University of Pennsylvania, 1939), 165–66.

10   Oral stories say that this boy's origi-
      nal name was Ch'ichu'7ath, which
      Sayach'apis uses in his 1910 story. The
      name Ch'ichu'7ath, translates as "Cut-
      Person." Later, the boy took the name
      N'a'siya ato, also spelled Naasiya atu,
      which translates as "Day Comes Down,"
      in Golla, "Legendary History of the
      Tsisha'ath," 167, 169, and in McMillan
      and St. Claire, *Ts'ishaa*, 8.

11   See Golla, "Legendary History of the
      Tsisha'ath, 167, and McMillan and St.
      Claire, *Ts'ishaa*, 8.

12   I do not know why Sapir writes the
      name as Day-Dawn here, rather than
      Day-Down.

13   Sayach'apis, in Sapir and Swadesh,
      *Native Accounts of Nootka Ethnogra-
      phy* (Bloomington: Research Center in
      Anthropology, Folklore, and Linguis-
      tics, Indiana University, 1955), 52–53.

14   Richard Atleo, *Tsawalk: A Nuu-chah-
      nulth Worldview* (Vancouver: UBC
      Press, 2004), 3.

15   Ibid., 10.

16   Sayach'apis, in Sapir and Swadesh,
      Native Accounts of Nootka Ethnography,
      53–56.

17   McMillan and St. Claire, *Ts'ishaa*,
      10–11; Golla, "Legendary History of the
      Tsisha'ath," 138–39.

18   In *Tsawalk*, Umeek says that Nuu-chah-
      nulth-aht referred to their houses as big
      houses rather than longhouses (p. 1).

19   Sayach'apis was born around 1843. See
      McMillan and St. Claire, *Ts'ishaa*, 23.

20   Ibid., 9–10.

21   Ibid., 10.

22   In 1882 the Tseshaht group was allocated
      nine reserve sites that were located on
      the islands and shores in Barkley Sound,
      along the Alberni Inlet, and along the
      Somass River. McMillan and St. Claire,
      Ts'ishaa, 205.

23   Veronica Strang, *Uncommon Ground,*
      217–19; Angèle Smith, "Landscape
      Representation: Place and Identity in

Nineteenth-Century Ordinance Survey
Maps of Ireland," in *Landscape, Memory
and History*, ed. Pamela J. Stewart and
Andrew Strathern (London: Pluto Press,
2003), 71–72.

24   Thomas F. Thornton, "Anthropological
      Studies of Native American Place Nam-
      ing," *American Indian Quarterly* 2, no. 2
      (Spring 1997): 215–16.

25   Thomas F. Thornton, *Being and Place
      among the Tlingit* (Seattle: University of
      Washington Press, 2008), 31.

26   John J. Bradley, "Wirriyarra Awara:
      Yanyuwa Land and Sea Scapes," *The
      South Atlantic Quarterly* 98, no. 4 (Fall
      1999): 801.

27   Keith Basso, "'Speaking with Names':
      Language and Landscape among the
      Western Apache," *Cultural Anthropol-
      ogy* 3, no. 2 (1988): 103.

28   Thornton, *Being and Place*, 6.

29   Thornton, "Anthropological Studies of
      Native American Place Naming," 209.

30   Pamela J. Stewart and Andrew Strath-
      ern, "Introduction," in *Landscape,
      Memory and History*, ed. Stewart and
      Strathern, 5–6.

31   Julie Cruikshank, "Getting the Words
      Right: Perspectives on Naming and
      Places in Athapaskan Oral History,"
      Arctic Anthropology 27, no. 1 (1990):
      63–64.

32   Ibid., i.

33   McMillan and St. Claire, *Ts'ishaa*, 10.

34   Ibid.

35   Ibid.

36   Basso, "'Speaking with Names,'" 122.

37   Ibid., 103; Basso, "'Stalking with Stories':
      Names, Places, and Moral Narratives
      among the Western Apache," in *Text,
      Play, and Story: The Construction and
      Reconstruction of Self and Society*, ed.
      Stuart Plattner (proceedings editor), 1983
      Proceedings of the American Ethnologi-
      cal Society (Washington, D.C.: Ameri-
      can Ethnological Society, 1984), 27.

38   Keith Basso, *Wisdom Sits in Places:*

Landscape and Language among the Western Apache (Albuquerque: University of New Mexico Press, 1996), 146.

39 Thornton, *Being and Place*, 68–115; Stewart and Strathern, *Landscape, Memory, and History*, 3–4; Basso, *Wisdom Sits in Places*, 143–49.

40 Bradley, "Wirriyarra Awara," 804; Ian J. McNiven, "Saltwater People: Spiritscapes, Maritime Rituals and the Archaeology of Australian Indigenous Seascapes," *World Archaeology* 35, no. 3 (December 2003): 330–34.

41 Sonny McHalsie, "Halq'eméylem Place Names in Stó:lō Territory," in *A Stó:lō Coast Salish Historical Atlas*, ed. Keith Thor Carlson et al. (Vancouver: Douglas and McIntire, 2001), 135.

42 McMillan and St. Claire, *Ts'ishaa*, 10.

43 Our whaling *haw'iih* ceremonial washing houses or shrines were the most sacred of all sites in Nuu-chah-nulth territories. These sites were kept secret and were hidden in the dense forests or on secluded islands. At these sacred sites, the *haw'ilth* would conduct rituals to implore supernatural beings for assistance in whaling. Aldona Jonaitis, *The Yuquot Whaler's Shrine* (Seattle: University of Washington Press, 1999).

44 Craig Howe, "Keep Your Thoughts Above the Trees: Ideas on Developing and Presenting Tribal Histories," in *Clearing a Path: Theorizing the Past in Native American Studies*, ed. Nancy Shoemaker (New York: Routledge, 2002), 161–64.

45 Jan Vansina, *Oral Tradition as History* (Madison: University of Wisconsin Press, 1985), xi.

46 Jan Vansina, *Oral Tradition: A Study in Historical Methodology* (Chicago: Aldine Publishing Company, 1961 and 1965), 19, 20.

47 Julie Cruikshank, *The Social Life of Stories: Narrative and Knowledge in the Yukon Terrirory* (Vancouver: UBC

1998); Alex Carroll, "Oral Traditions," in *American Indian Religious Traditions: An Encyclopedia*, ed. Suzanne J. Crawford and Dennis F. Kelly (Santa Barbara: ABC-CLIO, 2005).

48 Carroll, "Oral Traditions," 633–37.

49 Colleen Boyd, "Oral Traditions, Northwest Coast," in *American Indian Religious Traditions*, ed. Crawford and Kelly, 665.

50 Michael Chi'XapKaid Pavel, "Decolonizing through Storytelling," in *For Indigenous Eyes Only: A Decolonization Handbook*, ed. Waziyatawin Angela Wilson and Michael Yellowbird (Santa Fe: School of American Research Press, 2005), 131–32.

51 Ibid., 136, 137.

52 Kwaatie is the trickster character in Makah and Nuu-chah-nulth legends. Ishkus is the evil woman in Makah legends, and Snot Boy is the character who saves young Makahs from being taken and killed by Ishkus. Linda J. Goodman and Helma Swan, *Singing the Songs of My Ancestors: The Life and Music of Helma Swan, Makah Elder* (Norman: University of Oklahoma Press, 2003), 283.

53 Goodman and Swan, *Singing the Songs*, 64–65.

54 Quoted in Kimberly M. Blaeser, *Gerald Vizenor: Writing in the Oral Tradition* (Norman: University of Oklahoma Press, 1996), 72.

55 Angela Cavender Wilson, "Grandmother to Granddaughter: Generations of Oral History in a Dakota Family," in *Natives and Academics. Researching and Writing about American Indians*, ed. Devon A. Mihesuah (Lincoln: University of Nebraska Press, 1999), 27.

56 From the Introduction to Part 10 of the Sapir Texts, *The Whaling Indians: Tales of Extraordinary Experience* (Ottawa: Canadian Museum of Civilization, 2000), x.

57 Charlotte Coté, review of "The Whaling Indians: Legendary Hunters" by Edward Sapir et al., *American Review of Canadian Studies* (Fall 2005).

58 Ibid.

59 Many of these stories are recorded in Sapir and Swadesh, *Nootka Texts: Tales and Ethnological Narratives* (Philadelphia: University of Pennsylvania, 1939). The Mink story is on page 80.

60 My mother passed away in 1986.

61 Bruce Ballenger, "Methods of Memory: On Native American Storytelling," *College English* 59, no. 7 (November 1997): 792.

62 Throughout the last thirty years, Denis St. Claire has worked extensively with the Tseshaht people and has compiled numerous materials for us. He has worked with many of our elders, many of whom have since passed on. He held our elders in the greatest respect and has always acknowledged them in his research.

63 Sapir and Swadesh, *Nootka Texts*, 9.

64 This is based on the information Sapir collected from Sayach'apis, which was included in the 1910–14 notebook. Documented in St. Claire, *Thomas Family History and Genealogy*, 25–26.

65 Wiitsah's father, Tuutaa ap, had the fourth *haw'ilh* seat of the Ts'ishaa-aht, according to Sapir's conversations with Tseshaht ancestors. In St. Claire, *Thomas Family History and Genealogy*, 49–50.

66 Ibid., 50.

67 Ibid.

68 My grandmother came from the neighboring Nuu-chah-nulth village of Hupacasath.

69 St. Claire, *Thomas Family History and Genealogy*, 25, and pers. comm., October 24, 2008.

70 Sapir, "Sayach'apis, a Nootka Trader," in *American Indian Life*, ed. Elsie Parsons (Lincoln: University of Nebraska Press, 1922), 312.

71 Denis St. Claire, pers. comm., October 18, 2007.

72 Sayach'apis, in Sapir and Swadesh, *Native Accounts of Nootka Ethnography*, 53.

73 "Sayachapis, "Stands-Up-High-Over-All," Tseshaht First Nation Web site, http://www.tseshaht.com/tradition_history/figures/sayachapis.php. Denis St. Claire, pers. comm., October 18, 2007.

74 Sapir et al., *The Whaling Indians: Tales of Extraordinary Experience* (Ottawa: Canadian Museum of Civilization, 2000), xxii.

75 The symbols used in the story are from Sapir's language system and are different from those used by the Nuu-chah-nulth today.

76 E. Y. Arima et al., *Between Ports Alberni and Renfrew* (Ottawa: Canadian Museum of Civilization, 1991), 29.

77 Sapir et al., *The Whaling Indians: Legendary Hunters* (Ottawa: Museum of Civilization, 2004), 216.

78 Basso, "Speaking with Names," 110.

79 Ibid.

80 Ibid.

81 Cruikshank, *The Social Life of Stories*, 2–4, 26–36, 145–53.

82 Julie Cruikshank, *Life Lived Like a Story: Life Stories of Three Yukon Elders* (Lincoln: University of Nebraska Press, 1990).

83 Ibid.

84 McHalsie, "Halq'eméylem Place Names," 135.

85 Basso, *Wisdom Sits in Places*, 146.

86 Angèle Smith, "Landscape Representation," 78.

87 Nuu-chah-nulth elder Tlii-shin, Spencer Peters (Huu-ay-aht), quoted in Martha Black, *Huupukanum Tupaat, Out of the Mist: Treasures of the Nuu-chah-nulth Chiefs* (Victoria: Royal British Columbia Museum, 1999), 135.

88 Michael Chi'XapKaid Pavel, "Decolonizing through Storytelling," in *For*

Indigenous Eyes Only: A Decolonization Handbook, ed. Waziyatawin Angela Wilson and Michael Yellow Bird (Santa Fe: School of American Research Press, 2005), 131–33.

89 Goodman and Swan, *Singing the Songs*, 127.

90 Ibid.

91 Helen H. Roberts and Morris Swadesh, *Songs of the Nootka Indians of Western Vancouver Island* (Philadelphia: The American Philosophical Society, 1955), 201–3; Linda J. Goodman and Helma Swan, "Makah Music," in *Spirit of the First People: Native American Music Traditions of Washington State*, ed. Willie Smyth and Esmé Ryan (Seattle: University of Washington Press, 1999), 83; Linda Goodman, *Music and Dance in Northwest Coast Indian Life* (Tsaile, Ariz.: Navajo Community College Press, 1977), 10–11.

92 Roberts and Swadesh, *Songs of the Nootka Indians*, 202–3; Loren Olsen, "Native Music of the Pacific Northwest," in *Spirit of the First People*, ed. Smyth and Ryan, 107–8.

93 Goodman and Swan, "Makah Music," 83–85.

94 Roberts and Swadesh, *Songs of the Nootka Indians*, 202–3.

95 Loren Olsen, "Native Music of the Pacific Northwest," 110–11.

96 Roberts and Swadesh, *Songs of the Nootka Indians*, 323.

97 Goodman and Swan, *Singing the Songs*, 206–7.

98 Ibid.

99 Sapir et al., *The Whaling Traders*, xiv.

100 Roberts and Swadesh, *Songs of the Nootka Indians* 199.

101 Ibid., 316.

102 Ibid., 315.

103 Ibid.

104 Ibid., 312.

105 Linda Goodman, *Music and Dance in Northwest Coast Indian Life* (Tsaile,

Ariz.: Navajo Community College Press, 1977), 26.

106 Sapir and Swadesh, *Nootka Texts*, 159. Roberts and Swadesh, *Songs of the Nootka Indians*, 312.

107 In Roberts and Swadesh, *Songs of the Nootka Indians*, 312.

108 In Makah and Nuu-chah-nulth pre-contact societies, only free persons had rights to names. Individuals from the slave ranks were given names by their chiefs. Golla, "Legendary History of the Tsisha'ath," 163; Ruth Kirk, *Tradition and Change on the Northwest Coast: The Makah, Nuu-chah-nulth, Southern Kwakiutl, and Nuxalk* (Seattle: University of Washington Press, 1986), 56.

109 Golla, "Legendary History of the Tsisha'ath," 164–66.

110 Kirk, *Tradition and Change*, 55.

111 *Nuu-chah-nulth Traditional Whaling*, 10 (Teacher's Resource Book, Native Studies Programme, School District No. 70, Port Alberni, B.C.).

112 Sapir, "Sayach'apis, a Nootka Trader," 298.

113 Ibid.

114 Ibid.

115 Sayach'apis, in Sapir et al., *Native Accounts of Nootka Ethnography*, 53.

116 Sapir, "Sayach'apis, a Nootka Trader," 298. Denis St. Claire, pers. comm., October 18, 2007.

117 Alan D. McMillan, "Early Nuu-chah-nulth Art and Adornment: Glimpses from the Archaeological Record," in *Nuu-chah-nulth Voices*, ed. Alan Hoover, 250.

118 Aldona Jonaitis, *Art of the Northwest Coast* (Seattle: University of Washington Press, 2006), 41–44.

119 McMillan, "Early Nuu-chah-nulth Art and Adornment," 235, 237.

120 Ibid. Jeffrey Mauger "Shed-Roof Houses at Ozette and in a Regional Perspective," in *Ozette Archaeological Project Research Reports*, vol. 1 (Pullman:

Washington State University, 1991), 110; Aldona Jonaitis, *Art of the Northwest Coast* (Seattle: University of Washington Press, 2006), 41.

121 E. N. Anderson, ed., *Bird of Paradox. The Unpublished Writings of Wilson Duff* (Surrey, B.C.: Hancock House, 1996), 61–63; Hillary Stewart, *Cedar* (Seattle: University of Washington Press, 1984), 29.

122 Jonaitis, *Art of the Northwest Coast*, 229.

123 Ibid., 198–219.

124 The picture of this basket is in Jonaitis, *Art of the Northwest Coast*, 202.

125 Gary Wyatt, *Mythic Beings: Spirit Art of the Northwest Coast* (Seattle: University of Washington Press, 1999), 14.

126 Ibid., 138.

127 Art Thompson had many Nuu-chah-nulth names during his lifetime: Cha-chuck-mii-ah, Thlop-kee-tupp, Pul-kii-num, Chiiq-meek, and Tsaq-wassup (most people knew him by the latter). He received his final name, Gahnos, just before he succumbed to cancer in April 2003, at the age of fifty-four.

128 Art was interviewed by Kanawake scholar Taiaiake Alfred just before he passed away. Dr. Alfred printed his interview in the University of Victoria's publication *Celanen*. The interview is titled "My Grandmother, She Raised Me Up Again: A Tribute to the Memory of Art Tsaqwassupp Thompson," *Celanen: A Journal of Indigenous Governance*; http://www.uvic.ca/igov/research/journal/articles_taiaiake.htm.

129 Art Thompson, pers. comm.

130 In Alfred, "My Grandmother, She Raised Me Up Again," 4.

131 In Nuu-chah-nulth and Makah oral tradition, Pook-ubs (pook-oobs) was a whaler who was lost at sea while hunting whales. After an extended period in the water, his body would occasionally wash ashore, transformed into a spirit

being. He would still have his hair tied back in a whaler's knot but his skin would be wrinkled and white from being in the ocean water for so long.

132 Alfred, "My Grandmother, She Raised Me Up Again," 4.

133 Evelyn Thompson, pers. comm., November 2008.

134 "wcw Attends Panel on Indigenous Whaling," *World Council of Whalers News* (October 1999), 2.

135 Ibid., 7.

4 / MUU

1 When the U.S. government attempted to assert authority over the Makah, it seized a sealing vessel owned by a Makah member for not complying with the sealing ban. With the counsel of James Swan, the Makah sued, in *United States v. The* James G. Swan (1892), arguing that the ban violated their 1855 treaty, which guaranteed their fishing rights. Cary C. Collins, "Subsistence and Survival: The Makah Indian Reservation, 1855–1933," *Pacific Northwest Quarterly* 87, no. 4 (1996): 187–88.

2 Quoted in Joel Geffen and Suzanne Crawford, "First Salmon Rites," in *American Indian Religious Freedoms: An Encyclopedia*, ed. Suzanne J. Crawford and Dennis F. Kelly (Santa Barbara: ABC-CLIO, 2005), 313.

3 Geffen and Crawford, "First Salmon Rites," 311–20; Jovanna J. Brown, "Fishing Rights and the First Salmon Ceremony," in Crawford and Kelly, *American Indian Religious Freedoms*, 320–24; Hilary Stewart, *Indian Fishing: Early Methods on the Northwest Coast* (Seattle: University of Washington Press, 1977, 1982), 161–71.

4 Quoted in *Uncommon Controversy: Fishing Rights of the Muckleshoot, Puyallup, and Nisqually Indians*, a report prepared for the American Friends

Service Committee (Seattle: University of Washington Press, 1970, 1975), 82–83.

5   *Uncommon Controversy*, 83.

6   David H. Getches et al., *Federal Indian Law* (Minneapolis: West Publishing Co., 1993), 158–62, 862–63; *Uncommon Controversy*, 84–85.

7   Getches et al., *Federal Indian Law*, 158–62, 862–63; Charles Wilkinson, *Messages from Frank's Landing: A Story of Salmon, Treaties, and the Indian Way* (Seattle: University of Washington Press, 2000), 52, 53.

8   Fay G. Cohen, *Treaties on Trial: The Continuing Controversy over Northwest Indian Fishing Rights* (Seattle: University of Washington Press, 1986), 63.

9   *Uncommon Controversy*, 88–89.

10 Paul Chaat Smith and Robert Allen Warrior, *Like a Hurricane: The Indian Movement from Alcatraz to Wounded Knee* (New York: The New Press, 1996), 44–46; Stephen Cornell, *The Return of the Native: American Indian Political Resurgence* (New York: Oxford University Press, 1988), 189–90; Vine Deloria Jr., *Behind the Trail of Broken Treaties: An Indian Declaration of Independence* (Austin: University of Texas Press, 1974, 1990), 25–28. See also Wilkinson, *Messages*, 34; *Uncommon Controversy*, 86–87.

11 Chat Smith and Warrior, *Like a Hurricane*, 44–47; Wilkinson, *Messages*, 32–48.

12 Deloria Jr., *Behind the Trail of Broken Treaties*; Charles Wilkinson, *Blood Struggle: The Rise of Modern Indian Nations* (New York: W. W. Norton, 2005). Chaat Smith and Warrior, *Like a Hurricane*; Troy Johnson, Joane Nagel, and Duane Champagne, *American Indian Activism: Alcatraz to the Longest Walk* (Chicago: University of Illinois Press, 1997); Peter Matthiessen, *In the Spirit of Crazy Horse* (New York: Penguin Books, 1980, 1992); Wilkinson, *Messages*.

13 Alexandra Harmon, *Indians in the Making: Ethnic Relations and Indian Identities around Puget Sound* (Berkeley: University of California Press, 1998), 228, 231.

14 Quoted in Wilkinson, *Messages*, 33.

15 *Uncommon Controversy*, 92–97; Cohen, *Treaties on Trial*, 76–77.

16 *Uncommon Controversy*, 113–14.

17 Ibid., 113.

18 Cohen, *Treaties on Trial*, 72.

19 Ibid., 72–78; Wilkinson, *Messages*, 49–50.

20 Cohen, *Treaties on Trial*, 6–7.

21 Ibid., 4–5.

22 Wilkinson, *Messages*, 52–55.

23 *U.S. v. Washington*, 384 F. Supp. 312, 1974, U.S. Dist., 8–11.

24 Ibid., 10.

25 Ibid., 11.

26 Ibid., 323.

27 Ibid., 48–50.

28 In 1979 the U.S. Supreme Court upheld the Boldt Decision in *Washington v. Washington State Commercial Passenger Vessel Association*, 443 U.S. 658 (1979).

29 Charlotte Coté, "Historical Foundations of Indian Sovereignty in Canada and the United States: A Brief Overview," *American Review of Canadian Studies* (Spring/Summer 2001). 15, 16.

30 Christopher McKee, *Treaty Talks in British Columbia: Negotiating a Mutually Beneficial Future* (Vancouver: UBC Press, 1996), 17–23; Paul Tennant, *Aboriginal Peoples and Politics: The Indian Land Question in British Columbia, 1849–1989* (Vancouver: UBC Press, 1990), 39–52; Brian Titley, *A Narrow Vision: Duncan Campbell Scott and the Administration of Indian Affairs in Canada* (Vancouver: UBC Press, 1986), 134–63.

31 Michael Asch, *Home and Native Land: Aboriginal Rights and the Canadian Constitution* (Toronto: Methuen, 1984), 9.

32 Harold Cardinal, *The Unjust Society: The Tragedy of Canada's Indians* (Edmonton: M. G. Hurtig Ltd. Publishers, 1969), 1.

33 Peter McFarlane, *Brotherhood to Nationhood: George Manuel and the Making of a Modern Indian Movement* (Toronto: Between the Lines, 1993), 115–21.

34 Tim Schouls, "The Basic Dilemma: Sovereignty or Assimilation," in *Nation to Nation: Aboriginal Sovereignty and the Future of Canada*, ed. John Bird et al. (Toronto: Irwin Publishing, 2002), 19–21; Asch, *Home and Native Land*, 8–9, 63–64.

35 Section 35 (1) of the Constitution Act (1982) states that "the existing aboriginal and treaty rights of aboriginal peoples of Canada are hereby recognized and affirmed." Canadian Department of Justice Web site, http://www.laws.justice .gc.ca/en/const/annex_e.html#II.

36 Peter Kulchyski, *Unjust Relations: Aboriginal Rights in Canadian Courts* (Toronto: Oxford University Press, 1994), 61–126.

37 Originally, sixteen bands came under the name West Coast Allied Tribes; the West Coast District Council assumed administrative responsibility for only thirteen of these bands, with the other bands acting on their own; in "Chiefs Council Assumes Duties," *AV Times* (February 8, 1974). The NTC is composed of fourteen groups. Frank Cassidy and Robert L. Bish, *Indian Government: Its Meaning in Practice* (Lantzville, B.C.: Oolichan Books, 1989); Tennant, *Aboriginal People and Politics*, 123–24.

38 Tennant, *Aboriginal People and Politics*, 124.

39 Frank Cassidy and Norman Dale, *After Native Claims? The Implications of Comprehensive Claims Settlements for Natural Resources in British Columbia* (Lantzville: Oolichan Books, 1988), 7;

Cassidy and Bish, *Indian Government*, 92.

40 Quoted in Cassidy and Bish, *Indian Government*, 91. My cousin Hugh Braker was the first Nuu-chah-nulth male to achieve a law degree and the first B.C. Native lawyer to be made a Queen's Counsel (Q.C.).

41 George Watts, a well-known political leader, was my uncle; he passed away in 2005 at the age of fifty-nine.

42 Quoted in *Aboriginal Self-Determination*, ed. Frank Cassidy (Lantzville, B.C.: Oolichan Books, 1991), 163.

43 Cassidy and Bish, *Indian Government*, 90–94. *George Watts . . . Creating Greatness: A Tribute to George Watts through Recipes, Stories and Much More!* (Port Alberni: Nuu-chah-nulth Economic Development Corporation, 2007), 5–28.

44 Tennant, *Aboriginal People and Politics*, 223.

45 Des Kennedy, "Belonging to the Land. The Meaning of Meares Island," *The Canadian Forum* 65 (June/July 1985): 13.

46 Morley Eldridge, "The Significance and Management of Culturally Modified Trees," final report prepared for the Vancouver Forest Region and CMT Standards Steering Committee, Millennia Research Ltd. (January 13, 1997), 1; http://www.tsa.gov.bc.ca/archaeology/ docs/culturally_modified_trees_ significance_management.pdf.

47 Des Kennedy, "Belonging to the Land: The Meaning of Meares Island," *Canadian Forum* 65 (June/July 1985): 13. In the early 1980s, the Nuu-chah-nulth Tribal Council contributed funding for a project to inventory the culturally modified trees on Meares Island. Morley Eldridge, "Significance and Management of Culturally Modified Trees," 3.

48 Hilary Stewart, *Cedar* (Seattle: University of Washington Press, 1984), 17–19.

49 Kennedy, "Belonging to the Land."

50 Dimitri Portier, "The Meares Island

Case: Nuu-chah-nulth vs. the Logging Industry," *European Review of Native American Studies* 14, no. 1 (2000): 33.

51 Tennant, *Aboriginal People and Politics*, 223.

52 Quoted in ibid., 293.

53 Quoted in Portier, "The Meares Island Case," 35.

54 The continual demands of First Nations in Canada led to the eventual recognition and affirmation of their "existing Aboriginal and treaty rights" in the Constitution Act of 1982.

55 *Regina v. Dick* (June 25, 1993) upheld our hunting rights; *Regina v. NTC Smokehouse* (June 25, 1993) ruled that the Nuu-chah-nulth did not have a commercial right to fish; *Regina v. Jack, John and John* (December 20, 1995) upheld Nuu-chah-nulth fishing rights. See "Jerry Jack Wins Big in Court of Appeal," *Ha-Shilth-Sa* (February 8, 1996), 5; Thomas Isaac, *Aboriginal Law: Cases, Materials and Commentary* (Saskatchewan: Purich Publishing, 1995), 224–39; Canadian Native Law Reports (1993), 158–220, and (1996), 113–36; Hugh Braker, "A Shot in the Dark: Issues in Aboriginal Hunting Rights," paper presented at the Native Investment and Trade Association Conference, Aboriginal Law in Canada, September 26–27, 1996, Vancouver, B.C. Information on the cases is available on the Ministry of Aboriginal Relations and Reconciliation Web site, http://www.gov.bc.ca/arr/treaty/landmark_cases.html.

56 The Nuu-chah-nulth Research and Litigation Project, NTC Web site, http://www.nuuchahnulth.org/tribalcouncil/fisheries.html.

57 "Litigation," NTC Fisheries Department site, http://uuathluk.ca/treaty.htm.

58 "Nuu-chah-nulth Nations Conclude Presentation of Case," NTC Fisheries Department Web site, http://www.uuathluk.ca/treaty.htm.

59 *Ha-shilth-sa* 36, no. 21 (November 5, 2009): 1.

60 Larry Pynn, *Vancouver Sun*, November 3, 2009.

61 *Ha-shilth-sa.*

62 "Nuu-chah-nulth Nations Conclude Presentation," NTC Fisheries Department, http://uuathluk.ca/treaty.htm.

63 Archaeological excavations had taken place at Ozette since the late 1940s, but not on such a massive scale. Stephan R. Samuels and Richard D. Daugherty, "Introduction to the Ozette Archaeological Project," *Ozette Archaeological Project Research Reports*, vol. 1 (Pullman: Washington State University; Seattle: National Parks Service).

64 David Huelsbeck, "The Utilization of Whales at Ozette," *Ozette Archaeological Project Research Reports*, vol. 1 (Pullman: Washington State University; Seattle: National Parks Service), 267–391. Ruth Kirk, with Richard Daugherty, *Hunters of the Whale: An Adventure in Northwest Coast Archaeology* (New York: Morrow and Company, 1974), 92–119.

65 Huelsbeck, "Utilization of Whales at Ozette," 293–97.

66 Jeff Mauger, "Makah Cultural and Research Museum Collections Manager," in *A Gift from the Past* (film), Media Resources Association, Washington, D.C., 1994.

67 Samuels and Daugherty, "Introduction to the Ozette Archaeological Project," 17, 18.

68 *A Gift from the Past* (film).

69 Ibid.

70 Samuels and Daugherty, "Introduction to the Ozette Archaeological Project," 18, 19.

71 Patricia Pierce Erikson, "A-Whaling We Will Go: Encounters of Knowledge and Memory at the Makah Cultural and Research Center," *Cultural Anthropology* 14, no. 4 (1999): 557–58.

72   *A Gift from the Past* (film).

73   Melissa Peterson and the Makah Cultural and Research Center, "The Makah," in *Native Peoples of the Olympic Peninsula. Who We Are*, ed. Jacillee Wray (Norman: University of Oklahoma Press, 2002), 159.

74   Micah McCarty became chair of the Makah Tribal Council in January 2008.

75   Micah McCarty, pers. comm., June 18, 2000, and December 5, 2007.

76   "Might Whale Meat Once Again Find a Place on the Menu?" *High North News*, 11 (November 1996), http://www.highnorth.no/mi-wh-me.htm. Patricia Erikson, "A-Whaling We Will Go," 556–57.

77   Micah McCarty, pers. comm., June 18, 2000.

78   Keith Johnson, "An Open Letter to the Public from the President of the Makah Whaling Commission," August 23, 1998, Native Americans and the Environment, http://cnie.org/NAE/docs/makaheditorial.html.

79   Micah McCarty, pers. comm., June 18, 2007.

80   From a lecture Keith Johnson gave to my class at the University of Washington on May 17, 2007.

81   Keith Johnson, "An Open Letter."

82   Representatives were from the U.S. Department of Commerce; the National Oceanic and Atmospheric Administration (NOAA), which is housed in the DOC; and the National Marine Fisheries Service (NMFS), which is part of NOAA. The United States is a whaling nation, and Alaskan Eskimos have continued an unbroken whaling tradition, hunting bowhead, gray, and beluga whales. About fifty Alaskan Eskimo communities harvest whales, with the bowhead whale being the primary species hunted. The Makah are the only tribe who have a treaty-protected right to hunt whales. The Alaskan whalers, along with the Chuckchi people in Russia, helped the Makah acquire their whaling quota from the IWC. The Alaskan Eskimo whalers agreed to share their bowhead quota with the Chukotkan whalers, who in turn gave part of their gray whale quota to the Makah tribe. *Whaling Around the World*, ed. Kathy Happynook (Ladysmith, B.C.: World Council of Whalers, 2004), 11–13.

83   Makah Indian Tribe Whaling Proposal, May 5, 1995. Signed by Hubert Markishtum, Makah Tribal Council chairman. Received from the Makah Tribal Council Office.

84   In Robert Sullivan, *A Whale Hunt: Two Years on the Olympic Peninsula with the Makah and Their Canoe* (New York: Scribner, 2000), 37.

85   Jennifer Sepez Aradanas, "Aboriginal Whaling: Biological Diversity Meets Cultural Diversity," *Northwest Science* 72, no. 2 (1998): 142.

86   International Whaling Commission: Convention text, 1946, http://www.iwcoffice.org/Convention.htm. International Whaling Commission home page, http://www.iwcoffice.org/commission/iwcmain.htm.

87   International Whaling Commission home page, http://www.iwcoffice.org/commission/iwcmain.htm#history.

88   G. P. Donovan, *The Adhoc Technical Committee Working Group on Development of Management Principles and Guidelines for Subsistence Catches of Whales by Indigenous (Aboriginal) Peoples*. International Whaling Commission and Aboriginal/Subsistence Whaling: April 1979 to July 1981, special issue 4, IWC, Cambridge, England. http://www.highnorth.no/Library/Culture/de-of-ab.htm.

89   Ibid.

90   Erikson, "A-Whaling We Will Go," 562.

91   International Whaling Commission, Chairman's Report, Aboriginal

Subsistence Whaling, 48th Annual Meeting, 1996, http:/luna.pos.to/whale/iwc_chair96_10.html.

92 Aradanas, "Aboriginal Whaling," 143.

93 The ICRW established a schedule of whaling regulations (Schedule) and granted the IWC power to amend the Schedule by adopting subsequent regulations, which included quotas.

94 Extract from Appendix II (changes in bold type), International Whaling Commission, 49th Annual Meeting, 1997, http://www.iwcoffice.org/commission/schedule.htm.

95 Micah McCarty, pers. comm., June 18, 2000. Scott Smullen, "Whaling Commission Approves Combined Russian-Makah Gray Whale Quota," IWC US Delegates News Release, October 23, 1997, http://www.noaa.gov/public-affairs/pr97/oct97/iwc2.html. IWC 49th Annual Meeting, 1997, http://www.iwcoffice.org/meetings/meetingsmain.htm.

96 Keith Johnson, "An Open Letter."

97 "The Makah Indian Tribe and Whaling: A Fact Sheet Issued by the Makah Whaling Commission," July 21, 1998. Posted on the Native Americans and the Environment Web site, http://cnie.org/NAE/docs/makahfaq.html.

98 Johnson, "An Open Letter."

99 Quanah Parker was also well-known from a photo taken of him in his whaling regalia in the 1920s by photographer Edward Curtis.

100 Theron Parker, pers. comm., June 17, 2000.

101 Management plan for Makah Treaty gray whale hunting for the years 1998–2002, Makah Tribal Council, http://www.ncseonline.org/NAE/docs/makahplan.html.

102 Theron Parker, pers. comm., June 17, 2000.

103 Darrell Markishtum, pers. comm., July 17th, 2008.

104 Ibid.

105 Donovan, *The Adhoc Technical Committee Working Group.*

106 Johnson, "An Open Letter."

107 The whale caught in 1999 took eight minutes to die from the moment it was struck by the harpoon. "A Review on the Technique Employed by the Makah Tribe to Harvest Gray Whales," submitted by the U.S. government to the IWC, June 2006.

108 Makah Whaling Commission management plan for Makah Treaty gray whale hunting for the years 1998–2001. On the Native Americans and the Environment Web site, http://cnie.org/NAE/docs/makahplan.html

109 Theron Parker, pers. comm., June 17, 2000.

110 Sullivan, *A Whale Hunt,* 254–58.

111 Ibid., 258.

112 Theron Parker, pers. comm., June 17, 2000.

113 Sullivan, *A Whale Hunt,* 260–63.

114 "Save the Whales for the Makah," *World Council of Whalers News* (June 1999): 2, 3.

115 Johnson, "An Open Letter."

116 Paula Bock, *Seattle Times Magazine* (November 26, 1995); http://www.highnoth.no/a-wh-pe-.htm.

117 Theron Parker, pers. comm., June 17, 2000.

118 Ibid.

119 Florangela Davila, "Makah Students Proudly Rebuild the Remains of a Sacred Whale," *Seattle Times* (April 4, 2000).

120 Ibid.

121 Theron Parker, pers. comm., June 17, 2000.

122 Ibid.

123 Quoted in Milton M. R. Freeman et al., *Inuit, Whaling, and Sustainablility* (Walnut Creek, Calif.: Alta Mira Press, 1998), 85.

124 Ibid., 86.

125 Micah McCarty, pers. comm., June 18, 2000.

126 *The Washing of Tears* (film).

127 Ibid.

128 Aldona Jonaitis, *The Yuquot Whaler's Shrine* (Seattle: University of Washington Press, 1999), xiii.

129 Elders' Whaling Workshop, December 4–5, 2005; audiotape held at the Nuu-chah-nulth Tribal Council Office.

130 Nelson Keitlah, pers. comm., June 9, 2000.

131 Ibid.

132 The B.C. treaty negotiations follow a six-stage process beginning with a statement of intent made by the tribal group; preparation for negotiations; negotiation of a framework agreement; negotiation of an agreement-in-principle; negotiation to finalize the treaty; and, finally, the implementation of the treaty. A Treaty Commission oversees the process and is made up of five commissioners, two of whom are chosen by the First Nations Summit (an organization representing the tribes participating in the B.C. Treaty Negotiation Commission process), one chosen by the federal government, one chosen by the provincial government (in 1990 the B.C. government agreed to participate in the process), and a chief commissioner chosen jointly by all three parties. See Robert J. Muckle, *The First Nations of British Columbia* (Vancouver: UBC Press, 1998, 2000), 80–81.

133 Happynook, *Whaling Around the World* (Ladysmith, B.C.: World Council of Whalers, 2004), 11–13.

134 Stanley Sam, pers. comm., June 9, 2000.

135 Ibid.

136 Ibid.

137 Tom Mexsis Happynook, "Securing Food, Health and Traditional Values through the Sustainable Use of Marine Resources," talk given at the University of Washington, March 2, 2005.

138 Huu-ay-aht, Uchucklesaht, Toquaht, Ucluelet, Ka:' yu:'k'th/Che:k'tles7et'h (negotiated together as one group), Ditidaht, Pacheedaht, and Hupacasath, Treaty Commission update, newsletter, B.C. Treaty Commission (July 2008), 8. See note 129 above. For further information, see Christopher McKee, *Treaty Talks in British Columbia: Negotiating a Mutually Beneficial Future* (Vancouver: UBC Press, 1996); Tony Penikett, *Reconciliation: First Nations Treaty Making in British Columbia* (Vancouver, B.C.: Douglas and McIntire, 2006); Robert J. Muckle, *The First Nations of British Columbia* (Vancouver: UBC Press, 1998, 2000), 80–81.

139 *Together in Treaties: A Nuu-chah-nulth Perspective on Governance*, published by the Nuu-chah-nulth Tribal Council, 1999. McKee, *Treaty Talks in British Columbia*, 47–49; Penikett, *Reconciliation*, 88; Cassidy and Dale, *After Native Claims?* 218, Muckle, *First Nations of British Columbia*, 80–81.

140 Section 35(1) of the Constitution says, "The existing aboriginal and treaty rights of the aboriginal peoples of Canada are hereby recognized and affirmed." This amendment extended constitutional protection over Native rights that can not be diminished or reduced except by the prescribed procedure (constitutional amendment).The full text of the Canadian Constitution of 1982 is at http://laws.justice.gc.ca/en/const/index.html; Maa-nulth First Nations Final Agreement, December 9, 2006.

141 Section 10.1.0 of the Agreement states: "Each Maa-nulth has the right to harvest, in accordance with this Agreement, Fish and Aquatic Plants for Domestic Purposes in the Domestic Fishing Area. . . . The definition of fish includes marine animals." Maa-nulth First Nations Final Agreement, December 9, 2006, 93, 266.

142 Maa-nulth First Nations Side Agree-

ment Summary. Maa-nulth First Nations: Harvesting of Grey Whales and Sei Whales; http://www.maanulth.ca/downloads/treaty/whale_letter_sum_v2.pdf.

143 Milton Freeman et al., *Inuit, Whaling, and Sustainability* (Walnut Creek: Alta Mira Press, 1998); Freeman et al., *Recovering Rights: Bowhead Whales and Inuvialuit Subsistence in the Western Canadian Arctic* (Alberta: The Canadian Circumpolar Institute, 1992); Happynook, *Whaling Around the World*, 11–13.

144 The James Bay Northern Quebec Agreement (1976), the Inuvialuit Final Agreement (1984), and the Nunavut Agreement (1993). Freeman et al., *Inuit, Whaling, and Sustainability*, 127–29; D. Goodman, "Land Claim Agreements and the Management of Whaling in the Canadian Arctic," Proceedings of the 11th International Symposium on Peoples and Cultures of the North, Hokkaido Museum of Northern People, Abashiri, Japan, 1996. High North Web site, http://www.highnorth.no/Library/Policies/National/la-cl-ag.htm.

145 Freeman et al., *Inuit, Whaling, and Sustainability*, 127; Freeman et al., *Recovering Rights*, 25–28; Goodman, "Land Claim Agreements."

146 Tom Mexsis Happynook, pers. comm., July 28, 2008.

147 The word "whale" is not written in the document.

148 Monks et al., "Nuu-chah-nulth Whaling," 73.

149 Kathy Happynook, pers. comm., July 28, 2008.

150 Ibid.

151 Ibid.

152 Ibid.

153 Ibid. Denise Titian, "BC/Nations Sign Final Treaty Agreement," *Ha-Shilth-Sa* 35, no. 14 (July 24, 2008): 1, 19.

154 Happynook, pers. comm., July 28, 2008. On June 19, 2008, eight Nuu-chah-nulth First Nations have initiated a landmark lawsuit against the Canadian and B.C. governments, asserting title and rights to their fisheries resources. They are asserting that not only do they have a right to harvest the fish in their territories, but they also have the right to trade, barter, and sell these resources. The lawsuit came about after years of frustrating and unproductive treaty negotiations. The Nuu-chah-nulth Research and Litigation Project, NTC Web site, http://www.nuuchahnulth.org/tribalcouncil/fisheries.html. The Nuu-chah-nulth First Nations are also closely watching the current negotiations between Canada and the United States, which focus on several chapters and annexes of the Pacific Salmon Treaty. The Nuu-chah-nulth are mainly concerned about the impact this will have on the Chinook annex, which they rely on for subsistence. See Titian, "BC/Nations Sign Final Treaty Agreement," 17; *Uu-a-thluk*, Nuu-chah-nulth Fisheries Department, vol. 3, no. 2 (2007): 2.

155 Chief Les Sam, Tseshaht First Nation, pers. comm., August 5, 2008.

156 Davila, "Makah Indian Students Proudly Rebuild."

157 Ibid.

158 "Whale Bones Tell Story of Tribe's Milestone Hunt," *Associated Press*, December 4, 2005; http://www.whale.story.htm.

5 / SUCHA

1 In 1977 Paul Watson founded the Sea Shepherd Conservation Society, an organization established to protect marine wildlife throughout the world; http://www.seashepherd.org/people/watson.html. The organization is also known as Sea Shepherd International.

2 In the 1970s, Greenpeace received a lot of criticism over its anti-sealing

campaigns and opposition to bowhead whaling by the Inuit in Alaska, which may be the reason Greenpeace did not join the campaign against Makah and Nuu-chah-nulth whaling.

3   Jennifer Aradanas, "Aboriginal Whaling: Biological Diversity Meets Cultural Diversity," *Northwest Science* 72, no. 2 (1998): 145.

4   Mark Baumgartner, "Disrupting the Makah Hunt: Sticking up for the Whale," http://abcnews.com/sections/science/DailyNews/whalehuntopponents_981110.html.

5   "Makah Whaling Commission Management Plan for Makah Treaty Gray Whale Hunting for the Years 1998–2001." Native Americans and the Environment Web site, http://cnie.org/NAE/docs/makahplan.html.

6   "Makah Whaling Commission Management Plan for Makah Treaty Gray Whale Hunting for the years 1998–2002." Makah Tribal Council. Native Americans and the Environment Web site, http://www.ncseonline.org/NAE/docs/makahplan.html.

7   Keith Johnson, "An Open Letter to the Public from the President of the Makah Whaling Commission," Native Americans and the Environment, August 23, 1998. http:cnie.org/NAE/docs/makaheditorial.html (accessed March 15, 2001).

8   The whale caught in 1999 took eight minutes to die after it was struck by the harpoon and shot with the rifle. Review of "Technique Employed by the Makah Tribe to Harvest Gray Whales," submitted by the U.S. government to the IWC, June 2006.

9   Travis Reavley, "Nuu-chah-nulth Whaling and Its Significance for Social and Economic Reproduction," Native Americans and the Environment Web site, 8; reprinted from *Chicago Anthropology Exchange Graduate Journal of*

Anthropology 28 (Spring 1998): 23–40.

10   *Oregonian*, quoted in Ter Ellingson, *The Myth of the Noble Savage* (Berkeley: University of California Press, 2001), 368.

11   Robert Berkhofer, *The White Man's Indian* (New York: Vintage Books, 1978), 29.

12   Daniel Francis, *The Imaginary Indian: The Image of the Indian in Canadian Culture* (Vancouver: Arsenal Pulp Press, 1992), 8, 59.

13   The Tseshaht have stories about conflicts with other Nuu-chah-nulth tribes that led to amalgamations of various groups way before we came in contact with non-Indians. Alan D. McMillan and Denis E. St. Claire provide an excellent study of precontact culture change among the Tseshaht in their book *Ts'ishaa: Archeology and Ethnography of a Nuu-chah-nulth Origin Site in Barkley Sound* (Burnaby, B.C.: Archeology Press, Simon Fraser University, 2005).

14   Cary C. Collins, "Subsistence and Survival: The Makah Indian Reservation, 1855–1933," *Pacific Northwest Quarterly* 87, no. 4 (1996): 183.

15   Ibid.

16   Alx Dark, "The Makah Whaling Conflict: Eco-Colonialism," Native Americans and the Environment Web site, http://www.cnie.org/NAE/Cases/Makah/M6.html, April 1999.

17   Keith Johnson, "Open Letter."

18   From the film *The Makah Nation: A Whaling People* (Makah Whaling Commission, 2002).

19   Michael Harkin, "A Tradition of Invention: Modern Ceremonialism on the Northwest Coast," in *Present Is Past: Some Uses of Tradition in Native Societies* (New York and London: University Press of America, 1997), 102.

20   Ibid., 103.

21   Patricia Pierce Erikson, "A-Whaling We Will Go: Encounters of Knowledge

and Memory at the Makah Culture and Research Center," *Cultural Anthropology* 14, no. 4 (1999): 564.

22 Michael Two Horses, "'We Know Who the Real Indians Are': Animal-Rights Groups, Racial Stereotyping, and Racism in Rhetoric and Action in the Makah Whaling Controversy," master's thesis, University of Arizona, 2001, 11–12.

23 Bryan Pease, quoted in Ter Ellingson, *The Myth of the Noble Savage* (Berkeley: University of California Press, 2001), 360.

24 Ellingson, *Myth of the Noble Savage*, 360.

25 Roy Harvey Pearce, *Savagism and Civilization: A Study of the Indian and the American Mind* (Berkeley: University of California Press, 1988), 10–12.

26 Berkhofer, *The White Man's Indian*, 118–20; Francis, *The Imaginary Indian*, 198–218.

27 Pearce, *Savagism and Civilization*, 11.

28 Jack Metcalf, "Tradition Renewed: Makah Kill Gray Whale," *Seattle Post-Intelligencer*, May 18, 1999, A1.

29 The person who went to Neah Bay with the other anti-whaling protesters to oppose the hunt was named Doryan Jarrell. Ken Short, "Makah Police, Foes Clash," *Peninsula Daily News*, November 1, 1998.

30 Louise Dickson, "Whalers and Protestors Vow to Stay as Long as Necessary," *Times Colonist*, May 12, 1999.

31 Ellingson, *Myth of the Noble Savage*, 367.

32 Quoted in Michael Two Horses, "We Know Who the Real Indians Are," 121.

33 "Tradition Renewed: Makah Kill Gray Whale," *Seattle Post-Intelligencer*, May 18, 1999, A1.

34 Quoted in Two Horses, "We Know Who the Real Indians Are," 134, and on the CERTAIN Web site, http://www.certain-natl.org./certain-info.html. See also *Animal People* 8, no. 5 (June

1999): 8; http://www.animalpeoplenews.org/99/t/6.99.swf.

35 James Huffman, "An Exploratory Essay on Native Americans and Environmentalism," 63 University of Colorado Law Review, 1992, 905.

36 Albert Furtwangler, *Answering Chief Seattle* (Seattle: University of Washington Press, 1997).

37 Philip J. Deloria, *Playing Indian* (New Haven: Yale University Press, 167).

38 http://www.aef.com/exhibits/social_responsibility/ad_council/2278

39 Berkhofer, *The White Man's Indian*, 138.

40 Francis, *The Imaginary Indian*, 58.

41 Bryan G. Norton, *Toward Unity among Environmentalists* (New York: Oxford University Press, 1991), 61–73.

42 Ibid., 65.

43 Ibid.

44 George Wenzel, *Animal Rights, Human Rights: Ecology, Economy and Ideology in the Canadian Arctic* (Toronto: University of Toronto Press, 1991), 40.

45 Tom Regan, *Defending Animal Rights* (Chicago: University of Illinois Press, 2001), 19–21.

46 Quoted in Wenzel, *Animal Rights, Human Rights*, 40.

47 Ibid., 36–41.

48 Ibid., 41.

49 http://www.en.wikipedia.org/wiki/Counting_coup.

50 Ellingson, *Myth of the Noble Savage*, 372.

51 From the Wikipedia Web site, "People for the Ethnic Treatment of Animals," http://www.en.wikipedia.org/wiki/People_for_the_Ethical_Treatment_of_Animals

52 From the PETA Web site, http://www.petaliterature.com/VEG297.pdf.

53 Russell Lawrence Barsh, "Food Security, Food Hegemony, and Charismatic Animals," in *Toward a Sustainable Whaling Regime*, ed. Robert L. Friedman (Seattle: University of Washington Press, 2001), 148.

54 Johnson, "Open Letter."

55   *Treaties and Trees: A Nuu-chah-nulth Perspective* (Port Alberni, B.C.: Nuu-chah-nulth Tribal Council, n.d.).

56   Keith Johnson, former chair of the Makah Whaling Commission, in the film *The Makah Nation: A Whaling People* (Makah Whaling Commission, 2002).

57   "Biologists remind public, 'Death is natural even for whales,'" editorial in *IWMC Newsletter*, June 1999.

58   David Sones in the film *The Makah Nation*.

59   Ibid.

60   Berkhofer, *The White Man's Indian*, 71.

61   Quoted in "Sovereignty Sustains Makah Tribal Traditions," 8.

6 / NUPU

1   Treaty between the United States and the Makah Tribe of Indians (1855), Article 4.

2   International Whaling Commission: Convention Text, 1946, http:www.iwcoffice.org/Convention.htm. International Whaling Commission home page, http://www.iwcoffice.org/commission/iwcmain.htm.

3   Makah Indian Tribe—Whaling Proposal, p. 562, Makah Tribal Council, May 5, 1995.

4   The ICRW established a schedule of whaling regulations (Schedule) and granted the IWC power to amend the Schedule by adopting subsequent regulations, which included quotas.

5   Extract from Appendix II (changes in bold type), International Whaling Commission, 49th Annual Meeting, 1997, http://www.iwcoffice.org/commission/schedule.htm.

6   In Lawrence Watters and Connie Duggers, "The Hunt for Gray Whales: The Dilemma of Native American Treaty Rights and the International Moratorium on Whaling," 22 *Columbia Journal of Environmental Law* (1997), 332n.99.

7   Quoted in Tim Wheeler, "Makah Indians Defend Their Treaty Rights," *People's Weekly World* (June 3, 2000), 10–11.

8   Micah McCarty, pers. comm., July 9, 2008.

9   Quoted in Eric Rosenberg, "Makah Hopeful about Whaling Again by 2010," *Seattle Post-Intelligencer*, http://www.seattlepi.com/local.347208-Makah14.html (accessed January 2008).

10   Wikipedia, http://en.wikipedia.org/wiki/Slade_Gorton.

11   Fay Cohen, *Treaties on Trial: The Continuing Controversy over Northwest Indian Fishing Rights* (Seattle: University of Washington Press, 1986), 90.

12   Jeffrey R. Dudas, *The Cultivation of Resentment: Treaty Rights and the New Right* (Stanford: Stanford University Press, 2008), 60–94.

13   Ibid., 120. Ken Toole, "Drumming Up Resentment: The Anti-Whaling Movement in Montana," *Montana Human Rights Network* (2000), 14; http://www.mhrn.org/publications/specialresearchreports/DrummingUp.pdf.

14   Quoted in Dudas, *Cultivation of Resentment*, 60. Also see Cohen, *Treaties on Trial*, 120.

15   Ibid., 90.

16   Quoted in Dudas, *Cultivation of Resentment*, 82.

17   Wheeler, "Makah Indians Defend Their Treaty Rights," 10. Also see Dudas, *Cultivation of Resentment*, 60–62, 82.

18   Dudas, *Cultivation of Resentment*, 79.

19   Quoted in Wheeler, "Makah Indians Defend Their Treaty Rights," 10.

20   Robert Crawford, "The Anti-Indian Movement," *Building Progressive Community in the West* (Fall 1998): 3; http://speedy.wscpdx.org/publications/views/views18/anti-indian.pdf. Also see Wheeler, "Makah Indians Defend Their Treaty Rights," 10.

21   Michael Two Horses, "'We Know Who the Real Indians Are': Animal-Rights Groups, Racial Stereotyping, and Racism in Rhetoric and Action in the Makah Whaling Controversy," master's thesis, University of Arizona, 2001, 134.

22   Wikipedia, http://en.wikipedia.org/wiki/Jack_Metcalf.

23   Cohen, *Treaties on Trial*, 184–85.

24   Two Horses, "We Know Who the Real Indians Are," 133; Crawford, "The Anti-Indian Movement," 19; Toole, "Drumming Up Resentment," 14.

25   Crawford, "The Anti-Indian Movement," 3.

26   Two Horses, "We Know Who the Real Indians Are," 133–34; Crawford, "The Anti-Indian Movement," 3; Robert Crawford, "Jack Metcalf: 'Save the Whales.' An Anti-Indian Activist Finds New Allies," *Dignity Report* (Winter 1998), 16.

27   As a right-wing politician, he actively opposed affirmative action and co-sponsored a bill to abolish the Fourteenth Amendment citizenship rights of children born in the United States to undocumented workers. Crawford, "The Anti-Indian Movement," 19.

28   Toole, "Drumming Up Resentment," 23–24; M. J. Milloy, "Paul Watson Allies with a Far-Right Republican in His Fight against Aboriginal Whaling," *Hour Magazine*, posted on Web site, August 5, 1999.

29   "Rep. Metcalf—A Savior of the Cetaceans? Congressman Led Campaign to Stop Whaling," *Seattle Times*, June 30, 1996; http://www.search.nwsource.com/search?offset=120&from=ST&rs=1&similarto=PIArchives%3Api_archive8901050312.

30   Crawford, "The Politics of Whales," *Dignity Report* (Fall 1998), 5.

31   Watters and Duggers, "The Hunt for Gray Whales," 334.

32   "Rep. Metcalf—A Savior of the Cetaceans?"

33   Quoted in "Metcalf's Indian History," http://www.indianz.com/News/show.asp?ID=tc/692000–4.

34   In Crawford, "The Politics of Whales," 5.

35   Two Horses, "We Know Who the Real Indians Are," 132. Jack Metcalf died March 15, 2007.

36   Milloy, "Paul Watson Allies."

37   The group alleged that the federal government violated the National Environmental Policy Act (NEPA), the National Marine Sanctuaries Act, and the Whaling Convention Act.

38   National Environmental Policy Act, 1969, http://www.nps.gov/history/local-law/FHPL_NtlEnvirnPolcy.pdf.

39   http://www.mms.gov/eppd/compliance/nepa/index.htm.

40   The one difference in the second agreement was the requirement that the Makah confine their hunting activities to open waters, which would exclude the local or resident gray whale population that lived year-round in the Strait of Juan de Fuca. *Metcalf v. Daley*, 214 F.3d 1135, 9th Cir.2000, 6.

41   Ibid., 7.

42   Ibid.

43   The U.S. Representative united with the most vocal of the anti-whaling groups, the Sea Shepherd Conservation Society, and together they waged a relentless campaign to stop Makah from whaling.

44   *Metcalf v. Daley*, 2.

45   The plaintiffs in *Metcalf v. Daley* were U.S. Representative Jack Metcalf, Australians for Animals, Beach Marine Protection, Alberta Thompson (Makah member), The Fund for Animals, and other members of anti-whaling groups; the defendants were Secretary William Daley, U.S. Department of Commerce, other officials from federal fisheries and oceans, and the Makah Tribe.

46   *Metcalf v. Daley*, 12–13.

47   Ibid., 9.

48   Ibid., 13.

49 Ibid., 9.

50 http://www.en.wikipedia.org/wiki/
NationalEnvironmentalPolicyAct.

51 *Metcalf v. Daley*, 10. A. W. Harrris,
"Making the Case for Collective Rights:
Indigenous Claims to Stocks of Marine
Living Resources," 15 *Georgetown Inter-
national Environmental Law Review* 379
(Spring 2003), 418–19.

52 A. W. Harrris, "Making the Case," 419.

53 *Metcalf v. Daley*, 17.

54 Although the NEPA requires an environmental impact statement, which is
tougher than the EA, the court ordered
that only an EA be required (*Metcalf v.
Daley*, 17).

55 There are two populations of gray
whales in the North Pacific: the eastern
North Pacific population that migrates
along the western coast of North
America and the western North Pacific
population that migrates along the coast
of eastern Asia. "Draft Environmental
Assessment on Issuing a Quota to the
Makah tribe for a Subsistence Hunt
on Gray Whales for Years 2001–2002,"
National Marine Fisheries Service,
National Oceanic and Atmospheric
Administration, January 12, 2001, 12–13,
18–23.

56 Ibid., 7–8, 39–51.

57 Peggy Anderson, "Hearing on Federal
Whaling Report Draws Indians, Animal
Activists, Hunters," Associated Press,
February 1, 2001.

58 John Dougherty, "Resurrection: After
a seventy-year hiatus and a confrontation with the world, the Makah tribe
resumes its communion with the gray
whale," July 12, 2001, http://www.pitch
.com/content/printVersion/141514.

59 Draft EA, 18.

60 Ibid., 18.

61 The PBR definition is included in the
"Application for a Waiver of the Marine
Mammal Protection Act Take Morato-
rium to Exercise Gray Whale Hunting
Rights Secured in the Treaty of Neah
Bay, February 11, 2005," Makah Tribal
Council, iii.

62 Draft EA, 56–58.

63 Micah McCarty, pers. comm., July 9,
2008.

64 "Activist Trying to Save 'Swimming
Rocks,'" *Peninsula Daily News,* November 2, 1998, A1.

65 Final EA, 70–72.

66 NOAA reversed the order of Alternatives
1 and 2 in the final EA so that Alternative 1, the preferred alternative, would
include a limited hunt on the PCFA (EA,
10). In its revised plan, the Makah Tribe
eliminated some of the time and area
restrictions, which included a limited
hunt on the PCFA (EA, 3–4).

67 At its annual meeting in December
2002, the IWC renewed the U.S. gray
whale quota for the Makah Tribe, allowing them to take four whales in one year
and no more than a total of twenty in a
five-year period. IWC 54th annual meeting, 2002.

68 EA, 10.

69 Ibid.

70 The Marine Mammal Protection Act of
1972 (amended 2007), http://www.nmfs
.noaa.gov/pr/pdfs/laws/mmpa.pdf.

71 Marine Mammal Protection Act of 1972,
http://ipl.unm.edu/cwl/fedbook/mmpa
.html.

72 *Anderson v. Evans*, 314 F.3d 1006, Ninth
Circuit Court, December 20, 2002, 9–10.

73 Ibid., 18.

74 Ibid., 8, 16.

75 EA, 72

76 *Anderson v. Evans*, 25.

77 EA, 56–58.

78 *Anderson v. Evans*, 25–40.

79 The court also expressed concerns
over how the Makah Tribe obtained its
whaling quota from the IWC, which led
them to conclude that an EIS needed to
be prepared. The court believed that the
language concerning the IWC aboriginal

79. subsistence exception was vague and could open the door to other countries to declare subsistence needs for their aboriginal groups. "If such an increase in whaling occurs," the court noted, "there will obviously be a significant impact on the environment" (*Anderson v. Evans*, 40).

80. Ibid., 44–45.

81. Section 1372, (a)(2), MMPA.

82. International Whaling Commission Convention Text, 1946, http:www.iwcoffice.org/Convention.htm. International Whaling Commission home page, http://www.iwcoffice.org/commission/iwcmain.htm.

83. G. P. Donovan, *The Adhoc Technical Committee Working Group on Development of Management Principles and Guidelines for Subsistence Catches of Whales by Indigenous (Aboriginal) Peoples.* International Whaling Commission and Aborginal/Subsistence Whaling: April 1979 to July 1981, Special Issue 4, International Whaling Commission, Cambridge, England, http://www.highnorth.no/Library/Culture/de-of-ab.htm.

84. The amendment reads: "The taking of gray whales . . . is permitted, but only by aborigines or a Contracting Party on behalf of the aborigines, and then only when the meat and products of such whales are to be used exclusively for local consumption by the *aborigines whose traditional aboriginal subsistence and cultural needs have been recognized.*" Extract from Appendix II (changes in italic type), International Whaling Commission, 49th annual meeting, 1997; http://www.iwcoffice.org/commission/schedule.htm.

85. *Anderson v. Evans*, 34.

86. Ibid.

87. *United States v. Fryberg*, 622 F.2d, 1010 (Ninth Cir., 1980).

88. *Anderson v. Evans*, 38.

89. Ibid., 39.

90. EA, 17.

91. International Whaling Commission Report, 2000.

92. IWC Report of the Scientific Committee, 2000, 23, RSC 2003, 31, IWC office, Cambridge, UK.

93. Jonathan Dube, "Gray Whales Dying Ashore," http://www.abcnews.comgo.com/sections/science/DailyNews/graywhale990420.html.

94. Ibid.

95. "West Coast Whale Deaths Could Be Due to Food Supply," *Science Daily*, May 24, 1999), http://www.sciencedaily.com/releases/1999/05/990524035753.htm.

96. IWMC World Conservation Trust, June 1999 newsletter, 1.

97. David L. Roghair, "*Anderson v. Evans*: Will Makah Whaling under the Treaty of Neah Bay Survive the Ninth Circuit's Application of the MMPA?" *Journal of Environmental Law and Litigation* 189 (2005): 191.

98. David H. Getches, Charles F. Wilkinson, and Robert A. Williams Jr., *Federal Indian Law: Cases and Materials* (Minneapolis: West Publishing Co., 1993), 157.

99. Robert J. Miller, "Exercising Cultural Self-Determination: The Makah Indian Tribe Goes Whaling," 25 *American Law Review* 165 (2000–2001): 190–91.

100. Alexandra Harmon, *Indians in the Making: Ethnic Relations and Indian Identities around Puget Sound* (Berkeley: University of California Press, 1998), 230.

101. George Gibbs, "Treaty of Neah Bay," transcript of Journal Proceedings, Microcopy No. T-494, roll 5, National Archives, Washington, D.C.

102. Ibid., 2.

103. The Makah Indian Tribe and Whaling Fact Sheet, Makah Tribal Council, http://www.ncseonline.org/nae/docs/makahfaq.html.

104. Roghair, "*Anderson v. Evans*," 199–200.

105. *Anderson v. Evans*, 40.

106 Ibid., 40–41.

107 Ibid., 38–39.

108 Roghair, "*Anderson v. Evans*," 200–201.

109 Ibid., 202.

110 Jeremy Firestone and Jonathan Lilley, "An Endangered Species: Aboriginal Whaling and the Right to Self-Determination and Cultural Heritage in a National and International Context," *Environmental Law Reporter* 34 (September 2004): 10778.

111 Section 14 of Pub.L. 103–238, 1994 Amendment to the Marine Mammal Protection Act of 1972.

112 Lewis Lamb, "Court Rebuffs Makah's Appeal over Whaling," *Seattle Post-Intelligencer*, June 8, 2004.

113 "Application for a Waiver of the Marine Mammal Protection Act Take Moratorium to Exercise Gray Whale Hunting Rights Secured in the Treaty of Neah Bay," February 11, 2005, Makah Tribal Council, 1.

114 Ibid., 2.

115 Ibid.

116 Micah McCarty, pers. comm., July 9, 2008.

117 Four of the men were part of the whaling crew that killed a gray whale in the tribally sanctioned and federally approved hunt in 1999.

118 Lynda Mapes, "Hunter Not Ashamed of Killing Whale without a Permit," *Seattle Times*, September 10, 2007.

119 Mike Lewis and Paul Shukovsky, "Tribe Vows Prosecution for Killing Whale," *Seattle Post-Intelligencer*, September 10, 2007.

120 Ibid.

121 Paul Shukovsky, "Makah 'Treaty Warriors': Heroes or Criminals?" *Seattle Post-Intelligencer*, March 16, 2008.

122 Statement by the Makah Tribal Council, *Seattle Times*, September 10, 2007.

123 In January 2008, Micah McCarty became chair of the Makah Tribal Council.

124 Micah McCarty, pers. comm., September 9, 2007.

125 Mapes, "Hunter Not Ashamed."

126 Ibid.

127 Shukovsky, "Makah 'Treaty Warriors.'"

128 Lynda Mapes, "Makah Whalers Plead Not Guilty," *Seattle Times*, October 12, 2007.

129 Mapes, "Hunter Not Ashamed."

130 Ibid.

131 "Seattle Times: Reader Feedback," *Seattle Times*, September 10, 2007.

132 Ibid.

133 Ibid.

134 Ibid.

135 Quoted in Mapes, "Makah Whalers Plead Not Guilty."

136 Quoted in Mapes, "Hunter Not Ashamed."

137 Shukovsky, "Makah 'Treaty Warriors.'"

138 Darrell Markishtum, pers. comm., July 16, 2008.

139 Ibid.

140 Paul Shukovsky, "3 Makah Whalers Plead Guilty in Deal to Avert Jail," *Seattle Post-Intelligencer*, March 28, 2008.

141 Paul Shukovsky, "Part of Case against Makah Whale Killers Tossed," *Seattle Post-Intelligencer*, February 19, 2008. A Makah tribal judge has deferred prosecution of the five men. "Makah Court Defers Prosecution for 5 Who Killed Gray Whale," *Seattle Times*, May 15, 2008.

142 Lynda Mapes, "2 Makahs to Serve Time for Illegally Killing Whale," *Seattle Times*, July 6, 2008.

143 Jack Fiander, pers. comm., July 18, 2008.

144 The men discussed this in a private conversation with Makah Tribal Council Chair Micah McCarty. McCarty, pers. comm., July 16, 2008.

145 Mapes, "2 Makahs to Serve Time."

146 Paul Shukovsky, "3 Makah Whalers"; Jack Fiander, pers. comm., July 18, 2008.

147 Paul Shukovsky, "Judge Finds Whalers

Guilty," *Seattle Post-Intelligencer*, April 7, 2008.

148   Jack Fiander, pers. comm., July 18, 2008.

149   Mapes, "2 Makahs to Serve Time." When Judge Arnold sentenced Andy Noel and Wayne Johnson on June 30 for violating the MMPA, he made reference to his own personal library of books on tribal issues, noting that local Native writer Sherman Alexie was his favorite author, as if attempting to demonstrate that he, in fact, liked Native people. But he very openly showed his displeasure with these two men and his annoyance with Johnson for not showing "an ounce of remorse" for his actions. Both Johnson and Noel come from whaling lineages and were members of the whaling crew that harvested the whale in 1999. We tribal members ask, Why would Johnson be remorseful? He was just doing something that he believed was a birthright: his right to whale.

150   Paul Shukovsky, "3 Makah Whalers."

151   Shukovsky, "Makah 'Treaty Warriors.'"

152   Stephen L. Pevar, *The Rights of Indians and Tribes* (New York: New York University Press, 2002), 32.

153   *Cherokee Nation v. Georgia* 30 U.S. 1 (1831): 58, 71, and *Worcester v. Georgia* 31 U.S. 515 (1832).

154   *Cherokee Nation v. Georgia*, 17. In this case, tribes were described as "denominated domestic dependent nation[s]." Also, *Worcester v. Georgia*, 31.

155   *Cherokee Nation v. Georgia*, 75.

156   Ibid., 58, 71. *Worcester v. Georgia*.

157   David E. Wilkins, *American Indian Politics and the American Political System*, 2d ed. (New York: Rowman and Littlefield, 2007), 49.

158   McCarty, pers. comm., July 9, 2008.

159   "Draft Environmental Impact Statement for Proposed Authorization of the Makah Whale Hunt," United States Department of Commerce and National Oceanic and Atmospheric Administra-

tion, May 2008, Executive Summary, 1, 2.

160   Ibid., 2–12.

161   Ibid., 2–14, 2–15.

162   McCarty, pers. comm., July 9, 2008.

163   Ibid.

164   Ibid.

165   http://www.en.wikipedia.org/wiki/Culture.

166   Anthropologists such as Tylor, Boas, Sapir, Kroeber, Mead, Benedict, Lowie, and Wolf have analyzed and defined culture. See *The Dictionary of Anthropology*, ed. Thomas Barfield, 98–101.

167   Robert J. Miller, "Exercising Cultural Self-Determination: The Makah Indian Tribe Goes Whaling," *American Indian Law Review* 25: 233.

168   Dr. William Bradford, "'Save the Whales v. Save the Makah': Finding Negotiated Solutions to Ethnodevelopment Disputes in the New International Economic Order," *St. Thomas Law Review* 13 (2000–2001): 199–200.

7 / ATLPU

1   Harriet Kuhnlein et al., "Indigenous Peoples' Food Systems for Health: Finding Interventions That Work," *Public Health Nutrition* 9, no. 8 (2006): 1013.

2   T. Kue Young, "Recent Health Trends in the Native American Population," *Population Research and Policy Review* 16 (1997).

3   Laurel Lemchuk-Favel and Richard Jock, "Aboriginal Health Systems in Canada: Nine Case Studies," *Journal of Aboriginal Health* (January 2004): 31–32. The studies looked at contributing factors to low overall health and well-being, such as poor employment opportunities, low income and education, poor health behaviors, inadequate housing and community infrastructure, and overcrowding in Native communities.

4   *Diabetes: Lifetime Solutions* (film) (Gryphon Productions, 1998).

5   Type-2 diabetes is a not insulin-dependent and is the most common form of diabetes. It typically occurs in men and women over the age of forty. A high proportion of individuals with type-2 diabetes are overweight. *Diabetes in Canada,* 2d ed. (Health Canada, 2002), 19–21; http://www.phac-aspc.gc.ca/publicat/dic-dac2/pdf/dic-dac2_en.pdf.

6   "First Nations and Inuit Health," Health Canada; http://www.hc-sc.gc.ca/fniah-spnia/diseases-maladies/diabetes/index-eng.php. *Diabetes in Canada,* 64; George Pylychuk et al., "Diabetes Risk Evaluation and Microalbuminuria (Dream) Studies: Ten Years of Participatory Research with a First Nation's Home and Community Model for Type 2 Diabetes Care in Northern Saskatchewan," *International Journal of Circumpolar Health* 67, nos. 2–3 (2008): 190–93.

7   Lucy Barney of the Canadian Diabetes Association, in the film *Diabetes: Lifetime Solutions.*

8   Andrew Jin et al., "A Diabetes Mellitus in the First Nations Population of British Columbia, Canada. Part One: Mortality" and "Part Two: Hospital Morbidity," *International Journal of Circumpolar Health* 61, no. 3 (2002).

9   Nilka Rios Burrows et al., "Prevalence of Diabetes among Native Americans and Alaska Natives, 1990–1997," *Diabetes Care* 23, no. 12 (December 2000): 1786. Schumacher et al. argue that sweeping generalizations should be avoided when conducting studies with Alaska Natives. In Alaska, there are numerous indigenous groups with diverse lifestyles. Studies have found that heart disease is rising in some northern Native communities but in others, where members were more likely to eat a traditional diet, especially one rich in sea mammal oil and engage in physical activities, hypertension and/or diabetes is less prevalent. Schumacher et al., "Cardiovascular Disease among Alaska Natives: A Review of the Literature," *International Journal of Circumpolar Health* 62, no. 4 (2003): 357–59. Naylor et al. found that dietary changes among some indigenous groups in Alaska have caused a rise in diabetes, but the Eskimo communities that consume sea mammal and fish oil have lesser risks of developing this disease. "Diabetes among Alaska Natives: A Review," *International Journal of Circumpolar Health* 62, no. 3 (2003): 383–84.

10 *Diabetes: Lifetime Solutions* (film).

11 Quoted in *Diabetes: Lifetime Solutions.*

12 Ibid.

13 Kelly J. Acton et al., "Trends in Diabetes Prevalence among American Indian and Alaska Native Children, Adolescents, and Young Adults," *American Journal of Public Health* 92, no. 9 (September 2002): 1487. The study focused only on Native youth and adults who used Indian Health Service or tribal health facilities. However, the prevalence of the disease would likely be comparable in other Native communities since the same risk factors exist (obesity, inactivity, and genetic susceptibility) that cause diabetes to develop, 1488–89.

14 "Diabetes on the Rise in Young Native Americans," *Morbidity and Mortality Weekly Report* 849 (November 9, 2006); http://www.indigenousNewsNetwork@topica.com.

15 Acton et al., "Trends in Diabetes Prevalence," 1485, 1488; *Diabetes in Canada.*

16 Noreen D. Willows, "Overweight in First Nations Children: Prevalence, Implications, and Solutions," *Journal of Aboriginal Health* (March 2005).

17 *Diabetes in Canada*, 65.

18 Willows, "Overweight in First Nations Children."

19 Stewart B. Harris et al., "The Impact of

Diabetes on Cardiovascular Risk Factors and Outcomes in the Native Canadian Population," *Diabetes Research and Clinical Practice* 55 (2002); Raffaele De Caterina et al., "N-3 Fatty Acids in the Treatment of Diabetic Patients," *Diabetes Care* 30, no. 4 (April 2007): 1012.

20   Kibbe Conti, "Nutrition Status of American Indian Adults and Impending Needs in View of the Strong Heart Dietary Study," *Journal of the American Dietetic Association* 108, no. 5 (May 2008); Barbara V. Howard et al., "Rising Tide of Cardiovascular Disease in American Indians: The Strong Heart Study," *Circulation: Journal of the American Heart Association* (May 11, 1999); http://www.circ.ahajournals.org. Kathryn A. Myers, "Cardiovascular Disease and Risk in the Aboriginal Population," *Canadian Medical Association Journal* 166, no. 3 (February 2002); http://www.cmaj.ca/cgi/content/full/166/3/355.

21   Todd S. Harwell et al., "Defining Disparities in Cardiovascular Disease for American Indians: Trends in Heart Disease and Stroke Mortality among American Indians and Whites in Montana, 1991 to 2000," *Circulation: Journal of the American Heart Association* (October 11, 2005); http://www.circ.ahajournals.org. S. Anand et al., "Risk Factors, Atherosclerosis, and Cardiovascular Disease among Aboriginal People in Canada: The Study of Health Assessment and Risk Evaluation in Aboriginal Peoples (SHARE-AP)," *Lancet* 358 (2001).

22   *Aboriginal Health*, Canadian Institutes of Health Research (CIHR); http://www.cihr-irsc.gc.ca.

23   Anand et al., "Risk Factors, Atherosclerosis, and Cardiovascular Disease," 1147–52.

24   Conti, "Nutrition Status of American Indian Adults"; Howard et al., "Rising Tide of Cardiovascular Disease in American Indians."

25   *Diabetes: Lifetime Solutions.*

26   Nuu-chah-nulth hereditary chief Tom Mexsis Happynook, pers. comm., June 4, 2000. Also see Happynook, "Securing Nuu-chah-nulth Food, Health and Traditional Values through the Sustainable Use of Marine Mammals," *World Council of Whalers*, Brentwood Bay, B.C., 2001.

27   Happynook, "Securing Nuu-chah-nulth Food, Health and Traditional Values." Harriet Kuhnlein and Olivier Receveur, "Dietary Change and Traditional Food Systems of Indigenous Peoples," *Annual Review of Nutrition* 16 (July 1996), 419–23, 428–32; http://arjournals.annualreviews.org.offcampus.lib.washington.edu/toc/nutr/16/1 (accessed July 28, 2008).

28   De Caterina et al., "N-3 Fatty Acids in the Treatment of Diabetic Patients," 1012–14.

29   H. V. Kuhnlein et al., "Vitamins A, D, and E in Canadian Arctic Traditional Food and Adult Diets," *Journal of Food Composition and Analysis* 19 (2006): 495–506; Carole Blanchet et al., "Contribution of Selected Traditional and Market Foods to the Diet of Nunavik Inuit Women," *Canadian Journal of Dietetic Practice and Research* 61, no. 2 (Summer 2001).

30   De Caterina et al., "N-3 Fatty Acids in the Treatment of Diabetic Patients," 1012; Carole Blanchet et al., "Contribution of Selected Traditional and Market Foods"; Jan L. Breslow, "N-3 Fatty Acids and Cardiovascular Disease," *American Journal of Clinical Nutrition* 83 (2006): 1477–82; Yvon A. Carpentier, Laurence Portois, and Willy J. Malaisse, "N-3 Fatty Acids and the Metabolic Syndrome" *American Journal of Clinical Nutrition* 83 (2006): 1499–1504; William E. Connor, "N-3 Fatty Acids from Fish and Fish Oil: Panacea or Nostrum?" *American Journal of Clinical Nutrition*

74 (2001). Eric Dewailly et al., "N-3 Fatty Acids and Cardiovascular Disease Risk Factors among the Inuit of Nunavik," *American Journal of Clinical Nutrition* 74 (2001): 464–73; Eric Dewailly et al., "Cardiovascular Disease Risk Factors and N-3 Fatty Acid Status in the Adult Population of James Bay Cree," *American Journal of Clinical Nutrition* 76, no. 1 (July 2002).

31 Dewailly et al., "N-3 Fatty Acids and Cardiovascular Disease," 464.

32 Although there is a high prevalence of obesity and smoking in these communities, the people's diet, high in n-3 fatty acids, counters the occurrence of high blood pressure and lowers their mortality rates from heart disease. Dewailly, "N-3 Fatty Acids and Cardiovascular Disease," 471.

33 Ibid., 464–73.

34 De Caterina, "N-3 Fatty Acids in the Treatment of Diabetic Patients," 1021; Blanchet, "Contribution of Selected Traditional and Market Foods," 50–58.

35 April Kinghorn et al., "Reconstructing Historical Mercury Exposure from Beluga Whale Consumption among Inuit in the Mackenzie Delta," *Journal of Ethnobiology* 26, no. 2 (2006): 310–26.

36 Quoted in Doug O'Harra, "Experts Extol Tasty, Nutritious Whales: Benefits Beyond the Vitamins and Minerals, There's a Spiritual Element," *Anchorage Daily News* (November 24, 2003).

37 Whale skin is the most concentrated source of selenium. Carole Blanchet et al., "Contribution of Selected Traditional and Market Foods to the Diet of Nunavik Inuit Women," *Canadian Journal of Dietetic Practice and Research* 61, no. 2 (Summer 2001), 51.

38 Quoted in O'Harra, "Experts Extol Tasty, Nutritious Whales."

39 Hing Man Chan and Olivier Receveur, "Mercury in the Traditional Diet of Indigenous Peoples in Canada," *Envi-ronmental Pollution* 110 (2000).

40 Final Report, 1st Annual Interior of B.C. Indigenous Food Sovereignty Conference, prepared by Dawn Morrison, September 2006, p. 8.

41 Milton M. R. Freeman, Eleanor E. Wein, and Darren E. Keith, *Recovering Rights: Bowhead Whales and Inuvialuit Subsistence in the Western Canadian Arctic*, Canadian Circumpolar Institute and Fisheries Joint Management Committee (Edmonton: University of Alberta, 1992), 43.

42 Milton M. R. Freeman et al., *Inuit, Whaling, and Sustainability* (Walnut Creek, Calif.: Alta Mira Press, 1998), 22.

43 Ibid., 29. James Magdanz and C. J. Utermohle, "Family Groups and Subsistence," *Cultural Survival Quarterly* 22, no. 3 (September 1998).

44 Freeman et al., *Inuit, Whaling, and Sustainability*, 24.

45 Quoted in ibid., 30–32.

46 Magdanz and Utermohle, "Family Groups and Subsistence," 51–52.

47 Carol Zane Jolles, with Elinor Mikaghaq Ooseva, *Faith, Food, and Family in a Yupik Whaling Community* (Seattle: University of Washington Press, 2002).

48 Harry Brower Jr., "Subsistence Hunting Activities and the Inupiat Eskimo," *Cultural Survival Quarterly* 22, no. 3 (September 1998); http://www.209.200.101.189.offcampus.lib.washington.edu/publications/csq/index.cfm?id=22.3.

49 Brower Jr., "Subsistence Hunting Activities and the Inupiat Eskimo."

50 *Muktuk* means the same as *mattak*.

51 Eleanor Wein, Milton Freeman, Jeanette Makus, "Use and Preference for Traditional Foods among the Belcher Island Inuit," *Arctic* 49, no. 3 (1996): 256.

52 Quoted in Freeman et al., *Inuit, Whaling, and Sustainability*, 45.

53 Earl George, *Living on the Edge: Nuu-chah-nulth History from an Ahousaht*

Chief's Perspective (master's thesis, University of Victoria, 1994), 43–44.

54   Denise Ambrose, "Thousands Enjoy Makah Traditional Feast," *Ha-shilth-sa* 26, no. 11 (June 3, 1999).

55   Ann M. Renker, "Whale Hunting and the Makah Tribe: A Needs Statement." International Whaling Commission Report, April 2007; www.iwcoffice.org/ document/commission/iwc59docs/ 59-ASW%209.pdf (accessed October 15, 2007).

56   Ibid., 24–25.

57   Ibid., 24–25.

58   Russel L. Barsh, "Food Security, Food Hegemony, and Charismatic Animals," in *Toward a Sustainable Whaling Regime*, ed. Robert L. Friedheim (Seattle: University of Washington Press, 2001), 147–48.

59   Ibid.

60   Robert L. Friedheim, "Introduction. The IWC as a Contested Regime," in *Toward a Sustainable Whaling Regime*, 16.

61   Michael Marker, "Up with the Makah: Yodas of the Deep? Woe to Anyone, Especially Native, Who Fails to Sentimentalize the Whale," *Vancouver Sun* (July 14, 1999).

62   Tom Mexsis Happynook, "Whaling and the Nuu-chah-nulth People." A symposium at the Autry Museum of Western Heritage, Griffith Park, Los Angeles, March 24, 2001. Paper presented in conjunction with the exhibit Out of the Mist: Treasures of the Nuu chah nulth Chiefs.

63   Ibid.

64   Mexis Happynook, "Securing Nuu-chah-nulth Food, Health and Traditional Values."

65   Freeman et al., *Recovering Rights*, 41.

66   Barsh, "Food Security, Food Hegemony," 148–49.

67   "Death of a Whale," *Times Colonist* (May 18, 1999), A2.

68   Robert Sullivan, *A Whale Hunt: Two Years on the Olympic Peninsula with the Makah and Their Canoe* (New York: Scribner), 267.

69   *The Makah Nation: A Whaling People* (film), The Makah Whaling Commission, 2002.

Bibliography

Acoose, Janice. "Post Halfbreed: Indigenous Writers as Authors of Their Own Realities." In *Looking at the Words of Our People: First Nations Analysis of Literature*, edited by Jeanette Armstrong, 28–44. Penticton, B.C.: Theytus Books, 1993.

"Activists Trying to Save 'Swimming Rocks.'" *Peninsula Daily News*, November 2, 1998, A.1.

Acton, Kelly J., Nilka Rios Burrows, Kelly Moore, Linda Querec, Linda S. Geiss, and Michael M. Engelgau. "Trends in Diabetes Prevalence among American Indian and Alaska Native Children, Adolescents, and Young Adults." *American Journal of Public Health* 92, no. 9 (September, 2002).

Adams, David W. *Education for Extinction: American Indians and the Boarding School Experience, 1875–1928*. Lawrence: University of Kansas Press, 1995.

Alfred, Taiaiake. *Peace, Power, Righteousness: An Indigenous Manifesto*. New York: Oxford University Press, 1999.

———. "My Grandmother, She Raised Me Up Again: A Tribute to the Memory of Art Tsaqwassupp Thompson." *Celanen: A Journal of Indigenous Governance* 1, no. 1 (February 2004); http://www.uvic.ca/igov/research/journal/articles_taiaiake .htm (accessed July 10, 2004).

———. *Wasáse: Indigenous Pathways of Action and Freedom*. Peterborough, Ont.: Broadview Press, 2005.

Ambrose, Denise. "Thousands Enjoy Makah Traditional Feast." *Ha-shilth-sa* 26, no. 11 (June 3, 1999).

Ames, Kenneth M., and Herbert D. G. Maschner. *Peoples of the Northwest Coast: Their Archaeology and Prehistory*. London: Thames and Hudson, 1999.

Anand, S. Yusuf, R. Jacobs, A. D. Davis, Q. Yi, H. Gerstein, P. A. Montague, and E. Lonn. "Risk Factors, Atherosclerosis, and Cardiovascular Disease among Aboriginal People in Canada: The Study of Health Assessment and Risk Evaluation in Aboriginal Peoples (SHARE-AP)." *Lancet* 358 (2001): 1147–52.

Anderson, E. N., ed. *Bird of Paradox: The Unpublished Writings of Wilson Duff*. Surrey, B.C.: Hancock House, 1996.

Anderson v. Evans and Makah Indian Tribe. 314 F.3d 1006, Ninth Circuit Court, December 20, 2002.

Aradanas, Jennifer Sepez. "Aboriginal Whaling: Biological Diversity Meets Cultural Diversity." *Northwest Science* 72, no. 2 (1998): 142–45.

Arima, Eugene Y. *The West Coast (Nootka) People: The Nootkan of Vancouver Island and Cape Flattery.* Special publication no. 6. Victoria: British Columbia Provincial Museum, 1983.

——. "Thoughts on the Nuu-chah-nulth Canoe." In *Nuu-chah-nulth Voices: Histories, Objects and Journeys,* edited by Alan L. Hoover, 306–29. Victoria: Royal British Columbia Museum, 2000.

Arima, Eugene, and John Dewhirst. "The Nootkans of Vancouver Island." In *Handbook of North American Indians,* vol. 7: *Northwest Coast,* edited by Wayne Suttles, 391–411. Washington, D.C.: The Smithsonian Institution Press, 1990.

Arima, E. Y., Denis St. Claire, Louis Clamhouse, Joshua Edgar, Charles Jones, and John Thomas. *Between Ports Alberni and Renfrew: Notes on West Coast Peoples.* Ottawa: Canadian Museum of Civilization, 1991.

Arsdell, Jon Van. "B.C. Whaling: The Indians." In *Raincoast Chronicles, First Five: Stories and History of the B.C. Coast,* edited by Howard White, 20–28. Madeira Park, B.C.: Harbour Publishing, 1976.

Asch, Michael. *Home and Native Land: Aboriginal Rights and the Canadian Constitution.* Toronto: Methuen, 1984.

Atleo, Richard E. Umeek. *Tsawalk: A Nuu-chah-nulth Worldview.* Vancouver: UBC Press, 2004.

Barman, Jean, et al. *Indian Education in Canada,* vol. 1: *The Legacy.* Vancouver: UBC Press, 1986.

Barsh, Russel L. "Food Security, Food Hegemony, and Charismatic Animals." In *Toward a Sustainable Whaling Regime,* edited by Robert L. Friedheim, 147–79. Seattle: University of Washington Press, 2001.

Basso, Keith. "'Stalking with Stories': Names, Places, and Moral Narratives among the Western Apache." In *Text, Play, and Story: The Construction and Reconstruction of Self and Society,* edited by Stuart Plattner.

1983 Proceedings of the American Ethnological Society. Washington, D.C.: The American Ethnological Society, 1984.

——. "'Speaking with Names': Language and Landscape among the Western Apache." *Cultural Anthropology* 3, no. 2 (May 1988): 99–130.

——. *Wisdom Sits in Places: Landscape and Language among the Western Apache.* Albuquerque: University of New Mexico Press, 1996.

Baumgartner, Mark. "Disrupting the Makah Hunt. Sticking up for the Whale"; http://www.abcnews.com/sections/science/DailyNews/whalehuntopponents_981110.html (accessed January 1999).

Benedict, Ruth. *Patterns of Culture.* Boston: Houghton Mifflin, 1934.

Berkhofer, Robert. *The White Man's Indian.* New York: Vintage Books, 1978.

Black, Martha. *Huupukanum Tupaat, Out of the Mist: Treasures of the Nuu-chah-nulth Chiefs.* Victoria: Royal British Columbia Museum, 1999.

Blaeser, Kimberly M. *Gerald Vizenor: Writing in the Oral Tradition.* Norman: University of Oklahoma Press, 1996.

Blanchet, Carole, Eric Dewailly, Pierre Ayotte, Suzanne Bruneau, Olivier Receveur, and Bruce John Holub. "Contribution of Selected Traditional and Market Foods to the Diet of Nunavik Inuit Women." *Canadian Journal of Dietetic Practice and Research* 61, no. 2 (Summer 2001): 50–59.

Boas, Franz. *The Mind of Primitive Man.* New York: Macmillan, 1911.

Bock, Paula. "A Whaling People: The Makah Hunt for Tradition and Memories of Whaling. *Seattle Times Magazine* (November 26, 1995); http://www.highnoth.no/a-wh-pe.htm (accessed January 5, 2006).

Boyd, Colleen. "Oral Traditions, Northwest Coast." In *American Indian Religious Traditions,* edited by Suzanne J. Crawford and Dennis F. Kelly, 663–72. Santa Barbara: ABC-CLIO, 2005.

Boyd, Robert T. *The Coming of the Spirit of Pestilence: Introduced Infectious Diseases and Population among Northwest Coast Indians, 1774–1874*. Seattle: University of Washington Press, 1999.

Bracken, Christopher. *The Potlatch Papers: A Colonial Case History*. Chicago: University of Chicago Press, 1997.

Bradford, William. "'Save the Whales v. Save the Makah': Finding Negotiated Solutions to Ethnodevelopment Disputes in the New International Economic Order." *St. Thomas Law Review*, 13 (2000–2001): 155–220.

Bradley, John J. "Wirriyarra Awara: Yanyuwa Land and Sea Scapes." *The South Atlantic Quarterly* 98, no. 4 (Fall 1999): 801–16.

Braker, Hugh. "A Shot in the Dark: Issues in Aboriginal Hunting Rights." Paper presented at the Native Investment and Trade Association Conference, "Aboriginal Law in Canada," September 26–27, 1996, Vancouver, B.C.

Breslow, Jan L. "N-3 Fatty Acids and Cardiovascular Disease." *American Journal of Clinical Nutrition* 83 (2006): 1477–82.

Bridge, Kathryn. *Extraordinary Accounts of Native Life on the West Coast: Words of the Huu-ay-aht Ancestors*. Canmore, Alberta: Altitude Publishing, 2004.

British Columbia Indigenous Food Sovereignty. 1st annual conference for interior B.C.; final report prepared by Dawn Morrison, September 2006; http://www.fooddemocracy.org/docs/IFS_Conf06_Report.pdf (accessed October 19, 2007).

Brower, Harry, Jr. "Subsistence Hunting Activities and the Inupiat Eskimo." *Cultural Survival Quarterly* 22, no. 3 (September 1998); http://www.209.200.101.189.offcampus.lib.washington.edu/publications/csq/index.cfm?id=22.3 (accessed July 28, 2008).

Brown, Jovanna J. "Fishing Rights and the First Salmon Ceremony." In *American Indian Religious Traditions: An Encyclopedia*, edited by Suzanne J. Crawford and Dennis F. Kelly, 355–60. Santa Barbara: ABC-CLIO, 2005.

Burrows, Nilka Rios, Michael M. Engelgau, Linda S. Geiss, and Kelly J. Acton. "Prevalence of Diabetes among Native Americans and Alaska Natives, 1990–1997." *Diabetes Care* 23, no. 12 (December 2000): 1786–90.

Cairn, Elizabeth Crawford. "Nuu-chah-nulth Labour Relations in the Pelagic Sealing Industry, 1868–1911." Master's thesis, University of Victoria, 2006.

Calambokidis, John, Gretchen Steiger, and David Ellifrit. "Distribution and Abundance of Humpback Whales and Other Mammals off the Northwestern Washington Coast." *National Oceanic and Atmospheric Administration Fishery Bulletin* 102, no. 4 (2004), http://www.fishbull.noaa.gov/1024/calam.pdf (accessed July 10, 2007).

Calloway, Colin. *First Peoples: A Documentary Study of American Indian History*. Boston: Bedford, 1999.

Carpentier, Yvon A., Laurence Portois, and Willy J. Malaisse. "N-3 Fatty Acids and the Metabolic Syndrome." *American Journal of Clinical Nutrition* 83 (2006): 1499–1504.

Carroll, Alex K. "Oral Traditions." In *American Indian Religious Traditions: An Encyclopedia*, edited by Suzanne J. Crawford and Dennis F. Kelly, 633–37. Santa Barbara: ABC-CLIO, 2005.

Cassidy, Frank, ed. *Aboriginal Self-Determination*. Lantzville, B.C.: Oolichan Books, 1991.

Cassidy, Frank, and Robert L. Bish. *Indian Government: Its Meaning in Practice*. Lantzville, B.C.: Oolichan Books, 1989.

Castile, George Pierre, ed. *The Indians of Puget Sound: The Notebooks of Myron Eells*. Seattle: University of Washington Press, 1985.

Chan, Hing Man, and Olivier Receveur. "Mercury in the Traditional Diet of Indigenous Peoples in Canada." *Environmental Pollution* 110 (2000): 1–2.

Cherokee Nation v. Georgia 30 U.S. 1 (1831).

Chief Seattle's speech. http://www.synaptic
.bc.ca/ejournal/seattle.htm.

Clutesi, George. *Potlatch*. Sidney, B.C.: Gray's
Publishing, 1969, 1973.

Cohen, Fay. *Treaties on Trial: The Continuing
Controversy over Northwest Indian Fishing Rights*. Seattle: University of Washington Press, 1986.

Cole, Douglas, and Ira Chaikin. *An Iron Hand
Upon the People: The Law against the Potlatch on the Northwest Coast*. Vancouver:
Douglas and McIntyre; Seattle: University
of Washington Press, 1990.

Collins, Cary C. "Subsistence and Survival:
The Makah Indian Reservation, 1855–
1933." *Pacific Northwest Quarterly* 87, no.
4 (1996): 180–93.

Colson, Elizabeth. *The Makah Indians: A
Study of an Indian Tribe in Modern
American Society*. Minneapolis: Univer-
sity of Minnesota Press, 1953.

Connor, William E. "N-3 Fatty Acids from
Fish and Fish Oil: Panacea or Nostrum?"
American Journal of Clinical Nutrition 74
(2001): 415–16.

Conti, Kibbe. "Nutrition Status of American
Indian Adults and Impending Needs in
View of the Strong Heart Dietary Study."
*Journal of the American Dietetic Associa-
tion* 108, no. 5 (May 2008): 781–84.

Cornell, Stephen. *The Return of the Native:
American Indian Political Resurgence*.
New York: Oxford University Press, 1988.

Coté, Charlotte. "Historical Foundations of
Indian Sovereignty in Canada and the
United States: A Brief Overview." *Ameri-
can Review of Canadian Studies* (Spring–
Summer 2001): 15–23.

——. "Whaling, Religious and Cultural
Implications." In *American Indian Religious Traditions: An Encyclopedia,* edited
by Suzanne J. Crawford and Dennis F. Kelly,
1141–53. Santa Barbara: ABC-CLIO, 2005.

——. Review of *The Whaling Indians:
Legendary Hunters* by Edward Sapir,
Morris Swadesh, Alexander Thomas, John

Thomas, and Frank Williams. Told by
William Sayach'apis, Frank Williams, Big
Fred, Captain Bill, and Qwishanishim.
The American Review of Canadian Studies
(Fall 2005).

Crawford, Robert. "The Politics of Whales:
Makah Whaling Brings Animal Rights
Activists and the Anti-Indian Right
Together." *The Dignity Report* 5, no. 3 (Fall
1998): 4–7.

——. "Jack Metcalf: 'Save the Whales,' an
Anti-Indian Activist Finds New Allies."
The Dignity Report (Winter 1998): 16–17.

——. "The Anti-Indian Movement." *Building
a Progressive Community in the West* (Fall
1999): 3–19; http://www.speedy.wscpdx.org/
publications/views/views18/anti-indian
.pdf (accessed August 11, 2008).

Crawford, Suzanne. "Guardian Spirit Complex." In *American Indian Religious Traditions: An Encyclopedia*, edited by Suzanne
J. Crawford and Dennis F. Kelly, 355–60.
Santa Barbara: ABC-CLIO, 2005.

Cruikshank, Julie. "Getting the Words Right:
Perspectives on Naming and Places in
Athapaskan Oral History." *Arctic Anthro-
pology* 27, no. 1 (1990): 52–65.

——. *Life Lived Like a Story: Life Stories of
Three Yukon Elders*. Lincoln: University of
Nebraska Press, 1990.

——. *The Social Life of Stories: Narrative and
Knowledge in the Yukon Territory*. Vancouver: UBC Press, 1998.

Dark, Alx. "The Makah Whaling Conflict:
Eco-Colonialism." *Native Americans and
the Environment* (April 1999); http://www
.cnie.org/NAE/Cases/Makah/M6.html
(accessed November 18, 1999).

Davidson, Matthew. "Studies in Southern
Wakashan (Nootkan) Grammar." Ph.D.
diss., State University of New York, 2002.

Davila, Florangela. "Makah Students Proudly
Rebuild the Remains of a Sacred Whale."
Seattle Times, April 4, 2000.

Death of a Whale." *Times Colonist*, May 18,
1999, A2.

De Caterina, Raffaele, Alessandra Bertolotto,

Rosalinda Madonna, and Erik Berg Schmidt. "N-3 Fatty Acids in the Treatment of Diabetic Patients." *Diabetes Care* 30, no. 4 (April 2007): 1012–26.

Deloria, Philip J. *Playing Indian*. New Haven: Yale University Press, 1998.

Deloria, Vine, Jr. *Behind the Trail of Broken Treaties: An Indian Declaration of Independence*. Austin: University of Texas Press, 1974, 1990.

Densmore, Frances. *Nootka and Quileute Music*. Bureau of American Ethnology Bulletin 12. Washington, D.C.: Smithsonian Institution, 1939,

Dewailly, Eric, Carole Blanchet, Simone Lemieux, Louise Sauvé, Suzanne Gingras, Pierre Ayotte, and Bruce John Holub. "N-3 Fatty Acids and Cardiovascular Disease Risk Factors among the Inuit of Nunavik." *American Journal of Clinical Nutrition* /4 (2001): 464–73; http://www.ajcn.org.offcampus.ib.washington.edu/cgi/content/full/76/1/85 (accessed July 14, 2007).

Dewailly, Eric, Carole Blanchet, Suzanne Gingras, Simone Lemieux, and Bruce John Holub. "Cardiovascular Disease Risk Factors and N-3 Fatty Acid Status in the Adult Population of James Bay Cree." *American Journal of Clinical Nutrition* 76, no. 1 (July 2002): 85–92.

Diabetes: Lifetime Solutions (film). Gryphon Productions, 1998.

Diabetes in Canada. 2d ed. Health Canada (2002); http://www.phac-aspc.gc.ca/publicat/dic-dac2/english/01cover_e.html (accessed August 1, 2008).

"Diabetes on the Rise in Young Native Americans." *Morbidity and Mortality Weekly Report* 849 (November 9, 2006); IndigenousNewsNetwork@topica.com (accessed September 12, 2007).

Dickason, Olive Patricia. *Canada's First Nations: A History of Founding Peoples from Earliest Times*. Toronto: McClelland and Stewart, 1992.

Donovan, G. P. *The Adhoc Technical Committee Working Group on Development of Management Principles and Guidelines for Subsistence Catches of Whales by Indigenous (Aboriginal) Peoples*. International Whaling Commission and Aborginal Subsistence Whaling, April 1979 to July 1981. Special issue 4. Cambridge; http://www.highnorth.no/Library/Culture/de-of-ab.htm (accessed March 10, 2007).

Dougherty, John. "Resurrection after a Seventy-Year Hiatus and a Confrontation with the World, the Makah Tribe Resumes Its Communion with the Gray Whale," July 12, 2001; http://www.pitch.com/content/printVersion/141514 (accessed August 2001).

Draft Environmental Assessment on Issuing a Quota to the Makah Indian Tribe for a Subsistence Hunt on Gray Whales for the Years 2001 and 2002. U.S. Department of Commerce, National Oceanic and Atmospheric Administration, National Marine Fisheries Service, January 12, 2001.

Drucker, Philip. "Diffusion in Northwest Coast Culture Growth in the Light of Some Distributions." Ph.D. diss., University of California, Berkeley, 1936.

——. "Rank, Wealth, and Kinship in Northwest Coast Society." *American Anthropologist* 41 (1939): 53–65.

——. *The Northern and Central Nootkan Tribes*. Bureau of American Ethnology. Bulletin 144. Washington, D.C.: Smithsonian Institution. 1951.

——. *Indians of the Northwest Coast*. New York: Natural History Press, 1955.

——. *Cultures of the North Pacific Coast*. Scranton, Pa.: Chandler Publishing, 1965.

——. "Nootka Whaling." In *Indians of the North Pacific Coast*, edited by Tom McFeat, 22–27. Ottawa: Carleton University Press, 1989.

Dube, Jonathan. "Gray Whales Dying Ashore." http://www.abcnews.comgo.com/sections/science/DailyNews/graywhale990420.html (accessed September 14, 1999).

Dudas, Jeffrey R. *The Cultivation of Resentment: Treaty Rights and the New Right.* Stanford: Stanford University Press, 2008.

Duff, Wilson. *The Indian History of British Columbia*, vol. 1: *The Impact of the White Man.* Victoria: Royal British Columbia Museum, 1969.

"Elders Whaling Workshop." Campbell River, December 4–5, 1998. Audiotape held at the Nuu-chah-nulth Tribal Council Media Department, Port Alberni, B.C.

Eldridge, Morley, "The Significance and Management of Culturally Modified Trees." Final report prepared for the Vancouver Forest Region and CMT Standards Steering Committee, Millennia Research Ltd. (January 13, 1997), 1; http://www.tsa.gov.bc.ca/archaeology/docs/culturally_modified_trees_significance_management.pdf (accessed July 20, 2008).

Ellingson, Ter. *The Myth of the Noble Savage.* Berkeley: University of California Press, 2001.

"Environmental Assessment on Issuing a Quota to the Makah Indian Tribe for a Subsistence Hunt on Gray Whales for the Years 2001 and 2002." U.S. Department of Commerce, National Oceanic and Atmospheric Administration, National Marine Fisheries Service, July 12, 2001.

Erikson, Patricia Pierce. "A-Whaling We Will Go: Encounters of Knowledge and Memory at the Makah Cultural and Research Center." *Cultural Anthropology* 14, no. 4 (1999): 556–83.

Extract from Appendix II (changes in bold type), International Whaling Commission, 49th Annual Meeting, 1997; http://www.iwcoffice.org/commission/schedule.htm (accessed April 4, 2007).

Firestone, Jeremy, and Jonathan Lilley. "An Endangered Species: Aboriginal Whaling and the Right to Self-Determination and Cultural Heritage in a National and International Context." *Environmental Law Reporter* (September 2004): 10763–87.

Fisher, Robin. *Contact and Conflict: Indian-European Relations in British Columbia, 1774–1890.* Vancouver: UBC Press, 1981.

Fixico, Donald L. "Ethics and Responsibilities in Writing American Indian History." In *Natives and Academics: Researching and Writing about American Indians,* edited by Devon A. Mihesuah, 84–100. Lincoln: University of Nebraska Press, 1999.

Francis, Daniel. *The Imaginary Indian: The Image of the Indian in Canadian Culture.* Vancouver: Arsenal Pulp Press, 1992.

Freeman, Milton M. R., Lyudmila Bogoslovskaya, Richard A. Caulfield, Ingmar Egede, Igor I. Krupnik, and Marc G. Stevenson. *Inuit, Whaling, and Sustainability.* Walnut Creek, Calif.: AltaMira Press, 1998.

Freeman, Milton M. R., Eleanor E. Wein, and Darren E. Keith. *Recovering Rights: Bowhead Whales and Inuvialuit Subsistence in the Western Canadian Arctic.* Canada: Canadian Circumpolar Institute and Fisheries Joint Management Committee, 1992.

Friedheim, Robert L. "Introduction: The IWC as a Contested Regime." In *Toward a Sustainable Whaling Regime,* edited by Robert L. Friedheim, 3–48. Seattle: University of Washington Press, 2001.

Furtwangler, Albert. *Answering Chief Seattle.* Seattle: University of Washington Press, 1997.

Geertz, Clifford. *The Interpretation of Cultures: Selected Essays.* New York: Basic Books, 1973.

Geffen, Joel, and Suzanne J. Crawford. "First Salmon Rites." In *American Indian Religious Freedoms: An Encyclopedia,* edited by Suzanne J. Crawford and Dennis F. Kelly, 311–20. Santa Barbara: ABC-CLIO, 2005.

George, Earl. "Living on the Edge: Nuu-chah-nulth History from an Ahousaht Chief's Perspective." Master's thesis, University of Victoria, 1994.

George Watts . . . Creating Greatness: A Tribute to George Watts through recipes, stories and much more! Port Alberni:

Matilda Watts, Nuu-chah-nulth Economic Development Corporation, 2007.

Getches, David H., Charles F. Wilkinson, and Robert A. Williams Jr. *Federal Indian Law*. 3d ed. Minneapolis: West Publishing Co., 1993.

Gibbs, George. "Treaty of Neah Bay," transcript of *Journal Proceedings*, microcopy no. T-494, roll 5, National Archives, Washington, D.C.

——. "Tribes of Western Washington and Northwestern Oregon." *Contributions to North American Ethnology* 1. Washington, D.C.: U.S. Department of the Interior, 1877.

Gibson, James R. "Smallpox on the Northwest Coast, 1835–1838." *BC Studies* 5 (1982–83): 61–81.

A Gift from the Past. Film. Media Resources Association, Washington, D.C., 1994.

Gillis, Alix Jane. "The History of the Neah Bay Agency." *American Indian Ethnohistory: Indians of the Northwest*, edited by David E. Horr. New York/London: Garland Publishing, 1974.

Golla, Susan. "He Has a Name: History and Social Structure among the Indians of Western Vancouver Island." Ph.D. diss., Columbia University, 1987.

——. "Legendary History of the Tsisha'ath: A Working Translation." In *Nuu-chah-nulth Voices: Histories, Objects and Journeys,* edited by Alan L. Hoover, 133–71. Victoria: British Royal Museum, 2000.

Goodman, D. "Land Claim Agreements and the Management of Whaling in the Canadian Arctic." Proceedings of the 11th International Symposium on Peoples and Cultures of the North, Hokkaido Museum of Northern People, Abashiri, Japan, 1996; http://www.highnorth.no/Library/Policies/National/la-cl-ag.htm (accessed April 2008).

Goodman, Linda J., and Helma Swan. *Music and Dance in Northwest Coast Indian Life*. Tsaile, Ariz.: Navajo Community College, 1977.

——. "Makah Music." In *Spirit of the First People: Native American Music Traditions of Washington State*, edited by Willie Smith and Esmé Ryan, 81–105. Seattle: University of Washington Press, 1999.

——. *Singing the Songs of My Ancestors: The Life and Music of Helma Swan, Makah Elder*. Norman: University of Oklahoma Press, 2003.

Gregr, Edward J., Linda Nichol, John K. B. Ford, Graeme Ellis, and Andrew W. Trites. "Migration and Population Structure of Northeastern Pacific Whales of Coastal British Columbia: An Analysis of Commercial Whaling Records from 1908 to 1967." *Marine Mammal Science* 16 (2002): 699–727.

Guillod, Harry. "Report to the Deputy Superintendent-General, Indian Affairs" (Alberni, Barclay Sound), September 22, 1881. Victoria: Provincial Archives of B.C.

——. "Annual Report of the Department of Indian Affairs" (West Coast Agency), October 16, 1882. Ottawa: Maclean, Roger and Co.

——. "Annual Report of the Department of Indian Affairs" (West Coast Agency), October 1, 1884. Ottawa: Maclean, Roger and Co.

——. "Annual Report of the Department of Indian Affairs" (West Coast Agency), August 13, 1885. Ottawa: Maclean, Roger and Co.

Gunther, Erna. "Reminiscences of a Whaler's Wife." *Pacific Northwest Quarterly* 1, no. 1 (January, 1942): 65–69.

——. *Makah Marriage Patterns and Population Stability*. Seattle: University of Washington Press, 1960.

Guo, Pei-yi. "'Island Builders': Landscape and Historicity among the Langalanga, Solomon Islands." In *Landscape, Memory and History,"* edited by Pamela J. Stewart and Andrew Strathern, 189–209. London: Pluto Press, 2003.

Haig-Brown, Celia. *Resistance and Renewal: Surviving the Indian Residential Schools.*

Vancouver, B.C.: Tillicum Library, 1989.

Happynook, Kathy, ed. *Whaling Around the World*. Ladysmith, B.C.: World Council of Whalers, 2004.

Happynook, Tom Mexsis. "Securing Nuu chah nulth Food, Health and Traditional Values through the Sustainable Use of Marine Mammals." *World Council of Whalers Report*. Brentwood Bay, B.C., 2001.

——. "Whaling and the Nuu-chah-nulth People." Paper presented at a symposium at the Autry Museum of Western Heritage, Griffith Park, Los Angeles, March 24, 2001, in conjunction with the exhibit Out of the Mist: Treasures of the Nuu chah nulth Chiefs.

——. "Securing Food, Health and Traditional Values through the Sustainable Use of Marine Resources." Talk given at the University of Washington, March 2, 2005.

Harkin, Michael. "A Tradition of Invention: Modern Ceremonialism on the Northwest Coast." In *Present Is Past: Some Uses of Tradition in Native Societies*, edited by Marie Mauzé, 97–111. New York: University Press of America, 1997.

Harmon, Alexandra, *Indians in the Making: Ethnic Relations and Indian Identities*. Berkeley: University of California Press, 1998.

Harris, A. W. "Making the Case for Collective Rights: Indigenous Claims to Stocks of Marine Living Resources." *Georgetown International Environmental Law Review* 15 (Spring 2003): 379–428.

Harris, Stewart B., Bernard Zinman, Anthony Hanley, Joel Gittelsohn, Robert Hegele, Phillip W. Connelly, Baiju Shah, and Janet E. Hux, "The Impact of Diabetes on Cardiovascular Risk Factors and Outcomes in the Native Canadian Population." *Diabetes Research and Clinical Practice* 55 (2002): 165–73.

Harwell, Todd S., Carrie S. Oser, Nicholas J. Okon, Crystelle C. Fogle, Steven D. Helgerson, and Dorothy Gohdes. "Defining Disparities in Cardiovascular Disease for American Indians: Trends in Heart Disease and Stroke Mortality among American Indians and Whites in Montana, 1991 to 2000." *Journal of the American Heart Association* (October 2005): 2263–67; http//www.circ.ahajournals.org (accessed July 27, 2008).

Hawley, Donna Lea. *The Indian Act Annotated*. Calgary: The Carswell Company Ltd., 1984.

High North Publication. *The International Harpoon* 4 (1995); http//www.highnorth.no/ma-wh-cl.htm (accessed March 1996).

Howard, Barbara V., Elisa T. Lee, Linda D. Cowan, Richard B. Devereux, James M. Galloway, Oscar T. Go, William James Howard, Everett R. Rhoades, David C. Robbins, Maurice L. Sievers, and Thomas K. Welty. "Rising Tide of Cardiovascular Disease in American Indians: The Strong Heart Study." *Journal of the American Heart Association* (May 1999); http//www.circ.ahajournals.org (accessed July 27, 2008).

Howe, Craig. "Keep Your Thoughts above the Trees: Ideas on Developing and Presenting Tribal Histories." In *Clearing a Path: Theorizing the Past in Native American Studies,* edited by Nancy Shoemaker, 169–79. New York: Routledge, 2002.

Huelsbeck, David. "The Utilization of Whales at Ozette." In *Ozette Archaeological Project Research Reports,* edited by Stephan Samuels, 267–415. Pullman: Washington State University and the National Parks Service, 1994.

——. "Whaling in the Precontact Economy of the Central Northwest Coast." *Arctic Anthropology* 25, no. 1 (1998): 1–15.

Huffman, James. "An Exploratory Essay on Native Americans and Environmentalism." *University of Colorado Law Review* 63 (1992): 901–20.

Indian Act, R.S.C. s. 149, 1951, 1962.

Indian Residential Schools: The Nuu-Chah-Nulth Experience. Port Alberni: Nuu-chah-nulth Tribal Council, 1996.

———. "Whaling in the Precontact Economy of the Central Northwest Coast." *Arctic Anthropology* 25, no. 1 (1998): 1–15.

Inglis, Richard I., and James C. Haggarty. "Provisions or Prestige: A Reevaluation of the Economic Importance of Nootka Whaling." Victoria: B.C. Provincial Museum, 1983.

———. "Humpback off Port Bow." *Wildlife Review* (Spring 1985): 25–27.

The International Harpoon, no. 4, 1995 (High North Publication); http://www.highnorth.no/ma-wh-cl.htm (accessed March 1996).

International Whaling Commission (IWC). 49th Annual Meeting. 1997; http://www.iwcoffice.org/meetings/meetingsmain.htm (accessed November 15, 2007).

———. Convention Text, 1946; http:wwwiwcoffice.org/Convention.htm (accessed June 18, 2007).

———. Chairman's Report. Aboriginal Subsistence Whaling, 48th Annual Meeting (1996); http://luna.pos.to/whale/iwc_chair96_10.html (accessed June 1998).

Isaac, Thomas. *Aboriginal Law: Cases, Materials and Commentary*. Saskatchewan: Purich Publishing, 1995.

IWMC World Conservation Trust. June newsletter, 1999.

Jewitt, John R. *The Captive of Nootka, or, The Adventures of John R. Jewitt*. Washington: Ye Galleon Press, 1854.

Jin, Andrew, J. David Martin, and Christopher Sarin. "A Diabetes Mellitus in the First Nations Population of British Columbia Canada. Part 1: Mortality." *International Journal of Circumpolar Health* 61, no. 3 (2002): 251–53.

———. "A Diabetes Mellitus in the First Nations Population of British Columbia Canada. Part 2: Hospital Morbitity." *International Journal of Circumpolar Health* 61, no. 3 (2002): 254–59.

Johnson, Keith. "The Makah Manifesto." *Seattle Times,* August 23, 1998, B9.

———. An Open Letter to the Public from the President of the Makah Whaling Commission. Native Americans and the Environment, August 23, 1998; http:cnie.org/NAE/docs/makaheditorial.html (accessed March 15, 2001).

Johnson, Troy, Joane Nagel, and Duane Champagne, eds. *American Indian Activism: Alcatraz to the Longest Walk.* Chicago: University of Illinois Press, 1997.

Jolles, Carol Zane, with Elinor Mikaghaq Ooseva. *Faith, Food, and Family in a Yupik Whaling Community.* Seattle: University of Washington Press, 2002.

Jonaitis, Aldona. *The Yuquot Whalers' Shrine.* Seattle: University of Washington Press, 1999.

———. *Art of the Northwest Coast.* Seattle: University of Washington Press, 2006.

Kan, Sergei. *Symbolic Immortality: Nineteenth Century Tlingit Potlatch.* Washington, D.C.: Smithsonian Institution Press, 1989.

Kehoe, Alice. *North American Indians: A Comprehensive Account.* Englewood Cliffs, N.J.: Prentice-Hall Inc., 1981.

Kennedy, Des. "Belonging to the Land: The Meaning of Meares Island." *The Canadian Forum* 65 (June/July 1985): 10–17.

Kew, J. E Michael. "History of Coastal British Columbia since 1846." In *Handbook of North American Indians,* vol. 7: *Northwest Coast,* edited by Wayne Suttles, 159–68. Washington, D.C.: Smithsonian Institution, 1990).

Kim, Eun-Sook. "Theoretical Issues in Nuu-chah-nulth Phonology and Morpology." Ph.D. diss., University of British Columbia, 2003.

Kinghorn, April, Murray Humphries, Peter Outridge, and Hing Man Chan. "Reconstructing Historical Mercury Exposure from Beluga Whale Consumption among Inuit in the Mackenzie Delta." *Journal of Ethnobiology* 26, no. 2 (2006): 310–26.

Kirk, Ruth. *Tradition and Change on the Northwest Coast: The Makah, Nuu-chah-nulth, Southern Kwakiutl, and Nuxalk.* Seattle: University of Washington Press, 1986.

Kirk, Ruth, with Richard Daugherty. *Hunters of the Whale: An Adventure in Northwest Coast Archaeology.* New York: Morrow and Company, 1974.

Knight, Rolf. *Indians at Work: An Informal History of Native Labour in British Columbia, 1858–1930.* Vancouver, B.C.: New Star Books, 1978.

Kool, Richard. "Northwest Coast Indian Whaling: New Considerations." *Canadian Journal of Anthropology* 3, no. 1 (1982): 32–44.

Kroeber, Alfred, L. *The Nature of Culture.* Chicago: University of Chicago Press, 1952.

Kroeber, Alfred, Clyde Kluckhohn, Alfred G. Meyer, and Wayne Untereiner. *Culture: A Critical Review of Concepts and Definitions.* Cambridge, Mass.: Peabody Museum, 1952.

Kuhnlein, Harriet, Bill Erasmus, Hilary Cree-Kanashiro, Lois Englberger, Chinwe Okeke, Nancy Turner, Lindsay Allen, and Lalita Bhattacharjee. "Indigenous Peoples' Food Systems for Health: Finding Interventions That Work." *Public Health Nutrition* 9, no. 8 (2006): 1013–19.

Kuhnlein, H. V., V. Barthet, A. Farren, E. Falahi, D. Leggee, O. Receveur, and P. Berti. "Vitamins A, D, and E in Canadian Arctic Traditional Food and Adult Diets." *Journal of Food Composition and Analysis* 19 (2006): 495–506.

Kuhnlein, Harriet, and Olivier Receveur. "Dietary Change and Traditional Food Systems of Indigenous Peoples." *Annual Review of Nutrition* 16 (July 1996): 417–42; http://www.arjournals.annualreviews .org.offcampus.lib.washington.edu/toc/ nutr/16/1 (accessed July 28, 2008).

Kulchyski, Peter. *Unjust Relations: Aboriginal Rights in Canadian Courts.* Toronto: Oxford University Press, 1994.

Langlois, W. J., ed. *Nutka: Captain Cook and the Spanish Explorers on the Coast. Sound Heritage* 7, no. 1. British Columbia: Provincial Archives of British Columbia, 1978.

LaViolette, F. E. *The Struggle for Survival: Indian Cultures and the Protestant Ethic in B.C.* Toronto: University of Toronto Press, 1973.

Leeming, David Adams, "Creation." In *Storytelling Encyclopedia: Historical, Cultural, and Multiethnic Approaches to Oral Traditions Around the World.* Phoenix: Oryx Press, 1997.

Lemchuk-Favel, Laurel, and Richard Jock. "Aboriginal Health Systems in Canada: Nine Case Studies." *Journal of Aboriginal Health* (January 2004): 28–33.

Lillard, Charles, ed. *Gilbert M. Sproat: The Nootka: Scenes and Studies of Savage Life.* Victoria, B.C.: Sono Nis Press, 1987.

———. *Mission to Nootka, 1874–1900.* Sidney, B.C.: Gray's Publishing, 1977.

Lutz, John, "After the Fur Trade: The Aboriginal Labouring Class of British Columbia, 1849- 1890." *Journal of the Canadian Historical Association* 3, no. 1 (1992): 69–93.

Magdanz, James, and C. J. Utermohle. "Family Groups and Subsistence." *Cultural Survival Quarterly* 22, no. 3 (September 30, 1998): 51–52; http://www.209.200.101.189 .offcampus.lib.washington.edu/ publications/csq/index.cfm?id=22.3 (accessed July 28, 2008).

"The Makah Indian Tribe and Whaling: A Fact Sheet Issued by the Makah Whaling Commission, July 21, 1998." Posted on the Native Americans and the Environment Web site; http://www.cnie.org/NAE/docs/ makahfaq.html (accessed June 15, 2000).

Makah Indian Tribe v. Schoettler, 192 F.2d 224, 226, 9th Cir. Court (1951).

Makah Whaling Commission. "Management Plan for Makah Treaty Gray Whale Hunting for the Years 1998–2002." Makah Tribal Council. Native Americans and the Environment Web site; http://www .ncseonline.org/NAE/docs/makahplan .html (accessed June 15, 2000).

The Makah Nation: A Whaling People. Film. The Makah Whaling Commission, 2002.

Mapes, Lynda V. "Hunter Not Ashamed of

Killing Whale without Permit." *Seattle Times*, September 10, 2007.

The Marine Mammal Protection Act of 1972.

Marino, Cesare. "History of Western Washington since 1846." *Handbook of North American Indians*, vol. 7: *Northwest Coast*, edited by Wayne Suttles, 169–79. Washington, D.C.: Smithsonian Institution, 1990.

Marker, Michael. "Up with the Makah: Yodas of the Deep? Woe to anyone, especially native, who fails to sentimentalize the whale." *Vancouver Sun*, July 14, 1999.

Markishtum, Hubert. Makah Tribal Council Whaling Proposal, Makah Tribal Council, May 5, 1995.

Matthiessen, Peter. *In the Spirit of Crazy Horse*. New York: Penguin Books, 1980, 1992.

Mauger, Jeffrey. "Shed-Roof Houses at Ozette and in a Regional Perspective." In *Ozette Archaeological Project Research Reports*. Vol. 1, edited by Stephen R. Samuels, 29–169. Pullman: Washington State University, 1991.

Mauss, Marcel. *The Gift: The Form and Reason for Exchange in Archaic Societies*. Translated by W. D. Halls. London: Routledge, 1990.

Mauzé, Marie. "Potlatching as Ever." *European Review of Native American Studies* 9, no. 2 (1995): 25–31.

McFeat, Tom, ed. *Indians of the North Pacific Coast*. Ontario: Carleton University Press; Seattle: University of Washington Press, 1966–67.

McHalsie, Albert (Sonny). "Halq'eméylem Place Names in Stó:lō Territory." In *A Stó:lō Coast Salish Historical Atlas*, edited by Keith Thor Carlson, 134–35. Vancouver: Douglas and McIntire; Seattle: University of Washington Press, 2001.

McKee, Christopher. *Treaty Talks in British Columbia: Negotiating a Mutually Beneficial Future*. Vancouver: UBC Press, 1996.

McMillan, Alan D. *Since the Time of the Transformers: The Ancient Heritage of the Nuu-chah-nulth, Ditidaht, and Makah*. Vancouver: UBC Press, 1999.

——. "Early Nuu-chah-nulth Art and Adornment: Glimpses from the Archaeological Record." In *Nuu-chah-nulth Voices: Histories, Objects, and Journeys*, edited by Alan L. Hoover, 230–56. Victoria: Royal British Columbia Museum, 2000.

McMillan, Alan D., and Denis E. St. Claire. *Alberni Prehistory: Archeological and Ethnographic Investigations on Western Vancouver Island*. Penticton, B.C.: Theytus Books, 1982.

——. *Ts'ishaa: Archaeology and Ethnography of a Nuu-chah-nulth Origin Site in Barkley Sound*. Burnaby, B.C.: Simon Fraser University Archaeology Press, 2005.

McNiven, Ian J. "Saltwater People: Spiritscapes, Maritime Rituals and the Archaeology of Australian Indigenous Seascapes." *World Archaeology* 35, no. 3 (December 2003): 329–49.

Metcalf v. Daley, 214 F.3d 1135, 6, 9th Cir. Court, 2000.

"Metcalf's Indian History." Indianz.com, posted June 9, 2000; http://www.indianz.com/News/show.asp?ID=tc/692000-4 (accessed August 11, 2008).

"Might Whale Meat Once Again Find a Place on the Menu?" *High North News* 11 (November 1996); http://www.highnorth.no/mi-wh-me.htm (accessed November 15, 2000).

Mihesuah, Devon A. "Introduction" to *Natives and Academics: Researching and Writing about American Indians*, edited by Devon A. Mihesuah, 1–22. Lincoln: University of Nebraska Press, 1999.

Miller, Beatrice. "Neah Bay: The Makah in Transition." *Pacific Northwest Quarterly* 43, no. 4 (1973): 262–72.

Miller, J. R. *Shingwuak's Vision: A History of Native Residential Schools*. Toronto: University of Toronto Press, 1996.

Miller, Robert J. "Exercising Cultural Self-Determination: The Makah Indian Tribe Goes Whaling." *American Indian Law*

Review 25, no. 165 (2000–2001): 165–273.

Milloy, M. J. "Paul Watson Allies with a Far-right Republican in His Fight against Aboriginal Whaling." *Hour Magazine*, posted August 5, 1999; http://www .archives.econ.utah.edu/archives/ pen-1/1999m08.a/msg00089.htm (accessed August 11, 2008).

Monks, Gregory G., Alan D. McMillan, and Denis E. St. Claire. "Nuu-chah-nulth Whaling: Archaeological Insights into Antiquity, Species Preferences, and Cultural Importance." *Arctic Anthropology* 38, no. 1 (2001): 60–81.

Moziño, José Mariano. *Noticias de Nootka: An Account of Nootka Sound in 1792.* Translated and with an introduction by Iris Higbie Wilson. Seattle: University of Washington Press, 1970.

Muckle, Robert J. *The First Nations of British Columbia.* Vancouver: UBC Press, 1998.

Myers, Kathryn A. "Cardiovascular Disease and Risk in the Aboriginal Population." *Canadian Medical Association Journal* 166, no. 3 (February 5, 2002): 355; http:// www.cmaj.ca/cgi/content/full/166/3/355.

National Environmental Policy Act, 1969.

National Marine Fisheries Service. "Environmental Assessment on Issuing a Quota to the Makah Indian Tribe for a Subsistence Hunt on Gray Whales for the Years 2001 and 2002." U.S. Department of Commerce, National Oceanic and Atmospheric Administration, July 12, 2001.

Naylor, J. L., C. D. Schraer, A. M. Mayer, A. P. Lanier, C. A. Treat, and N. J. Murphy. "Diabetes among Alaska Natives: A Review." *International Journal of Circumpolar Health* 62, no. 3 (2003): 363–87.

Nichol, Linda M., Edward J. Greg, Rowenna Flinn, John K. B. Ford, Riccoh Gurney, Linda Michaluk, and Allison Peacock. "British Columbia Commercial Whaling Catch Data 1908 to 1967: A Detailed Description of the B.C. Historical Whaling Database." Canadian Technical Report of Fisheries and Aquatic Sciences

2396, Fisheries and Oceans Canada; http://www.pac.dfo-mpo.gc.ca/sci/sa/ cetacean/Nichol%20et%20al.%202002 .pdf (accessed July 10, 2007).

Nootka. British Columbia Heritage Series. Province of British Columbia, 1966.

Norton, Bryan G. *Toward Unity among Environmentalists.* New York: Oxford University Press, 1991.

"Nuu-chah-nulth Nations Conclude Presentation of Case." NTC Fisheries Department; http://www.uuathluk.ca/treaty.htm (accessed August 15, 2008).

Nuu-chah-nulth Phrase Book and Dictionary. Barkley Sound Dialect. Banfield: Barkley Sound Working Group, 2004.

The Nuu-chah-nulth Research and Litigation Project. http://www.nuuchahnulth.org/ tribalcouncil/fisheries.html (accessed June 2008).

Nuu-chah-nulth Traditional Whaling. Teacher's Resource Book, Native Studies Programme, School District No. 70; copy held at the Nuu-chah-nulth Tribal Council Offices.

O'Harra, Doug. "Experts Extol Tasty, Nutritious Whales: Benefits Beyond the Vitamins and Minerals, There's a Spiritual Element." *Anchorage Daily News*, November 24, 2003.

Ohnishi, Mutsuko. *Mrs. Ohnishi's Whale Cuisine.* Tokyo: Kodansha, 1995.

Olsen, Loren. "Native Music of the Pacific Northwest." In *Spirit of the First People: Native American Music Traditions of Washington State,* edited by Willie Smyth and Esmé Ryan, 106–16. Seattle: University of Washington Press, 1999.

Our World: T'aat'aaqsapa Cultural Dictionary. Book One. Nuu-chah-nulth Tribal Council, 1989.

Our World: T'aat'aaqsapa Cultural Dictionary. Book Two. Nuu-chah-nulth Tribal Council, 1991.

Pascua, Maria. "Ozette: A Makah Village in 1491." *National Geographic* 180, no. 4 (October 1991): 38–54.

Paterson, T. W. "Foreign Competition: Too Much Hunting Threat to Whalers." *The Daily Colonist*, July 4, 1965.

Pavel, Michael Chi'XapKaid. "Decolonizing through Storytelling." In *For Indigenous Eyes Only: A Decolonization Handbook*, edited by Waziyatawin Angela Wilson and Michael Yellow Bird, 127–37. Santa Fe: School of American Research Press, 2005.

Pearce, Roy Harvey. *Savagism and Civilization: A Study of the Indian and the American Mind*. Berkeley: University of California Press, 1988.

Penikett, Tony. *Reconciliation: First Nations Treaty-Making in British Columbia*. Toronto: Douglas and McIntire, 2006.

People for the Ethical Treatment of Animals (PETA). http://www.petaliterature.com/VEG297.pdf.

Peterson, Jan. *The Albernis, 1860–1922*. Lantzville, B.C.: Oolichan Books, 1992.

Peterson, Melissa, and the Makah Cultural and Research Center. "The Makah." In *Native Peoples of the Olympic Peninsula: Who We Are*, edited by Jacilee Wray, 151–67. Norman: University of Oklahoma Press, 2002.

Pevar, Stephen L. *The Rights of Indians and Tribes*. New York: New York University Press, 2002.

Portier, Dimitri. "The Meares Island Case: Nuu-chah-nulth vs. the Logging Industry." *European Review of Native American Studies* 14, no. 1 (2000): 31–37.

Reavely, Travis. "Nuuchahnulth Whaling and Its Significance for Social and Economic Reproduction." *Chicago Anthropology Exchange Graduate Journal of Anthropology* 28 (Spring 1998): 23–40. Native Americans and the Environment (2000); http://www.ncseonline.org/nae/docs/reaveley.html (accessed July 5, 2000).

Regan, Tom. *Defending Animal Rights*. Chicago: University of Illinois Press, 2001.

Reid, Martine J., ed. *Paddling to Where I Stand: Agnes Alfred, Qwiqwasutinuxw Noblewoman*. Vancouver: UBC Press; Seattle: University of Washington Press, 2004.

Renker, Ann M. "Whale Hunting and the Makah Tribe." Prepared for the Makah Fisheries Management Office; submitted in the IWC Makah Whaling Proposal, Makah Tribal Council, May 5, 1995. (Held at the Makah Tribal Council Office.)

———. "Whale Hunting and the Makah Tribe: A Needs Statement." International Whaling Commission Report, April 2007; www.iwcoffice.org/document/commission/iwc59docs/59-ASW%209.pdf (accessed October 15, 2007).

Renker, Ann M., and Erna Gunther. "Makah." In *Handbook of North American Indians*, vol. 7: *Northwest Coast,* edited by Wayne Suttles, 422–30. Washington, D.C.: Smithsonian Institution, 1990.

"Rep. Metcalf—A Savior of the Cetaceans? Congressman Led Campaign to Stop Whaling," *Seattle Times*, June 30, 1996; http://www.search.nwsource.com/search?offset=120&from=ST&rs=1&similarto=PIArchives%3Api_archive8901050312 (accessed August 11, 2008).

Reyner, Jon, and Jeanne Eder. *American Indian Education: A History*. Norman: University of Oklahoma Press, 2004.

Richardson, Scott. "Washington State Status Report for the Gray Whale." Seattle: Department of Fisheries and Oceans, July 1997; http://www.wdfw.wa.gov/wlm/diversty/soc/status/graywhal/graywhal.pdf (accessed September 11, 2007).

Riley, Carroll L. "The Makah Indians.: A Study of Political and Economic Organization." *Ethnohistory* 15 (1968): 57–95.

Roberts, Helen H., and Morris Swadesh. *Songs of the Nootka Indians of the Western Vancouver Island*. Philadelphia: The American Philosophical Society, 1955.

Roghair, David L. "*Anderson v. Evans*: Will Makah Whaling under the Treaty of Neah Bay Survive the Ninth Circuit's Application of the MMPA?" *Journal of*

Environmental Law and Litigation 189
(2005): 189–211.

Rohner, Ronald P., and Evelyn C. Rohner. *The Kwakiutl Indians of British Columbia.* New York: Holt, Rinehart and Winston, 1970.

Rosman, Abraham, and Paula G. Rubel. *Feasting with Mine Enemy: Rank and Exchange among Northwest Coast Society.* Long Grove, Ill.: Waveland Press, 1986, 2001.

Samuels, Stephan R. "Introduction to the Ozette Archaeological Project." In *Ozette Archaeological Project Reports,* edited by Stephan R. Samuels and Richard D. Daugherty, 1–24. Pullman: Washington State University and the National Parks Service, 1994.

Sapir, Edward. "Sayach'apis, a Nootka Trader." In *American Indian Life,* ed. Elsie Clews Parsons. Lincoln: University of Nebraska Press, 1922.

Sapir, Edward, and Morris Swadesh. *Nootka Texts: Tales and Ethnological Narratives, with Grammatical Notes and Lexical Materials.* Philadelphia: Linguistic Society of America, 1939.

———. *Native Accounts of Nootka Ethnography.* Bloomington: Indiana University Press, 1955.

Sapir, Edward, Morris Swadesh, Alexander Thomas, John Thomas, and Frank Williams. *The Whaling Indians: West Coast Legends and Stories.* Part 10 of the Sapir-Thomas Nootka Texts, told by Tom Sayach'apis, William, Dick Lamahos, Captain Bill, and Tyee Bob. Ottawa: Canadian Museum of Civilization, 2000.

———. *The Whaling Indians: Legendary Hunters.* Part 9 of the Sapir-Thomas Nootka Texts, told by Sayach'apis, William, Frank Williams, Big Fred, Captain Bill, and Qwishanishim. Ottawa: Museum of Civilization, 2004.

"Save the Whales, for the Makah." *World Council of Whalers News* (June 1999): 2, 3.

Sayach'apis. "Stands Up High Over All." Tseshaht First Nation; http://www.tseshaht.com/ tradition_history/figures/sayachapis.php (accessed July 14, 2007).

Schouls, Tim, "The Basic Dilemma: Sovereignty or Assimilation." In *Nation to Nation: Aboriginal Sovereignty and the Future of Canada,* edited by John Bird, Lorraine Land, and Murray Macadam, 12–26. Toronto: Irwin Publishing, 2002.

Schumacher, Catherine, Michael Davidson, and Gretchen Ehrsam. "Cardiovascular Disease among Alaska Natives: A Review of the Literature." *International Journal of Circumpolar Health* 62, no. 4 (2003): 343–62.

Sea Shepherd Conservation Society. http://www.seashepherd.org/people/watson.html.

Service, Elman R. *Profiles in Ethnology.* New York: Harper and Row, 1950.

Short, Ken, "Whalers and Protestors Vow to Stay as Long as Necessary." *Peninsula Daily News,* November 1, 1998.

Smith, Angèle, "Landscape Representation: Place, and Identity in Nineteenth-Century Ordinance Survey Maps of Ireland." In *Landscape, Memory and History,* edited by Pamela J. Stewart and Andrew Strathern, 71–88. London: Pluto Press, 2003.

Smith, Linda Tuhiwai. *Decolonizing Methodologies: Research and Indigenous Peoples.* New York: St. Martin's Press, 1999.

Smullen, Scott. "Whaling Commission Approves Combined Russian-Makah Gray Whale Quota." IWC US Delegates News Release, October 23, 1997; http://www.noaa.gov/public-affairs/pr97/oct97/iwc2.html (accessed November 15, 2007).

Smyth, Willie. "Preface" to *Spirit of the First People: Native American Music Traditions of Washington State,* edited by Willie Smyth and Esmé Ryan, ix–xii. Seattle: University of Washington Press, 1999.

Spalding, David E. *Whales of the West Coast.* Madeira Park, B.C.: Harbour Publishing, 1998.

Sproat, Gilbert M. *Scenes and Studies of Savage Life*. London: Smith, Elder and Co., 1868.

St. Claire, Denis. "Thomas Family History and Genealogy." Document based on accounts by Sayach'apis as told to Edward Sapir in 1910–14. Manuscript, 2003.

St. Germain, Jill. *Indian Treaty-Making Policy in the United States and Canada, 1867–1877*. Lincoln: University of Nebraska Press, 2001.

"Statement by the Makah Tribal Council." *Seattle Times*, September 10, 2007.

Stewart, Hilary. *Indian Fishing: Early Methods on the Northwest Coast*. Seattle: University of Washington Press, 1977, 1982.

———. *Cedar*. Seattle: University of Washington Press, 1984.

Stewart, Pamela J., and Andrew Strathern. "Introduction" to *Landscape, Memory and History*, edited by Pamela J. Stewart and Andrew Strathern, 1–15. London: Pluto Press, 2003.

Stonham, John. *A Concise Dictionary of the Nuu-chah-nulth Language*. New York: Edwin Mellon Press, 2005.

Strang, Veronica. *Uncommon Ground: Cultural Landscapes and Environmental Values*. New York: Oxford University Press, 1997.

Sullivan, Robert. *A Whale Hunt: Two Years on the Olympic Peninsula with the Makah and Their Canoe*. New York: Scribner, 2000.

Suttles, Wayne. "Affinal Ties, Subsistence, and Prestige among the Coast Salish." *American Anthropologist*, n.s., 62, no. 2 (April 1960): 296–305.

———. "Coping with Abundance: Subsistence on the Northwest Coast." In Suttles, *Coast Salish Essays*, 45–63. Vancouver, B.C.: Talon Books, 1987.

Suttles, Wayne, and Aldona C. Jonaitis. "History of Research in Ethnology." In *Handbook of North American Indians*. vol. 7: *Northwest Coast*, edited by Wayne Suttles, 73–88. Washington, D.C.: Smithsonian Institution, 1990.

Swan, James. *The Indians of Cape Flattery, at the Entrance to the Strait of Fuca, Western Washington Territory*. Washington, D.C.: Smithsonian Institution, 1870.

Swanson, Earl. "Nootka and the California Gray Whale." *Pacific Northwest Quarterly* 47, no. 2 (1956): 52–56.

Taylor, Herbert C., Jr. "Anthropological Investigation of the Makah Indians Relative to Tribal Identity and Aboriginal Possession of Lands." In *American Indian Ethnohistory: Indians of the Northwest*, edited by David A. Horr. New York: Garland Publishing, 1974.

Tennant, Paul. *Aboriginal Peoples and Politics: The Indian Land Question in British Columbia, 1849–1989*. Vancouver: UBC Press, 1990.

Thornton, Thomas F. "Anthropological Studies of Native American Place Naming." *American Indian Quarterly* 2, no. 2 (Spring 1997): 209–28.

———. *Being and Place among the Tlingit*. Seattle: University of Washington Press, 2008.

Titian, Denise. "BC/Nations Sign Final Treaty Agreement." *Ha-shilth-sa* 35, no. 14 (July 24, 2008).

Titley, E. Brian. *A Narrow Vision: Duncan Campbell Scott and the Administration of Indian Affairs in Canada*. Vancouver: UBC Press, 1986.

Toole, Ken. "Drumming Up Resentment: The Anti-Whaling Movement in Montana." *Montana Human Rights Network* (2000), 14; http://www.mhrn.org/publications/specialresearchreports/DrummingUp.pdf (accessed August 11, 2008).

Treaties and Trees: A Nuu-chah-nulth Perspective. Nuu-chah-nulth Tribal Council, Port Alberni, British Columbia.

Treaty of Neah Bay, 1855.

Two Horses, Michael. "'We Know Who the Real Indians Are': Animal-Rights Groups, Racial Stereotyping, and Racism in Rhetoric and Action in the Makah Whaling

Controversy." Master's thesis, University of Arizona, 2001.

Tylor, Edward B. *Primitive Culture: Researches into the Development of Mythology, Philosophy, Religion, Art, and Custom.* London: Murray, 1881.

Uncommon Controversy: Fishing Rights of the Muckleshoot, Puyallup and Nisqually Indians. Report prepared for the American Friends Service Committee. Seattle: University of Washington Press, 1970, 1975.

U.S. v. Washington, 384 F. Supp. 312, 1974, U.S. Dist. Court.

Uu-a-thluk. Nuu-chah-nulth Fisheries Department. Volume 3, no. 2 (2007), Nuu-chah-nulth Tribal Council; http://www.nuuchahnulth.org/tribalcouncil/fisheries.html (accessed August 12, 2008).

Vansina, Jan. *Oral Tradition: A Study in Historical Methodology.* Chicago: Aldine Publishing Company, 1961 and 1965.

——. *Oral Tradition as History.* Madison: University of Wisconsin Press, 1985.

The Washing of Tears. Film. Nootka Sound and Picture Company, Inc./National Film Board of Canada, 1994.

Waterman, T. T. *The Whaling Equipment of the Makah Indians.* University of Washington Publications in Anthropology, 1920.

Watters, Lawrence, and Connie Duggers. "The Hunt for Gray Whales: The Dilemma of Native American Treaty Rights and the International Moratorium on Whaling." *Columbia Journal of Environmental Law* 22 (1997): 319, 352.

"wcw Attends Panel on Indigenous Whaling." *World Council of Whalers News*, October 1999.

Webb, Robert L. *On the Northwest: Commercial Whaling in the Pacific Northwest, 1790–1967.* Vancouver: UBC Press, 1988.

Webster, Peter. *As Far As I Know: Reminiscences of an Ahousaht Elder.* Campbell River, B.C.: Campbell River Museum and Archives, 1983.

Wein, Eleanor, Milton Freeman, and Jeanette Makus. "Use and Preference for Traditional Foods among the Belcher Island Inuit." *Arctic* 49, no. 3 (1996): 256–66.

Wenzel, George. *Animal Rights, Human Rights: Ecology, Economy, and Ideology in the Canadian Arctic.* Toronto: University of Toronto Press, 1991.

"West Coast Whale Deaths Could Be Due to Food Supply." *Science Daily* (May 24, 1999); http://www.sciencedaily.com/releases/1999/05/990524035753.htm (accessed May 2001).

"Whale Bones Tell Story of Tribe's Milestone Hunt." Associated Press, December 4, 2005; http://www.whale.story.htm (accessed December 15, 2005).

Wheeler, Tim. "Makah Indians Defend Their Treaty Rights." *People's Weekly World* (June 3, 2000): 10–11.

Wheeler, Winona. "Social Relations of Indigenous Oral Histories." In *Walking a Tightrope: Aboriginal People and Their Representation.* Ontario: Wilfred Laurier University Press, 2005.

Wike, Joyce. "Social Stratification among the Nootka." *Ethnohistory* 5, no. 3 (1958): 219–41.

Wilkins, David E. *American Indian Politics and the American Political System.* 2d ed. New York: Rowman and Littlefield Publishers, Inc., 2007.

Wilkinson, Charles. *Blood Struggle: The Rise of Modern Indian Nations.* New York: W. W. Norton and Company, 2005.

——. *Messages from Frank's Landing: A Story of Salmon, Treaties, and the Indian Way.* Seattle: University of Washington Press, 2000.

Willows, Noreen D. "Overweight in First Nations Children: Prevalence, Implications, and Solutions." *Journal of Aboriginal Health* (March 2005): 76–84.

Wilson, Angela Cavender. "American Indian History or Non-Indian Perceptions of American Indian History?" In *Natives and Academics: Researching and Writing*

about American Indians, edited by Devon
A. Mihesuah, 23–36. Lincoln: University
of Nebraska Press, 1999.

Worcester v. Georgia 31 U.S. 515 (1832).

Wyatt, Gary. *Mythic Beings: Spirit Art of the
Northwest Coast*. Seattle: University of
Washington Press, 1999.

Young, Y. Kue. "Recent Health Trends in the
Native American Population." *Population Research and Policy Review* 16 (1997):
147–67.

Index

Page numbers in italics refer to illustrations.

Cruikshank, Julie, 76

culinary imperialism, 204

culture: changes in, 7, 13, 56, 61, 68, 79, 154; definition of, 68, 192, 221n119; disruption to, 5, 6, 42, 75; as dynamic, 153; effect on ceremonial positions and family lineages, 49; effect on spirituality, 49, 50; imperialism of, 163, 192, 204; revitalization of, 14, 127, 141, 143, 169

D

dances: connected to whaling tradition, 39, 66, 102, 148, 202; cultural significance of, 95; owned by chiefs, 96; prohibition on, 53–55; and Wolf Ritual, 36, 55. *See also* ceremonies; potlatch

David, Winnie/Winifred, 19

Deep Ecology Movement, 160–61. *See also* animal rights; environmental movement; Pinchot, Gifford; Muir, John

Department of Indian Affairs (DIA), 58, 121, 123, 124; health statistics of, 193

diabetes, 193–98, 242n5, 242n13. *See also* disease; health

disease: depopulation as a result of, 47; and effect on the Nuu-chah-nulth and Makah, 47–50, 57, 59, 68; epidemics, 7, 19, 47; present-day, 193–98. *See also* health

Ditidaht, xiv, 48, 109

E

economy: changes to Makah and Nuu-chah-nulth, 50–51, 55, 59–64, 66–68; market, 6, 7, 61; pre-contact, 6, 20, 36; wage-labor, 60, 64, 66, 67

education: as federal Indian policy, 44, 50–51, 57; traditional, 81, 83, 94, 110–11. *See also* missionaries; schools

Endangered Species list, 5, 7, 130, 164

environmental assessment (EA), 171, 172, 173, 176. *See also Anderson v. Evans*; *Metcalf v. Daley*

environmental impact statement (EIS), 172, 173, 176, 177, 190, 191. *See also Anderson v.*

Evans; *Metcalf v. Daley*

environmental movement, 158–70. *See also* Pinchot, Gifford; Muir, John

epidemics, 217n22. *See also* disease; smallpox

Erickson, Patricia Pierce, 155

ethnography, 10, 20, 31, 60, 72, 82–83

explorers, 16, 42, 48, 75, 103

F

Faroe Islands, 197

feast. *See* potlatch

federal trust responsibility, 179, 182, 184, 188–89

Fiander, Jack, 187, 188

finding of no significant impact (fonsi), 172, 173, 175. *See also Anderson v. Evans*

First Nations Summit, 232n132

First Salmon Ceremony, 116, 204

First Species Ceremony, 204

fishing: and canning industry, 61, 71; commercial, 71; rights struggles of the 1960s, 116–21; Indian Fisheries Association (IFA), 118; in oral tradition, 15, 96; non-Indian, 46; Nuu-chah-nulth fishing rights case, 125–26, 148–49; subsistence, 6, 23–24, 28, 31–32, 44, 45, 59–61, 66, 71; treaty rights, 116–20, 168–70, 180. *See also* Boldt Decision

Fixico, Donald, 10

food: and position in society, 23, 25; ceremonial distribution of, 22, 36, 54, 55, 79; cultural importance of eating traditional, 198–204; gathering, 20, 39, 44, 91, 136; hegemony, 204–5; introduction of new, 65–66, 153; and Makah generosity with neighbors, 18; stores, 61; traditional, 5, 6, 8, 14, 121, 146, 148, 197–204; whale meat and blubber as, 15, 20–21, 41, 65–66, 127, 132. *See also* whales

Francis, Daniel, 153

Frank, Billy, 117–18. *See* fishing: rights struggles of the 1960s

Frank, Trudy, 194

Friendly Cove, 19, 43

Fund for Animals, 168, 237n45

G

Gambell, Alaska, 200
Georg, Evelyn, 80, 84, *86*, *89*
Georg, Jack, *86*
George, Chief Earl, 40, 144, 201, 215n102
Gibbs, George, 52–53, 60, 216n11
Golla, Susan, 221nn7,8
Gonzales, Bruce, *203*
Gonzales, Frankie, 183, 187–88
Gorton, Slade, 119, 158, 168–69. *See also* anti-whaling coalition
Gray's Harbor whaling station, 220n101
gray whale: and the Endangered Species List, 5, 7, 130, 131, 132, 164; bones, 30; deaths of, 131, 164, 179; decline in, 4–6, 7, 130, 134, 162, 167; IWC quota of, 135, 166, 167, 170–79, 190–91; *maa'ak*, 30, 77; population, 7, 65, 130, 135, 164, 166, 174, 175, 177, 179, 192; recent whaling of, 3, 131–32, 138–40, *139*, 144, 147, 150, 156, 164, 166–67, 181–183, 185, 191, 192, 202; *sih-xwah-wiX*, 30, 138, 140; species, 62, 77, 163; traditional whaling of, 30, 63, 64–65, 75. *See also* Makah whaling; whales
Greenland, 197
Greenpeace, 150, 161, 233–34n2
Guardian Spirit Complex, 23–24
Guillod, Harry, 54, 55, 59
Gus, Gail Peterson, *83*

H

haahuupa (education/teaching), 24, 81, 212n30
Haggard, Eileen, 24
ha-he-to-ak (lightning serpent, Makah), 30. *See also* art; stories
ha-houlthee (land), 143
halibut, 5, 20, 61, 120, 202, 203. *See also* fishing; food
Happynook, Tom Mexsis, 40, 146, 147, 205, 206
haquum. See whaler's wife
Harkin, Michael, 155
Harmon, Alexandra, 117
haw'iih. See under chiefs

haw'ilth. See under chiefs
health: problems, 8, 13, 14, 132, 133, 148, 167, 193–95; whale oil and, 193–206. *See also* diabetes; disease; heart disease
Health Canada, 193
heart disease, 193–98, 240, 242. *See also* health
herring, 27, 62, 65. *See also* fishing; food
Hesquiaht, 40, 49–50, 194
Hiikwis, 71, 87
hishuk ish tsawalk (heshook-ish tsawalk), 42, 67–68, 73, 207
housing, 20, 22–23, 26, 35, 39, 40, *74*, 74–75; changes to after contact, 50, 56, 59, 67. *See also* cedar; longhouses
Humane Society of the United States (HSUS), 168
humpback whale: bones, 30; *ch'ih-ch'ih-wad* (Makah), 30; and commercial fishing, 62, 63, 65; *iihtuup* (Nuu-chah-nulth), 30; in stories, 29–30, 92, 148; species, 31. *See also* whales; whaling
Hunter, Anne, 71, 129, 130
Hunter, Chief Arnie, 186, 206
Huu-ay-aht, 213n54

I

iihtuup (Nuu-chah-nulth). *See* art; humpback whale; stories; whales
Indian Act, Canada (1876), 58, 147, 218n61, 218n63. *See also* Indian policy
Indian Agent, 19, 47, 49–57, 59, 61, 65, 105
Indian Health Service (IHS), 195
Indian images: "noble Indian," 156; "savage Indian," 157–58; "ecological Indian," 158–59; as "other," 152
Indian policy, 6, 43–51, 52, 57, 58, 59, 105, 117, 121–22; based on assimilation, 45–61, 121–22, 154, 156; British Columbia, 44–46. *See also* Indian Act, Canada; White Paper
indigenous rights struggles, 121–22
Ingling, Allen, 138, 151. *See also* Makah whaling
International Convention for the Regulation of Whaling (ICRW), 133–35, 151, 166, 178
International Whaling Commission (IWC), 132–35, 138, 147, 151, 164, 166–67, 170–75, 178–79, 181; and aboriginal subsistence

whaling definition, 133–35, 152, 167, 178

Inuit, 147, 161, 197, 199, 201, 233–34n2

Inupiat, 199, 200

Iron Eyes Cody, 159–60. *See also* environmental movement

itl'ik (lightning or sea serpent), 15, 103, 106, 201n1. *See also* art; stories

J

Jack, Chief Jerry, 27, 143

Japan, health studies in, 197

Johnson, Ben, Jr., 168

Johnson, Keith, 8, 130, 132, 136, 141, 154, 165, 192, 206

Johnson, Wayne, 183, 184, 187, 188, 241n149

Jonaitis, Aldona, 105

K

Kapkimyis, 72, 73, 74, 75, 77, 221nn8,9

Keesta (Kista), 25–26, 32, 40, 41. *See also* whaling rituals

Keitlah, Nelson, 144–45

Klachote, Chief, 44, 180. *See also* Stevens treaties

Klasset. *See* Makah: villages

klukwalle (*cloqually*, Makah). *See* Wolf Ritual

kohl. See also rank; slaves

Kwatyat, 15, 81

Kyuquot, 63–64

L

labor (indigenous): changes to, 66–67; and its impact on chiefs' authority, 66–67; seasonal, 59– 64; wage-labor, 60, 64, 66

land claims, 122, 123, 124, 125, 143, 146, 147. *See also* Meares Island

language: Chinook Jargon, 24, 35; Interior Salishan, 198–99; Nootkan, 210n4; and oral tradition, 78–85, 90, 114; orthography, xiv–xviii; repression of, 42, 52, 145; revitalization of, xiv, xv, 7–8, 128–29, 141, 143, 146; Tsehaht, 11, 12, 18, 19, 31, 35, 75, 123, 205; Wakashan, xiv, 16

lawsuits, 233n154

lineage group (*ushtakimilh*), 18, 22, 23, 58, 67, 88, 89, 102

linguistics. *See* language

logging, 46, 60, 61, 124, 125

longhouses, 38, 50, 54, 87, 104, 115, 124, 222n18

Lucas, Simon, 194, 195, 196

M

maa'ak (gray whale, Nuu-chah-nulth), 30, 77. *See also* gray whale

Maa-Nulth, 141, 146–149. *See also* treaties

Makah (*kwih-dich-chuh-ahtX*): and the Boldt decision, 120; community, 4, 130, 131–33, 135, 141, 142, 166, 167, 186, 187; culture, 79, 97, 105, 128, 134, 141, 154, 155; language, xiv, xv, xviii, 31, 128; Makah Cultural and Research Center (MCRC), 128; Makah Days, 98; reservation, 51, 55, 128, 157, 219n77; school, 51; trade, 60; villages, 16, 18, 216n16; whaler's song, 97–98

Makah Indian Tribe et al. v. Schoettler (1951), 117

Makah Tribal Council, xi, 58, 129, 131, 132, 135, 168, 174, 183–84

Makah whaling: Household Whaling Survey, 202–4; and 1999 whale hunt, 135–41; and 2007 whale hunt, 166, 183–92; and Whale Management Plan, 134, 135, 167, 171, 175, 181, 187. *See also* whales; whaling

Makah Whaling Commission (MWC), 135, 151, 184; and gray whale management plan, 231n108

mamalhn'i (non-Indians). *See* contact

mammals: marine, 160, 163, 176, 177, 181, 196; in the Alaska Native and Inuit diet, 197–201; and mercury toxins, 196–98. *See also* Marine Mammal Protection Act

Maquinna, 27–28, 54, 103, *104*

Marine Mammal Protection Act (MMPA) (1972), 176–78, 181, 182, 183, 187, 191; and Alaska Natives exemption, 176–78, 181–82; Makah waiver process, 183, 187, 191

marine space, importance of in signing treaties, 44–45; importance of names, 76– 78; Tseshaht names of, 75–77

People for the Ethical Treatment of Animals (PETA), 162–63

Pérez, Juan, 42

Pinchot, Gifford, 160. *See also* animal rights; Deep Ecology Movement; environmental movement

Pook-ubs, 226n131

Port Alberni, 221n7

potential biological removal (BPR), 175

potlatch, 22, 24, 31, 35–40; ban, 218n63; changes to after contact, 53–56, 57, 58, 66; and coming of age, 24; naming, 101, 108; *pa-chitle* (to give), 35, 52; prohibition against, 49–56; resistance to prohibition, 54, 56, 57; Sayach'apis', 90, 101; whale-oil, 38–40. *See also* ceremonies

Powell, Israel Wood, 53, 71

Progressive Animal Welfare Society (PAWS), 154

Puyallup Tribe v. The Department of Game et al. (1968), 118

Q

Quadra, Juan Francisco de la Bodega y, 31

R

rank (social), 18, 22–23, 49; changes to after contact, 58–59; and housing, 211n17; and marriage, 23, 96; and prestige system, 22; and privileges, 35, 36, 49, 58–59

"Red Power" movement, 121–22

Regan, Tom, 160–61. *See also* animal rights

religion: beliefs of, 56, 68, 120, 188, 192; and conversion, 50, 52, 157; and groups, 50; and training, 51, 137. *See also* missionaries

resistance: writing, 10; 1960s, 118–23; "Red Power" movement, 122

Ross, Lena, xvi

S

salmon: fishing, 20, 80, 118–21, 186; as resource, 5, 116–20, 202, 203; species of, 27, 116, 163. *See also* First Salmon Ceremony; fishing; food

Sam, Les, 126

Sam, Stanley, 144, 145–46

Sapir, Edward, 54–55, 59; fieldwork of, xiv, 10–11, 65, 82, 85–87, 99, 100; publications of, 82–83, 87, 90; and Sayach'apis, 37–38, 72, 74, 74, 76, 82, 85–87, 90, 95, 99, 100. *See also Nootka Texts*

Sayach'apis, xiii, 25, 37, 38, 72, 74, 76, 82, 85–89, 94–103; potlatch of, 90, 101

schools: Alberni Indian Residential School, 109; boarding schools, 13, 50–52, 57, 71, 82, 84, 109, 113, 145, 194

Scott, Duncan Campbell, 51. *See also* Indian policy

Sea Defense Alliance, 157. *See also* anti-whaling coalition

sealing: commercial, 60–63; Makah involvement in, 60–61, 153, 180, 226n1; Nuu-chah-nulth involvement in, 61, 66, 153; protests against, 161, 163. *See also* trade

sea otter, 43, 73, 100–101. *See also* trade

sea serpent, 15, 103, 106. See also art; *itl'ik*

Sea Shepherd Conservation Society, 150, 152, 155, 171, 233n1, 237n43. *See also* anti-whaling coalition; Watson, Paul

Sea Shepherd International, 233n1

Seattle, Chief, 158–59

Seattle Times, 158, 183, 184, 185

Sechart whaling station, 220n103

Secor, William, Sr., 183, 187, 188

self-determination, 7–8, 105, 115, 117, 122, 125, 146, 206

shellfish, 5, 20, 77, 92, 93, 194, 202, 203

sih-xwah-wiX (gray whale, Makah), 30, 138, 140. *See also* gray whale

Singer, Peter, 161. *See also* animal rights

slaves, 22, 23, 36, 59, 92, 100–101, 225n108. *See also* rank

smallpox, 18, 47–50. *See also* disease

Smith, Linda Tuhiwai, 11

Sohappy v. Smith (1968), 119

Somass River, 71, 80, 84, 87, 126

Sones, David, 164

songs: belonging to chiefs, 49, 96, 98; chorus of, 35, 97–101; connected to whaling, 15, 24, 26, 34, 35, 39, 68, 69, 93, 97–100, 140, 205; importance of, 6, 94–101; ownership of, 96; Sayach'apis', 99–100; transfer of, 96, 97; types of, 97–99

sovereignty: British, 155, 158, 167; indigenous, 117, 119, 122; and the federal trust responsibility, 188–89

spirits of our ancestors, 69, 77, 206

Sproat, Gilbert M., 19, 37, 46, 48, 53, 66. *See also* Indian policy

St. Clair, Denis, 85, 224n62

Steelhead/Salmon Protection Action for Washington Now (S/SPAWN), 170

Stevens, Governor Isaac. *See* Stevens treaties

Stevens treaties, 116, 119–20, 159, 180. *See also* treaties; Treaty of Neah Bay

stories: and storytelling, 78–85, 90, 93–95; whaling, 82, 91–94, 97–98, 110, 132, 145, 226n131. *See also* oral tradition

subsistence activities, 23, 25, 27, 29, 44, 45, 60, 68

Swadesh, Morris, xiv, 10, 72, 82, 99

Swan, Helma, 79, 95, 97–98

Swan, James, 16, 31, 47, 59, 210n5, 226n1

T

Tatooche. *See* Makah: villages

Thlu-kluts (Thunderbird, Makah), 29–30. *See also* Thunderbird

Thomas, Alex, xiv, 10–11, 72, 82, 87, 96, 99

Thomas, Eva (Laal), 84, 86

Thompson, Art, 3, 108–14, 143, 226n127

Thompson, Charlene, 108, 112

Thompson, Evelyn, 112, 113

Thompson, Jeanie, 149

Thompson, Katherine, 3

Thornton, Thomas, 76

Thunderbird: connection to whaling, *107, 111*; in art, 69, *74*, 75, 104, 106, *107, 111*, 112, 127; in carving, 108; in dance, 112; in regalia, 100, 108, 112, 114; in stories, 6, 9, 15–16, 28, 81, 201, 210n1. *See also* art; stories

T'iick'in (Thunderbird, Nuu-chah-nulth), 15. *See also* art; stories; Thunderbird

Tla-o-qui-aht, 124–125

Tloo-qua-nah (Nuu-chah-nulth). *See* Wolf Ritual

tourism, 61, 105, 128, 148, 150

trade: fur, 43; general, 31, 47, 54, 120, 125; whale meat, 93; whale oil, 38, 45, 60, 66, 180

traditional food. *See* food

treaties, 43–46, 57–58, 116–22, 145, 146–49, 178, 182, 216n8; NTC negotiations of, 126, 146–49, 230n132; Stevens treaties, 44, 116, 119–20, 159, 180; treaty rights, 7, 14, 44–45, 64, 115, 116–22, 130, 134, 136, 145, 158, 166, 168–70, 177, 178–82, 184, 203. *See also* Boldt Decision; Maa-Nulth; Stevens treaties; Treaty of Neah Bay

Treaty of Neah Bay (1855), 18, 45, 57, 132, 134, 153, 179–82, 184–92

Trutch, Joseph, 44. *See also* Indian policy

tsawalk, as a theory, 67, 68. See also *hishuk ish tsawalk*

Tseshaht: chiefs (*haw'iih*), 46, 47, 53, 74; creation story, 72–75; fishing rights, 125–26; history, 69–75; origin of name, 74; traditional territory, 71, 85, 94; whaling sites, 75–77, 78. *See also* Ts'ishaa

Ts'ishaa (Ts'ishah'ath, Ts'ishah'aht), 9, 38, 69, 71, 73, 74, 75, 76, 77, 88, 209n5

Tsoo-yess (Tsu-yess, T'sues). *See* Makah: villages

Tulee v. Washington (1942), 116

tumanos, tamanawas, 24. *See also* Guardian Spirit Complex

tuupaati (ceremonial prerogatives), 38, 49, 97, 98–100, 102, 103. *See also* chiefs

Two Horses, Michael, 155

U

Umeek, Chief, 215n1. *See also* Atleo, Richard

United Property Owners of Washington (UPOW), 170

United States v. Fryberg (1980), 178, 181

United States v. Oregon (1969), 119

United States v. State of Washington (1974). *See* Boldt Decision

United States v. Winans (1905), 116, 120

Universal Declaration on Human Rights (UN), 205, 206–7

Ushtakimilh. See lineage group

V

Vancouver, George, 31

Vancouver Island: development of industries on, 48–49, 53; non-Indian settlement on, 63–64

Vizenor, Gerald, 81

W

Wa'atch (Wayatch). *See* Makah: villages

Wakashan: language, xiv, xv, xviii, 4; speaking, 16

warfare, 18, 22, 31, 49, 71, 73, 75, 153, 162; and firearms, introduced during trade, 43

washing houses, 223n43

Washington: coast, 64; Territory, 43, 44; tribes, 116, 119, 168

Watson, Paul, 150, 233n1. *See also* Sea Shepherd Conservation Society

Watts, George, 123, 124, 125, 228n41

Watts, Grace, 79–80

Watts, Hughie, 79–80, 89

weaving. *See* art; cedar

Webster, Peter, 24, 25, 38

Wenzel, George, 161

West Coast Allied Tribes, 20, 123, 228n37. *See* Nuu-chah-nulth Tribal Council

West Coast Anti-Whaling Society, 168

West Coast District Council. *See* Nuu-chah-nulth Tribal Council

whaler's wife (*haquum*), 26–27, 35

whales: in art, 103, 114; blubber of, 4, 5, 14, 15, 20, 21, 29, 35, 38, 40, 65, 89,127, 131, 133, 140, 142, 151, 179, 196–98, 200–203; bones of, 20, 30, 75, 103, 104, 127, 149; *ch'ih-t'uh'pook* (whale, Makah), 29–31, 213n60; dividing up the, 6, 35, 38, 76, 200; drift, 27, 40, 99, 100; drums made from, 97; health benefits of, 14, 193–206; *iihtuup* (whale, Nuu-chah-nulth), 6, 15, 30, 31, 34, 106, 112; meat, 4, 15, 21, 40, 60, 65, 93, 131, 198, 199, 202, 203; migration of, 30, 75, 173, 174; oil, 8, 38, 39, 45, 46, 59, 60, 62, 65, 76, 89, 127, 133, 142, 144, 167, 180, 196, 200, 201, 203; population, 6, 7, 63, 64, 65, 130, 135, 162, 164, 166, 174, 175, 177, 179, 180, 191, 192;

and potlatches, 35–39; spirit of, 27, 34, 35, 93, 98–99, 139, 140; and trade, 38, 45, 60, 66, 180. *See also* beluga whale; bowhead whale; gray whale; humpback whale

whaling: as birthright, 90, 133, 184; and canoes, 32, 77, 93, 105, 110; charms/supernatural power of, 26, 28–29, 100, 101; collapse of Makah and Nuu-chah-nulth, 64–66; commercial, 5, 6, 7, 41, 60, 62–65, 130, 133, 134, 162, 167, 171, 180; crews, 4, 11, 32, 34, 67, 77, 93, 99, 129, 130, 135–41, 149, 151, 152, 157, 185, 186, 191, 200; equipment, 62, 93; and harpoons, 4, 15, 28, 31, 32, 34, 62, 64, 72, 73, 75, 91–93, 104, 110, 127, 130, 137, 138–39, 151, 153, 156, 166, 175, 183, 185; and marriage, 38; MMPA waiver, 176–78, 181–83, 191; preparation for, 30–35; rights, 147, 166, 168, 180–82, 188; schedule, 231n93, 236n4; songs, 98–100; stations, 220n103, 220n109. *See also* Makah whaling

Whaling Convention Act, 172, 187

whaling rituals: for drift whales, 27–28, 143; for the dorsal fin (*chakwa'si*), 35, 100, 103, 104, 127, 140; feathers associated with, 4, 25–26, 38, 100, 104; for good luck, 29–30; prayers, 25, 28, 34, 39, 137; purification, 24, 27, 29, 34, 109, 110, 132, 137–38, 144, 147, 143, 151; for strength (*cheesum*), 27–29

whaling shrines (washing houses), 27–28, 143–44. *See also* whaling rituals

Wheeler, Winona, 12

White Paper (1969), 121–22. *See also* Indian policy

Wilson, Angela Cavender, 9, 81, 85

Wolf Ritual, 36, 55, 97, 99,109; headdresses in, 107, 108, 112

women, 48, 93, 141; as basket weavers, 61, 105, 107; as slaves, 22. *See also* whaler's wife

Worcester v. Georgia (1832), 188

World Council of Whalers (WCW), 206

World Wildlife Fund, 150

Y

Yupik, 200

Charlotte Coté is associate professor of American Indian Studies at the University of Washington, Seattle. She is a member of the Tseshaht First Nation, one of fifteen culturally and linguistically related groups in British Columbia under the name Nuu-chah-nulth. She and many of her extended family are shown here celebrating her doctoral graduation at UC Berkeley in 2001. Coté is currently doing research for a book on indigenous food sovereignty.

LIBRARY OF CONGRESS CATALOGING-IN-PUBLICATION DATA

Coté, Charlotte J.
Spirits of our whaling ancestors : revitalizing Makah and Nuu-chah-nulth traditions /
Charlotte Coté ; foreword by Micah McCarty. — 1st ed.
    p. cm. — (Capell family book)
Includes bibliographical references and index.
ISBN 978-0-295-99046-0 (pbk. : acid-free paper)
1. Makah Indians—Ethnic identity.
2. Makah Indians—Hunting.
3. Makah Indians—Social life and customs.
4. Whaling—Social aspects—Northwest, Pacific.
I. Title.
E99.M19C68 2010   305.897'954–dc22   2010007787